Animist Poetics

SUNY series, Philosophy and Race

Robert Bernasconi and T. Denean Sharpley-Whiting, editors

Animist Poetics

Ancestral Trauma and Regeneration
in African Literature

RYAN TOPPER

Cover Credit: Egúngún Masquerade Dance Costume, Yorùbá-style Maker, Nigeria, West Africa, 1900s. Cotton, velvet, flannel, leather, dye, probably wood, cowrie shells, metal, 60 × 23 × 16 inches. The Cleveland Museum of Art, gift of Katherine C. White, 1976. https://www.clevelandart.org/art/1976.188

Published by State University of New York Press, Albany

© 2025 State University of New York

All rights reserved

Printed in the United States of America

No part of this book may be used or reproduced in any manner whatsoever without written permission. No part of this book may be stored in a retrieval system or transmitted in any form or by any means including electronic, electrostatic, magnetic tape, mechanical, photocopying, recording, or otherwise without the prior permission in writing of the publisher.

Links to third-party websites are provided as a convenience and for informational purposes only. They do not constitute an endorsement or an approval of any of the products, services, or opinions of the organization, companies, or individuals. SUNY Press bears no responsibility for the accuracy, legality, or content of a URL, the external website, or for that of subsequent websites.

EU GPSR Authorised Representative:
Logos Europe, 9 rue Nicolas Poussin, 17000, La Rochelle, France
contact@logoseurope.eu

For information, contact State University of New York Press, Albany, NY
www.sunypress.edu

Library of Congress Cataloging-in-Publication Data

Name: Topper, Ryan, 1989- author.
Title: Animist poetics : ancestral trauma and regeneration in African literature / Ryan Topper.
Other titles: SUNY series, philosophy and race.
Description: Albany : State University of New York Press, [2025]. | Series: SUNY series, Philosophy and Race | Includes bibliographical references and index.
Identifiers: LCCN 2024057046 | ISBN 9798855803259 (hardcover : alk. paper) | ISBN 9798855803266 (ebook) | ISBN 9798855803273 (pbk. : alk. paper)
Subjects: LCSH: African literature—History and criticism. | Animism in literature. | Animism—Africa. | Postcolonialism—Africa.
Classification: LCC PR9340 .T67 2025 | DDC 809.1/9382—dc23/eng/20250131
LC record available at https://lccn.loc.gov/2024057046

To Jade Rose

Contents

Acknowledgments ix

Introduction: African Literature's Animist Poetics 1

Chapter 1 Ancestral Trauma and the Regenerative Death Drive:
Toward an Animist Revision of Psychoanalysis 31

Chapter 2 Animist Poetics' Realism-Ritual Spectrum:
Aminatta Forna, Delia Jarrett-Macauley,
Oswald Mbuyiseni Mtshali, Uhuru Portia Phalafala 67

Chapter 3 Cosmic Personhood in the Animist Lyric:
Reading Wole Soyinka's Prison Poetry with and
against New Materialism 101

Chapter 4 Animist Tragedy's Biopolitical Mediation:
Staging Human Sacrifice in Wole Soyinka's
Death and the King's Horseman 143

Chapter 5 Multidimensional Memory: Environmental Wounds
and the Architecture of Animism in Yvonne Vera's
The Stone Virgins 183

Conclusion: Principles of Animist Criticism 227

Notes 231

Works Cited 257

Index 277

Acknowledgments

This book began as my doctoral dissertation at the University of Leeds. I am indebted to Sam Durrant's supervision. He carefully read, discussed, critiqued, reread, and sharpened this project. I am grateful for the criticism and guidance from my examiners, Ato Quayson, Brendon Nicholls, and Graham Huggan, and to the late Jane Taylor's and Harry Garuba's comments on portions of an early draft. I am thankful for Nicholas Ray's and Griselda Pollock's conversations on psychoanalytic theory when I was first formulating these ideas, as well as the many conversations on postcolonial studies and cultural theory with members of University of Leeds's Quilting Points and Creaturely Life reading groups and the Finding Africa seminar series. During this time, I also learned from my colleagues while interning at the National Commission for the Fight against Genocide (CNLG) in Kigali, Rwanda, and co-organizers and participants in the "Interpreting Violence and Trauma in Africa" symposium at the Johannesburg Holocaust and Genocide Centre.

Arthur Rose and Dominic O'Key generously read and responded to countless drafts of this project. I am thankful for their friendship, intelligence, and support. Michael Allan, Philip Dickinson, and Nathan Suhr-Sytsma provided feedback on portions of early drafts, which helped me sharpen my argument. Jeanne-Marie Jackson's, Nicole Rizzuto's, Lily Saint's, and Madhu Krishnan's comments on a draft of my proposal helped me nuance this book's framing. My peer reviewers' generous commentary and criticism, and Rebecca Colesworthy's guidance, made this book significantly better. My colleagues Henry Hughes's and Rob Troyer's comments on the introduction made my ideas more readable. My students consistently challenge me to make literary theory and criticism make sense. I am grateful for all this support.

I presented an abridged version of the introduction as the Presidential Plenary Talk at Western Oregon University in 2024, an early version of chapter 3 as a lecture for the Postcolonial Research Group at the University of Leeds's School of English in 2023, and an early draft of chapter 5 as a lecture for Wits University's English Department in 2016. In 2020, Ama Bemma Adwetewa-Badu invited me to discuss an early version of chapter 4 on Zoom with a group of graduate students at Cornell University's Department of Literatures in English. I am grateful for all these invitations and the generous feedback I received. I am also thankful for all the comments and criticism I have received on this project from friends in African literary studies, postcolonial studies, and literary theory at conferences over the years. Every chapter of this book was test driven at the ACLA, ACLALS, MLA, ALA, and others, and during each test drive I learned something new.

The librarians at the Brotherton Library Special Collections at University of Leeds and the Clara Thomas Archives and Special Collections at York University helped me access archival material indispensable to this book.

An early version of a portion of chapter 2 is published as "Trauma and the African Animist Imaginary in Aminatta Forna's *The Memory of Love* and Delia Jarrett-Macauley's *Moses, Citizen and Me*" (*English Language Notes*, vol. 57, no. 2, 2019, pp. 86–98). An early version of chapter 4 is published as "The Sacrificial Foundation of Modernity in Wole Soyinka's *Death and the King's Horseman*" (*Research in African Literatures*, vol. 50, no. 1, 2019, pp. 53–79). I thank Duke University Press and Indiana University Press for permission to reprint this material.

I am grateful to Judah and Eden for their welcomed interruptions to my writing and for teaching me about the animism of childhood we too quickly lose. Above all, I am thankful for Jade Rose: Your love, companionship, and support has sustained me throughout the writing of this book.

Introduction

African Literature's Animist Poetics

In the late 1960s, Nigerian writer, activist, and future Nobel laureate Wole Soyinka looked out from his prison cell to stare at lizards mating. "They copulate incessantly," he writes in his prison memoir, *The Man Died* (1972), turning what he calls the "crypt" of imprisonment into an "orgiastic spectacle of sex." Through this spectacle, he claims, the prison could well have become a "lizard sanctuary" but for Ambrose, the prison guard, who, when overtaken by "the spirit of boredom," began hunting the lizards: "he piles up bodies and proudly points at the day's bag." Soyinka is struck by one lucky lizard who escapes Ambrose's "stone and baton" (269). Watching his head bob up and down, Soyinka writes, "There are reasons, undoubtedly, in folk-lore why the lizard constantly nods his head. . . . Whatever ancestral trauma plagues the lizard still, will, I hope, be exorcised some day at some great lizard meet" (270).

    This passage is a mise-en-scène of postcolonial African literature. The lizards transform a space of enforced death, a crypt in which the unruly are buried, into a locus of life's regeneration, an "orgiastic spectacle." But this transformation is fleeting. By hunting the reptiles, the prison guard transforms the would-be "sanctuary" back into a space of neocolonial punishment. That the guard's name, Ambrose, derives from the Greek *ambrosios*, signifying immortality or divinity, connects him with a Western mythos and its conception of a divinely ordained sovereign rule over the colonies. This animal spectacle thereby comes to symbolize humanity in the African postcolony. In a locale marked by both the history of European imperial expansion and its perpetuation in post-independent African politics, the lizards attempt to create new life. This investing of life in a *polis* continually marked by death—in a word, hope—is a core premise

1

of any literary writing worth its salt in postcolonial Africa. Despite this hope, the lizards are slaughtered. Yet one survives, bearing what Soyinka terms an "ancestral trauma" marked by his bobbing head. Soyinka then daydreams of a "great lizard meet" at which this trauma is communally "exorcised." This passage becomes a more specific mise-en-scène, which articulates the aesthetic strategy centered in this book. If this spectacle symbolizes life in the African postcolony, Soyinka's hope for a reptilian *eschaton* at which the lizard's ancestral trauma will be ritually mended represents the utopian horizon of the form of writing he practices, a form I describe as animist poetics.

In this book I propose three, interrelated theoretical concepts: ancestral trauma, animist poetics, and the regenerative death drive. Ancestral trauma, a term I pull from this passage and place at the center of postcolonial African literature in English, names the cultural inheritance of colonial modernity's incision of planetary wounds. The advent of global capitalism under European imperial expansion hinges on both material and spiritual wreckage: the mutilation of Indigenous economies and ecosystems and with this mutilation the extirpation of the perceived kinship between the living and the dead and the human and more-than-human world embodied in the colonized subject. This latter extirpation, the spiritual outworking of colonial modernity's material damage, is inherited by the colonized subject as an erasure of ancestral ties. Animist poetics names the widespread creative appropriation and reinvention of Indigenous cosmologies as strategic responses to this erasure across the postcolonial social imaginary. The regenerative death drive, a term alluding to Freud's infamous theory of the death drive, names the hydraulics of this poetics. As the force undergirding animist poetics' multifarious attempts to mend the ancestral trauma conditioning its historical emergence, the regenerative death drive is the logic of animist poetics' symbiotic relation to ancestral trauma. Drawing on Indigenous understandings of nature, this logic views death as generative of new life. Through this final concept, I offer an animist revision of psychoanalytic theory by flipping the Freudian death drive on its head. Freud famously claims that the aim of all life is death. But for the postcolonial African writer, the aim of all death is a new form of collective life: the "great lizard meet."

In chapter 1, I argue that psychoanalytic and deconstructive trauma theory—reconsidered through the lens of Frantz Fanon's conceptualization of colonial trauma—gives language to ancestral trauma, the form of collective wounding immanently theorized in so many African literary texts. Yet these texts push Fanon's social critique of psychoanalysis into an ecological totality, opening an animist mode of theory I develop across this book. Throughout chapters 2 to 5, I then articulate the logic of animist poetics, an aesthetic tactic formed in response to ancestral trauma, the philosophical dynamics of which is the primary focus of this introduction. Through animist poetics, writers like Soyinka, I argue, creatively recreate Indigenous cosmologies in response to their erasure under the pressures of colonial modernity.[1]

By formulating these concepts and articulating their relationship—a problem of ancestral trauma and a solution, spurred by the regenerative death drive, of animist poetics—I intervene in debates surrounding the intersection of trauma theory and postcolonial studies by reframing the assumed subjects of these discourses beyond their anthropocentric coordinates. My hope is that through this epistemic intervention, my argument allows the internal logics of African literature to speak to the state of literary and cultural criticism at large. Canonical trauma theory focuses on the individual, the human, and the living. Yet many postcolonial African writers, I argue throughout this book, propose a theory of trauma that is transpersonal, transspecies, and transtemporal. From an animist perspective, trauma always incorporates forms of collectivity connecting the living and the dead, and the human and more-than-human, because subjectivity is an ongoing environmental process. An animist trauma theory is thus, in the language of cultural criticism, posthumanist,[2] postsecular,[3] and ecopoetic.[4] In other words, postcolonial African literature, through its conceptualizations of trauma and survival, has always been "doing theory," and theory as practiced in Euro-American academia is only recently catching up with this literature.

This book began with a practical question: What kind of trauma theory is intrinsic to postcolonial African literature? Colonization, civil war, genocide, rape, displacement: There can be no doubt that trauma saturates postcolonial African literature's foundational texts, as well as its contemporary iterations—from Okonkwo's suicide in Chinua Achebe's *Things Fall Apart* (1958) to Sissie's racial alienation in Ama Ata Aidoo's *Our Sister Killjoy* (1977), from Darling's migration in NoViolet Bulawayo's *We Need New Names* (2013) to The Ada's rape in Akwaeke Emezi's *Freshwater* (2018). As many critics have argued, however, the theories of trauma assumed by literary scholars are too Eurocentric to make sense of the everyday suffering of life throughout the colonized world. As I will argue in chapter 1, although this critique is widely accepted, literary scholarship that theorizes the metapsychological coordinates of Indigenous frameworks and that considers how such frameworks conceptualize trauma is severely lacking.[5] Thando Njovane frames the problem of postcolonial trauma theory this way:

> Despite current contestation around the uses of trauma theory in reading postcolonial texts, critics nonetheless agree that traumatic histories are inassimilable and that they are transmitted across generations. Frantz Fanon (1961), Paul Gilroy (2005), and Toni Morrison, for example, contend that racist histories have lasting effects on the psychic lives of the oppressed and their descendants. If we accept Neil J. Smelser's contention that "it is possible to describe social dislocations as traumas if they disrupt organised social life" . . . , then colonialism, which was predominantly grounded on racism, constitutes a particular type of historical trauma. (171–72)

A straightforward application of Euro-American trauma theory to postcolonial contexts misses what Njovane highlights as the historical particularity of colonial trauma. As she implies, however, some sort of trauma theory remains necessary for any serious postcolonial criticism because colonial modernity is conditioned by "social dislocations" constituting distinct forms of "historical trauma." How then does African literature conceptualize the forms of collective wounding historically conditioning its variegated aesthetic forms?

This problem was my motivating premise as I began to write this book. Oddly enough, it quickly led me to the spirit world. All of the texts I analyze in this book (and so many more) conceptualize trauma and survival by creatively engaging with Indigenous conceptions of the spiritual. This spiritual focus is by no means peripheral within African literature. It fills canonical texts: the encounters with ghosts and strange creatures modeled by Amos Tutuola's "drinkard"; the ritual incantations crystallized in Christopher Okigbo's poetry; the priestly, mediatory function of Achebe's Ezeulu. It also fills contemporary African literature: Chris Abani's diasporic reimagining of Okigbo's ritual aesthetics, the ancestral curse made modern myth by Jennifer Nansubuga Makumbi, the enmeshed relations between ecologies and subjectivities in Nnedi Okorafor's fiction. This list is by no means exhaustive. Indeed, the spiritual life of African literature is vast and varied, yet too often sidelined by scholarship.

Inspired in part by Soyinka, scholars such as Caroline Rooney and Harry Garuba have brought spiritual life a renewed importance in African literary criticism by way of animism.[6] Blurring boundaries between people and things, human and animal, living and dead, and other binaries central to post-Enlightenment European humanism, animism invests all these categories with spirit, placing them in mutual animation. At its core, then, animism is an umbrella term for Indigenous knowledge systems that reject the ipseism of the Cartesian subject, conceptualizing instead a subject infinitely implicated with the rest of the cosmos. Soyinka terms this logic "the animist interfusion of all matter and consciousness" and places it at the core of what he perceives as the African Weltanschauung (*Myth* 145). Rooney agrees, further arguing that this logic assumes ontological systems that together form an alternative to the European metaphysical tradition and consequently a politics aligning with deconstructive theory. Garuba, too, argues that this logic contains a critique of capitalist modernity and therefore a politics aligning with historical materialism. I draw on both of these arguments throughout this introduction, but my opening gambit is that animism implicitly reframes how we should theorize cultural trauma and survival in postcolonial contexts by moving away from a solely individual, living, human subject.

In an animist framework, trauma cannot be conceptualized as the rupture of the "receptive cortical layer" functioning as an individual psyche's protective shield against external stimuli, as Freud famously hypothesizes in *Beyond the Pleasure Principle* (229). From at least this hypothesis onward, psychoanalytic trauma theory has presupposed an individual, bordered subject whose consciousness becomes breached by an experience deemed overwhelming to the psyche. If, however, subjectivity is mutually animated by the living and the dead as well as various life forms within given environments, then consciousness is constitutively transsubjective—always open to what Freud deems "external stimuli." *External* is a misnomer if we lose Freud's Cartesian dualism. If animism assumes subjective coordinates spread across various life forms, a paradigm shift away from Freud's ipseitic coordinates is necessary when theorizing many of the traumas experienced by Indigenous populations colonized under European rule.[7] Trauma in an animist framework is necessarily transpersonal: It emerges not from a breach in an individual psyche's protective shield (such a hypothesis makes no sense if we do not buy into the illusion of bordered ipseity to begin with), but rather from a rupture in the networks of life forces animating a given environment and historical moment.

From an animist standpoint, then, any division between individual and collective trauma makes no sense: Trauma is necessarily always *cosmological*[8] because the subject is inextricably linked to the totality of the cosmos. Thus, as Sam Durrant and I argue in "Cosmological Trauma and Postcolonial Modernity," the trauma of colonization must be conceptualized less as an individual rupture than as a collective severance from a sense of co-animacy with the world, a rupture that affects humans and the more-than-human world alike. We write, "If trauma studies is not yet postcolonial, it is because its secular, anthropocentric coordinates cannot conceive of trauma as a spiritual, environmental, and cosmological rupture, as something that happens—and keeps on happening—not simply to individuals, nor even to a people, but to the broader network of relations by which life itself is animated" (195). To make this argument, we draw on Max Horkheimer and Theodor Adorno's claim at the beginning of *Dialectic of Enlightenment* that "[t]he disenchantment of the world means the extirpation of animism" (2). Modern logic, in other words, emerges through an uprooting of animist logic (nowhere is this process more apparent than in colonial education systems). When theorizing trauma throughout the colonized world, then, we must take seriously the primary wound of "being thrown" (to collectivize and posthumanize Martin Heidegger's formulation) out of animist interconnectivity and into the individuated world of colonized modernity: the trauma of losing a living connection to the cosmos that Soyinka takes to be a core tenet of African cultures.

Conceptualizing trauma as cosmological, the rupture of a world-system perpetually constituted by networks of living forces, resonates with current turns to the more-than-human dimension of African literature. I am thinking, for example, of Evan Maina Mwangi's call to focus on the "porous" divide between human and nonhuman life in African literature (12) or Cajetan Iheka's notion of African literature's "distributed agency" (50): an approach to subjective agency as never owned by individual humans, but rather distributed across various life forms. Moreover, approaching trauma as cosmological resonates with much of contemporary literary and cultural theory outside Africanist scholarship: for example, critical posthumanism's decentering of human sovereignty, postsecular criticism's reinvestment in questions of spirituality, or the environmental humanities' challenge to any clear-cut nature/culture divide. These connections will become more apparent as my argument unfolds, but it should first be noted that tethering the psyche to the cosmos necessarily, from an animist view, also tethers trauma to the ancestral. If colonization historically ruptured Indigenous cosmologies, colonial trauma also ruptured, and continues to rupture, perceived relations between the living and the dead, past and present, and thus the very process of cultural memory and inheritance (in short, history). Although cosmological trauma is an intrinsically more-than-human process (we might think of the destruction of the Congo's ecosystem throughout Joseph Conrad's *Heart of Darkness* as a canonical example of this process), ancestral trauma names the cultural outworking of cosmological trauma as experienced in the passing of time.

In chapter 1 I articulate in more detail this concept of ancestral trauma and its formal relation to the regenerative death drive, but for now I wish to highlight the role that temporality plays in my argument. This understanding of ancestral trauma's temporal nature leads directly to my theory of the regenerative death drive—a process immanent in African literature's animist poetics. For Freud, trauma names the rupture of a protective border around a decidedly *living* subject's consciousness, from which this subject seeks escape in the stasis of death. This quest for escape is what Freud terms the death drive. In this book, by taking seriously the animist notion that subjectivity is the outworking of entangled forms of cosmic co-animation—human and nonhuman, living and dead—I revise the philosophy of time assumed by the Freudian death drive. For Freud, death is the endpoint of the subject's movement through linear time. From an animist standpoint, however, death can be a transition into a new form of life (Azaro in Ben Okri's *The Famished Road* is a prominent example of such nonlinear temporality). The ontological possibility of such transitions, I would argue, provides the postcolonial social imaginary with the impetus for the cultural development of animist poetics as an aesthetic strategy. The texts I examine in this book portray worlds once mutually animated by the living and the dead as desecrated under colonization while simultaneously depicting the reinscription of the dead into the world of the living as a path through which a colonized people may survive modernity. In sum, animist poetics reinvents (rather than recovers) precolonial cosmologies as strategic responses[9] to the ancestral trauma of colonized modernity.[10] As the outworking of what Uhuru Portia Phalafala perceives as the animistic process through which "the traditional evolves and continually shapes and synthesises with the modern" ("Time" 36), animist poetics is not a nostalgic logic of historical redemption, but a modernist embrace of the cosmological regeneration always taking place across the more-than-human world.

The regenerative death drive I uncover at the heart of animist poetics both extends and overturns Freud's most radical insight. By writing death not as the blank space of ontological stasis at the horizon of teleologic time, but rather as a transitional space of collective transformation, animist poetics functions as an entry point for articulating a postcolonial theory of trauma and survival. But this theory cannot be reduced to a product of the academic discourse dubbed "trauma studies." Since the corpus of postcolonial African literature is composed of aesthetic responses to colonial modernity, which is conditioned by historical trauma, all critical reckoning with African literature must at some point theorize trauma (whether critics recognize this fact or not). In this book, by taking animist cosmologies seriously, I theorize through this trauma a form of postcolonial subjectivity more broadly. This subject operates beyond the secularized anthropocentric coordinates that Euro-American trauma theory often assumes. Rethinking Freudian thought through African Indigenous knowledge produces a "psychoanalysis whose cure does not stop at the human subject," writes Brendon Nicholls, but includes "the animal, the vegetable, and the environmental" (53). My textual analyses throughout this book therefore address, through a structural revision of trauma theory by way of animism, theoretical discourses outside psychanalysis and cultural trauma studies, particularly those set on remapping subjectivity beyond human/nonhuman and nature/culture dualisms.

Finally, it is my hope that the affirmative approach to the aesthetic modeled in this book's explication of animist poetics and, consequently, the affirmative approach to the death drive I posit in my animist revision of Freud, challenges a predominant style of pessimism in literary and cultural criticism at large. In what is arguably the most influential interpretation of the death drive within literary criticism over the past two decades, for example, Lee Edelman equates its politics with pure negativity. For him, the death drive's radical choice of death over life, and therefore its rejection of the future, is part and parcel to theory as a disruptive mode of inquiry. From this standpoint, the horizon of theory is not a future form of collectivity, but instead the embrace of pure, disruptive negativity: "Fuck the social order," he writes, "and the future that serves as its prop" (29). This pessimism can be recognized far beyond Edelman's intervention in queer theory—most notably in Frank B. Wilderson III's style of Afropessimist "critique without redemption" (174). As I demonstrate throughout this book, animist poetics' salient critiques of modernity's "social order" do not minimize its radical affirmation of life otherwise. Moreover, animist poetics' implicit revision of the death drive into a regenerative force provincializes the negative mode of critique exemplified by Edelman and Wilderson within a post-Enlightenment tradition of humanity individuated from the rest of the world, a world in which death always generates future life. Against the pessimism of so much contemporary cultural criticism, the writers examined in this book break out of this tradition to posit a resolutely future-oriented, affirmative poetics even as they respond to the traumas of the past and present. It is my contention that criticism has much to learn from them.

Thus, by exegeting the three interrelated concepts of ancestral trauma, animist poetics, and the regenerative death drive from African literature and articulating these concepts in the language of contemporary theory, I model throughout this book an affirmative method of animist criticism. Animist criticism can be summed up as the practice of a twofold hermeneutic strategy. First, animist criticism reads in response to the cosmological wounding that has extirpated Indigenous forms of more-than-human, nonlinear kinship across the colonized world and continues, through global capitalism, this extirpation process (which is both material and spiritual) on a planetary scale. Second, following the posthumanist, post-secular, and ecological logic intrinsic to animist poetics, animist criticism formulates its exegesis as a strategic, dialectical act aimed at conjuring a regenerated kinship with the wounded cosmos. Throughout the rest of this introduction, I explain how African literature's animist poetics models the dynamics of this dialectical, regenerative act. Its radically affirmative nature is most apparent, I will argue, when we recognize the manner in which the ritualized side of its aesthetic spectrum operates beyond the process of historical representation and into the conjuring of a new dispensation (what Soyinka depicts as the reptilian *eschaton*). It is this aesthetics-as-conjuring process that results in the logic of collective survival through death that unites so many of African literature's most striking texts. Before laying out this argument in more detail, I wish to first of all consider some examples of this regenerative death in contemporary African art and film, which will function as a point of departure for a more detailed articulation of animism and its relationship to Euro-American theory.

Posthumous Transfigurations

Wanuri Kahiu's short film *Pumzi* (2009) depicts life in the Maitu Community, a postapocalyptic, East African compound, thirty-five years after World War III. Asha, the protagonist, is an archivist in the Virtual

Natural History Museum, which documents the natural prehistory of the outside world, now a barren desert. In the museum newspaper clippings detailing the earth's loss of water stand beside specimens of previous life forms, including the dead, charred roots of the earth's last tree. Upon discovering a mysterious box containing a soil sample, however, Asha dreams of another tree—hope of life outside the compound. Taking the soil and a seed labeled the Maitu Seed, Asha escapes the compound to journey through a radioactive desert in search of the tree she witnessed in her dream. She walks to exhaustion, discovering no sign of life. With her last remaining strength, she plants the seed, which has begun to sprout within the mysterious soil, watering it with her own sweat. Lying beside the seed, shading it from the sun, Asha dies. As the camera pans upward, her body transfigures into a tree, sprouting through her decomposition the realization of her dream. The audience witnesses her, in becoming the Maitu Seed of her archive, become, through death, an archivist of future life: a prophet.

Similar prophecies abound in contemporary African art. In Wangechi Mutu's animated short *The End of Carrying All* (2015), an African woman undertakes a journey across a savanna while the basket on her head is increasingly filled with symbols of European, capitalist expansion: a bicycle wheel, a satellite dish, an oil rig. Upon reaching a single tree at the edge of a cliff, she, like Asha, collapses from exhaustion. Transfiguring into molten lava, she is absorbed into the earth; the earth ripples, and the film begins again. Through this loop, Mutu ritualizes Kahiu's vision of posthumous transfiguration, re-situating the process from a postapocalyptic future to the cyclic foundation of history—that which has always animated existence. The trees in each film, symbols of a (re)genesis, cast each protagonist as a new Eve, a source of collective life. *Maitu* (mother), deriving from the Kikuyu roots *maa* (truth) and *itu* (ours), philologically suggests, like the biblical Eve, a primal germination of community. Deriving from the Arabic *A'isha*—"she who lives"—Asha denotes both life and, in English, ash (as in the Book of Common Prayer's "ashes to ashes"). Through Asha's transfiguration into the Maitu Tree, *Pumzi* asks its audience to imagine a future form of communal life germinated in death, a life emerging through its own ashes, while *The End of Carrying All* suggests that this future form is somehow already immanent in life itself.

That both protagonists shed any perceived human differentiation from nature during their deaths, becoming a tree or molten lava, is vital to their shared vision of life. This prophetic loss of creaturely difference abounds in African art. In Nandipha Mntambo's photographic composite *Europa* (2008), for instance, an African woman with a bull's head leans forward, gazing upon the viewer, seemingly roused by her newly acquired therianthropic form. Whereas Europa of Greek mythology was raped by Zeus disguised as a bull, Mntambo's *Europa* appears transfigured—even empowered—by the experience. On the one hand, she embodies the association between the Indigenous and the animal that Frantz Fanon famously places at the core of colonization. The "zoological terms" historically used by imperial regimes to associate Indigenous people with "the bestiary" gestures beyond the rhetorical, he argues, revealing the political structure of the colony (33). The colonial world functions as a *polis* only as it "dehumanizes the native" and "turns him into an animal" (32). This process of dehumanization not only constitutes the political structure of the colony, he argues, but also of global modernity, the European metropole included. Since European progress comes "from the soil and from the subsoil of that underdeveloped world," a "world which has been forced down to animal level by imperial powers," for Fanon, "Europe is literally the creation of the Third World" *as animal* (76, 79, 81). In other words, Europe is not a habitus we can understand as distinctly separate from the Global South; rather, Europe only exists through its process of animalizing the rest of the world. Hence his mocking of post-Enlightenment European humanism, in particular its notion of a universalized Man, in the conclusion to *The Wretched of the Earth*. "When I search for Man in the technique and the style of Europe," he writes, "I see only a succession of negations of man" (252). Mntambo's *Europa* embodies this dehumanizing humanism as the rape of her African, female body, but also depicts a future life emerging through this rape.[11] Printed with archival ink on cotton rag paper, both used for preservation, the image archives the "social death," to use Orlando Patterson's term, at the core of colonial and, indeed, European history. Similar to Kahiu's and Mutu's protagonists, Mntambo's subject becomes an archivist of life after the death of the (European) human—what Sylvia Wynter, building on Fanon, describes as humanity "After Man." Flaunting a form of life neither fully animal, nor fully human, *Europa* sheds the legacy of her namesake by re-crafting the death Europe bestowed upon her into new life.

It may be tempting to interpret each of these artworks as examples of the Afrofuturism currently in vogue. Blending generic conventions across science fiction, fantasy, and magical realism to reconfigure historical realities of the African diaspora, Afrofuturism is a speculative aesthetic that imagines possible futures for Black life. *Pumzi*, for example, reconfigures modernity as a postapocalyptic dystopia in order to imagine a future beyond the subjugation of Black life as the space of the political. Like Michel Foucault's metanarrative of European modernity, inhabitants of the Maitu Community live in constant surveillance by "the council," producing kinetic energy through mandatory exercise routines and water by filtering urine and sweat, ensuring the compound remains self-enclosed and self-sustaining. Dream suppressant pills keep inhabitants from imaging life outside their political structure, but Asha's pills fail to suppress her visions. The Maitu Seed and the unknown soil bear the promise, Asha believes, of a community no longer rooted in the political capture of life (the interpellation from *zoê* to *bios* Giorgio Agamben places at the root of all political structures), but rather the natural regeneration of life in death. But this prophetic vision exceeds Afrofuturism, Kahiu (*Pumzi*'s writer and director) argues. Much like Asha, "my job is to be a seer, not just a historian," she claims, which has always been the task of the African storyteller ("Afrofuturism"). Components of what critics now term Afrofuturism exist in all forms of African narrative, she explains: the solar system in Dogon cosmology, the prophecies of colonial conquest told by Mugo wa Kibiru, the presence of the spirit world in Ben Okri's writing, even the stories told to Kahiu by her mother. For Kahiu, *Pumzi*'s narrative of Asha becoming the Maitu Tree is a "continuation of storytelling" passed down from such sources ("No More"). According to this framework, *Pumzi*, *The End of Carrying All*, and *Europa* become archives of the future by becoming archives of their ancestral sources—recasting their Afrofuturist aesthetics as techniques of a broader logic: animist poetics.

Indeed, similar posthumous transfigurations abound in forms of African art not typically interpreted as Afrofuturism, forming something of a leitmotif within postcolonial African literature. These transfigurations often merge humanity and the land into an organic whole, a more-than-human world, as in the earth's inheritance of Okonkwo's curse at the end of Achebe's *Things Fall Apart* (1958), passing on the need for "sacrifices to cleanse the desecrated land" (187). In Bessie Head's *A Question of Power* (1973), the protagonist, Elizabeth, discovers a form of "belonging" within the land: "As she fell asleep, she placed one soft hand over her land. It was a gesture of belonging" (206). Likewise, in Mia Couto's *Sleepwalking Land* (1992) Kindzu's words themselves join this belonging with an image of the literary as ecopolitical: "Then, one by one, the letters turn into grains of sand, and little by little, all my writings are transformed into pages of earth" (213). Head's and Couto's novels both end by casting the desecrated union Achebe depicts uniting the colonized African subject and ecosystem as regenerative.

In other works, characters themselves transfigure, much like Kahiu's, Mutu's, and Mntambo's protagonists. In the final chapter of Uzodinma Iweala's *Beasts of No Nation* (2005), for instance, Agu the child soldier sits in a rehabilitation program dreaming of posthumous transfiguration:

> I am wanting to lie down on the warm ground with my eye closed and the smell of mud in my nose. . . . I am wanting to feel how the ground is wet all around my body so that if I am sweating, I am feeling like it is the ground sweating through me. And I am wanting to stay in this same place forever, never moving for anything, just waiting waiting until dust is piling on me and grasses is covering me and insect is making their home in the space between my teeths. I am telling her that I am thinking one Iroko tree will be growing from my body, so wide that its trunk is separating night and day, and so tall that its top leaf is tickling the moon until the man living there is smiling. (176)

Agu dreams of dying like Asha, sprouting through his death a new life form, much like the speaker of Jared Angira's "A Look in the Past" (1972):

> I shall go back
> to the formless clouds
> and melt myself into rain
> then shall I land in the plantation
> and mate with the secondary roots
> of the old fig tree. (62)

Such transfigurations, by imaging new forms of collective life regenerating through death, offer a theory of trauma and survival through which we can interpret the everyday violence of postcolonial life. Yet interpreting the subject of these posthumous transfigurations through a lens of post-Enlightenment secular humanism results in pessimism: Death is the only form available to the colonized subject (hence the "negative ontology" exemplified by Edelman and Wilderson). From an animist perspective, however, this death drive is affirmative because the subject is not an individual human, but rather an environment, an entire cosmos, a network of life forces perpetually undergoing destruction and creation. In this sense, through animist poetics, African literature theorizes trauma in a manner that speaks to a broad range of literary and cultural criticism insofar as it envisions subjectivity as endlessly relational and thus environmental in the most expansive sense imaginable (in a word, cosmic). This cosmic alternative to the Cartesian subject is both an extension of the poststructuralist critique of ipseity and the posthumanist critique of theory's tendency to quarantine human culture from nature. It is therefore my hope that scholars in disparate fields of criticism—from Indigenous and postcolonial studies to modernist studies the environmental humanities—can find in my exegesis of African literature a theory of trauma and survival that, because it speaks to the axiology of contemporary theory, a hermeneutic tool for analyzing the myriad disasters of global capitalism. In short, if traditional trauma theory focuses on the individual, the human, and the living, an animist theory of trauma focuses instead on the transpersonal, the transspecies, and the transtemporal. This focal shift requires criticism to turn from a theory of trauma to a more primary topic: a theory of the subject.

Situating Animist Poetics in Contemporary Theory

Since E. B. Tylor's *Primitive Culture* (1871) and James Frazer's *The Golden Bough* (1890), animism has typically been conceptualized as a pre-monotheistic religion of spirits: an investment of *anima* across the nonhuman world. More recently, anthropologists, philosophers, theologians, and environmental activists have returned to the animism first envisioned by colonial anthropology, seeking to transgress its post-Enlightenment European paradigm, which rendered animism primitive (as in Freud's association of children, neurotics, and Indigenous people).[12] Graham Harvey terms this return "the new animism": a positive exploration of Indigenous modes of dwelling with nonhuman subjects.[13] For him, if the animism of colonial anthropology contrasted a primitive "belief in spiritual beings" (Tylor 383) with the scientific rationality of modern Europe, the new animism recuperates the term to posit a more-than-human redefinition of personhood. This animism locates *anima* "'in between,' in the relating together of persons (often of different species), rather than 'within'" ("Introduction" 3). This new animism should thus be historically contextualized alongside contemporary theory's widespread turn away from the purely human realm—from ecocriticism to animal studies to new materialism. These discourses offer ways to imagine, through Euro-American theory, Nurit Bird-David's description of animism as a "relational epistemology" (67).

In this sense, the recent interest in animism among largely non-Indigenous scholars located in the North Atlantic makes sense. As literary and cultural theory undergoes a posthumanist turn, what David Abram describes as animism's "participatory mode of perception" (27) into humanity's "consanguinity" with the rest of the world (16) appears more intelligent than Tylor or Freud would have liked to admit.[14] By "posthumanist turn," I mean the current attempt to move beyond the focus on exclusively human culture that united so much of the twentieth century's literary and cultural theory. By swapping this myopic vision of human culture severed from the more-than-human world for a vision of the social more attuned to the networks of relations between subjects and objects, people and things, humans and nonhumans, posthumanism (which is by no means a united theoretical dogma) begins from a critical disposition away from anthropocentrism. This disposition casts subjectivity as a space to be remapped by theory that gestures outside the realm of (purely human) semiotics. In Rosi Braidotti's words, "Critical posthuman thought wants to re-assemble a discursive community" (42) rooted in a "non-dualistic understanding of nature-culture interaction" (3). Such a project makes a "focus on subjectivity necessary," she writes, because "issues such as norms and values, forms of community bonding and social belonging as well as questions of political governance both assume and require a notion of the subject" (42). In other words, while the posthumanist discourses have pried the sovereignly bordered human from the throne of subjectivity—incorporating animals, things, plants, and a host of other nonhuman actors—their political stakes remain tethered to the dynamics of a redefined, more-than-human subject. A core question for theory in the wake of posthumanism is, then, if subjectivity has never been a matter of individual human ownership, in what form of agency or notion of personhood does the subject participate?[15]

This question (implicitly asked across disparate fields of contemporary criticism) is just one example of the manner in which theory is playing catch-up with, in Soyinka's words, Africa's "primal systems of apprehension" (*Myth* xii). Indeed, much like the *post* in postsecularism, the *post* in posthumanism is misleading if we do not take European humanism as our philosophical starting point. That the human is never a solely human category, but rather inextricably part of a more-than-human world, may be exciting news to literary critics in the world of Euro-American academia, but it is a logical a priori for many African writers. Indeed, a subjectivity spread across various life forms is central to African literature's animist poetics. Consider Lenrie Peters's poem "On a Wet September Morning" (1967). The speaker, upon viewing a West African seascape, perceives the anima undergirding his experience of life as proliferated across the expanse of evolution. The speaker hears a "silent yell" ring through "time's corridors," beginning at

> . . . the farthest end
>   Where the amoeba becomes
> The fire, water and air.
>   Where the primeval fruit still hangs.
> So to the other end
>   Where plants are but continents
> Deep in the future
>   That is darker and older
> Than the past. (67)

This stanza depicts the earth's deep time as a corridor and, visually, a ladder or series of stepping stones for the animist to scale. On one end an amoeba becomes primal elements and on the other lies a somehow more ancient future. Across this corridor/ladder the "silent yell" of the earth's shared anima reverberates. "The echo burst inside me," the speaker goes on to declare, like a "pagan trumpet blast" (67). This pagan reverberation ties the speaker to both the primeval fruit at the beginning of time and the continental plants of the future, shaping his present view of the seascape:

> The world under the sea
>   The sea under the earth
> The sky under the sea
>   Were elemental changes of a world.
> As the true life is death
>   Which is the idea inside us
> So distinction ends.
>   The plagued centuries

	In a weeping jelly-fish.
	The pebble that will be a crown
	The moon reflected in a starfish. (66)

Dividing the sea, earth, and sky becomes impossible as all "distinction ends." The entire world is connected (the moon in a starfish, humanity's "plagued centuries" in a jellyfish), the speaker recognizes, through an eternally recurring process of life and death. This recognition informs his sense of self. His feet buried in the sand become "already prehistoric," sprouting "symbiosing weeds" that anchor him to the anima functioning as evolution's impetus (66). This endlessly expansive vision of subjectivity mirrors the ecological subject Jason Allen-Paisant finds in the practice of spirit possession across the African diaspora. He writes, "Spirit possession . . . conveys the idea that not only humans, animals and trees are alive but that so are mountains, boulders, winds and fire. If all the world pulses and acts and nothing is merely acted upon, then the urge to be possessed by the god, the ancestor, the snake, the river and so on, is the deep awareness of the animacy of the world acting upon self, of billions of neutrinos constantly penetrating our human bodies, and so on" (43). To return to the question of subjectivity that Braidotti's account of posthumanism raises, Peters's poem, like Allen-Paisant's ecological approach to possession rites, envisions subjectivity as irreducibly cosmic,[16] an animist remapping of the subject highly pertinent to contemporary theory.[17] What might theory look like, for example, if this subjectivity became a starting point?

	This question brings us to Garuba's notion of animist realism: an aesthetic genre that performs a "continual re-enchantment of the world" disenchanted by Western modernity ("Explorations" 284). As Garuba argues, this process challenges what Max Weber, borrowing a term from Friedrich Schiller, famously describes as Western modernity's "disenchantment of the world" (Weber 155). Weber's historical narrative of secularized rationalization proves useful for analyzing the public sphere that emerges with capitalism and consequently colonization, Garuba admits. This framework, however, misses the other rationalities, such as animist epistemologies, he claims, which flourish despite the modernization of the so-called third world. By appropriating animist cosmologies for the present, literary writers open, in Garuba's words, "avenues of agency for the dispossessed in colonial and postcolonial Africa" ("Explorations" 285). Moreover, Garuba contextualizes animist realism within a cultural logic of animist materialism, the former term placing Indigenous modes of thought in proximity to Marxism. Such proximity casts Marx's concept of commodity fetishism, the process by which material objects are endowed with spiritual power, as a critique of the disavowed animist structure of capitalism. If, in Wendy Brown's words, "material life is always already fetishized," (qtd. in Garuba, "On Animism"), then animism is not only a mode in which the Empire "writes back," to use Bill Ashcroft et al.'s phrase, but, as Garuba writes, "animism is the spectral Other that simultaneously constitutes and haunts the modern. Rather like Giorgio Agamben's reading of the status of the *homo sacer* of ancient Roman law, it is always already included by its exclusion" ("On Animism"). Modernity, from this standpoint, functions through the repression of its animistic form—what Marx diagnoses as the commodity fetishism central to capitalism—and its secular rationality is the logic of this repression.

In this book I build on Garuba's definition of animist realism: a literary genre that assumes a political philosophy he dubs animist materialism—a postcolonial, Marxist critique of capitalism as, despite its disenchanted appearance, animistic. Crucially, though, I locate Garuba's theory within a larger realism-ritual aesthetic spectrum. His theory remarkably articulates the realist side of this spectrum, but cannot quite grasp the ritual side. Just as Garuba places magical realism under the umbrella term of animist realism, I situate his definition of animist realism under the umbrella term of animist poetics: the widespread creative appropriation and reinvention of Indigenous cosmologies as strategic responses to modernity across the postcolonial social imaginary. By limiting the role of animism to a logic of realism, Garuba's definition implies that the modern, capitalist, colonized world of ancestral trauma can be critiqued through an animist style of representation, but not ritually mediated or transformed (the dispensational hope embedded in Soyinka's reptilian *eschaton*). Thus, in chapter 2 I focus on animist poetics' realism-ritual spectrum, beginning with realist-oriented novels, analyzed as a limit case for Garuba's method of reading animism, and ending with ritualized poems, analyzed as exemplary of the method of reading animism I employ in the rest of this book. The texts of chapters 3 through 5 explicitly cross the threshold of representational critique within which Garuba's theory remains, embracing a conceptualization of literature as a ritual process aimed at collective transformation.

Here I build on Rooney's *African Literature, Animism and Politics*. Alongside an array of philosophical and literary texts, she explicates the ontology assumed in Birago Diop's poem "Breath" (1947):

> Listen more to things
> Than to words that are said.
> The water's voice sings
> And the flame cries
> And the wind that brings
> The woods to sighs
> Is the breathing of the dead
> And repeats each day
> The Covenant where it is said
> That our fate is bound to the law,
> And the fate of the dead who are not dead
> To the spirits of breath who are stronger than they. (427)

Translated most often as "Breath," (though Langston Hughes opts for "Forefathers"), Diop's "*Souffles*" (Breaths/Spirits) is, in Soyinka's words, a "poetic exegesis of animism" (*The Burden* 171). This exegesis is not, Soyinka argues, a "manifesto in verse-form," but a glimpse of the "quiet enthusiasm of the initiate, the sharing instinct of the votive who has experienced immersion in a particular dimension of reality and calls out from within his spiritual repletion" (*Myth* 131). The poem appears in the short story "Sarzan," part of Diop's transcription of stories told by his family griot, Amadou Koumba. Upon returning to his village from serving the French in World War II, Sarzan intends to bring European rationality to his people. Sarzan becomes possessed by ancestral spirits, however, who voice the poem through his voice. These spirits urge the reader to listen more to Things (*Choses*) than Beings (*Etres*). The ancestors speak through rivers, trees, and fire, they explain, as well as the breasts of women and the noises of wailing children. The above designated "things" are natural phenomena, living beings. Calling natural spirit mediums things implies that the thing/being difference in the poem is not related to any conceivable divide between the cultural and the natural or the living and the nonliving. In fact, the logic that produces these differences is the logic against which Sarzan's ancestral spirits warn.

Through this conceptualization of being as the participation in a shared force dispersed across life forms rather than an experience of individuated presence,[18] Diop's poem bears resemblance to new materialism. New materialism names the "new ways of thinking about matter and processes of materialization" (Coole and Frost 2) attentive to "matter's immanent vitality" (8) now prevalent throughout the social sciences and humanities. It begins by rejecting the severance of epistemology from ontology undergirding so much of the twentieth century's semiotically oriented theories. This rejection means it is a materialism that, like Diop's animist poetics, refuses to separate the living matter designated as human from the material life of the more-than-human world. By swapping a human subject for a Deleuzean multiplicity or Latourian network of various forms of matter, new materialism expands the borders of the subject to include anything and everything that exists. Similarly, in Diop's poem all matter is "vibrant" (Bennett), "intra-active" (Barad), and "trans-corporeal" (Alaimo), as the new materialists would have it.

The poem's material vitality is composed, however, from a series of reverberations emanating from the voices of ancestral spirits: the "living forces" perpetually voicing the world into being (Rooney 22). This difference highlights an important distinction between new materialism and my view of animist poetics. If new materialism posits a subject-object continuum in order to displace human agency from the center of Euro-American theory, animist poetics utilizes such a continuum to constitute a postcolonial form of human agency. In this sense the political horizon of animist poetics is more aligned with Sylvia Wynter's "planetary humanism" or Gloria Anzaldúa's "New Consciousness" than it is with new materialism's flattened ontology.[19] Indeed, a signature move of new materialism is to pragmatically discard human subjectivity. As Jane Bennett admits in *Vibrant Matter*, "[S]ubjectivity . . . gets short shrift so that I may focus on the task of developing a vocabulary and syntax for, and thus a better discernment of, the active powers issuing from nonsubjects" (ix). This concept of a nonsubject is absent from the philosophical grammar of African literature's animist poetics. "Breath," for example, preemptively theorizes what Bennett later calls the "curious ability of inanimate things to animate, to act, to produce effects" in the world (6), but their animating nature leads the initiate of the lyric deeper into the experience of a more radically expansive form of subjectivity, a form connecting the living and the dead. Since the move from colonized object to postcolonial subject is the political horizon of so much African literature, Diop's writing included, there is a jarring disjoint between animism's expansion of subjectivity and the monist utopia of nonsubjects many new materialists propose.[20] Thus, as I argue in chapter 3, although animist poetics resembles aspects of new materialism, animist poetics' resolute focus on postcolonial subject formation through Indigenous cosmologies, especially through its engagement with ancestral life, highlights animism's distinctly postsecular relevance to contemporary theory.

That this vision of postcolonial subject formation incorporates the living and the dead is key to understanding animist poetics' proximity to Euro-American theory. Rooney argues that "Breath" suggests a philosophy of death at odds with the metaphysical concept of absence. This philosophy is described in the poem as "The Covenant." The poem perceives death as a process of "succumbing to stronger *living forces*—rather than succumbing to non-being—and . . . the dead, whilst losing their own breath, live on as part of the on-going stronger forces of life," she writes (22). This covenant between life and death, I would add, can be found throughout much of African literature. Consider, for example, Richard Ntiru's "To the Living" (1971):

> Only those
> Who have survived
> The final anaesthetization;
> Those who have enacted the final epilogue;
> Only those
> Have the prescient perception
> Of the inner idea of life
> And can partake of the spectral dance; (48–49)

Death in this poem gifts the subject an understanding of life. Those who have paradoxically (for the non-animist, at least) "survived" death (figured, in Holocaust-inspired terms, as the "final anaesthetization") are able to perceive "the inner idea of life" by joining in the collective dance of ancestral spirits. "Who but they," the poem goes on to ask, "Know the revitalizing power of the stilled blood?" (49). As Kwesi Brew's "Ancestral Faces" (1958) makes clear, these dead subjects who experience posthumous revitalization remain inextricably linked to the actions of the living:

> They sneaked into the limbo of time,
> But could not muffle the gay jingling
> Brass bells on the frothy necks
> Of the sacrificial sheep that limped and nodded after them;

Through ritual performances (e.g., the sacrifice of a sheep), this stanza declares, the living keep the dead tethered to their community as ancestral forces. The poem's use of the semicolon marks both the break and continuation, death and life, these rituals embody. More-than-human nature, moreover, joins in this process of communal binding, revealing that the ancestral forces voicing the world likewise keep the living tethered to the dead:

> They could not hide the moss on the bald pate
> Of their reverent heads;
> And the gnarled barks of the wawa tree; (43)

The dead reveal themselves in the moss and the bark of the wawa tree. The latter is associated in Akan cosmology with perseverance, as in the Andrinka symbol of the *wawa aba*, emphasizing that the dead in Brew's poem, as in Ntiru's and Diop's, persevere into a form of living experienced through death. Against the European metaphysical concept of absence as the opposition to presence, death in these poems reveals a "Covenant," in Diop's words, anchored in the natural world, binding together the living and the dead as well as the human and the more-than-human.[21] Central to these poems is thus the belief that, because the dead are not dead, nonexistence is nonexistent. Death is thus regenerative, a transition into a new form of life.

What is more, like Derridean deconstruction, Diop's animist approach to the lyric (an approach practiced by many African writers), Rooney argues, points readers beyond metaphysical ontology as it has been defined by Western philosophy. Since the ontology assumed in the poem does not define being in opposition to nonbeing, the binaries of metaphysical ontology overseeing the history of Western philosophy such as presence/absence do not hold a sovereign position, Rooney argues. Instead, "being," for lack of a better word, is at its core "a question of movement" posed by a subject caught in a network of mutually constitutive life forces (1).[22] Following Diop's vision of a world of spirits as one "living text that creates itself in a writing-voicing of being," Rooney pins the animist concept of being against the being of European metaphysics (21). The latter relies upon its opposition to nonbeing, as Heidegger and Jacques Derrida have both influentially argued, while the former envisions being as creative movement: the "writing of being in a living world that must necessarily continue to be written or inscribed" (23). Crucially, however, Rooney does not inoculate African animism from Euro-American theory, as many postcolonial critics may be tempted to do, but rather utilizes their productively agonistic relation as a springboard for modeling an alternative method of critical thought. Throughout this book I take a similar approach.

For example, if within the world of Diop's poem (as in my other examples) nonexistence is nonexistent, casting the world not as an economy of individual beings but as a regenerative interplay of mutually enforced being-as-movements, we may then ask, is animist reading a step ahead of deconstructive reading? Rooney narrates such a distinction through a hypothetical encounter between two anthropologists, one European and one African: "The Western anthropologist might say: 'Where you see and speak of other "living creatures" or "spirits" as other beings, even other *subjects*, so to speak, we sometimes speak of "non-being" or "ghosts."' While the African anthropologist (not native informant) might say: 'Where you talk of "non-being" or "ghosts," we speak of spirits or the actuality of other being, of subjects, so to speak, beyond your the one-and-only subject'" (81). In this hypothetical discussion between the European metaphysician and the African animist, two hermeneutic schemes are demonstrated. The metaphysician interprets the world according to what Derrida calls the "onto-hermeneutic presupposition": there is a one-and-only subject (*Spurs* 113). The animist interprets through, in Francis Nyamnjoh's words, "ontologies of incompleteness" (2) that counter this myth of the sovereign subject with a re-enchantment of the world—the endowment of spiritual subjectivity to that which has been desubjectivized by European metaphysical ontology. What the metaphysician deems nonbeing or ghosts are, as Derrida describes in *Specters of Marx*, memories of those who haunt the presence/absence binary producing the illusion of the sovereign subject: the presence of absence that reveals the subject's absence of presence (to use Derridean terms). On the other hand, what the animist deems spirits are those other-subjects who live within a regenerative interplay of forces differently than you and I do. The animist reader does not therefore disagree with the deconstructive reader, but nonetheless, according to Rooney's hypothetical discussion, reads the world differently: Why deconstruct the European myth of sovereign subjectivity when one can re-enchant the worlds this myth disenchanted through colonial expansion? Consequently, if Derrida famously invites the deconstructive reader to learn to live with ghosts, Rooney calls the animist reader to (re)inscribe the world with spirits.

Chapter Outline and Philosophical Orientation

In response to this call, this book's chapter organization follows a theoretical logic rather than a historical, linear logic. This book does not offer a detailed literary history of how ancestral trauma developed as a structuring principle of postcolonial African literature across the twentieth and twenty-first centuries, or a genealogy of how animist poetics developed in response. Similarly, this book is not a site-specific study of the ancestral trauma and animist poetics dialectic (articulating, for example, frameworks distinct to Nigeria or Zimbabwe). Such projects require their own books. To be sure, I draw on social, historical, and cultural context as I offer formal analyses of animist texts throughout this book, but my main focus is understanding how a reckoning with the internal logics of postcolonial African literature might reframe theoretical paradigms undergirding literary and cultural criticism at large. This philosophical focus provides the impetus behind this book's organization.

In chapter 1, I espouse in more detail what I, following Soyinka, call ancestral trauma. Fanon in particular helps elucidate this concept by depicting colonial trauma as the constitutive erasure of the Indigenous past. While much scholarship in postcolonial theory and Black studies places constitutive erasure at the core of colonial modernity, my focus on animism allows for a recognition of the affirmative logic through which African literature dialectically responds to this trauma. This logic is revealed in a process I describe as the regenerative death drive. By drawing on African literature's cosmological expansion of subjectivity (as outlined in this introduction) alongside Fanon's "sociodiagnostic" critique of Freud, as well as his appropriation of Freud's primal patricide plot, I posit an animist revision of psychoanalytic theory. This revision finds in Freudian metapsychology a more-than-human death and regeneration dialectic, which Freud actively represses. Recuperating this dialectic, I argue, provincializes Euro-American trauma theory and the Manichaeism of its postcolonial critique, highlighting the need for contemporary theory to reexamine the psychoanalytic theory of trauma beyond the epistemic framework of post-Enlightenment European humanism.

In chapter 2, I demonstrate how texts at different ends of animist poetics' realism-ritual spectrum process the form of colonial trauma I theorize in chapter 1. Aminatta Forna and Delia Jarrett-Macauley, two contemporary British–Sierra Leonean novelists, exemplify the realist side of animist poetics through their narrations of post–Civil War Sierra Leone. In my analysis, *The Memory of Love* (2010) and *Moses, Citizen and Me* (2005) form a limit case for the standard postcolonial critique of trauma theory's Eurocentrism and Garuba's approach to animism. For these novelists and these theories, literature can represent colonial modernity and critique its trauma-producing social structures, but no more. The ritual side of animist poetics, however, endows aesthetics with a more affirmative role, envisioning literature as a process of collective transformation. Drawing on Michael Taussig's and Paul Stoller's anthropological studies of postcolonial spirit possession, I model an alternative method of reading trauma and animism, a method focused less on a text's representational content than on its formal processing of history. I use two works of South African poetry—Oswald Mbuyiseni Mtshali's apartheid-era "An Abandoned Bundle" (1971) and Uhuru Portia Phalafala's recent collection *Mine Mine Mine* (2023)—as examples of this ritualized animism. This poetry ritually mediates the ancestral trauma of apartheid by activating the regenerative death drive. In this way, the ritual side of animist poetics more fully incorporates the posthumanist and postsecular dimensions of Indigenous cosmologies.

This comparative case study between realist and ritual animism functions as a springboard for chapters 3, 4, and 5. In chapters 3 and 4, I focus on Anglophone African literature's paradigmatic practitioner and theorist of animism and ritual, Soyinka. In chapter 5, I focus on Yvonne Vera, a writer who appropriates Soyinka's literary experiments with animism to craft an ecopoetics of cultural memory. These chapters demonstrate how the ritual side of animist poetics revises resting assumptions within psychoanalytic theory and new materialist ecology (chapter 3); political theology as construed in European and Black biopolitics (chapter 4); and cultural memory studies (chapter 5). Thus, while I propose a postcolonial, posthumanist, postsecular, and ecological revision of psychoanalytic trauma theory in chapter 1, then model how this animist reframing of trauma allows critics to read across a spectrum of African literature's animist poetics in chapter 2, I spend the rest of this book more explicitly demonstrating why and how this approach to postcolonial practices of animism matter to literary and cultural criticism. And I do so through extended theoretical and formal analyses of two paradigmatic figures of animist poetics, Soyinka and Vera, whose writings I place in dialogue with philosophers and critics at the forefront of the theoretical humanities. Moreover, in organizing these final chapters by genre—poetry (chapter 3), drama (chapter 4), and fiction (chapter 5)—I seek on the one hand to leave behind Anglophone postcolonial criticism's usual myopic focus on the novel as the only significant literary form throughout the Global South. On the other, I also seek to invest "the new modernist studies" (Mao and Walkowitz), which often pays lip service to the nebulous existence of African modernism, but rarely trains critical focus on specific forms of African modernism, with interpretive lenses through which to begin appreciating how modernism operates in postcolonial poetry, drama, and fiction.

In chapter 3, I posit a theory of the animist lyric. By incanting what I call cosmic personhood, this form functions as a tactic of postcolonial subject formation. Its logic partially resonates with psychoanalysis and new materialist ecology, but implicitly revises their secular assumptions. The lyrical spells Soyinka wrote while in prison are paradigmatic of this revision. I interpret their appropriation of Yoruba cosmology's "creative-destructive principle" in dialogue with Catherine Malabou's new materialist revision of the Freudian death drive, "destructive plasticity." Like destructive plasticity, the creative-destructive principle is tied to the material cosmos and thus operates beyond the humanist coordinates of Freudian psychoanalysis. Venturing beyond new materialism's (and thus Malabou's) purely spatial expansion of subjectivity, however, these spells also temporally expand subjectivity by way of Yoruba cosmology's cyclic time. Incorporating the living, the dead, and the unborn (and with them the past, present, and future) into the structure of cosmic personhood, the animist lyric invests ecological subjectivity with a transtemporality central to the politics of animist poetics.

In chapter 4, I propose an animist theory of tragedy. Through its ritual activation of the regenerative death drive, animist tragedy transforms the constitutive erasure of Indigenous subjectivity under the pressures of colonial modernity into the foundation of a new community. By ritualizing ancestral trauma, this form makes the wounding it stages politically generative. Soyinka's *Death and the King's Horseman* (1975) is paradigmatic of this process. Framing my analysis of the play is my placement of Soyinka's theory of Yoruba tragedy as a sacrificial rite in dialogue with the theories of political and racial sacrifice in European and Black biopolitical theology. Animist tragedy resonates with the biopolitical critiques of modernity's theological structure exemplified by Derrida, Agamben, and Wilderson, among others, I argue. Crucially, though, this form operates outside European biopolitics' post-Enlightenment cosmological coordinates and, in doing so, offers an affirmative aesthetic, rooted in an animist philosophy of life-death symbiosis, to Black biopolitical critique. This affirmative aesthetic, I argue, implicitly critiques the pessimism exemplified by Wilderson, contextualizing him within the tradition of post-Enlightenment rationality he seeks to diagnose.

In chapter 5, I model an animist approach to cultural memory. More specifically, I posit a theory of multidimensional memory, approaching

Vera's animist narrations of Zimbabwean cultural memory as paradigmatic of this theory. Analyzing her novel *The Stone Virgins* (2002) alongside her scholarship on the genealogy of the colonial prison in Africa and public writing on Zimbabwean culture and politics, I argue that Vera approaches cultural memory as a strategy of combat against what she takes to be the spatial ideology of colonialism undergirding contemporary African subjectivity. This approach hinges on Vera's filtering of Soyinkan animism through Fanonian dialectical materialism, a synthesis enabling a practice of memorialization that necessitates discarding the secular cosmopolitanism exemplified by Michael Rothberg's *Multidirectional Memory* (2009). Hence my employment of the term multi*dimensional*. For Rothberg (who voices much of cultural memory studies' resting assumptions), the work of memorialization should be aimed at the construction of globally informed identities. But if modernity extirpated the more-than-living, more-than-human dimensions of Indigenous subjectivity, this theory of memory forecloses animist subjectivity from its vision of a global public sphere: This public sphere only exists through animism's extirpation. Animist poetics must therefore dialectically produce, through the work of memory, new dimensions for a postcolonial subject to emerge, dimensions reconnecting the living with the dead and the human with the more-than human world.

From Cosmological Rupture to the Regeneration of Animacy

In terms of philosophical orientation, this chapter ordering demonstrates a movement from proposing and applying a postcolonial, posthumanist, postsecular, and ecological revision of psychoanalytic trauma theory—in short, an animist revision—to this project's next theoretical step: the more fundamental question of how to reimagine the *polis*'s theological structure. If animist subjectivity is not one, but cosmic—and therefore infinite—not an individuated human, but an expansive environment of space and time, atoms and ancestors, then not only must our understanding of the psyche's coordinates be remapped, but so must our understanding of the *polis*.

In post-Enlightenment European thought, the *polis* has been anchored to the monotheistic inheritance of the illusion of sovereign subjectivity. To return to Horkheimer and Adorno's claim that "[t]he disenchantment of the world means the extirpation of animism" (2), they go on to argue that extirpated animism has never been replaced by a less "mythic" logic. Instead, modernity takes root when animism is replaced by monotheism in secularized form. "In their mastery of nature," they write, "the Creative God and the ordering mind are alike. Man's likeness to God consists in sovereignty over existence, in the lordly gaze, in the command" (6). The "ordering mind" of the ipseitic subject, a mind that invents its own individuated borders, thereby divorcing itself from the universe, is for Horkheimer and Adorno the structuring principle of the post-Enlightenment European *polis*.

As this book unfolds, I therefore shift my theoretical lexicon from psychoanalysis proper to other theoretical discourses aimed at critiquing the myth of the sovereign subject (e.g., new materialist ecology, biopolitics) before I return, in light of these critiques, to theoretical ground more familiar to trauma theory via an animist revision of cultural memory. Ironically, these philosophical focal shifts mirror Freud's own vision of trauma theory. As his late metapsychological works such as *Civilization and Its Discontents* (1930) and *Moses and Monotheism* (1939) demonstrate, psychoanalytic trauma theory leads directly to the question of the Euro-American *polis*'s monotheistic structure. Moreover, for Freud, this question amplifies the stakes of theorizing the process of cultural memory because, as he continuously argues, the psychodynamics of memory never trace back to a single, sovereign source, but instead an infinitely relational subjectivity—not monotheism, but animism, at least in terms of structure. Contemporary theory's varied critiques of sovereignty are therefore not as far removed from psychoanalysis—or animism—as critics might believe.

In this book's brief conclusion, I distill the main points of my argument as developed across my theoretical and textual analyses. Instead of summarizing the distinct arguments of each chapter or reviewing my readings of individual writers and theorists, I offer a succinct abstraction of this book's main claims—moving from the interrelated concepts of ancestral trauma, animist poetics, and the regenerative death drive; to the implications of these concepts for interpreting trauma; to the need for an animist criticism to pass through a posthumanist, postsecular, and ecological reframing of cultural trauma to arrive at a broader theory of postcolonial subject formation as the process of reanimating the protean coordinates of cosmic personhood. In its most basic form, animist criticism, as I have suggested, involves two hermeneutic steps: (a) read in strategic response to the cosmological wounding at the heart of colonial modernity, and (b) dialectically aim this act of reading toward regeneration of the more-than-human, transtemporal kinship we all have lost (albeit in highly uneven ways) under the pressures of colonial modernity. To return to the lizard spectacle with which I began, it is Soyinka the interpreter—the critic—who from his cell envisions, against Ambrose's violent declarations of human sovereignty, a kinship between his condition of neocolonial imprisonment and the plight of his evolutionary ancestors. How might such a regenerative hermeneutics reshape our approaches to postcolonial studies, transatlantic Black studies, the environmental humanities, or our understanding of modernism as a global practice?

Chris Abani describes this regenerative turn as "The New Religion" (2006). As the Latin *religare*, "to bind," suggests, the speaker of Abani's poem discovers in his own body—marked by colonial modernity as "dark," "snubbed," and "savage"—the seed of renewed communal bonds between the subject and the world. "The body is a nation I have not known," he begins, voicing the subjective alienation to which the poem responds. Then, mimicking "God's desire to smell his own armpit"—a carnal animism hidden under monotheism's abstraction of theology from the earth—the speaker voices a cosmologically oriented corporeal sacrality. This renewed sacrality emerges in dialectical combat to "the safety of the mind" internalized by the Cartesian dualism of the post-Enlightenment European subject as "virtue/not cowardice." And the speaker voices this critical sacrality as epiphanic memory. In an "unguarded moment," he encounters The New Religion, the rites of an unknown body politic, which replace his individuating borders with the memory of a lost cosmic personhood:

> I remember the cowdung-scent
> Of my childhood skin thick with dirt and sweat
> And the screaming grass. (56)

Dung-scent, dirt, sweat, and grass adorn the speaker's skin, draping the body in its consanguinity with a fertile world, a world in which even the grass carries the screaming voice of a coming postcolonial subject. To become animist is to burst our Cartesian borders and regenerate our extirpated kinship.

Chapter 1

Ancestral Trauma and the Regenerative Death Drive

Toward an Animist Revision of Psychoanalysis

> Colonialism is not satisfied merely with holding a people in its grip and emptying the native's brain of all form and content. By a kind of perverted logic, it turns to the past of the oppressed people, and distorts, disfigures and destroys it.
>
> —Frantz Fanon, *The Wretched of the Earth*

> In contrast to the Jewish memory of the Holocaust, there is, properly speaking, no African memory of slavery; or, if there is such a memory, it is one characterized by diffraction. At best, slavery is experienced as a wound whose meaning belongs to the domain of the unconscious—in a word, witchcraft.
>
> —Achille Mbembe, "African Modes of Self-Writing"

These epigraphs place the erasure of memory at the core of colonial trauma. As Fanon argues, postcolonial conditions emerge through the historiographic trauma of the colonial encounter. I do not use the modifier *historical*, experienced during an identifiable moment in history, but *historiographic*: at once historic and hermeneutic. The historic event of colonialism erases native access to the recollection and interpretation of Indigenous history, replacing this process with a new history, Fanon argues. He calls this erasure "the settler's violence *in the beginning*," casting colonialism as a violent (re)genesis of Indigenous culture (*Wretched* 73, my emphasis). As the colonizer becomes he who "makes history," Fanon claims, he becomes "the absolute beginning" of the Indigenous world (39–40). The "historiographic perversion" of colonization is also for Fanon cosmological.[1] As Ben Grant argues, through this historiographic process Fanon casts the colonizer as an ancestor who creates a new form of ancestry; more precisely, the colonizer takes on the structural role of the ancestor through the colonization of the ancestral itself. "It is not . . . the colonizer who all unknowingly wears the mask of ancestor," Grant writes, "but the ancestors who henceforth cannot help falling into the place hollowed out by the colonizer, a place named Origin, Source, Author, etc. In other words, the ancestor is a colonizer, *by the self-definition of the latter*" (594). I describe this process as ancestral trauma.

Unlike Marianne Hirsch's influential theory of the intergenerational transmission of traumatic memory, postmemory, or Michael Rothberg's influential theory of the cross-cultural transmission of traumatic memory, multidirectional memory, ancestral trauma is not only historical, but also, as Fanon implies, cosmological. Colonization severs the link between a colonized people and their ancestral tradition by rupturing the cosmological frame of reference upon which their cultural memory depends. This rupture functions to "abolish any idea of ancestry and thus any debt with regard to a past," Mbembe writes ("African Modes" 269). By enforcing an alien frame of reference, colonial modernity makes an ancestral claim that paradoxically erases ancestry. Consequently, as Mbembe suggests, interpreting the events that historically inaugurated the everyday traumas of modern African life—the transatlantic slave trade being his example—requires transgressing the concept of cultural memory undergirding scholarship such as Hirsch's and Rothberg's. The exigency of memory loses potency in a form of life that is itself constituted through forgetting and therefore cut off from remembering.[2] Rather than Hirsch's description of a generation, or for Rothberg a culture, creatively recollecting the memories of another, ancestral trauma names the process in which the colonization of an Indigenous memory framework desecrates a social form of intergenerational, cultural remembrance. As Okonkwo puts it in Chinua Achebe's *Things Fall Apart*, "What is it that has happened to our people?" (99).

In explicating these claims from Fanon and Mbembe, I am in one sense returning to well-trodden territory within postcolonial theory—namely its intersect with poststructuralism's uses of psychoanalytic theory. We may recall Homi Bhabha's argument that a primal scene of collective and unrecoverable forgetting, the "signification of a minus in the origin," is precisely what "constitutes the *beginning* of the nation's narrative," for instance (230). Such Freudian appropriations are also foundational to Black studies outside of my focus on continental Africa. Saidiya Hartman's argument in *Lose Your Mother* (2006) that due to the "disaster of the slave trade" (29) the only return to cultural roots available to the Black subject is to "avow the loss that inaugurates one's existence" (100), for example, points to a similarly constitutive erasure, though focalized from the other side of the Atlantic. Hortense Spillers similarly writes:

> Those African persons in "Middle Passage" were literally suspended in the "oceanic," if we think of the latter in its Freudian orientation as an analogy for undifferentiated identity: removed from the indigenous land and culture, and not-yet "American" either, these captive persons, without names that their captors would recognize, were in movement across the Atlantic, but they were also *nowhere* at all. Inasmuch as, on any given day, we might imagine, the captive personality did not know where s/he was, we could say that they were the culturally "unmade," thrown in the midst of figurative darkness that "exposed" their destinies to an unknown course. (72)

Drawing on psychoanalytic terminology, Spillers emphasizes the Middle Passage's erasure of African subjectivity, which functions as the ground zero of Black subjectivity in the modern epoch.

As Bhabha, Hartman, and Spillers demonstrate in different ways, the theory of ancestral trauma I am proposing is relevant to postcolonial and Black studies outside of African studies.[3] By focusing specifically on African forms of animism, I am both joining a multidisciplinary discussion of the constitutive erasure at the core of colonial modernity and pointing this conversation in a new direction. This chapter's second epigraph gestures toward this direction. Mbembe proposes a fusing of theory of colonial trauma with vernacular forms of thought to produce an alternative to the discourse of cultural memory. For him, the "theoretical" language of the unconscious and the "vernacular" language of witchcraft both instate a logic of collective wounding and survival operating outside the logic of memorialization. So does a significant tradition of postcolonial African literature, I would add. On the one hand, African literature aesthetically represents ancestral trauma. K's "story with a hole in it" in J. M. Coetzee's

The Life and Times of Michael K (110) and Nyasha "shredding her history book between her teeth" in Tsitsi Dangarembga's *Nervous Conditions* (205) are just two examples (amid many) of characters embodying ancestral trauma. What is more, the inauguration of a tactic through which to recover from this trauma, opening the possibility of a new history—a postcolonial dispensation—is the genesis of animist poetics, the aesthetic tactic centered in this book.

Here I build on Emmanuel Chukwudi Eze's argument that postcolonial African literature is not merely a representation of modern African experience, but more fundamentally an attempt to collectively heal from the temporal rupture conditioning this experience. For him, what makes Achebe so important is that he "was the first to grasp—and in a series of criticisms, aesthetically articulate—the full dimensions of the modern African sense of tradition as that which is in need of artistic healing and repair" ("Language" 26). As Achebe claims, quoting James Baldwin, the African writer must creatively utilize language to "bear the burden" of collective experience. To bear this burden, language must be molded, Achebe argues, to operate in "communion with its ancestral home but altered to suit its new African surroundings" (*Morning* 62). For Eze, this process means utilizing "language to mend time" after colonization ruptured Indigenous experiences of historical continuity (26). In other words, in response to the ancestral trauma of colonization, African literature must operate beyond an aesthetics of representation, engaging instead with what Wole Soyinka calls "art as a ritual process" ("Ritual" 7) and Achebe calls "regeneration" (*Morning* 45). To be sure, many postcolonial African writers choose a mode of purely representational aesthetics disinterested in Eze's framing of the Achebean tradition. While it may be true that literature has a powerful role to play in representing cultural trauma, in this book I focus on the process through which certain postcolonial African writers utilize literature to create new forms of collective life emerging through such trauma. Such literature shares its affirmative, agential—indeed, ritual—act, Mbembe's quote implies, with witchcraft, though, as I have made clear in this book's introduction, I opt for the term *animism*.[4]

As I explained in the introduction, throughout this book I focus on an aesthetic response to ancestral trauma I find in postcolonial African literature, animist poetics, the best of which moves, through ritual aesthetics, beyond the process of historical representation and into the conjuring of a new dispensation in which the kinship between the subject and the cosmos is regenerated. Like the *egungun* mask on this book's cover, animist poetics is less representational than mediatory, ritually connecting the living with the dead as well as the human with the more-than-human world. Since colonial modernity, as Fanon claims, "distorts, disfigures and destroys" Indigenous coordinates of ancestral mediation, animist poetics must mediate a wound disabling its own ritual efficacy (*Wretched* 169). This auto-mediation operates through a logic of collective survival through death, a process I term the regenerative death drive, on which I focus in this chapter. If animist poetics is a strategic response to ancestral trauma, the regenerative death drive is the hydraulics of this response, the force spurring its formal dynamics.

Since the corpus of postcolonial African literature immanently theorizes each of these categories, the language of contemporary theory is not necessary to recognizing the regenerative death drive I map out in this chapter. However, by alluding to a term central to Freudian psychoanalysis, my formulation of the phrase "regenerative death drive" highlights the revision of psychoanalytic theory implicit within animist poetics. In this chapter, I argue that psychoanalytic and deconstructive trauma theory, reframed through Fanon, gives language to the ancestral trauma depicted by so many African writers.[5] By staging this dialogue between theory and African literature, I also demonstrate how the affirmative logic of the regenerative death drive opens the possibility of developing what Edward Said would call a "contrapuntal" reading of Freudian theory as animist.[6] By proposing animist revision of Freud—drawing on animist poetics' cosmological expansion of subjectivity in dialogue with Fanon's critique of Freud—I outline a collective trauma and regeneration dialectic constantly taking place throughout the more-than-human world. This ecological scope provincializes Euro-American trauma theory and the Manichaeism of its typical postcolonial critique, highlighting the need for contemporary theory to reexamine the concept of trauma beyond the epistemic framework of post-Enlightenment European humanism. To contextualize this argument, I first turn to the problem of Eurocentrism within psychoanalytic theory.

Trauma Theory in the Postcolony

In "Geopsychoanalysis: '. . . and the rest of the world,'" Derrida critiques the Euro-American blindfold of psychoanalysis, asking us to consider what sort of global *polis* is imagined when psychoanalytic theory's "ongoing worldification" ignores the majority of the globe, those spaces, mostly colonized spaces, where "*Homo psychoanalyticus* is unknown or outlawed" (66, 87). To push Derrida's polemic further, "the rest of the world" appears within the psychoanalytic paradigm as a "dark continent," to use Henry Morton Stanley's infamous phrase, a phrase Freud himself employs in "The Question of Lay Analysis" to refer to female sexuality. As Ranjana Khanna convincingly argues, Freud's use of Stanley's phrase (in its original English)—the (non)translation of a geopolitical metaphor into the realm of sexual difference—reveals two regimes that historically produced the subject of psychoanalysis: patriarchy and empire. This pairing implies a question pertinent to trauma theory. If, after the influence of *écriture féminine*, sexual difference and thus the problem of phallogocentrism is an obligatory concern of psychoanalytically informed literary and cultural theory, what of the colonial relation and thus the problem of Eurocentrism?[7]

This problem is pertinent to the collective of comparatists who, during high theory's "ethical turn" in the early 1990s, began to theorize trauma as the fundamental experience of twentieth-century history as well as an ethically motivated mode of reading culture—the most influential of whom has been Cathy Caruth.[8] In one of the most debated phrases in contemporary trauma studies, Caruth posits that trauma offers the "possibility, in a catastrophic era, of a link between cultures" (*Unclaimed* 56). Taking the current state of literary and cultural studies as a litmus test, however, we must admit that, a few decades in, the link produced by theory's turn to traumatic memory is unequal. As the work of Giorgio Agamben, Roberto Esposito, Eric Santner, and others attest, the Holocaust—and perhaps more specifically, Auschwitz—has been cast as the primal scene of modernity. Forget the entire history of European imperial expansion; it is not until we reach the Nazi death camp that, as Agamben famously puts it, the "*nomos* of the modern" is revealed (*Homo*, 166). This tunnel vision is precisely the problem Derrida raises in "Geopsychoanalysis." By leaving "the rest of the world," to borrow the International Psychoanalytic Association's words, "[d]isremembered and unaccounted for" (274), to borrow Toni Morrison's words, psychoanalysis, Derrida argues, faces a problem of futurity. He writes, "The size of these psychoanalytically virgin territories, in terms both of their physical extension and of their (present and future) demographics, as well as their cultural and religious foundations, means that they constitute a vast problem for the future of psychoanalysis. For that future is far from being structured like a space opening up ahead—a space yet to come, as it were, for psychoanalysis"

(87). In our globalized world, the future of psychoanalysis, Derrida argues, is not pre-given. Rather, it hangs upon the eclipse of Western worldification. In short, psychoanalysis can only survive by being reframed through postcolonial criticism.

Rather than rejecting psychoanalytic thought in order to understand the multitude of traumas that emerge outside the narrow world of psychoanalysis, Derrida reads psychoanalysis against itself, arguing that the reality of disremembered traumas throughout the globe traumatizes psychoanalytic trauma theory, threatening its survival from an unknown future. As he puts it in "Autoimmunity: Real and Symbolic Suicides," "A traumatic event is not only marked as an event by the memory, even if unconscious, of what took place." He continues, "I believe we must complicate this schema (even if it is not completely false); we must question its 'chrono-logy,' that is, the thought and order of temporalization it seems to imply. We must rethink the temporalization of traumatism" (96). A traumatic event, he claims, temporally "proceeds neither from the now that is present nor from the present that is past but from an im-presentable to come (á venir)" (97). Such a temporal logic is, despite being pinned against psychoanalysis, the core of psychoanalytic trauma theory. How does one think this strange history? How does one interpret that which is not present? Such entangled historicity raised by the everyday, disremembered wounds of the postcolony is in fact the central concern, according to Derrida, of any serious theory of trauma.

Both Freud and Caruth bring this concern to the fore. The most influential text undergirding contemporary debates on trauma across the theoretical humanities, Caruth's *Unclaimed Experience* (1996), begins with Freud's analysis of a scene of haunting from Torquato Tasso's *Jerusalem Liberated*. One of the most influential critiques of Caruth, Ruth Leys's *Trauma: A Genealogy*, culminates in a conflicting interpretation of this scene. This dispute emblematizes the logic of the typical postcolonial critique of psychoanalytic trauma theory—a logic that, despite offering useful critiques of theory's blind spots, remains too limited by post-Enlightenment European humanism to recognize how animist cosmologies frame trauma.

In Tasso's epic, Tancred, who accidentally killed his lover, Clorinda, slashes a tree with his sword. Blood streams down the bark, and Tancred hears Clorinda's voice crying. He is shocked to find that his lover's spirit resides within this tree. In *Beyond the Pleasure Principle*, Freud interprets this passage as a depiction of the repetition compulsion. Like survivors returning to their traumatic experiences within their dreams, Tancred returns to his scene of trauma, re-wounding Clorinda against his conscious desire.[9] Caruth filters Freud's interpretation through post-deconstructive ethics, claiming this passage stages the ethical stakes of trauma theory. Tancred is addressed by trauma, she argues, just as subjectivity is addressed by "the other"; in other words, in the fashion of 1990s theory, Freudian trauma substantiates Levinasian ethics.[10]

Most striking to me about Freud's and Caruth's interpretations is the fact that they both repress the animism of the passage under consideration. For them, the text is decidedly not about a tree spirit, but is instead an allegory of the human psyche's secular coordinates. Leys doubles down on this repression, arguing that Freud and Caruth cast the perpetrator, Tancred, as the victim, instead of Clorinda (an Ethiopian princess who is for Amy Novak "the female voice of black Africa" [32]). Clorinda, Leys argues, is the "undisputable victim of wounding," and Freud's and Caruth's shared mistake bears ethical consequences (294). Following their logic "would turn the executioners of the Jews into victims and the 'cries' of the Jews into testimony to the trauma suffered by the Nazis," she writes (297). According to this logic, Freud's and Caruth's interpretations are not secular enough. Even though they allegorize the tree spirit, they still challenge the post-Enlightenment belief that subjectivity is individuated, that there are clear borders between persons; for Leys, functional ethics requires a retainment of these borders.

Leys's argument is exemplary of the standard critique of psychoanalytic and deconstructive trauma theory across literary and cultural criticism. Lauren Berlant, Rob Nixon, Ann Cvetkovich, and Veena Das, for example, have each faulted the discourse for ignoring the ordinary violence of everyday life—what Berlant calls "crisis ordinariness"—be they economic, environmental, sexual, or racial. Each concludes that, in short, the theory of trauma brought into the spotlight by Caruth and her "Yale School" affiliates bypasses *realpolitik* for that late deconstructive nowhereland, the ethical.[11] What I am arguing, however, is that while Caruth's and Leys's interpretations might appear opposed (Levinasian totality vs historicist specificity), they share the assumption that only a secularized, anthropocentric approach to Tancred's haunting can make sense of the passage's claims for trauma theory. In *Multidirectional Memory*, Rothberg brings this assumption to the spotlight of this metadebate. He critiques Leys's conflation of trauma with the status of victimhood (perpetrators can also become traumatized), arguing that Clorinda cannot actually be the passage's embodiment of trauma because, unlike Tancred, she is dead; "trauma implies some 'other' mode of living on" (90).

From classical psychoanalysis to post-deconstructive theory to historicist genealogy, each of these arguments shares the assumption that there is a clear division between the living and the dead, the human and the more-than-human world. Read from a standpoint primarily concerned with developing a postcolonial trauma theory, the problem of contingency versus universality overseeing this debate is less illuminating than the fact that every major intervention in this debate ignores the animistic qualities of Tasso's passage. Sam Durrant and I therefore write:

> What if Leys is misguided in her conflation of trauma and morality, political justice and stably bordered identities, but correct (perhaps unwittingly so) in her claim that dead people can be traumatized? What is repeated is not only Tancred's initial wounding of Clorinda but monotheism's attempted extirpation of animism. In voicing its own wounding, the spirited tree thus testifies both to its own animacy and to the ties that bind Tancred not just to Clorinda but to all life forms. (195)

Read in light of Max Horkheimer and Theodor Adorno's claim that "[t]he disenchantment of the world means the extirpation of animism" (2), this passage shifts from an image of the repetition compulsion undergirding a solely human subject to the cosmological return of a repressed animistic subject whose extirpation constitutes European modernity. In an epic of the First Crusade—a poem memorializing the European seizing of the center of monotheism—the dead Clorinda and the wounded forest address themselves to Tancred as a shared animacy ruptured by the sociohistorical and theological structures he embodies. It is only through my interest in animist poetics that I recognize this animist revision of trauma theory already within the corpus of psychoanalysis. In this way, African literature enables a contrapuntal reading of psychoanalysis, allowing us to recognize in a manner that Freud never could the wound of Tasso's spirited tree as embodying a cosmological rupture incorporating the living and the dead as well as the human and the more-than-human: in a word, modernity.

The posthumous transfigurations I briefly examined in the introduction demonstrate a recrafting of the Tancred and Clorinda parable around a regenerative death drive central to modern African aesthetics—from which I explicate a trauma theory that both takes into account "the rest of the world," in Derrida's polemic and, perhaps more enigmatically, the world of the ancestors—including our nonhuman ancestors. Such an epistemic shift in theory amounts to a simultaneously postcolonial and posthumanist remapping of psychic coordinates around environmental ruptures, which in the Tancred and Clorinda debate amounts to a postsecular revision of trauma theory. While postsecular criticism focuses primarily on the public spheres tied to Christianity and Islam (the focal points of Tasso's poem), I instead focus on texts that seek to regenerate a public sphere tied to the Indigenous spiritualities predating monotheism's advent: animism (the unconscious focal point of Tasso's poem). But if ancestral trauma names a severance of the colonized subject from Indigenous cosmology, how can animist poetics actually be animist? What is especially fruitful about the Tancred and Clorinda passage is that its animism emerges as a wound, a dialectical response to its extirpation under European modernity's monotheistic inheritance of the myth of the sovereignly bordered individual. Similarly, none of the literary texts I analyze in this book assume frames of reference that preexist the ancestral trauma of colonization. Rather, their animist cosmologies emerge as strategic responses to this collective wounding, articulated by Fanon in this chapter's first epigraph as the distortion, disfiguration, and destruction of Indigenous frames of reference.

Consider, for example, how Achebe's narrator in *Things Fall Apart* represents the precolonial Igbo world with recourse to biblical (that is, colonial) symbolism: the locust as an omen of cultural collapse (an allusion to Exodus 10), or the description of ancestral voices speaking through the *egwuwu* as "tongues of fire" (an allusion to Acts 2:3). The intricately detailed Indigenous cosmology of *Things Fall Apart*'s opening, established through the narrator's ethnographic impulse, is narrated from the beginning with reference to Christian symbolism; this aspect of the novel suggests that, for Achebe, there is no return to a purely precolonial world, even at the level of aesthetic imagination. For the postcolonial African writer, animist poetics is always an act of creatively appropriating a lost frame of reference as a strategic response to the colonial modernity that distorted said frame.

I am here building on claims made by Durrant and David Lloyd. In one of the first studies to place the theoretical turn to trauma partially opened by Caruth in dialogue with postcolonial literature, *Postcolonial Narrative and the Work of Mourning*, Durrant demonstrates a formal relation between theories of post-traumatic mourning in Freud and Derrida and the historiography envisioned within postcolonial fiction. Contra claims made by many postcolonial critics of trauma theory (on which I train focus in the next chapter), Durrant locates within postcolonial narrative a primary, irrecoverable act of forgetting: a prehistoric foreclosure through which the colonized subject historically emerges as traumatized (5). And postcolonial fiction, he suggests, functions as acts of mourning this trauma, thereby aiding postcolonial recovery (a claim that resonates with Eze's view of African literature as an act of mending broken time). In "Colonial Trauma/Postcolonial Recovery?" Lloyd argues that such recovery cannot be conceptualized as the "retrieval of a lost self or lost culture" because colonial trauma erases the past self, constituting a new "subject whose very condition is a transformation" (215). Despite this transformational erasure, or traumatic subject formation, Lloyd argues, there lurk "melancholy survivals" of precolonial, precapitalist forms of collective living scattered through the postcolonial present (219). A "non-therapeutic relation to the past, structured around the notion of survival or living on rather than recovery" should therefore "ground a different mode of historicization" for postcolonial critique, he claims (219–20). In other words, if fragments of the precolonial past haunt the postcolonial present from which they have been excluded—spectrally surviving despite being erased, like the animism haunting Tasso's poem—then postcolonial recovery paradoxically founds itself on a refusal to heal, a continual openness toward being haunted by the past from which the subject has been severed.

In response, Durrant writes, "Lloyd in effect reverses the formula that he sets out to question in his title; instead of postcolonial mourning as the cure for colonial trauma, the 'living on' of colonial trauma disrupts the therapeutic culture of postcolonial modernity" ("Undoing" 96). Durrant thus recognizes that what Lloyd calls postcolonial recovery requires a rethinking of history as the temporality of traumatic survival. By way of the terms "recovery" and "mourning," then, Lloyd and Durrant perceive the connection between the psychoanalytic concept of trauma and postcolonial theory to be the challenge of crafting out of an irrecoverable erasure a form of living on, surviving otherwise—like Tasso's animist forest. Similarly, animist poetics is a logic of survival. As an aesthetic logic emerging from colonized modernity, animist poetics challenges dichotomies between the Indigenous and the modern, Africa and the West—or, as the Tancred and Clorinda interpretive debate demonstrates, the logics of animism and Euro-American theory. This book consequently challenges both a therapeutic framework of recovery and the Manichaeism of the standard critique of psychoanalysis as too Eurocentric and totalizing—even if these critiques are partially correct.

Fanon is a helpful model for this productively agonistic relationship to psychoanalytic theory. A fierce critic of Freudian Eurocentrism, he also argues that "only a psychoanalytical interpretation of the black problem can lay bare the anomalies of affect that are responsible for the structure of the complex" (*Black Skin* 10). Ogaga Ifowodo expands Fanon's focus on race to account for the traumatic nature of colonialization (an expansion Fanon himself models in *The Wretched of the Earth*), writing that psychoanalysis's unique salience for postcolonial studies is due to the fact that "psychoanalytic procedure inexorably refers us to the exterior world of lived experience, a space in the postcolony riddled with the original and transgenerational traumas of colonialism. But it does so while also keeping us focused on the interior world of the traumatized. In other words, a psychoanalytic interpretation of the postcolonial problem is invariably a Janus-faced methodology that compels us to look both inward and outward at the same time" (20). Ironically, this inward and outward movement of postcolonial interpretation that psychoanalysis enables also challenges a core assumption of Freudian trauma theory: that there is a discernible inside and outside to the subject. Formally, this challenge is the starting point for Fanon's "sociodiagnostic" appropriation of psychoanalysis, his refusal to quarantine the internal space of individual subjectivity from the external space of social and political dynamics. He writes, "Freud insisted that the individual factor be taken into account through psychoanalysis. He substituted for a phylogenetic theory the ontogenetic perspective. . . . [T]he black man's alienation is not an individual question. Beside phylogeny and ontogeny stands sociogeny. . . . [L]et us say that this is a question of a sociodiagnostic" (*Black Skin* 11). This claim, that a psychoanalysis of race and colonization must be sociogenic, is in many ways a radical expansion of Lacan's socialization of Freud, which is itself an expansion of Freud's late metapsychology—which does not neatly separate the individual from the social. Fanon's critique of psychoanalysis is, in other words, an extension of a logic intrinsic to the discourse. What Fanon makes abundantly clear is that in the postcolony the mode of critique psychoanalysis enables must continuously be expanded. One implication of this continuous expansion is that the "society" implied by the word "sociodiagnostic" must venture beyond the domain of the solely human to include whole environments, and even the living and the dead. In this way, Fanon's appropriation of psychoanalysis leads directly to animist critique.

Édouard Glissant models a similar expansion of Fanon in a Caribbean context in his *Poetics of Relation* (1990). His concept of the "abyssal" intertwinements between subjects constituting a postcolonial collective subject who mirrors the "oceanic" form of the Middle Passage should not be separated from his use of psychoanalytic theory to conceptualize the postcolonial condition. As he rhetorically asks elsewhere:

> Would it be ridiculous to consider our lived history as a steadily advancing neurosis? To see the Slave Trade as a traumatic shock, our relocation (in the new land) as a repressive phase, slavery as the period of latency, "emancipation" in 1848 as reactivation, our everyday fantasies as symptoms, and even our horror of "returning to those things of the past" as a possible manifestation of the neurotic's fear of his past? Would it not be useful and revealing to investigate such a parallel? What is repressed in our history persuades us, furthermore, that this is more than an intellectual game. (*Caribbean* 66)

Glissant's development of a "poetics of relation" to transform the "oceanic" erasure of African subjectivity into the starting point for an expansive theory of postcolonial subjectivity is a response to his view of colonial history as a cultural trauma. As his poetic and philosophical writings consistently suggest, Fanon's critical expansion of psychoanalysis's field of vision must be totalizing. It must be pushed beyond secular, anthropocentric coordinates to include the living, the dead, and their ecosystems. In short, it must become animist. Unfortunately, the academic discourse dubbed "trauma studies" does not follow this trajectory.

Interpreting Trauma: A Critique of "Trauma Studies"

According to psychoanalysis, trauma is, at its core, a hermeneutic phenomenon. Prior to its status as a psychic experience, trauma's origination is interpretive, which is to say that any theory of trauma is necessarily a hermeneutics, or theory of interpretation. The word *hermeneutics* derives from Hermes, the messenger of the gods, and the interpretation of an overwhelming message is precisely what is at stake in a traumatic experience. That certain survivors of horrific events are forever shaped by their experience while others move on means that no event, no matter how violent, is itself traumatic. Any experience, from the most extreme act of violence to the most quotidian aspect of modern life, has the potential to be or not to be traumatic. The decisive factor, according to psychoanalysis, is the gap between experience and interpretation. Freud makes this point in *Moses and Monotheism* when he claims that the "quantitative" nature of trauma implies a certain relativity: "If we may assume that the experience acquires its traumatic character only as a result of a quantitative element—that is to say, that in every case it is an excess in demand that is responsible for an experience evoking unusual pathological reactions—then we can easily arrive at the expedient of saying that something acts as a trauma in the case of one constitution but in the case of another would have no such effect" (316). Here Freud conceptualizes trauma as the experience of an event that overwhelms the subject, but may not overwhelm others, casting trauma theory as a comparative hermeneutics. If "What does this experience mean?" is the question that, in its unanswerability, shapes an experience into trauma, then the theorization of trauma requires an examination of the various and often contradictory frameworks through which subjective experiences take on meaning—in a word, culture.

In literary criticism, trauma studies has for the past three decades focused on this cultural aspect. Divorcing itself from psychoanalysis, however, the discourse has mostly neglected the problem of interpretation. As Petar Ramadanovic described in 2014:

> [T]he MLA database lists over twelve hundred works published after 1999 with the term "trauma" in the title, most of which are applying the simplest of formulas—"trauma in X," where X can be anything from a Shakespeare tragedy to Native American hip-hop. The newfound ubiquity of trauma does not, however, imply that the very basic concepts of this theory are well understood, including issues like how trauma is present in a work of art or who is traumatized exactly. Is it the character? The audience? The author? To complicate matters, with the work of Jacques Lacan . . . psychoanalysis stopped psychoanalyzing literary characters and authors and moved beyond reading narratives as representations. After his seminar on Edgar Allan Poe's short story "The Purloined Letter," Lacan defined a whole new task for analysis that concerned the nature of interpretation and consisted of investigating the structure of meaning, the role of the signifier, and so on. (1–2)

The problem identified here has only intensified since Ramadanovic voiced this critique. As he laments, most critics working within trauma studies "apply" psychoanalytic terms to literary and social texts in hopes of diagnosing certain sociohistorically situated moments of individual trauma (rape, death of a loved one) or collective trauma (World War II, September 11), typically represented by a traumatized character (Septimus Smith, Paul D), author/artist (Fyodor Dostoevsky, Marguerite Duras), or basic narratological techniques (nonlinearity, the flashback). Even skeptical critics follow this formula: "apply" psychoanalytic terms to literary and social texts in order to demonstrate this application's failure and thus argue that certain sociohistorically situated individual and collective traumas (domestic abuse, structural racism, subaltern genocides) are underrepresented by theory.[12] This common practice has by and large severed trauma studies from Lacan's turn to "the nature of interpretation," as Ramadanovic puts it. With notable exceptions, most work in the field is motivated by the belief that art functions as a diagnostic representation of the social reality of trauma.

Many critics, however, remain skeptical of the very category of trauma. Responding to the widespread appeal of trauma within cultural criticism, Leys calls for a Foucauldian "genealogical approach" to the subject (8). According to Jeffrey Alexander, this approach helps overcome the "naturalistic fallacy" tethering trauma theory to wider cultural obsessions with witnessing and memorializing trauma. These obsessions have induced zeitgeist titles from cultural critics such as our "trauma culture," (Kaplan), our "post-traumatic culture" (Farrell), or our "musealizing culture" (Huyssen). For Didier Fassin and Richard Rechtman, scholarship should respond to this zeitgeist by "denaturalizing trauma and repoliticizing victims" (xii). As they document, following the post-Vietnam implementation of post-traumatic stress disorder (PTSD) into the West's cultural lexicon, the concept of trauma has morphed into our era's "central reality of violence" (22). Allan Young dubs this perceived reality a "harmony of illusions," which has become "glued together" through the "practices, technologies, and narratives" of modernity (5). Similarly, Roger Luckhurst describes trauma as a "knot" of "hybrid assemblages" arising from the practices of a "statistical society" attempting to calculate the modern "accident" (14, 25). These critiques are all attempts to combat a cultural shift—what Fassin and Rechtman describe as the reshaping of our "moral economy" into a "politics of trauma"—through the de-universalizing tactic of new historicist genealogy (7, 8).

On top of genealogy, many critics attempt to combat this shift through sociocultural contextualization. Pushing Judith Herman's germinal study of the relation between trauma and female experience further, for instance,

Laura Brown influentially argues that to conceptualize trauma as an *extraordinary* experience is to ignore the "normative, quotidian" (*Cultural* 18) traumas of minorities that structurally sustain the ordinary, nontraumatic life patterns of "white, young, able-bodied, educated, middle-class, Christian men" ("Not Outside" 101). In other words, because normality is ideological, the phenomenological, event-based focus of trauma as a disruption of the normal—single-blow trauma theory—ignores the traumas of those denied subject positions on the stage of the normal. Moreover, it misses the ongoing political forces that, by producing ordinary experience and thereby defining what counts as an extraordinary experience, constitute trauma (invisible or not) in the first place.

In the following chapter, I will demonstrate how these genealogical and contextual critiques are employed in the postcolonial critique of trauma studies exemplified by Stef Craps's *Postcolonial Witnessing* (2012), and I will demonstrate the limits of this form of critique. For now, though, I wish to emphasize something that many critics attempting to construct a postcolonial trauma theory forget. If a traumatic event is traumatic not because of the horrific essence of the event itself, but because of its non-position within an interpretive framework, its act of undoing a hermeneutic field from without, then a properly postcolonial trauma theory can only be realized through comparative hermeneutics—that is, by actively engaging with incongruous ways of meaning making. In this chapter I am attempting precisely this task by placing deconstructive, psychoanalytic trauma theory and African literature in dialogue. As will become clear, one of my wagers is that the theoretical critiques of sovereignty assumed in the relational subjectivities envisioned by both Freud and Derrida share a formal relation with the animist cosmologies in the African literary texts I examine throughout this book. Thus, as I will detail in the next chapter, contra many critics of trauma theory, I take as a given that psychoanalysis and deconstruction are both critiques of Eurocentrism, not Eurocentric thought itself. In this sense, of course their scope is Eurocentric: Europe is their subject of critique. Consequently, a better route to "decolonize the mind," as Ngũgĩ wa Thiong'o famously puts it, is a comparative hermeneutics that holds critiques of Eurocentrism in one hand and alternative cosmological structures in another. By modeling this strategy throughout this book, I demonstrate that African literature's animist poetics ultimately thinks beyond the confines of Euro-American theory—not because animism is less Western (despite this claim being true), but because animist poetics ventures beyond critique and into a mode of ritually mending a world extirpated by, to employ Derrida's term again, Western worldification.

This *beyond* of theory leads us to the problem of political theology, a problem that will take an increasingly prominent role in this book. For now, I will raise this problem as a question: What if the myth of the sovereign subject that is traumatized by theory—wounded by Freud, deconstructed by Derrida—no longer held its sway on our imagination? Although critiquing sovereignty has its place, it also has its limit, and the only way to transgress this limit is to enter a new hermeneutic field. As Achebe explains in "Chi in Igbo Cosmology," for the Igbo worldview, "Wherever Something stands, Something Else will stand beside it. Nothing is absolute. *I am the truth, the way and the life* would be called blasphemous or simply absurd[,] for is it not well known that a man may worship Ogwugwu to perfection and yet be killed by Udo?" (*Morning* 94). Likewise, Soyinka describes a "harmonious will" at the center of Yoruba tragedy, a will that "accommodates every alien material or abstract phenomenon within its infinitely stressed spirituality" (*Myth* 146). What would a hermeneutic field that incorporates *every* alien phenomenon look like? Freud's hypothesis of the "receptive cortical layer . . . suspended in the middle of an external world charged with the most powerful energies," the breach of which constitutes trauma, would no longer apply (*Beyond* 298). The breakdown of sovereignly bordered subject positions would not be trauma, but fact (which is the utopian horizon of Fanon's disruption of Freud's division between internal psyche and external society). Moreover, what would an "infinitely stressed spirituality" look like? A cosmology in which the "stress" of the external breaking into the internal would no longer be "stress," but instead an infinite state of movement? Are these questions ways of approaching animism as a cosmology without a sovereign subject, as Achebe suggests?

If our mode of theory resides solely in the realm of negative critique, questions like these fall on deaf ears. Yet these questions are central to my placement of theory and postcolonial African literature in dialogue. If psychoanalysis and deconstruction both in their own ways observe the moment in which the demystifying, disenchanting hermeneutic scheme of the sovereignly bordered subject of Western metaphysics breaks down, animist poetics attempts to re-enchant the world, the text, and the subject otherwise than sovereignly. Furthermore, if animist cosmologies do not operate according to such metaphysical calculations, could animist poetics help us articulate forms of life beyond the limit of deconstruction, beyond the threshold of mourning at the eclipse of metaphysics to which the late Derrida remained tethered? I am not so naive as to believe I can speak outside the grasp of metaphysics simply by analyzing African literature, but what I am suggesting is that placing these hermeneutic frameworks together may help us articulate new hermeneutic possibilities. As long as postcolonial studies operates purely as ideology critique, however, such possibilities will remain unrealized. One of the implications of my argument throughout this book is therefore that postcolonial criticism must read not only to expose colonial and neocolonial ideology sedimented in global modernity's cultural forms, but to craft a new hermeneutic framework to battle these forms: a hermeneutics of re-enchantment, to return to Harry Garuba's term from this book's introduction.

Caruthian Trauma Theory in the Postcolony

Caruth consistently advances three hypotheses. First, deconstruction and psychoanalysis can together craft a historiography rooted in the logic of traumatic temporality and literary language. Both discourses foster a "rethinking of reference" that allows "*history* to arise where *immediate understanding* may not," she claims (*Unclaimed* 11). More specifically, an unconscious, traumatic (un)knowledge of non-referential historicity arises at the intersect between the "psychoanalytic theory of traumatic experience" (3) and the "enigmatic language of the literary" (*Literature* 90), that space "between knowing and not knowing" (*Unclaimed* 3) that deconstruction and psychoanalysis both explore. In *Literature in the Ashes of History*, this project shifts from the question of how to articulate non-referential historicity to how to conceptualize history as disappearance. Although this shift demonstrates a transition from the de Manian language of rhetoric (semiology) to late Derridean language of ashes (ontology), Caruth remains focused on the same problem: How can we inaugurate a hermeneutic scheme through which to conceptualize history beyond the metaphysical trope of the self-presencing sovereign subject who uses language to directly signify historical reality? This question is far more pertinent to the trauma of colonization than critics have perceived. If Freud's temporality of trauma casts the traumatic blow as never historically locatable in the past, but always in the differed/deferred space/time of the repetition compulsion, the temporality of *Nachträglichkeit* that Caruth (like Derrida) takes to be Freud's stroke of genius, then this form of trauma theory may provide a language useful for conceptualizing the constitutive erasure of cultural memory Fanon places at the core of colonization. What has been critiqued as "canonical trauma theory" by postcolonial critics is, I am suggesting, more useful for understanding the starting point of animist poetics than such criticism has recognized.

Second, Caruth argues, this rethinking of reference and history around trauma implies a politics. If one's history always emerges through the traumatic temporality of the repetition compulsion, and if this emergence always takes place with others, then "history, like trauma, is never simply one's own"; rather, "history is precisely the way we are implicated in each other's traumas" (*Unclaimed* 24). Such is the context of Caruth's promise of the "possibility" of a "link between cultures" (56). If cultural history is structured around cultural trauma, which is always multiplicitous, then trauma theory is also a theory of transcultural links. Here Caruth precedes Judith Butler's turn to the politics of vulnerability. For Butler, it is not that the human is vulnerable because she or he exists in community, but rather that vulnerability, susceptibility to traumatic loss, is the precondition of community, which requires a rethinking of politics through ontological precarity. In "Undoing Sovereignty," Durrant takes Butler's project in *Precarious Life* to be the political horizon of trauma theory. "Against the normative, psychoanalytic account of mourning as a reconstitution of the subject's borders, a withdrawing of the ties that bind or bound us to others," he writes, "Butler argues that traumatic losses are occasions for a kind of ethical growth, whereby we come to understand that 'we' were never simply ourselves but were always part of others" (92). In other words, when Butler celebrates traumatic subject deformation, becoming re-implicated through loss, she affirms Caruth's contested traumatic link: Trauma reveals our implicated existence ordinarily hidden by our culturally bordered subject positions.[13]

Third, Caruth argues the first two wagers are best grasped through the act of close reading. Geoffrey Hartman recognizes this exegetical dimension of what he terms trauma theory's "feverish quest" for knowledge of the "first encounter." In an early response to the then emerging discourse, he acknowledges its return to "an older question: what kind of knowledge is art, or what kind of knowledge does art foster?" (537). More specifically, trauma returns us to "basic literary questions," he claims: " 'Why is interpretation necessary?' or, 'Why are there texts?' or, 'Why literature, story, and not just events, history?' " (541). These questions raised by both trauma and literature, he argues, "produce their own mode of recognition," and it is the task of trauma theory, like literary theory, to inherit this epistemology, which operates outside the logic of our currently inherited hermeneutic scheme of text-history (i.e., word-world) referentiality (545).

Thus, Ramadanovic correctly takes the task of trauma theory to be the "study of the constitutive limitations of knowledge and experience" ("Intro"), reminding critics that the goal of the discourse is not to provide models of representing trauma, but theories of aesthetic encounter. "Caruth's . . . arguments are about interpretation and how we might define theory and its epochal role of breaking with the past," he writes ("The Time" 19). By asking what it would be like if "shattered frameworks and discontinuities are a permanent feature of the interpretive process," the goal of trauma theory is not only a clarified understanding of how trauma has been experienced and represented, but the more arduous goal of "defining a new aesthetic that itself would offer a way to create a different kind of reality, a new kind of culture that can exist despite the disruption of the frame of reference, and a new kind of theory of history" (18).

While my inquiry is influenced by this Caruthian trauma theory, I also move beyond its purveyance, which follows the narratological movements of *awakening* and *falling*. The former is the most cited motif in the body of criticism on Caruth and is expounded in her reading of Lacan's interpretation of "the dream of the burning child" from Freud's *The Interpretation of Dreams*. In this passage a father is haunted in his sleep by his dead son, during which the father awakens from bordered ipseity into relational existence—an awakening that provides a ghost-narrative form to the Levinasian ethics Caruth finds embedded in the act of witnessing trauma. Less cited is Caruth's insistence that this awakening from ontology to what Derrida terms hauntology in *Specters of Marx* takes the form of the Fall, a concept Caruth inherits from Paul de Man. *Unclaimed Experience*'s boldest claims emerge in Caruth's interpretation of de Man's rhetoric of falling, through which she casts her trauma theory as an attempt to catch up with de Man's intervention in the history of Western philosophy. As she puts it, "[T]he history of philosophy after Newton could be thought of as a series of confrontations with the question of how to talk about falling," and after de Man, this problem becomes a problem of reference, she argues, rewriting the question of how to linguistically refer to historical reality as *"how to refer to falling"* (76). This movement elucidates the productive agonism inherent to my placement of Caruthian trauma theory and postcolonial African literature in dialogue. This elucidation, however, requires an understanding of the contingent nature of the de Manian fall Caruth theorizes.

Near the end of de Man's influential reading of Heinrich von Kleist's "On the Marionette Theatre" as an allegory of aesthetic form, de Man claims that "by falling (in all the sense of the term, including the theological Fall), gracefully, one prepares the ascent" (*The Rhetoric* 287). He insists that this falling as ascending, or ascending as falling, is something like an indeterminable phenomenology of aesthetic form. "Rather than speaking of a synthesis of rising and falling," he goes on to write, "one should speak of a continuity of the aesthetic form that does not allow itself to be disrupted by the borderlines that separate life from death, pathos from levitation, rising from falling" (287). Justifying not quite a formalism but a certain experience of falling into the movement of form, de Man argues that as the rhetoric of aesthetics ignores metaphysically erected borders (e.g., living and dying), his proposed implicated phenomenology of falling, which somehow enables an ascent, is the modus operandi of literature. Literary interpretation, in sum, pushes the reader from the ontological world of truth claims into the hauntological world of aesthetics—which, like Tasso's animist forest, challenges binaries central to post-Enlightenment rationality.

Trauma theory, Caruth suggests, is a theory of, a giving words to, this epistemic fall, what de Man elsewhere describes as the crisis inaugurated by the advent of literary theory. He writes, "Well-established rules and conventions that governed the discipline of criticism and made it a cornerstone of the intellectual establishment have been so badly tampered with that the entire edifice threatens to collapse. One is tempted to speak of recent developments in Continental criticism in terms of a crisis" (*Blindness* 3). In this early proclamation (1967), reproduced in *Blindness and Insight*, de Man describes an interpretive crisis resembling trauma. We can no longer interpret the process of interpretation through our inherited interpretive frameworks, he argues, which is why literary criticism during the rise of theory "occurs in the mode of crisis" (8). Roland Barthes's dead author and Foucault's proverbial sandman erased by the sea are just two contemporaneous images of the force of the questions de Man pursued in "The Crisis of Contemporary Criticism," and Caruth takes this force to be literary criticism's twentieth-century trauma. It is thus striking that, despite the fact that the deconstructive severance of the speech act from the illusion of direct reference into the free fall of literary form is *the* philosophic trauma Caruth claims to be invoking, what Eleanor Kaufman dubs Caruth's "serendipitous fall" remains largely untouched throughout the critical reception of Caruthian trauma theory (49). The overlooked core of Caruth's argument is, then, this: Psychoanalysis and deconstruction together enable an epistemic fall, which is also an awakening, from the metaphysical world of direct reference into the world of "ghostly transmissions,"[14] hauntology, a world in which the subject is not sovereignly bordered but infinitely implicated.

Infinitely implicated subjectivity is, however, a state in which one awakens or falls into only if one begins with the (European) tradition of metaphysical ontology from which to awaken or fall. Therefore, the de Manian form of Caruth's project does not neatly translate outside the European tradition. In making this claim I am not repeating the battle cry for postcolonial Manichaeism made by the many critics of trauma theory, a battle cry I will further detail in the next chapter. Instead of beating this dead horse, I am calling for a more nuanced, comparative criticism, the likes of which would recognize the historical tradition in which Caruth situates her trauma theory—the deconstruction of the metaphysical ontology at the core of Western philosophy—and attempt a departure from this epistemic situation into other (in the case of this book, animist) cosmologies.

Here, we should return to Horkheimer and Adorno's argument that modernity's extirpation of animism leads to a secularized monotheism in which "Man's likeness to God consists in sovereignty over existence" (6) discussed in this book's introduction. Their argument allows us to see that the ipseitic subject Yale School trauma theory aims to deconstruct is modeled on a theological notion of sovereignty. This form's hold on collective consciousness differentiates European modernity from animism. The goal of Yale School trauma theory is thus in part an attempt to articulate in Eurocentric terms that which was extirpated under colonial modernity: a sense of being-with-others that Freud's "protective cortical layer" represses, the cosmic co-implication that Tasso's poem voices as irrevocably wounded. Viewed from this angle, Yale School trauma theory attempts to explicate from Freud a post-sovereign reconceptualization of Freud's tethering of psychoanalysis to what Horkheimer and Adorno call "the ordering mind." Animistic modes of ordering the mind, however, are able to more radically depart from the logic of sovereignty that the Yale School critiques.

To illustrate this comparative departure, consider the subject envisioned in the novels of Amos Tutuola, a formative figure of African literature's animist poetics. Infinitely implicated subjectivity is within Tutuola's fiction not a state into which one awakens or falls. In fact, *The Palm-Wine Drinkard* (1952) begins with relational or implicated existence, which, if we follow Caruth's Eurocentric plot, is the horizon of trauma theory. The narrator, who is the novel's drinkard, can only be a drinkard through his economic relation to the palm-wine tapster. Since his sole task, his lifework, is to drink "from morning till night and from night till morning," when his tapster dies, not only does the narrator's quest to find the tapster's spirit begin, but the narrator's subjectivity is itself at stake, severed from its original relationality and forced into a bordered existence out of which he continuously and briefly morphs (191).[15] That which animates the novel's narrative movement is therefore a fall from implicated existence into the ill-fitting illusion of sovereignly bordered subjectivity. This falling movement is not only the inverse of Caruthian trauma theory, but the structure of colonial subjection: being thrown into an illusively bordered, European form of life, severed from one's ancestral history (which, as Fanon puts it, has been distorted, disfigured, and destroyed by colonization). Tutuola's narratives thus begin by simultaneously mapping subjectivity beyond the logic of sovereignty, yet also dragged within its grasp: both beyond yet within the purveyance of Caruthian trauma theory.

This beyond-yet-within leads us to the centrality of the death drive to animist poetics, which, I will soon suggest, both affirms and overturns Freud's infamous theory. In a well-known passage from *The Palm-Wine Drinkard*, Tutuola gives us a glimpse of an animist death drive in the form of a parable. He describes a woman trailing a beautiful and "complete gentleman" she finds at the market, only to discover he is not actually "complete": "As they were travelling along in this endless forest then the complete gentleman in the market that the lady was following, began to return the hired parts of his body to the owners and he was paying them the rentage money. When he reached where he hired the left foot, he pulled it out, he gave it to the owner and paid him" (203). The woman observes the gentleman she mistook as absolute returning his body parts to those from whom he rents, culminating in his reduction to a skull—severed not only from ipseitic beauty, but from life. Yet the skull somehow lives on. Although the myth of sovereign subjectivity may be alluring, Tutuola warns us not be tricked, for life has no owner; the "I" is pastiched together by rented body parts of others. As Caroline Rooney succinctly puts it in her interpretation of the passage, "life in its totality is composed of temporarily leased forms." She continues:

> [W]e might just see here a shuttling between living and dying where death is not the *final* form. Rather, out of a minimal form of existence new life is woven in an increasing combination of forms or body parts until a final or complete form is attained. Once this has been attained, this final stage of a life form, there can only be a process of de-composition towards re-composition because at no point can there be a cessation of life which is a necessarily ongoing process. (*African Literature* 84)

This eternal de-composition/re-composition cycle of a life that is briefly composed of parts of other lives symbolizes the regenerative death drive at the core of animist poetics.

This drive demonstrates both my influence by and departure from Freud throughout this book. Tutuola's novel (unapologetically "plagiarizing" Yoruba folk-tales and even D. O. Fagunwa's earlier *Forest of a Thousand Daemons*) narrates what Soyinka calls the Yoruba "cyclic concept of time and the animist interfusion of all matter and consciousness" (*Myth* 145). In such a cosmology, all matter matters—trees, creatures, and corpses resound with agency (as they do in Freud's reading of Tancred and Clorinda)—and the ongoing process of subject formation/deformation/reformation ritually operates through a "disintegrating process within the matrix of cosmic creativity" (153). In other words, the subject is an ongoing environmental process of decay and renewal eternally taking place throughout the cosmos. While what has been critiqued as Eurocentric trauma theory celebrates the death of the post-Enlightenment sovereign subject (rightfully so), Tutuola's animist poetics, by reframing subjectivity as animist, narrates the perpetual regeneration of collective life beyond this death. Formally, we could speculate, Tutuola is post-deconstructive, which opens a path for a rereading of Freud's most radical insight.

The Regenerative Death Drive

In his restructuring of psychoanalytic theory from the Oedipal structure of the family to the traumatic structure of subjectivity, *Beyond the Pleasure*

Principle (1920), Freud thinks through the seemingly oppositional life and death drives. Ontologically, the former plots the evolution of matter into subjectivity: Nothing becomes inorganic material becomes organic material becomes animated by subjective life. The life drive thus pushes the subject forward in a Darwinian movement for survival, while the death drive plots this movement's inevitable collapse back into nonexistence. If we take the pleasure principle to be that which dictates psychoanalytic theory, Freud reasons, then we must interpret these oppositional drives toward life and death as partners of the pleasure principle, laws that, despite contradictory appearances, work together to bring the subject pleasure. Through its Darwinian narrative the life drive fits more clearly within the pleasure principle (all forms of life desire the continuation of life), but the death drive can also fit within this framework.

The latter drives the subject simultaneously backward and forward (backward by way of forward); the subject is driven toward death through a desire for that state before they experienced life and consequently the possibility of death. Following again the Darwinian narrative, every subject, Freud argues, wishes to return to the state before nothing became the inorganic became the organic became the subject. As he puts it, the subject wishes to "*restore an earlier state of things* which the living entity has been obliged to abandon" (308). Thus, just as the life drive, by way of plotting the survival of the species, fits within the pleasure principle, so does the death drive, by way of throwing the subject toward the ultimate Sabbath, or pleasurable rest from the struggle of existence. We could thus conceptualize the death drive as a materialist reformulation of the Augustinian *felix culpa* (a reformulation Caruth's "serendipitous fall" rewrites in relation to deconstruction). For Augustine, the fall into sin is a "happy fall" insofar as falling from paradise produces the conditions through which the narrative of redemption, the return to paradise, is able to take place. Though less "happy," for Freud, like Augustine, falling into life—the originary, universal trauma—enables the narrative of return, a return to the paradisiacal stasis of inorganic matter in which subjectivity becomes nonexistent. In sum, through Freud's materialist-theological metanarrative, the subject is unconsciously driven toward a postlapsarian transubstantiation of the material body into a prelapsarian state of static, inorganic matter, before life (and therefore death) existed, thereby negating, after the fact, death.

But ultimately, Freud argues, the death drive points toward a new foundation for psychoanalysis: the repetition compulsion. Here the phenomenon of trauma becomes vital. Freud notes that many victims of "severe mechanical concussions, railway disasters and other accidents involving risk to life" survive an unexpected accident only to return, through recurring dreams, flashbacks, and images, to the scene of the accident, despite their wishes (281).[16] This claim seems to contradict Freud's earlier theory of dreams as wish fulfillment, a contradiction that, he reasons, undermines the pleasure principle. Despite the subject's desire for pleasure, traumatic repetition captures the subject, a capture he terms the repetition compulsion. The death drive is itself an expression of the repetition compulsion—we repeat a way of being that is not being, return to a time that is not time—recasting subjective life as operating through the form of traumatic neurosis. The subject is driven to repeat the experience of a lost origin, an origin of nonexistence, that time when we were not, that is itself nonexistent—if we were not, this time did not exist—and so, in a sense, this origin is not really an origin, but only an origin through its relation to our time of existence. The death drive consequently assumes through its ontological repetition compulsion a temporality emerging through its own negation, a time that is not, but is, precisely because of that fact that it is not; put differently, our origin does not exist apart from our lack of it, yet we desire to return to it, which is why *"the aim of all life is death"* (311).

In *Moses and Monotheism* (1937), Freud transposes this compulsion he first observes in victims of traumatic neurosis, defying wish fulfillment and transgressing the pleasure principle, culminating in the death drive, into a theory of collective subjectivity, or culture. He interprets the historical development of Judeo-Christian monotheism—and by implication the nomological structure of Western culture—through a framework of trauma. For the purposes of this chapter, I simply wish to point out that according to Freud, Moses was an Egyptian. More specifically, he was an Egyptian murdered by his Jewish followers, and over time another Moses, a Jew, came to embody the memory of the murdered Egyptian's deeds. For Freud, then, Judeo-Christian monotheism has no fixed, historical point; the "origin" is rather a primal, violent confrontation between cultures resulting in a web of memories emerging only in relation to each other, in latent repetition. In sum, for Freud, the collective subjectivity passed on by the Jewish tradition—as well as Christianity's reworking of this tradition—is, in its very form, traumatic. In other words, Freud views the nomology of Western culture inherited from monotheism as animated by ancestral trauma.

In *The Wretched of the Earth* (1961), Fanon conceptualizes the colonized *polis*, as well as the possibility of a postcolonial *polis*, in a similar manner to Freud. As I have previously described, he theorizes colonization as a traumatic (re)genesis of Indigenous culture, which recasts the colonizer as a new type of ancestor: "For it is the settler who has brought the native into existence and who perpetuates his existence," he writes (28). However, Fanon continuously stresses the possibility of the colonized creating a new "violence in the beginning," a "cleansing force" through which to "change the order of the world" inaugurated by colonial modernity (73–4, 27). The goal of this new, traumatic (re)genesis named "decolonization is quite simply the replacing of a certain 'species' of men by another 'species' of men," Fanon writes. "Without any period of transition, there is a total, complete and absolute substitution" (27). This substitutionary, generative violence—in many ways similar to what Walter Benjamin terms "divine violence," yet stripped of any divinatory origin—requires, Fanon argues, the death of the colonizer. "For the native," he writes, "life can only spring up again out of the rotting corpse of the settler" (73). This claim resembles Freud's plot of the primal patricide in *Totem and Taboo*, which raises the problem of agency in relation to ancestral trauma. In Freud's prehistoric plot, a group of jealous sons together murder their father and eat his corpse. Despite his physical death, the father lives on as a structuring concept, Freud argues, becoming stronger by transfiguring into the very idea of "the father," or sovereign authority, making possible the organization of society, morality, religion, etcetera. As Julia Kristeva writes, the sons "replaced the dead father with the image of the father, with the totem symbol of power, the figure of *the ancestor*" (12, my emphasis). If one implication of this argument is that rebellion can never lead to agency, then what of Fanon's calls for decolonization? If primal patricide must be the foundation of decolonization, as he claims, does this "cleansing violence" reconstitute the colonizer as, once again, the new ancestry of the modern?

This conundrum leads to the political importance of what I call the regenerative death drive. Freud explicitly embeds the death drive within a metaphysical framework in which death is equated with stasis. In one of the more famous passages of *Beyond the Pleasure Principle*, for example, he writes, "If we are to take it as a truth that knows no exception that everything living dies for *internal* reasons—becomes inorganic once again—then we shall be compelled to say that '*the aim of all life is death*' and, looking backwards, that '*inanimate things existed before living ones*'" (310–11). First, the subject dies sovereignly, Freud claims, for internal reasons (an ironic claim, considering the fact that the traumatic structure of collective subjectivity Freud posits exposes sovereign subjectivity as a myth, replacing it, as Caruth recognizes, with radically implicated subjectivity). This claim is the first in an intricately woven logical sequence. Next, sovereign death, death due to internal reasons, is aligned with a return to inorganic matter; this return reveals the death drive, which suggests, Freud concludes, that inanimate matter precedes animate life. Ultimately, then, this sequence of claims builds an argument centered on the relation between the animate and the inanimate:

1. The animate subject dies solely due to internal reasons.
2. Through this death, the subject returns to inorganic matter, which is inanimate.
3. In life, the animate subject, who is driven toward death, desires to return to an inanimate state.
4. Therefore, inanimate matter precedes animate matter, and thus subjectivity.

But this logic only works when inorganic matter is equated with stasis—the ontological Sabbath of nonexistence toward which Freud's subject is driven.

If all matter is vibrant (Bennett), intra-active (Barad), and transcorporeal (Alaimo), as animist cosmologies have claimed long before new materialist critique, then Freud's argument reformulates itself into a drive toward death that regenerates into new life. Put differently, if subjectivity is environmental, then the death drive must be more-than-human, which means it cannot actually end with an individual subject's death.[17] In this way, the contrapuntal reading of Freud I am offering through animism is also a mode of ecocriticism. However, my insistence that animist poetics emerges from the trauma of colonization adds to the growing body of postcolonial ecocriticism[18] a recognition that animist ecologies are modes of modernism, strategic responses to the colonial wounding of Indigenous ecologies. In this sense, Cajetan Iheka's categories of human and ecological proximity in African literature—"multispecies presence, interspecies relationship, and distributed agency" (50)—must all be conceptualized as dialectical responses to colonization's planetary wounds always in process: the multispecies regeneration of copresence, the renewal of interspecies relations, and the infinitely expanding redistribution of agency into a reanimated sociogenic order.

By extending Fanon's critical appropriation of psychoanalysis to include the living, the dead, and the more-than-human world into the "social" of sociodiagnostic analysis, animist cosmologies invest postcolonial critique with a posthumanist, postsecular logic that allows for an affirmative logic even in the bleakest of conditions of the postcolony. An animist revision of Freud is therefore one strategy of connecting Fanon's sociodiagnostic appropriation of psychoanalysis in *Black Skin, White Masks* (1952) to *The Wretched of the Earth*'s (1961) vision of a decolonized future liberated from post-Enlightenment European humanism's grasp on world history: "the Third World starting a new history of man" (254). This new form of collective life to which Fanon directs the project of decolonization—furthered by Sylvia Wynter's use of Fanon to remap subjectivity beyond Europe's sociogenic "Man" and toward a "planetary humanism"—can be conceived as a theoretical gesture, at the eclipse of European humanism, toward the a priori of animist subjectivity. The animist subject responds to its own extirpation under the advent of colonial modernity's sociogenic subject by regenerating an expansive relationality, a refusal to distinguish between the internal and external spaces of subjectivity dictated by post-Enlightenment rationality.

Consequently, if Freud's subject is driven toward death in order to return to a state of inorganic matter and therefore enter ontological rest, the animist subject is driven toward death in order to experience a transfiguration of subjective life, its redistribution into an extirpated animist habitus always in the process of regeneration. The regenerative death drive at the heart of African literature's animist poetics—a drive of which we have seen glimpses from African art and literature in this book's introduction—thus both extends and overturns Freud's theory. This extension and overturning allows us to return to Freud's four claims above in light of the animist explosion of the ipseitic subject and observe them tell a different metanarrative, in reverse order:

1. Inorganic matter, organic matter, human and non-human life (including past lives and unborn lives) all resound with shared agency.

2. In life, the animate subject, who is driven toward death, desires regeneration—not a return to stasis, but a transfiguration of the form in which the animation of subjectivity happens.

3. Through death, the animate subject returns to inorganic matter, changing form, yet remaining animated.

4. The animate subject dies neither internally nor externally.

If the jump between claim number 3 and claim number 4 is difficult to follow, that is because Freud's argument, which I am formally following, assumes a leap, which is never stated, between the hypothesis of static matter and the hypothesis of death for internal reasons. In my reversal of his argument, I am formally following and therefore logically reversing this jump. Freud's conception of sovereign death, death for internal reasons, falls apart when we conceptualize the entire material world as mutually animated. If there is no animate/inanimate binary, but rather a world in which all matter is mutually enforced, then the human subject (as animated organic matter) is no more sovereign over his or her animation than inorganic matter. The internal is animated by that which animates the external, or the internal is externally enforced just as the external is internally enforced.[19] We are back to Fanon's critique of Freud's inoculation of the internal from the external, though we have invested Fanon's sociodiagnostics with a cosmological resonance that overturns the conclusion of Freud's theory of the death drive. If the internal is always already enforced by the external, then nobody's death is sovereignly crafted, as Freud hypothesizes.

No wonder Freud continuously wards off what he calls the "mystical impression" (*Beyond* 328) of the death drive and the resemblance of the repetition compulsion to a state of being "possessed by some 'daemonic' power" (292). In his late restructuring of psychoanalysis around trauma theory, Freud ventures dangerously close to what he deems the animism of primitives, children, and neurotics, which he associates with narcissism.[20] As Rooney explains:

> Although Freud struggles with and evades the question of what the force or energy of this [death] drive would be, he tells us, however, that (what could be termed) the *motivation* of the death drive is the desire to return to an original inanimate, inorganic state of death, an original state of non-existence. But what if we were to affirm: 'The world is all that is the case.' In other words, what I am trying to get at is: if all that there is, is all that there is, then how can we think of something that

is *originally non-existent*? This original non-being could well create the mystical impression that Freud wishes to evade. What *on earth* would this original death 'be'? It would just not be; 'being' only a gap or lack without content that could be seen, but only retrospectively, to have strangely anticipated what comes to be in a being for this death. The way in which I tend to read Freud's account of the death drive is that it serves to deny or negate other-being as opposed to non-being at the origin, a question of foreclosure. Or, it negates a being with other being at the origin. (136)

To return to the Augustinian form of Freud's materialist theology of the subject, Rooney points out the unintentional "mysticism" in Freud's insistence that the subject returns to nonexistent stasis, a paradise lost and regained. This insistence takes the difference between being and nonbeing as the structuring principle of ontology (i.e., a metaphysical claim), thereby foreclosing any interaction with cosmologies that could be deemed animist and consequently associated with children, neurotics, and primitives.

In chapter 3 I return to this problem by way of Catherine Malabou's new materialist critique of Freud. For now, however, I simply wish to claim that if there is no nonexistence, but only forms of being-animated-with, including the animation of inorganic matter (that is, if we take seriously animist cosmologies), then we could follow Rooney's exegesis of African literature in claiming that the death drive and the repetition compulsion should be reconsidered in terms that Freud continuously attempts to avoid: possession. Being possessed or animated by a spirit implies that a force external to the subject has become internal to the subject—the subject is hailed from without—which is precisely what happens during an event of trauma. Out of nowhere, an event happens, so unexpectedly that it can't quite be experienced, at least not in the mythic time of teleology. The subject is thrown into the temporality of the repetition compulsion, in which they obsessively memorialize what Lacan terms the "missed encounter," realizing (as in making real) the trauma, through latent performance (dreams, flashbacks, enactments, etcetera) (55). The subject becomes animated, enforced, informed, possessed by the spirit of the missed encounter. If subjectivity, both individual and collective, is structured traumatically, as Freud claims in *Beyond the Pleasure Principle* and *Moses and Monotheism*, in this book I wish go a step further, following animist cosmologies, and consider subjectivity as a form of possession.

Jean Laplanche gestures toward this animist form of psychoanalysis, associating (with and against Freud) the psychoanalytic theory of the subject with possession. Freudian phrases such as "internal foreign body," "reminiscence," or "the unconscious as an alien inside me, and even one put inside me by an alien," illustrate that, "[a]t his most prophetic, Freud does not hesitate over formulations which go back to the idea of *possession*," he writes (66, my emphasis). He consequently asks:

> Would it not be possible, then, to maintain that the unconscious has a close link with the past, the past of the individual, *while at the same time abandoning the psychological problematic of memory* with its intentionality aimed at *my* past, but also its retrospective illusions and its ultimately undecidable nature? For Freud neglects here the innovative core of his own initial formulation: hysterics suffer, not from memories, forgotten or not, but from 'reminiscences'. The term could, of course, be reduced to memory—a memory cut off from its context—but it could equally be allowed to bear the value of *extravagance* . . . : something which returns as if from elsewhere, a pseudo-memory perhaps, coming from . . . the other. ("Unfinished" 72)

For Laplanche, psychoanalytic theory operates as what Mbembe deems witchcraft in this chapter's second epigraph—a discourse of trauma beyond memory, trauma as possession.

Yet this discourse of possession is already intrinsic to Freud's theory of ancestral trauma in *Moses and Monotheism*. It is thus this text, I would suggest, that influences Fanon's use of the primal patricide plot in *The Wretched of the Earth*, which leads us back to the problem of postcolonial agency. As Grant argues, Fanon reformulates this plot to open new forms of agency:

> [W]hen Fanon says that 'the native never ceases to dream of putting himself in the place of the settler', he immediately qualifies this with: 'not of becoming the settler but of substituting himself for the settler'. . . . A clear distinction is thus drawn between a desire to become the settler, and a desire to take his place, which is reinforced when Fanon goes on to say that what the natives 'demand is not the settler's position or status, but the settler's place'. . . . The colonizer will be, well and truly,

dead, and the natives will not, after his death, be compelled to respect his prohibitions, since they feel no remorse. In this way, Fanon rejects the implicit political logic of Freud's myth, namely that decolonization is impossible, because by killing him the figure of authority, become ancestral, will be rendered stronger than ever. (599)

If the sons in Freud's plot kill their father and thus constitute their ancestor, the colonized in Fanon's plot kill not only their colonizer but his reconstitution of the ancestral, thereby regenerating modes of copresence between the self and the ancestors stifled by the colonial paradigm of sovereign authority. "Fanon rewrites as he interprets Freud's narrative," Grant claims, "founding a new man and a new society on the rotting corpse of the Freudian father" out of which the "decolonization of the ancestral as such" takes place (608, 596). Grant perceives within Fanon's call for decolonization a regeneration of ancestral copresence through the death of the ancestral. What Grant underappreciates, however, is that similar avenues of agency are already contained in Freudian psychoanalysis.[21]

Animism Beyond Memory Representation

If part of the cultural work of animist poetics is to re-enchant the colonized world, then the political horizon of this literature cannot end with a critique of colonial modernity and the global capitalist system, but, more radically, a transformation of its structure. Similarly, animist poetics is not content with bringing cross-cultural memorialization of trauma into the public sphere (as the discourse of trauma studies and, as I will detail in the next chapter, its postcolonial critique, would have it). More fundamentally, it seeks a transformation of this sphere. At its best, animist poetics, operating beyond the mode of representational critique undergirding so much of literary and cultural criticism, is designed to inaugurate a transformative experience of ritual. For this reason, as this book unfolds, my theoretical lexicon will draw more on what has been termed political theology, or a theory of that which animates the *polis*, and thus a theory of the base structure in need of ritual mending.

Influenced by Benjamin, especially his digressive use of Carl Schmitt's jurisprudential theory, philosophers such as Jean-Luc Nancy, Agamben, and Derrida have brought the theological foundation of modern political subjugation to the forefront of European theory.[22] To be sure, theorists of transatlantic Black studies, notably Wynter, have long been examining this theological structure in relation to colonialism. I will therefore bring political theologies of Black studies and European theory into a more explicit dialogue in chapter 4. For now, though, I wish to highlight the fact that deconstructive political theology's appropriation of Schmitt bears implications for trauma theory as well as postcolonial criticism. For Schmitt, modernity is not "disenchantment," as Max Weber argues, but rather a reconstitution of theocracy's structure within the nation-state. As he famously puts it, "All significant concepts in the modern theory of the state are secularized theological concepts" (36). As I have previously suggested, Freud makes a similar claim by casting the nomology of Western culture as a Judeo-Christian inheritance formed around the concept of sovereignty, particularly the trauma of being subjected to a sovereign—be it the father, or, more effectively, the idea of the father.[23] This inheritance bears implications for conceptualizing the work of postcolonial African literature as a response to colonial modernity. If the colonized African *polis* is structured around this discursive formation of sovereignty, the political task facing animist poetics is not quite re-enchanting what has been disenchanted, but, more enigmatically, re-enchanting-otherwise-than-sovereignly.

This transformative task informs Benjamin's appropriation of Schmitt—for instance, through his concept of divine violence: a generative rupture of political sovereignty, which opens new modes of being-together beyond the subjugations structuring modern life. As I will argue in chapters 3 and 4, it also informs Soyinka's concept of the "creative-destructive principle" he appropriates from Yoruba cosmology and utilizes in his literary writing. In chapter 5, I demonstrate how Yvonne Vera appropriates this principle, which I cast as an implicit revision of the Freudian death drive, to her own context of twenty-first-century Zimbabwe. In these chapters, my analyses demonstrate that articulating life beyond the sovereign-subject relation inherited from monotheism, which oversees post-Enlightenment Western culture and thus the plotline of Caruthian trauma theory, is not primarily a task of memory representation, but of spiritual reimagination. The copresence of the living and the dead and the human and more-than-human envisioned in the art and poetry considered in the introduction and the eternally morphing subjectivity envisioned in Tutuola's "temporarily leased" life considered in this chapter, for instance, do not operate through the archival logic of memory cumulation. Rather, they assume a regenerative logic of ritual in which the past and present coconstitute a future. Animist poetics is in this sense less interested in critically representing the colonized *polis* than imagining a transition into a new *polis*. Theorizing these imaginative transformations reframes the project of postcolonial trauma theory from the latent liberal multiculturalism animating trauma and memory studies toward a more radical task: the invention of new political-theological structures to shed our monotheistic inheritance of the myth of sovereign subjectivity. These structures must be, in the language of cultural criticism, posthumanist, postsecular, and ecopoetic: incorporating the living and the dead as well as the human and more-than-human world. As I argue in the following chapter, not all texts we might categorize within animist poetics are up for this task. By juxtaposing examples of animist realism and animist ritual, I will argue that the ritualized side of animist poetics functions as paradigmatic of this aesthetic logic's politics. This political logic is less interested in representational critique than transformational experience, transitioning the colonized subject into what African Indigenous knowledge systems envision as polytheistic forms of being-in-common. Put somewhat differently, at its best, animist poetics does not only unmask the traumatic structure of modern, political life, which at its root assumes a secularized theology of sovereign authority, but, like Benjamin's "divine violence" and Fanon's "cleansing violence," opens the possibility of a political theology (better yet, political cosmology) of that which is not, but could be: an imaginative, ritualized inauguration of a post-sovereign political community yet to come, what Nancy calls the "deconstruction of monotheism" and David Marriot recognizes as Fanon's "non-sovereign form of politics" (255).

There is a passage in Tutuola's *My Life in the Bush of Ghosts* (1954) that illustrates such a project. A chief-ancestor spirit from the river gifts the narrator a six-foot smoking pipe with a monstrous bowl—four feet in diameter and three feet deep, nesting a half-ton of tobacco. As the narrator smokes, an unnamed spirit continuously refills the bowl with fresh tobacco from the spirit world. The narrator continues to inhale the eternally regenerative leaf, hitherto unsmoked by humankind, growing intoxicated while the surrounding spirits begin to celebrate:

> They were singing, clapping hands, ringing bells and their ancestral drummers were beating the drums in such a way that all the dancers were jumping up with gladness. But whenever the smoke of the pipe was rushing out from my mouth as if smoke is rushing from a big boiler, then all of them would

> laugh at me so that a person two miles away would hear them clearly. . . . So at this time I forgot all my sorrow and started to sing the earthly songs which sorrow prevented me from singing about since I entered this bush. (74)

Transitioning into this intoxicating mode of being-with-spirits allows the narrator to sing songs formerly inexpressible, songs he had forgotten. These "earthly" songs are not quite a recovery of the past, though, because they are now sung alongside the claps, bells, drums, and singing of ancestral spirits *in the present*. In other words, as the narrator enters a new relation to the ancestors, together they reinvent the past by performing new ancestral relations for the future.

The spirits stand agape above the narrator, struck by the beauty of this new music. Saliva then begins to drop from the spirits' open mouths onto the narrator until he is bathing in their spit. After this baptism into life-with-spirits, the chief-ancestor places the narrator on top of a three-hundred-foot-long coconut tree, uprooted from the ground and resting on the head of another unnamed spirit. Moved by the narrator's "earthly songs," this spirit jumps onto the head of the chief-ancestor and they all begin to dance with the surrounding spirits. The coconut tree, the unnamed spirit in the middle, and the chief-ancestor spirit on the bottom all then grow feathers to fly the singing narrator to their king. Through this song, then, the narrator briefly experiences a new form of political community, an experience toward which the questions I have raised in this chapter ultimately point. What if we divert the direction of trauma theory from (a) recovering and proliferating diverse representations of trauma and (b) critiquing our trauma-inducing *polis*? Instead, what if we attempt the more puzzling task of creatively joining the spirits of a coming tradition? In other words, I am asking us to imagine, like Tutuola in this passage, a transformation in the cosmological structure of the *polis* itself. Such a task has thus far resided beyond the purveyance of trauma theory. By reformulating psychoanalysis as animist, though, a future criticism can bring this task within its purveyance. An animist criticism can both renew trauma theory for postcolonial studies and invest posthumanism, postsecularism, and the environmental humanities with a necessary and expanded notion of (a) the collective, constitutive wounding at the core of colonial modernity and (b) the forms through which the ecological subjectivities of the postcolony emerge in dialectical response to this wound.

Chapter 2

Animist Poetics' Realism-Ritual Spectrum

Aminatta Forna, Delia Jarrett-Macauley,
Oswald Mbuyiseni Mtshali, Uhuru Portia Phalafala

In this chapter, I demonstrate how texts at different sides of animist poetics' realism-ritual spectrum chart onto the theory of ancestral trauma and the regenerative death drive I proposed in the previous chapter. Through literary case studies more truncated than the extended exegeses I will offer in chapters 3 through 5, I here argue that Harry Garuba's approach to reading animism, centered on the realism side of animist poetics, operates in the same field of vision, and with the same political limits, as what I describe as the trauma studies approach to reading literature. Alternatively, I extrapolate from the anthropology of postcolonial spirit possession modeled by Michael Taussig and Paul Stoller a way of reading animism at the level of formal process rather than magical content. This approach to animism, more useful for recognizing the force of the ritual side of animist poetics, ventures beyond academic trauma studies' limited field of vision by seeking to mend the ancestral trauma that animist realism critiques. Drawing on the terms of my previous chapter, I claim that this mediation takes place through the ritual activation of the regenerative death drive. In this way, the ritual side of animist poetics more fully incorporates animism's posthumanist and postsecular dimensions.

This chapter is the only one of its kind in this book: exemplary case studies juxtaposing the uses and limits of two approaches to reading trauma (the academic discourse of trauma studies—including its postcolonial critique—and mine) tied to two approaches to reading animism

(Garuba's and mine). My goal through this juxtaposition is to demonstrate the applicability and practical uses of the theory of cultural trauma and survival I laid out in chapter 1. Polemically, I do so by highlighting the limits of the trauma studies method and the method of reading animism through its proximity to realism, since these are typically the de facto approaches to studies of trauma and animism in literary criticism. It is my hope that by demonstrating these limits, this chapter can function as a threshold leading to the rest of this book, which is composed of more extended close readings of poetry, drama, and fiction by Wole Soyinka and Yvonne Vera, two paradigmatic figures of the ritual side of animist poetics.

In what follows, I argue that Aminatta Forna and Delia Jarrett-Macauley, two contemporary British–Sierra Leonean novelists, exemplify the realist side of animist poetics' realism-ritual spectrum through their narrations of post–Civil War Sierra Leone. In my analysis, Forna's *The Memory of Love* (2010) and Jarrett-Macauley's *Moses, Citizen and Me* (2005) form a limit case for the now widely accepted postcolonial critique of trauma studies and Garuba's approach to reading animism, the most influential approach to animism in literary criticism. Both of these modes of interpretation are centered on identifying representational content. As such, their political horizon is critique (which is, to be sure, a useful and necessary act). The ritual side of animist poetics, however, endows aesthetics with a more affirmative role, envisioning literature not only as a mode of representational critique, but also as a process of collective transformation. Animist ritual's formal operations thus venture beyond the aesthetic logic overseeing the academic apparatus of trauma studies and its postcolonial critique, as well as Garuba's approach to animism. In short, animist ritual swaps the discourse of trauma studies' secular assumptions for the posthumanist, postsecular method of trauma theory I proposed in the previous chapter.

Additionally, recognizing the dynamics of animist ritual requires that we discard Garuba's assumption that the locus of animism is represented content. A ritual approach, instead, casts the locus of animism as a text's formal process—a shift for which Taussig's and Stoller's studies of postcolonial spirit possession provide a useful frame of reference to articulate. To demonstrate this aesthetic-political juxtaposition, I conclude this chapter with a brief analysis of two examples of South African poetry that exemplify how ritualized animism ventures beyond politicized representations of trauma. Oswald Mbuyiseni Mtshali's apartheid-era lyric "An Abandoned Bundle" (1971) and Uhuru Portia Phalafala's recent collection *Mine Mine*

Mine (2023) each seek to ritually mediate their own inheritance of the ancestral trauma wrought by apartheid. In taking on this ritual function, these poems take animism more seriously than animist realism is able to do. These poems are thus exemplary texts of a mode of animism alternative to the limit case of the Forna and Jarrett-Macauley novels.

The majority of this chapter is dedicated to my analysis of Forna's and Jarrett-Macauley's employment of realism and animist realism to theorize postcolonial trauma. This focus is a consequence of this chapter's polemical function. Approaching these novels as a limit case, I frame my analysis with the question of how these exemplary texts of realism and animist realism speak to the academic debate over Euro-American trauma theory's applicability in postcolonial contexts—a debate into which these novels consciously join. While these novels utilize animism to critique trauma theory's Eurocentrism, I argue, they also critique the logic of a postcolonial Manichaeism that too quickly divides African texts from the claims of Euro-American theory. The crux of my analysis, however, is that this double critique forms the political limit of these texts. My concluding analysis of Mtshali's and Phalafala's poetry is briefer and punchier. Rather than polemically framing my reading with another scholarly discourse or even criticism on these writers or the apartheid and post-apartheid political economies in which they write, I simply demonstrate an exegesis of these texts in light of the differentiation between animist realism and animist ritual I propose throughout this chapter. In other words, this chapter ends with an example of close reading illustrative of how the animist revision of trauma theory I proposed in the previous chapter might be practiced by a literary criticism that no longer defines animism by way of its proximity to realism.

Animist Poetics' Realism-Ritual Spectrum

Animist poetics names the formal operations of the wide and multifaceted social imaginary through which postcolonial writers strategically appropriate Indigenous cosmologies as modern. Through these appropriations, as I argued in the introduction, animist poetics envisions—in dialectical opposition to the subject of post-Enlightenment European humanism—a postcolonial subjectivity uniting the living and the dead and the human and more-than-human world. As I further argued in the previous chapter, since colonial modernity is founded on the erasure of such cosmological kinship, an erasure inherited by the colonized subject as ancestral trauma, animist poetics is always a strategic response to trauma—a survival tactic. It follows that animist poetics cannot be reduced to a particular genre, such as Afrofuturism or speculative realism, as typical usage of the term *animism* in literary criticism often assumes. To be sure, such genres can and often do operate through animist poetics, but they do not define its limit. Instead, a formal analysis of any postcolonial appropriation or even reinvention of Indigenous knowledge, no matter the genre, will lead to a recognition of some aspect of animist poetics. This expansive definition means that comparatively identifying and categorizing different generic logics operating under the umbrella logic of animist poetics is necessary for practical criticism. Hence my heuristic concept of animist poetics' realism-ritual spectrum, the starting point for this chapter.

Garuba's theory of animist materialism, the most influential approach to animism in literary criticism, is limited to the realism side of this spectrum. For him, animist materialism names the cultural logic through which postcolonial societies challenge Western modernity's "disenchantment of the world" (Weber 155): the "changes in attitudes and practices occasioned by the increasingly secular rationalization of the world brought about by modernity and the rise of capitalism" (Garuba, "Explorations" 266). According to Garuba, this "re-enchantment" is continual, always happening at the level of the cultural unconscious, because, in postcolonial societies, "'magical elements of thought' are not displaced" by capitalist modernity's secular rationality, "but, on the contrary, continually assimilate new developments" (267). Garuba identifies the modus operandi of this assimilatory animism as the "spiritualiz[ation] of the object world" (267) as well as its seemingly opposite act: "according physical, often animate material aspect to what others may consider an abstract idea" (274). In this way, animist materialism is a cultural logic through which postcolonial societies tether spirituality to their material conditions and consequently spiritualize these material conditions.

The aesthetic outworking of this philosophy, Garuba argues, is animist realism. He differentiates this genre from magical realism insofar as the former is not limited to the "urban, cosmopolitan aspect" and "ironizing attitude" of the latter (274). This differentiation is key to recognizing the limits of Garuba's approach. At the level of cultural operations, animist realism works just like magical realism (but with more stylistic flexibility): Both use "magical thinking" to challenge the Weberian secularized rationalization intrinsic to colonial modernity, both do so to offer a political critique of the global capitalist order, and both ultimately offer this critique through their representational content (that is, their fantastical depictions of modernity). Thus, Paul D's tobacco tin heart in Toni Morrison's *Beloved* is for Garuba paradigmatic of the way animist realism accords physical matter to an abstract idea, the materialization of spirit that places animistic knowledge in proximity with Marx's theory of commodity fetishism.

This approach to reading animism is extremely useful for analyzing texts whose animistic features are primarily representational and thus African texts that resemble magical realism—from Ben Okri's *The Famished Road* (1991) to the new wave of animist realism such as Nnedi Okorafor's *Lagoon* (2014) or Wayétu Moore's *She Would Be King* (2018).[1] I would argue, however, that Garuba's stated goal of animist materialism, opening "avenues of agency for the dispossessed in colonial and postcolonial Africa" (285), requires an incorporation of animistic logic not only in a text's representations, but also into its formal operations. It may be true that *Beloved*, for instance, is filled with animistic content, such as Paul D's tobacco tin heart, but the novel's more primary animism is its formal process as a communal rite implicating not only the haunted characters, but the "Sixty Million and more" victims of the transatlantic slave trade to which the narrative is dedicated, culminating in the ritualized chant "It was not a story to pass on . . . It was not a story to pass on . . . This is not a story to pass on" in the final chapter (274–75).

I am not claiming Garuba is wrong, but rather that the analytical tool he has quite brilliantly formulated has its limits. In this book I am most interested in theorizing an animism operating at the level of formal process, which does not quite fit into Garuba's otherwise helpful focus on the spiritualized matter and materialized spirits typically populating the content of these same texts. I therefore place Garuba's animist realism under my macro-aesthetic of animist poetics. By truncating literary animisms through a logic of realism, Garuba's theory implies that colonial modernity can be critiqued through an animist style of representation, but not ritually mended. Such a task resides beyond the purveyance of realism and has nothing to do with whether or not a text contains "magical" content that may challenge secular rationality. For most critics, ascribing the work of ritual mending to literature—approaching the literary as the utilization of "language to mend time" ruptured under colonization, as Emmanuel Eze puts it ("Language" 26)—might appear to be taking animism too seriously. I am willing to take this risk, which is why I identify a ritual side of animist poetics that ventures beyond the representational limit of Garuba's model.

A useful analytical tool for reading animism at the level of formal process can be found in the anthropological study of spirit possession. Taussig's and Stoller's studies of shamanic healing rituals, for example, are less examples of precolonial religion than modes of postcolonial critique. They both uncover postcolonial critiques of the European nation-state in the structure of Indigenous possession rites as well as modes of subject formation in dialectical response to these critiques. Commenting on the West African Hauka spirit possession rituals, in which participants become possessed by the spirit of historical European colonizers in hopes of capturing through their performances the historical power of the European, Stoller argues that the animist experience of "spirit possession is a site of mimetic production and reproduction, which makes it a stage for the production and reproduction of power" (*Embodying* 37). In their performances of colonial power relations, he claims, the "Hauka embody difference," a difference, or alien spirit, that "generates power" in the possessed (12). This power is, as Taussig (drawing on Walter Benjamin) explains, the work of mimetic representation as production. For Taussig, shamans in postcolonial societies create healing rituals by recrafting material history (objects signifying capitalism and Christianity abound in rituals he examines), casting the shaman's magic as the magic of mimesis, the sorcery of history itself. "As the nature that culture uses to create second nature," he writes, "mimesis chaotically jostles for elbow room in this force field of necessary contradiction and illusion, providing the glimpse of the opportunity to dismantle that second nature and reconstruct other worlds" (*Mimesis* 70–71). The subject of postcolonial spirit possession, who is already possessed by the trauma of colonial history, crafts a form of recovery through a reworking of that history, a new way of becoming animated by it. As Taussig sums up Putumayo shamanism, "From the represented shall come that which overturns representation" (*Shamanism* 135).

This overturning of history through ritual modes of memorialization provides a framework for conceptualizing an animism operating at the level of a mimetic process that is relatively unconcerned with Garuba's focus on fantastical content's challenge to secularized rationality. In fact, many texts that fit snugly within a framework of animist realism due to their "magical" depictions also operate, at the level of form, through the ritualized mimetic process that Taussig and Stoller find in spirit possession rituals. What makes their method of reading animism so useful to literary criticism is its recognition that the overturning of history intrinsic to postcolonial shamanic practice happens not only through the iconography of this practice's content (e.g., appropriations of capitalist and Christian symbols), but more fundamentally through the formal, dialectical process structuring their acts of representation. Put differently, intrinsic to their method of reading animism is a belief that the locus of animism is not magical content represented, but the magical process of postcolonial representation's dialectical form. This form, as Taussig's and Stoller's studies suggest, emerges as the ritualized recreation of historical trauma into postcolonial subjectivity. The seeds of this process, to be sure, are operative in Garuba's theory of animist realism. However, in my literary case studies that follow, I place a realism-ritual spectrum within the broader logic of animist poetics, through which I differentiate two methods of animist responses to cultural trauma: the limited political logic exemplified by Forna's and Jarrett-Macauley's fiction and the more open political logic exemplified by Mtshali's and Phalafala's poems. These logics, in turn, coincide with what the academic discourse of trauma studies has reified into the trauma studies approach to literary interpretation, and the posthumanist, postsecular trauma theory I proposed in the previous chapter.

The Problem of Postcolonial Trauma

Forna's *Memory* and Jarrett-Macauley's *Moses* each plot a Western protagonist's failed attempt to help locals recover from the aftermath of the Sierra Leone civil war.[2] In *Memory*, Adrian Lockheart, a British psychologist volunteering with mental health services in Freetown, finds himself unable to help his patients, even with his bookshelf full of the latest psychiatric trauma theory: "He came here to help and he is not helping. *He is not helping*" (64). Likewise, at the beginning of *Moses*, the British-raised Julia cannot get her Sierra Leonean cousin Citizen—a silent, eight-year-old boy traumatized by his experience fighting in the Revolutionary United Front (RUF)—to say anything beyond *no* (9). This novel's core question is, can Julia, a Westernized diasporic protagonist, help her Sierra Leonean cousin Citizen and uncle Moses recover from their life-altering experiences of war? Julia's conundrum, like Adrian's, plots the much-debated problem of trauma theory in postcolonial contexts: Can a theoretical discourse invented in the West to make sense of Euro-American modernity, critics ask, make sense of the everyday traumas of the postcolonial world?

Since these novels explicitly plot this question, it is worth noting the resting assumptions framing how literary criticism approaches it. Building on the genealogical and contextual critiques of trauma studies I detailed in the previous chapter, Stef Craps and Gert Buelens's edited collection, "Postcolonial Trauma Novels," helped usher the task of "decolonizing trauma studies," as Michael Rothberg describes it, into literary criticism. The necessity of such a task, a necessity Adrian and Julia face in *Memory* and *Moses*, is widely accepted by scholars participating in trauma studies as a field of literary criticism. To redeem its lack of diversity, critics argue, trauma theory must turn toward "discursive intersections of trauma, gender, and neocolonialism" (Novak 48), toward "non-western, non-Eurocentric models of psychic disorder" (Visser 280), toward "vernacular representational practices" (Bennett and Kennedy 11), toward "local, non-western concepts of suffering, loss, and bereavement" as well as "recovery and healing" (Whitehead 15), etcetera.

Most critics making these claims believe they require distancing trauma studies from Euro-American theory, most notably psychoanalysis and deconstruction. For instance, as Greg Forter charges in "Colonial Trauma, Utopian Carnality, Modernist Form," a deconstructive, psychoanalytic approach to colonial trauma mistakenly "*analogizes* the social with the psychic," which, he claims, hinders any real social or psychic change after trauma (71). More explicitly than Forter, Kalí Tal argues that the focus on "Euro-American thinkers and scholars" such as Freud, Lacan, and Derrida coinciding with a neglect of the ways trauma has been theorized by other traditions demonstrates trauma theory's core problem: The discourse is "complacent within a racist structure" that "stand[s] in opposition to the very principles (of humanity, of cross-cultural connection) ostensibly espoused by critics concerned with trauma."[3] In this view, a postcolonial trauma theory must "link the phenomenal and the epiphenomenal dimensions of the trauma of colonialism" by way of a diversification of theorists and texts (Ifowodo 2). I will soon examine how Forna's and Jarrett-Macauley's novels respond to this view, but I first wish to highlight what I take to be its limited scope.

In the most influential monograph to pursue the problem of postcolonial trauma within literary criticism, *Postcolonial Witnessing*, Craps agrees with what is now a commonplace critique of so-called Yale School trauma theory: Its reliance on Euro-American cultural theory hinders its hermeneutic relevance in postcolonial contexts. But he rightly argues that the "decolonization" of the discourse, as Rothberg puts it, cannot be realized by simply broadening the corpus of trauma studies. Because examining global traumas from a Western vantage point repeats the categorical violence of colonial anthropology, Craps writes, "breaking with Eurocentrism requires a commitment not only to broadening the usual focus of trauma theory but also to acknowledging the traumas of non-Western or minority populations *for their own sake*" (19, my emphasis). This acknowledgment means not merely representing subaltern subjects, but taking seriously subaltern epistemic frameworks. Ethan Watters describes this problem to a popular audience in *Crazy like Us: The Globalization of the American Psyche*. "Indigenous forms of mental illness and healing are being bulldozed by disease categories and treatments made in the USA," he writes, including the category of trauma—and Craps's project could be conceptualized as an attempt to right this wrong through literary criticism (3). For Rothberg, like Craps, taking a "multidirectional" stance, which considers both Western and non-Western frameworks, fosters a "comparative thinking that, like memory itself, is not afraid to traverse sacrosanct borders of ethnicity and era" (*Multidirectional* 17). Craps and Rothberg, the most influential critics working at the intersection between postcolonial studies and trauma studies, rightly call for diverse representation paired with active engagement between subaltern ways of seeing, being, and consequently experiencing trauma—a step in the right direction, but a problem persists.

Their mode of critique rests on post-Enlightenment secular assumptions about the nature of art and subjectivity that keep them from actually taking non-Western frameworks of trauma and survival seriously. I will tease out the implications of this problem for Rothberg's project in chapter 5, but in this chapter I focus on Craps's project, which maps more neatly onto Forna's and Jarrett-Macauley's novels. Although Craps calls for the theorization of subaltern traumas on their own terms, throughout *Postcolonial Witnessing*, he does not quite step foot down this path. Instead, through diverse literary case studies (South African, British-Caribbean, Indian), he points out the incongruous relation between Eurocentric and "other" conceptions of trauma. His achievement is therefore the articulation of a failure, the failure of the Caruthian trauma theory I detailed in the previous chapter to live up to its ethical-political promise, but the articulation of this failure is the limit of his argument. This problem is by no means his own. Thus far, the postcolonial critique of trauma theory in Euro-American academia has been mostly that: a critique more than a sustained engagement with subaltern forms of theorizing trauma.[4] In this sense, the postcolonial critique of trauma studies is actually a critical reproduction of the trauma studies method: "apply" Euro-American terms to literary and social texts in order to demonstrate this application's failure, thereby highlighting the fact that certain sociohistorically situated traumas are underrepresented by Euro-American theory.

To be sure, this form of critique has its place, especially in an academic culture that refuses to provincialize its own epistemic frameworks. The problem I am pointing out, though, is that the widely accepted postcolonial critique of trauma studies does not provincialize its own epistemic framework. Instead, much like the discourse of trauma studies it believes itself to be critiquing, this mode of critique operates through the assumption that art functions as a diagnostic representation of the social reality of trauma. The missing step from Craps's undoubtably important argument is, then, to ask what it might mean for art to function as the means of mending (as many Indigenous aesthetic practices assume), rather than simply representing, such traumas. Put differently, the typical postcolonial critique of trauma studies demystifies but does not encounter anything new and therefore does not move beyond the problem it identifies: the categorical violence of the colonial gaze. Consequently, its limit is the same limit of trauma studies as a reified discourse in Euro-American academia: the elaboration of a politics of cultural difference.

In what follows, by tracing how Forna and Jarrett-Macauley, two British–Sierra Leonean writers, narrate collective trauma in post–civil war Sierra Leone, I pick up where Craps leaves off. That is, the following analysis is not first and foremost a critique of trauma theory's Eurocentric focus—such critiques already abound—but instead what I take to be this critique's necessary, yet too often missing next step: an explication of the trauma theory intrinsic to the writings of postcolonial authors attentive not only to their representations of trauma, but also to the formal processes through which their texts process this trauma.

Approaching Trauma through Realism and Animist Realism

Memory and *Moses* both invent modes of consciousness that become marked within each text as Indigenous, culminating in characters experiencing spiritual crossings and shamanic rituals. Sidestepping the question of the anthropological authenticity of these experiences, I interpret them as Forna's and Jarrett-Macauley's strategic engagements with animist poetics, and I focus my analysis on how their creative uses of Indigenous consciousness relate to the intervention their novels make in trauma studies. Forna and Jarrett-Macauley, I argue, each propose an animist reconsideration of trauma theory by representing Agnes, an internally displaced person (IDP) in *Memory*, and Citizen, a former child soldier in *Moses*, as suspended in states of spiritual possession and/or plague. Agnes "cross[es] back and forth between this world and the spirit world" (*ML*, 129), while Citizen "jump[s] to his feet, shouting into the air, hitting and punching in a way that suggest[s] combat with several ghostly enemies" (*MC*, 41). Each novel's plot hinges on these characters' need of new, communal rituals of recovery, which are also figured—much like Taussig's and Stoller's anthropological studies—as modes of ritual possession.

As I claimed in the introduction and in the previous chapter, one consequence of rethinking trauma theory from an animist viewpoint is that we must envision a subject that is always (traumatized or not) animated by external stimuli, to use the parlance of psychoanalysis. Thus, trauma cannot be conceived as the rupture of the "receptive cortical layer" functioning as the psyche's protective shield against external stimuli, as Freud famously hypothesizes (*Beyond* 229). Instead, an animist trauma theory must focus on ruptures within a nexus of mutually animating life forces always open to the spirit of external stimuli (which cannot properly be described as *external* since this subjective form does not adhere to the Cartesian divide between internality and externality). The logic of this consequence explains *Memory*'s and *Moses*'s insistence that post-traumatic survival is experienced not through a re-bordering of the traumatized subject's sense of self, but through the strategic creation of new possession rites through which to regenerate a transsubjective kinship.

Filtering Garuba's concept of animist realism through Taussig's and Stoller's theories of postcolonial spirit possession rituals functions as a useful springboard from which to consider how Forna and Jarrett-Macauley cast ritual possession as both trauma and transformation. It is through their novels' insistence that the historical possession of the colonized subject is both trauma and cure, I argue in what follows, that they intervene in the debate over trauma theory's applicability in postcolonial contexts. It is their nesting of this insistence within a logic that defines animism in proximity to realism, however, that limits these novels' ability to enact their own immanent theories of animism.

Jarrett-Macauley's fiction in particular is emblematic of Garuba's theory of animist realism. Forna's fiction, in contrast, is emblematic of realism. But animism is foundational to both *Memory*'s and *Moses*'s configurations of trauma, despite the novels' formal differences. In *Memory*, for example, Agnes is subjected to the disenchanted language of the *Diagnostic and Statistical Manual of Mental Health Disorders*; while Adrian believes that she has dissociative fugue, many locals believe her to be caught in between "this world and the spirit world" (*ML*, 129). In *Moses*, Julia is estranged from her cousin Citizen. When a shaman begins to visit Julia in her dreams, however, she learns rituals to help Citizen, whose name suggests he incarnates his ruptured nation. For Jarrett-Macauley, then, creatively reinventing rituals for the present opens, in Garuba's words, "avenues of agency for the dispossessed" ("Explorations" 285)—which is precisely what Forna represents as intrinsic to Agnes's consciousness. By harboring an alternative state within the consciousness of a subaltern character, *Memory* places an animist-realist consciousness within a traditionally realist textual ontology. By awakening Julia to an alternative state, *Moses* transitions the protagonist's realist consciousness into an animist-realist textual ontology. Through animist realism *Moses* ritualizes what is already intrinsic to the textual unconscious of *Memory*'s realism. Both novels are in this sense animist, not just in content or genre (Garuba's focus), but also in the functional process of their acts of narration (Taussig's and Stoller's focus). They each, through different genres, attempt to aesthetically mediate alternative states.

Yet, as I will argue, this mediatory act is ultimately limited by these novels' realist and animist-realist logics. Despite this limit, these novels productively utilize a process structurally similar to Taussig's and Stoller's theories of spirit possession rituals to critique humanitarian discourse in post–civil war Sierra Leone, a discourse these novels associate with much of Euro-American trauma theory. The crux of my argument, however, is that the limit of Forna's and Jarrett-Macauley's use of animism is precisely this critique. By representing two of humanitarian discourse's symbolic figures—an IDP and a child soldier—as harboring forms of consciousness that gesture toward alternative modes of spiritual community, these novels impressively lay the groundwork to theorize trauma beyond humanitarian ideology. But, as I demonstrate in this analysis and my argument throughout this book as a whole, shifting from a realist to a ritualized mode of animism more fully takes on the posthumanist and postsecular dimensions of animist cosmologies. The ritual side of animist poetics therefore incorporates more fully, into its very form, the process of postcolonial subject formation these novels, caught in a mode of animism defined by the proximity between magical and real depictions, envision but do not ultimately enact.

Before I lay out this argument in more detail, Z'étoile Imma's explanation of the Sierra Leone Truth and Reconciliation Commission (SLTRC)'s focus on the proliferation of cultural memory in the Sierra Leonean public sphere helps paint the picture of the cultural conundrum to which *Memory* and *Moses* respond. She writes:

> While the SLTRC advocates insistently promoted the formalized public space of the commission as the primary site where memory and forgiveness should be enacted, many Sierra Leoneans sought out family, community, and spiritual settings where collective memory-making, selective forgetting, and identity transformation rituals would better attend to a post-war transition. Misreading the suspicion of the SLTRC by locals as a willful silencing and negation of victims' perspectives, . . . international non-governmental agencies failed to consider how the SLTRC disrupted and obscured local practices of reconciliation. . . . Uneasy with the globalized and nationalist discourses that uphold public testimony and confession as the most appropriate and successful paths to reconciliation, many Sierra Leonean survivors of the war continued to cultivate intimate spaces as the focal location for forgiveness rituals. (130)

Memory and *Moses* likewise create animist "focal locations" for memorializing trauma, a process they aim not only at remembering the past but also at constructing a future. These novels thus demonstrate the political stakes of transitioning trauma studies away from perpetual calls for diversification and into a discourse that might finally start "acknowledging the traumas of non-Western or minority populations *for their own sake*" (Craps, *Postcolonial* 19, my emphasis). Despite the generic differences through which each novel represents trauma—realism and animist realism—they remain united by a shared aesthetic practice: the strategic reinvention of animist consciousness for the purpose of envisioning post-traumatic forms of collective life.

This vision is a contextualized instantiation of the political horizon of animist poetics I described in the introduction. However, as I argue in what follows, although Forna's and Jarrett-Macauley's writings respond to trauma by way of experiments with animist poetics, neither writer accepts the posthumanist, postsecular dimensions of animism as radically as the numerous aesthetic examples I provided throughout the introduction, or the texts upon which the rest of this book will focus. Hence these novels' lack of a key aspect of my argument throughout this book: the regenerative death drive. I thus conclude this chapter with a brief analysis of two works of poetry that share, from a different African context, *Memory*'s and *Moses*'s historically contingent, pragmatic utilization of animist poetics, but more radically accept its postsecular, posthumanist dimensions through their incorporation of the regenerative death drive.

An Alternative State

As Susan Shepler reports, for the United Nations and the majority of nongovernmental organizations in post–civil war Sierra Leone, the primary means of fostering recovery is a process called "sensitization," a model of public health spread through community awareness and social marketing projects. Sensitization, she writes, operates "top-down, the assumption apparently being that Sierra Leoneans [are] ignorant . . . and simply [need] more knowledge" ("Rites" 201). This knowledge is tied to Western ideas of psychological health. When Sierra Leoneans interpret their experience through English words like *psychosocial* and *trauma*, Shepler claims, they are rewarded with humanitarian aid, casting sensitization as a conglomerate of "power, rhetoric, and pedagogy" (204): a biopolitical apparatus through which Western conceptions of health and therefore subjectivity are proliferated.[5] One question postwar humanitarian work in Sierra Leone raises is, then, similar to the question postcolonial critics ask of trauma theory: How are we to conceptualize trauma and recovery without taking part in a process of globalized, Western subject formation?

This question is a clear impetus behind Forna's writing. Adrian becomes obsessed with diagnosing Agnes, for example, through a paradigm local doctors condemn as neocolonialism. On informing Adrian of a foreign medical team's six-week study, which concluded that 99 percent of Sierra Leoneans suffer from post-traumatic stress disorder (PTSD), Attila, head of the mental hospital, rhetorically questions Adrian: "When I ask you what you expect to achieve for these men, you say you want to return them to normality. So then I must ask you, whose normality? Yours? Mine? . . . This is their reality. . . . You call it a disorder, my friend. We call it *life*" (*ML*, 319). This conversation takes place while

Attila pulls over his car so Adrian can see the slums in which locals live. Post-traumatic recovery, Attila explains, assumes a state of normality to which the traumatized subject must return, but in Sierra Leone, he implies, this state is a priori unstable, arbitrary, falling apart; trauma is, in other words, the very stuff of Sierra Leonean life (which, as Laura Brown has influentially argued, challenges the American Psychiatric Association's definition of trauma). In his reading of the novel, Craps takes this scene as exemplary of an "inclusive, materialist, and politicized form of trauma theory" ("Beyond" 51) contra Eurocentrism, but his analysis focuses solely on the mode of critique characters like Attila offer, not any alternative mode of conceptualizing life that Forna's novel may enable.

Achille Mbembe has influentially theorized a foundational arbitrariness within postcolonial Africa that, as Attila claims, challenges psychiatric frameworks of trauma, especially psychiatry's assumption of normative stability. In "African Modes of Self-Writing" he conceptualizes "the state of war" as "part of the new African practices of the self." Through massacre and sacrifice under the state of war, the African subject "becomes a sort of work of art shaped and sculpted by cruelty." And this form demands a new theory of the subject, he claims. "[T]he African subject transforms his or her own subjectivity and produces something new—something that does not belong to the domain of a lost identity that must at all costs be found again, but rather something radically different, something open to change and whose theory and vocabulary remain to be invented" (269). Like Attila, Mbembe rejects the "lost and found" narrative of trauma and recovery within postwar African contexts, pointing instead toward a theory of trauma (and more fundamentally, subjectivity) yet to be articulated. An important aspect for such a theory is his concept of necropolitics: the violent logic of political sovereignty in the postcolony that "account[s] for the various ways in which . . . weapons are deployed in the interest of maximum destruction of persons and the creation of *death-worlds*, new and unique forms of social existence in which vast populations are subjected to conditions of life conferring upon them the status of *living dead*" ("Necropolitics" 40). As Agnes embodies the impossibility of recovery Attila articulates, she also incarnates Mbembe's living-dead status. In response to her death-world (witnessing her husband beheaded, fleeing to a refugee camp, surviving the war to find her daughter married to her husband's murderer), Agnes slips into alternative states of dreamlike wandering.

Adrian becomes convinced Agnes suffers from a rare case of dissociative fugue stemming from PTSD. What is more, the psychogenic structure of fugue informs *Memory*'s plot. Adrian's copy of *A History of Mental Illness*, for example, narrates the fuguer's unconscious in language mirroring the sociocultural questions intrinsic to the novel's setting: "*Fugue. Characterised by sudden, unexpected travel away from home. Irresistible wandering, often coupled with subsequent amnesia. A rarely diagnosed dissociative condition in which the mind creates an alternative state. This state may be considered a place of safety, a refuge*" (ML, 325). This description traces both the novel's plot and Adrian's position as the protagonist. In a fugue state, after catastrophe, the unconscious creates an alternative state, a refuge; in Sierra Leone, after the civil war, can anyone (*such as myself,* questions Adrian throughout the novel) create an alternative state, a refuge, for Agnes (an IDP) and millions like her?

Forna refuses to provide a positive or negative assessment of Adrian's diagnosis, but some Sierra Leonean characters (including Agnes herself) reject it, favoring Indigenous paradigms of psychic life. The novel's "European" and "African" paradigms, however, use similar language, implying that Forna's intention is to place what postcolonial critics often too hastily juxtapose in proximity. For example, the head nurse, Salia, explains to Adrian a local diagnosis of Agnes in this way: "[S]ometimes a person may be able to cross back and forth between this world and the spirit world. . . . And when they are in between the worlds, in neither world, then we say they are crossed. This woman is travelling between worlds" (*ML* 129). Despite cross-cultural disagreement, in the same way that Adrian's copy of *A History of Mental Illness* functions within the novel to associate dissociative fugue with the relation between the postwar state and the IDP, this animist diagnosis casts Agnes's symptoms as a matter of being "in between worlds, in neither world," not possessed—by a spirit or, for that matter, a nation-state—but crossed: in between worlds and thus in none.

Toward the end of the novel, local doctor Kai Mansaray, in diagnosing Agnes, uses the novel's transcultural diagnostics as a framework for interpreting its narrative. Thinking back on the mutilated survivors of village attacks, he considers: "[I]f you had asked any of the survivors how they had managed it, they would not have been able to tell you. It was as if those days in the forest, the escape to the city, had passed in a trance. *The mind creates an alternative state.*" Survival is phenomenologically produced as the experience of an alternative state. He elaborates: "Agnes isn't searching for anything. She is fleeing something. She is running away from intolerable circumstances. Escaping the house, her daughter, most of all, escaping JaJa": her son-in-law and husband's murderer.

"The difference between Agnes and the injured people who arrive at the hospital," Kai continues, "is that for Agnes there is no possibility of sanctuary." For Agnes, returning home (from abnormality to normality, as the psychiatric narrative would have it) is not a cure but a repetition of trauma. Her domestic conundrum thus reflects her position as an IDP: She is internally displaced from her home and nation. Inspired by his recognition, Kai removes "the book on the table," Adrian's copy of *A History of Mental Illness*, rejecting the categorical violence of Adrian's clinical paradigm with a gesture symbolic of the epistemic movement of the novel itself (*ML*, 326).

In literary terms, Kai recognizes that Agnes, rather than coming of age to her subject position within the *polis* like a traditional novelistic protagonist, performs her own internally displaced position within this *polis*. In her strange wandering, Agnes responds to what Mbembe terms the death-world inaugurated by the civil war. Performing her "living-dead" status by embodying a "crossed" or "fugue" state (depending on the paradigm of the reader), Agnes embodies a transcultural theory of trauma and survival (as opposed to the Manichaeistic logic intrinsic to most postcolonial critiques of trauma theory), which, the novel suggests, gestures toward the possibility of an alternative state. As an IDP, she incarnates a certain excess of the postcolonial nation-state, a person for whom "there is no possibility of sanctuary," in Kai's words. Through becoming crossed between this world and the spirit world, she dissociates herself from her constitutive dissociation from her nation-state, creating an alternative state, as Kai imagines it, by entering a dissociative fugue state, as Adrian imagines it.

Through this seemingly paradoxical agential double dissociation, Forna uses both the realist consciousness of the novel's narration and the animist consciousness of a subaltern character, Agnes, to transform this character's trauma into a logic of survival. The crossed Agnes performs an embodied memorialization of her constitutive trauma, which is aimed not at nation building through "sensitization," but at the survival of life inclusively excluded (to use Giorgio Agamben's framing of bare life) from such national consciousness. Ultimately, though, Agnes's consciousness remains for the reader a phenomenon to be diagnostically conceptualized. Through its realist aesthetic, *Memory* exceptionally represents the possibility of, but does not formally constitute, an alternative state rooted in animist consciousness. In *Moses*, Jarrett-Macauley moves from realism to animist realism in her attempt to cross this threshold.

Ritual Recovery

In *Moses* Julia ritually awakens to her role as her family's shaman. This role is juxtaposed to her uncle Moses, who responds to their familial trauma by archiving family photographs. Moses's aesthetic hero, J. P. Decker (a historical Creole photographer), photographed British "government buildings and military quarters" throughout Sierra Leone (Viditz-Ward, "Studio Photography" 37). While Moses models his response to trauma on an imperialist aesthetic, Julia is called to perform an Indigenous healing rite aimed at constructing a new form of collective life.

Each night in her dreams, Julia enters the Gola Forest, where the RUF initiated Citizen and other children as soldiers. Here she encounters Bemba G, a shaman who teaches her a healing rite. Sidestepping questions of the cultural authenticity of Julia's experience with rituals, I wish to focus on the narrative function of Jarrett-Macauley's strategically invented animism. Like the possession rituals that Taussig and Stoller examine, Bemba G's "Indigenous" rite is a translation/interpretation of a European text. He carries a book that holds two plays: Shakespeare's *Julius Caesar* and Thomas Decker's *Juliohs Siza* (a Krio translation of *Julius Caesar* from the late 1960s). Teaching the children Decker's translation is Bemba G's shamanic rite, which becomes the novel's route through which to imagine, like Agnes, an alternative state.

Considering the importance of colonial history to the shamans of Taussig's and Stoller's studies, Bemba G's technique is no surprise. Summarizing the historical importance of Decker's Shakespeare translation, Tcho Mbaimba Caulker writes:

> The very act of translating the English of Shakespeare's *Julius Caesar* into the Krio adaptation of *Juliohs Siza* was both (1) an act of linguistic and political independence done at a pivotal time in history when formerly colonized Africans were attempting to assert their own respective national sovereignties apart from England, and (2) an attempt to deliver an important political message to the new nation on the subject of governance through the example and representation of a once noble servant of the Roman people turned hubristic emperor. (209)

This second point is continuously emphasized in Decker's translation, which overtly politicizes the play. As Caulker writes, "The message to its national audience is one that sings the praises of democracy, while offering a stern warning to the nation that strays from the path of democracy" (212–13). For example, the soothsayer, rather than warning Caesar to "beware the Ides of March," exclaims, "Teyk tem Mach midul-mohnt," which, as Caulker explains, is "literally a call to Siza to halt his progress on the path to tyranny"—"Teyk tem" being "similar to the call of concern that a parental figure would offer to warn a young child headed for a dangerous fall" (216).

Decker's translation is therefore simultaneously a constitution of an imagined community, in Benedict Anderson's terms, and a warning against the political sovereignty of imagined communities. As Decker translated Shakespeare's play about a hubristic emperor en route to reshaping Roman democracy into a one-man state and hubristic revolutionaries who, in their attempts to defend democracy, reproduce tyranny, the newly independent Sierra Leone (whom Decker addresses) mirrored the drama. The shared irony of Shakespeare's and Decker's plays is that by killing Caesar/Siza, imperialism is established. In translating Shakespeare, Decker himself took on the role of the soothsayer. And like that of Shakespeare's soothsayer, his warning was ignored: Four years after the publication of *Juliohs Siza*, Sierra Leone became a one-party state (Caulker 222). Furthermore, since the historical Julius Caesar led the first invasion of Britain during the Gallic Wars, Jarrett-Macauley (much like Joseph Conrad) casts him as a precolonial, archetypal colonizer, colonizing the land that would later colonize Sierra Leone. Decker, as soothsayer, thus warns a new nation against the perils of entering a long history of imperialism, and Bemba G takes up Decker's call (Julia—the feminine form of Julius—even refers to Bemba G as a soothsayer). In sum, Bemba G's rite is an act of playing with history through a historical play directed at subjects implicated in this history. Like Taussig's and Stoller's studies, the performers of *Juliohs Siza* ritually construct a new reality out of the symbols history has handed them.

This ceremony takes place in the Gola Forest, already a ritual space. As Paul Richards explains, during the war the RUF's *sowo*, "sacred groves for the initiated" (81), provided a stage in the Gola Forest on which the RUF enacted a "drama of state recession" (32). Here, inspired by the Poro and Sande secret societies of West Africa, the RUF initiated children who had been denied political agency into sacred agency as warriors. Since this forest was once a space of refuge for Africans fleeing the slave trade, the RUF's rituals enter a mimetic relation with colonial history; by miming the RUF, so does Bemba G's play. These sacred groves in which the children were initiated as soldiers become the sacred groves in which they are initiated, through another ritualized performance, into what Julia witnesses as a new form of collective life.

This process is figured as spirit possession. For instance, Peter (the boy who plays Caesar) begins to distrust the other boys. In his performance of history, he becomes possessed by it; as another child puts it, "Caesar has gone to his head" (*MC* 174). Much like Citizen's post-traumatic flashbacks and Agnes's entrapment between worlds, Bemba G's mode of recovery, like the trauma to which it responds, is figured as a performance of possession through which an alternative state of being may emerge. Julia glimpses such a state:

> The child soldiers got it, meeting themselves in the play. They understood their place in the scheme of things. . . . The ancestors must be looking on. . . . I shouted out: "We are not alone, there are other people here watching us, listening—can't you feel them?" The child soldiers had stopped, frozen in their positions. A long time had passed since they first completed that scene but if I closed my eyes, I would find them in the same places, timeless human sculptures against the purplish night sky. (*MC* 159)

According to Julia, performing *Juliohs Siza* becomes a type of timeless ritual, freezing the children like sculptures perfectly positioned in relation to ancestral spirits. In this possessed state, the children break free of their possession by the trauma of war.

Bemba G's healing rite is thus a performative commemorative practice juxtaposing Moses's photographic archive, which reproduces the colonial history Bemba G uses as the building blocks for an alternative state. We should note that Foday Sankoh, leader of the RUF, was, like Moses, a photographer (the RUF was notorious for photographing its atrocities). As Richards argues, the RUF's warfare is a discursive performance of their political theory:

> The problem of understanding the basic political aims of the RUF is sometimes exaggerated. The leaders have made few *published* statements of their aims, but in large measure the political aims of the movement are manifest in its actions. RUF threats and acts of violence are dramatized messages to the

people about its view of the world, as well as military tactical ploys. Burning of houses and cutting off of villagers' hands and fingers inscribe, on the landscape and bodies of village people, a set of political messages rather more firmly than if they had been spoken over the radio. (6)

In their dramatized messages, Richards suggests, the rebels perform violence as responses to colonial history. For instance, in contrast to the rigid, uniformed marching of the postcolonial nation-state's military, so desperately attempting to reflect the propriety of colonial powers, "the cross-dressing, horror-comic-helmeted, young teenage rebel fighter was . . . brilliantly recapitulating an inventive pre-colonial tradition, where dress served to disguise and protect, rather than express, the true character of the warrior" (56). But this re-crafting of Indigenous practices produced the very atrocities that constitute the traumatic setting of *Moses*. Unlike Moses's reproduction of colonial aesthetics (and Sankoh's through his much-photographed guerrilla warfare), Bemba G's play mimetically (re)produces a new constellation of subjectivities forming a yet unexperienced *polis*.

For Bemba G, however, this ritual requires more performers: a global audience. The children perform *Juliohs Siza* within Julia's dream in front of an international audience. Moved by what they see onstage, the audience join the children, chanting, "Peace, Freedom, Liberty! Peace, Freedom, Liberty!" (*MC* 205). This global chant is the climax of the novel. "Whatever happens," Julia, shocked by the audience, tells herself, "this performance will not last forever." Though audience members from Africa, Europe, and North America join the children onstage, performatively constructing some sort of global community of ritualized possession, Julia recognizes this alternate universe—she claims the world becomes "ruled according to reverse laws, with reverse atoms coming from above"—as provisional (*MC* 209). In this provisional performance through which the foundations of liberal democracy (peace, freedom, and liberty) are spread from the Western world into Sierra Leone, does Jarrett-Macauley fall into the humanitarian dream of global interpellation? Can a more blatant picture of the ideology Forna's Sierra Leonean characters critique be imagined?

This scene is similar to the end of the film *Blood Diamond* (released a year after the novel) in which Solomon Vandy, a Mende fisherman, recently reunited with his son, a former child soldier of the RUF, stands before an international audience in Kimberly, South Africa. This scene represents a historic meeting in 2000 that led to the Kimberly Process, a scheme inaugurated to stop the international trading of conflict diamonds. By addressing a Western audience as the source of Sierra Leone's problems—the film continually points out that American women desire the diamonds fueling African warfare—and by ending on this scene of globalized liberal democracy, the ambivalent message of *Blood Diamond* is that Western intervention in Africa is both poison and cure. Unlike *Blood Diamond*, however, *Moses* signals its own limit. After all, "Peace, Freedom, Liberty!" is what the conspirators, following Brutus, chant after murdering Caesar, their hands freshly bathed in his blood, effectively laying the foundations of imperialism (Shakespeare 164). Bemba G's international performance therefore testifies against its own agenda. Like *Julius Caesar*, the defenders of democracy are guilty of what they seek to destroy. *Moses*'s animist realist form thus culminates in an autocritique that leaves the novel in the same position as *Memory*'s realism. In the end, like Agnes, Julia dreams of an alternative state.

Psychoanalytic Animism

It is no coincidence, then, that Jarrett-Macauley places her novel in dialogue with psychoanalytic trauma theory through the motif of dreaming. Not only do Julia's visits to the Gola Forest begin in her dreams, but the novel also, through Julia's dream-life, alludes to a passage from Freud's *The Interpretation of Dreams* central to psychoanalytic trauma theory. This allusion suggests that for Jarrett-Macauley, Indigenous approaches to trauma should not be neatly divorced from psychoanalytic theory, as the typical postcolonial critique of trauma studies suggests. Through Forna's continuous engagement with trauma theory, culminating in *Happiness* (2018), she similarly posits the need for a more nuanced, productive agonism between Indigenous knowledge and Euro-American theory.[6] For my purposes in this book, though, I demonstrate these two novels' shared call for a transcultural trauma theory by focusing on *Moses*'s allusion to Freud: This specific allusion demonstrates the conviviality between animism and psychoanalytic theory that postcolonial critiques of trauma studies too quickly dismiss.

While sleeping in Moses's home, Julia is awakened by a breeze. Unsure of whether she is awake or dreaming, Julia notices a light coming from Citizen's room. She opens the door to find Citizen's room on fire. Citizen is sleeping, and though flames cover the room, nothing burns: "[T]here was no crackle of burning wood, no sign of ash, no hissing of fire. The fire made no impact on the room." She then thinks, "*A child's bedroom is adapted to his life, his imaginings, his dreams*" (49). Since Citizen was a member of "number-one-burn house unit" during his time as a soldier, his room adapts, in Julia's words, to emulate his experience of burning houses throughout Sierra Leone, itself a repetition of Citizen's own loss of home in a rebel raid (58). Upon waking, Julia recognizes that Citizen's condition "involve[s] me. I need to take it in properly and learn more; only then can I see what I can do to make a difference" (50). Next, in the novel's most clunky scene, Anita (Moses's neighbor) twists Julia's hair in cornrows, performing a "hairdressing ritual" that transforms Julia's head into "a map of Sierra Leone," which allows Julia to finally "see" her role in Citizen's recovery (51).

The fire within the room that does not physically burn the room is an allusion to the burning bush narrative in Exodus (in which Moses approaches a bush on fire, yet never burning up). This allusion makes explicit Julia's connection to Uncle Moses. Unlike her uncle, who attempts to archive the past through imperialist photography, Julia must become a new Moses, someone who can lead her family into a livable future. As the viewer of the burning room, like Moses viewing the burning bush, Julia in this passage accepts her role as the novel's prophet. Hence her hair plait ritual: the rite of passage that allows Bemba G to visit her in her dreams and thus the rite upon which the novel's vision of post-traumatic recovery hinges.

Moreover, Julia's response to her dream of the burning room, a recognition of her own implication in her family's traumatic history, marks the passage as also an allusion to Freud's account of the dream of the burning child. In *The Interpretation of Dreams*, Freud records the story of a man who sleeps near the room containing the corpse of his recently deceased son. The dead son visits the father in a dream, grabbing his arm and asking, "*Father, don't you see I'm burning?*" (652). The father wakes up to find his dream is true: A candle has fallen on the corpse. Starting with the assumption that there is no clear-cut distinction between the fiction of dreams and the reality of waking existence, for Lacan, "The question that arises . . . is—*What is it that wakes the sleeper*? Is it not, *in* the dream, another reality?" (58). The son's address within the dreamworld, Lacan argues, carries "more reality" than the falling candle in the external world: "Is there not more reality in [the dream] than in the noise by which the father also identifies the strange reality of what is happening in the room next door?" (58). Thus, in Lacan's rereading, the father awakens, within the dream, to the relational constitution of his subjectivity, the fact that his life is, as Cathy Caruth claims in her reading of the case, "no longer simply his own," but implicated in the memory of his deceased son (*Unclaimed* 102).

In Julia's dream of the burning room, she has a similar awakening. Her "slippery self" (54) as she calls it, transforms, through both biblical-psychoanalytic allusion and a strategically crafted Indigenous ritual, in response to her awakening within a dream. In this sense the passage casts Julia as akin to Freud's Moses, who in *Moses and Monotheism* functions as the symbolic founder of a community (of which he is, like Julia, an outsider) operating through what Caruth describes as "implicated subjectivity."[7] Edward Said, more explicitly than Caruth, draws out the postcolonial politics implied by this form of implicated subjectivity incarnated in the figure of Moses. "[I]n excavating the archeology of Jewish identity," Said writes in *Freud and the Non-European*, "Freud insisted that it did not begin with itself but, rather, with *other identities*"—better yet, with an Arab (44). This view of "Moses as both insider and outsider" (16), Jew and Arab, suggests, Said claims,

> [T]here are inherent limits that prevent [community] from being incorporated into one, and only one, Identity. Freud's symbol of those limits was that the founder of Jewish identity was himself a non-European Egyptian. In other words, identity cannot be thought or worked through itself alone; it cannot constitute or even imagine itself without that radical originary break or flaw which will not be repressed, because Moses was Egyptian, and therefore always outside the identity inside which so many have stood. . . . (54)

Julia's dream of Citizen's burning room awakens, through a biblical-psychoanalytic script, a connection between herself and Citizen that, with Anita's help, awakens within Julia, through an invented Indigenous script, the ability to see through her dreams the possibility of a collective future. She thus embodies the "diasporic, wandering, unresolved, cosmopolitan consciousness of someone who is both inside and outside his or her community" that Said recognizes in Freud's Moses (53). Consequently, the passage in which she becomes cast as the novel's prophet is precisely the moment the novel shifts from a traditionally realist bildungsroman (the novel begins in Heathrow airport with Julia wondering what her trip to her ancestral home will teach her) to the undoing of the bildungsroman's individuated subject by way of animist realism.

A New Direction for Animism and Trauma Theory

While Jarrett-Macauley's critique of humanitarian ideologies of cultural memory coincides with her critique of postcolonial Manichaeism, thereby casting animist realism as convivial to both Indigenous knowledge and Euro-American theory, her novel's endpoint, as I have already argued, is the same horizon as Forna's realism. Each novel intelligently critiques the world as is, then dreams of a world otherwise. This shared limit demonstrates that postcolonial literary criticism, if it is to begin taking animism more seriously, must move beyond the notion that a text's proximity to realism is what constitutes its animism: Doing so imposes the former's limits on the latter's politics. To understand the affordances of animist poetics, which is a more expansive aesthetic logic than literary critics have recognized, we must identify a different form of aesthetics operating within its domain. Hence my insistence that animist ritual functions on the other side of an aesthetic spectrum.

To summarize my argument thus far, by reading an animist-realist novel alongside a realist novel, I have located forms of literary animism residing deeper than fantastic content or the generic framing of such content (Garuba's focus): animism at the level of formal process (Taussig's and Stoller's focus). By engaging with animist poetics, Forna and Jarrett-Macauley posit, through realism and animist realism, the possibility of an alternative state emerging through post-traumatic commemorative practices. But—and this is the crux of my polemic—this state remains for each a *polis* yet to come. Neither novel is able to fully voice a script to counter the humanitarian development narrative in post–civil war Sierra Leone that they critique by way of animism. The next step in a more fully animist criticism is to assume a more animistic approach to the literary itself.

I therefore conclude this chapter by illustrating what this assumption might look like in terms of practical criticism. In what follows, I offer brief close readings of two works of poetry from South Africa—Mtshali's "An Abandoned Bundle" and Phalafala's collection *Mine Mine Mine*—that, by way of ritual aesthetics, exemplify an animist approach to the literary.

This approach exemplifies an alternative to the limit case of Forna and Jarrett-Macauley I have been analyzing and critiquing. A more extended analysis of this poetry would require a study of apartheid law, political economy, and racialized ecology (with special attention to the region's mining industry), the thematic and formal relationships between these poets and South Africa's more recognizable poets (such as Dennis Brutus or Keorapetse Kgositsile), and a greater appreciation of this poetry's placement in the history of South Africa's Black Consciousness movement. For the purposes of this chapter, however, I approach these works of poetry as a case study in animist exegesis juxtaposing my polemical approach to Forna's and Jarrett-Macauley's fiction.

Much like my pairing of Forna's realism and Jarrett-Macauley's animist realism, my pairing of these two poets places Mtshali's seemingly less "spiritual" content in dialogue with Phalafala's explicitly spiritualized content. Indeed, what might be called the structural animism I have been analyzing throughout this chapter can be recognized throughout many African texts that appear relatively disinterested in typical iconographies of Indigenous cosmologies, lacking in what Euro-American critics deem fantastical content. Mtshali's "An Abandoned Bundle" is such a text, focused primarily on the material realities of township life under apartheid. Phalafala's poem, on the other hand, stages a conversation between its speaker and the spirit of Phalafala's deceased grandfather. Despite this apparent difference in representational content—material degradation and spiritual interlocution (as if these categories can be differentiated)—these poems share a formal animism through their ritual activation of the regenerative death drive I espoused in the previous chapter. Through the following brief close readings, I therefore shift this chapter's focus from the limits of trauma studies and the limits of animist realism to a key aspect of my theoretical argument throughout this book: the ritualization of the regenerative death drive. Although Forna and Jarrett-Macauley both experiment with animist poetics, neither, I have suggested, ventures beyond *dreaming* of the alternative states their novels attempt to construct. Alternatively, Mtshali's and Phalafala's poetry ritually voices this dream into a process of posthumous transfiguration resembling the art and film of Wanuri Kahiu, Wangechi Mutu, and Nandipha Mntambo I briefly analyzed in the introduction: collective life dialectically emerging through enforced death. Thus, on the one hand, the following close readings together function as a conclusion to this chapter's focus on how a practical criticism might approach the symbiotic relationship between cultural trauma and animism in African literature. On the other hand, they function as an exemplary threshold into the rest of the book, which is focused on the experimental animisms of Soyinka and Vera, writers paradigmatic of the way Mtshali and Phalafala ritualize the regenerative death drive.

A classic of Soweto poetry, Mtshali's 1971 poem demonstrates an animism that appears relatively disinterested in theological particularities of Indigenous cosmologies, focusing instead on offering a political critique of apartheid's political economy.[8] In this sense, critics might be tempted to view the poem's animism as akin to that of Forna's realism. Unlike Forna or Jarrett-Macauley, however, this poem assumes that part of literature's animistic quality is its ability to transfigure death into a new form of collective life: what I described in the previous chapter as the regenerative death drive operating, in response to ancestral trauma, at the core of animist poetics, and what I will describe in more detail through Soyinka's prison poetry in the next chapter as the "creative-destructive principle."

"An Abandoned Bundle" opens with an environmentally focused morning scene:

> A morning mist
> and chimney smoke
> of White City Jabavu
> flowed thick yellow
> as pus oozing
> from a gigantic sore. (144)

The "morning mist" and "chimney smoke" of the first two lines, images of the pastoral and the urban, set the poem within an environment structured by a symbiosis between transcendence (mist) and immanence (smoke). The setting is White City Jabavu, a Soweto township. Jabavu (a Xhosa surname denoting strength), an area formed by nineteenth-century Black squatters, and White City, an area created in the 1950s under the Group Areas Act, combine to name the force cruelly animating the township scene: white strength, the racist ideology structuring apartheid. The next line describes the symbiosis of morning mist and chimney smoke in the language of disease: "pus oozing from a gigantic sore." The opening stanza thus figures the township as a diseased body politic, and the pastoral/urban dialectic of the opening lines—reflecting the city/township, Johannesburg/

Soweto, or white/Black stratification of apartheid—is revealed as the locus of infection, that which, in the next line, "smothered our little houses / like fish caught in a net."

As the phrase "fish caught in a net" signals, the speaker's vocabulary of infection quickly shifts into one of predator and prey:

> Scavenging dogs
> draped in red bandanas of blood
> fought fiercely
> for a squirming bundle. (144)

The hard and soft alliterations "bandanas of blood" and "fought fiercely" create a tonal back-and-forth that mimes the poem's predator and prey dynamic, which itself mimes the predatory violence of township life: fishermen netting fish, dogs scavenging for food, and finally the speaker attacking the dogs:

> I threw a brick
> they bared fangs
> flicked velvet tongues of scarlet
> and scurried away,
> leaving a mutilated corpse -
> an infant dumped on a rubbish heap - (144)

Here, the abandoned bundle of the poem's title, a meal for wild dogs, is revealed as an infant's corpse. A narrative lyric composed of images from the quotidian violence of township life, the poem may appear more akin to realist materialism than what Garuba terms animist materialism. Quite simply, pollution, smoke fueling the apartheid political economy, smothers the speaker's shanty. The Black body politic of the poem is, in other words, animated not by the ancestral vitality central to my other lyric examples of animist poetics throughout this book's introduction, but rather the material conditions of 1970s South African culture and, as the first stanza suggests, its ideology of white supremacy. The poem's subject—a baby left for dead on a pile of trash—is, on the one hand, a revelation meant to shock readers with the despair central to Black life under apartheid, and on the other, an incarnation of an African subjectivity extirpated under the weight of colonial history. If in Birago Diop's "Breathe" (to name one example from the introduction), ancestral spirits breathe life into the material world, perpetually voicing their presence to the African subject, in Mtshali's poem the African subject has been severed from ancestral presence, left as carrion by the social stratification animating the apartheid *polis*.

This revelation, like the rest of the poem thus far, is spoken in the past tense, but the speaker shifts to the present tense for the next three lines, emphasizing the speaker's message to the corpse:

"Oh! Baby in the Manger
sleep well
on human dung."

Its mother
had melted into the rays of the rising sun,
her face glittering with innocence
her heart as pure as untrampled dew. (144)

Here, the speaker remediates what I will describe in the next chapter, through Soyinka's experiments with animist poetics during his imprisonment, as the temporal relation between the dead, the living, and the unborn. The rupture of this temporal relation, as I argued in the previous chapter, is precisely what ancestral trauma names. While Forna's and Jarrett-Macauley's engagements with animist poetics are likewise focused on the mediation of alternative states, neither goes as far as Mtshali in attempting to mediate a ruptured sense of time. Through the last two stanza's shifting tenses and addressees, it becomes clear the poem takes on an animist philosophy of the literary as a collective rite to "mend time itself," in Eze's words ("Language" 26). Lifting the poem out of the sequential temporality overseeing its language thus far, the speaker repositions the dead, abandoned subject as presently living (not dead, but "sleep[ing] well") and, moreover, in rejuvenated connection to ancestral vitality.

The theological imagery is not coincidental. To label the rubbish heap "the Manger" is to label the corpse a Christ, the township a Bethlehem. Human dung, further infecting the diseased body politic of the poem, becomes the locus of fertilization for renewed life—an "excremental genesis," in Soyinka's words (*Myth* 116). While christening the corpse, the speaker casts its lost mother as a new Mary, though her Assumption is not directed toward a heaven abstracted from nature, but instead back into her material environment: the sun, the dew. The last phrase, "untrampled dew," both figures the mother's "innocence" in regard to her baby's death and hearkens back to the "morning mist" of the poem's beginning. The poem thus concludes where it begins—a dialectic of transcendence and immanence—this time allowing the mother's posthumous transfiguration as becoming-environment to transfigure the oozing pus of the poem's first stanza into the dew of a new day.

Formally, this poem's movements resemble Taussig's and Stoller's dialectical readings of postcolonial spirit possession. By locating the text's animism within its formal processing of history's material conditions, we can recognize even in an exemplary text of Soweto poetry (an activist movement not typically read for its form) a strategic employment of animist poetics. We can also differentiate this strategy from that of Forna and Jarrett-Macauley. Rather than dreaming of an alternative state, "An Abandoned Bundle" more audaciously declares that this alternative state already is. By addressing the dead baby of its title, the poem reads within this lost life a dialectical, surrogate rite for the poem's Christian allusions. Its lyrical movement therefore becomes a liturgical celebration of the advent of an animist subjectivity emerging in dialectical response to its own state of abandonment under apartheid.

In conclusion, I wish to briefly consider how Phalafala's recent collection *Mine Mine Mine* (2023) employs the logic of animist ritual that Mtshali's poem exemplifies. Operating together as interwoven lyrical movements, the poems within this collection blend confessional, epic, and liturgical conventions to depict Phalafala's family's experience of Johannesburg's mining industry and place this experience within a broader vision of what I described in the previous chapter as the ancestral trauma at the heart of colonial modernity. Like Mtshali, even though Phalafala aims her poems at concrete historical experience, she is not content with merely representing historical trauma—even when these representations involve more explicit markers of animist iconography. More fundamentally, she aims her poetry at the ritual mending of her own inheritance of the ancestral trauma her poems depict: These poems are "A Litany of Loss," as the opening movement declares. Like "An Abandoned Bundle," then, the poems of *Mine Mine Mine* incorporate animist logic into their formal movements to the point at which they cross the threshold of animist realism and can be more accurately described as animist rites.

In the first stanza of the first poem, the speaker describes the death of Phalafala's Rakgolo, or grandfather:

> My grandfather is dead
> he was vomiting blood, my mother says
> lungs contaminated by history
> brimming full with mine dust. (3)

Phalafala's grandfather (addressed as Rakgolo throughout the poems) was a migrant mine worker who died from silicosis. This experience was so widespread that, as the collection's preface explains, in 2018 a class-action lawsuit against the South African mining industry was won in favor of the dead miners. As Rakgolo's lungs, like the lungs of so many Black South Africans under apartheid, became "contaminated by history," he began vomiting blood, replacing his own life source with "mine dust."[9] The collection thus begins with a striking image of the apartheid migrant labor system as a materialized form of spirit possession. Through a perversion of the process of ancestral vitality we saw in the poems analyzed in this book's introduction, crystalline silica dust here replaces the role of the ancestors as the breath/spirit (in Diop's terms) of Rakgolo's lungs until he is "[b]rimming full" with "history." Bodily wounding is here an outworking of historical wounding, history lodged in the lungs of Phalafala's immediate ancestor, her Rakgolo, and it kills him. The first two lines' slant rhyme (*dead/says*) charges the poem with inheriting this loss by voicing it in the present. This death, animating the speaking voice, must be spoken anew: The poem must re-vomit Rakgolo's blood as litany, as incantation, his contaminated lungs resounding within the speaker's.

As the speaker calls forth and questions Rakgolo, his spirit responds, emphasizing his inability to function as an ancestral presence for the poem and by extension Phalafala:

> *Where is the life I have come to live?*
> *I live in deadly conditions of protracted absences*
> *I am unavailable, a void in my family*
> *ringing with loss, longing, loneliness and shame*
> *I am battered by the whip of history*
> *there is no sanctuary. . . .* (6)

Rakgolo's spirit is severed from his "ancestral land" (5) by the "whip of history," leaving him searching for his own ancestral vitality, stuck as a void left to be inherited by "strangers who were once kin" (6). These poems consistently associate this familial loss not only with Rakgolo's forced migration from his home, severing him from his "stranger-family" (4), but of a larger history of colonial modernity conditioning this severance—a history incorporating British, Dutch, US, and South African forms of imperialism, slavery, and capitalism:

> We become the coal we mine
> the cotton we pick
> the sugarcane we reap
> the tobacco we cultivate
> the grapes we harvest . . . (34)

Here, the collective subject addressed in *Mine Mine Mine*, a colonized "we," is, like Rakgolo, "asphyxiated / by the chokehold of history" (32). Phalafala's inheritance of ancestral trauma is thus "Our inheritance" (38), the speaker continuously declares, a loss incorporating all "Collaterals / of colonial conquest" (51). The motif of Rakgolo's mining—"baking in earth's womb" (4)—thus comes to incarnate a collective "drilling / in the heart of / ancestral man" (47), the lodging of colonial modernity's planetary wounds within all colonized subjectivities.

Yet to be baked in earth's womb is to become a subterranean meal, buried sacrament awaiting extraction. This extraction, these poems declare, takes place through the poem's engagement with the speaker's body, the manner in which the lyrics themselves force the speaker's lungs to breath its litany and womb to prepare for conception. By addressing a familial loss that cannot be separated from a globalized ancestral trauma at the core of colonial modernity, these poems seek to regenerate a form of animist subjectivity by mending the speaker's own incarnation of ancestral trauma within her body:

> Our bodies are vaults
> storing trauma that still breathes.
> In.our.wombs . . . (72)

The speaker's womb incarnates the mines in which Rakgolo suffered, and his imprint as a void who *still breathes* (continuation and stilling) his contamination in the speaker's womb suggests that the horizon of this poetry is the act of mining the extirpated ancestral out of the colonized subject. Put differently, Phalafala's speaker must birth her own ancestor by breathing this poem, and thus its wounded ancestral voice, into renewed life. Hence the motif of birthing:

> A vicious modernity
> disfigures Black maternity
> turns Black women's wombs
> into factories producing blackness
> . . . .
> domestic middle passages
> forced to deliver sons
> into the mine tomb of the state (9)

The birth canal is a Middle Passage, an embodied enactment of historical loss, as the rhyme *womb* and *tomb* emphasizes. This Middle Passage transports both the unborn, who will toil for "the state," but also the ancestors who have been dislocated from their home—whose void resides in the speaker's womb, awaiting their birthing ritual (which is the vocalization of the poem itself).

The chantlike repetitions throughout the collection thus all hearken back to the postcolonial birth rite functioning as the force undergirding the poetry's formal movements. Even the chantlike repetition of the title, *Mine Mine Mine*, suggests a ritual mining of the ancestral. Interpreted as a verb, this thrice repeated *Mine* suggests mining the history from the dead Rakgolo's lungs, mining the ancestral from the colonized subject's womb, and mining through these acts an affirmative declaration of life (as in, *this history is Mine Mine Mine*). As a noun, this thrice-repeated *Mine* is a chanting of the site of Rakgolo's possession by crystalline silica dust and, through this ritual repetition, transforming the location of his enforced death into the regeneration of collective life ("earth's womb" [4]). Thus, in a dialectical move mirroring Mtshali's poem, the ritual repetition of the title distills the function of the poetry collection as whole: This poetry is the means through which Phalafala's speaker transforms her inheritance of ancestral trauma into a regenerated ancestral kinship.

This regeneration, like Mtshali's poem, emerges through death, a death Phalafala's speaker figures as the animist birthing ritual functioning as the litany's pinnacle:

> Yes we did die,
> in the blackness
> of destruction and creation.
> We part our hips
> like the sea
> and birth ourselves, (45)

Although the poem's "we" (its vision of animist collectivity) has died, the very act of voicing this poem turns auto-"destruction" into auto-"creation" (as I will argue in the next chapter, these two concepts are, in an animist view, symbiotic). This same "we" who has died moves like the sea of the Middle Passage and the Red Sea parting, like birthing hips, to deliver an enslaved people, to birth the conditions of a new form of collective life.

In sum, operating beyond the purveyance of Forna's and Jarrett-Macauley's uses of animist poetics, Mtshali's and Phalafala's poetry utilizes ritual aesthetics to activate the regenerative death drive as an animist response to ancestral trauma. While Forna's and Jarrett-Macauley's writings undeniably play with animism, neither accept its postsecular, posthumanist implications as radically as Mtshali's and Phalafala's poetry. In these poems, the dead join their degraded ecosystems—township dew (smog), the earth's womb (mines)—to be posthumously transfigured as a regenerated form of collective subjectivity uniting the living and the dead as well as the human and more-than-human world in dialectical response to colonial modernity's planetary wounds. While Forna and Jarrett-Macauley dream of an alternative state, Mtshali and Phalafala have the audacity to declare its presence, to call forth the animist subject. As Phalafala writes,

> Where is the ritual
> the song and prayer?
> Here, now. . . . (51)

Chapter 3

Cosmic Personhood in the Animist Lyric

Reading Wole Soyinka's Prison Poetry
with and against New Materialism

In 1967 Wole Soyinka was arrested and imprisoned in Nigeria for twenty-two months. Surprisingly, the poetry he wrote while incarcerated both prefigures and challenges, decades in advance, a discourse in vogue among literary and cultural theorists today: new materialism.[1] Like new materialism, this poetry envisions a spatial expansion of subjectivity to include the vitality of the more-than-human world, which he describes as the "organic totalism" of the African subject (*Art* 55). Venturing beyond new materialism, however, this poetry also proposes a temporal expansion of subjectivity to include past, present, and future life. This temporal expansion is an outworking of Soyinka's utilization of what he terms Yoruba cosmology's "cyclic consciousness of time" (*Myth* 2). Through this philosophy of time, his prison poetry casts living, dead, and unborn people as dwelling in a dynamic nexus they must perpetually negotiate, the act of which sustains an eternally moving temporal cycle in which the past, present, and future interpenetrate and co-constitute each other.[2] In contrast, for most theorists in Euro-American academia (new materialists included), the past is solely past, dead in the stasis left behind by linear time's unbendable movement toward sequential posterity and alive only by way of representation in the memory of the living. By taking seriously the vitality of both atoms and ancestors, thereby envisioning a spatial *and* temporal expansion of subjectivity, Soyinka's prison poetry prefigures new materialism's fundamentally ecological subject while thinking beyond the latent secular humanism undergirding its linear view of time.

In this chapter I utilize this differentiation to articulate how the animist lyric revises psychoanalytic theory and new materialist ecology, and, by extension, disrupts resting assumptions within contemporary theory at large. As I suggested in this book's introduction, animism in the modern epoch implicitly places psychoanalysis and new materialism in dialogue because (a) modernity is founded on colonial trauma (the subject of psychoanalysis) and (b) this trauma implicates the more-than-human world (the subject of new materialism). Using Soyinka's prison poetry as paradigmatic of the ritual function of the animist lyric, I argue in this chapter that this aesthetic form exceeds the post-Enlightenment secular assumptions retained by both psychoanalytic and new materialist theory even as they offer their most radical critiques of the Cartesian subject.

As I will demonstrate, Soyinka's prison poems ritualize what he terms the creative-destructive principle: an example from Yoruba cosmology of the regenerative death drive I have been casting as the hydraulics of animist poetics throughout this book. I juxtapose the implicit animist revision of the Freudian death drive intrinsic to Soyinka's prison poetry with Catherine Malabou's explicit new materialist revision of the Freudian death drive (what she terms destructive plasticity). Through this juxtaposition, I argue that central to the cultural work of the animist lyric is a spatial-temporal expansion of subjectivity activated through its regenerative death drive. The spatial aspect of this expansion resonates with new materialist ecology and thus Malabou's revision of Freud: Since the subject *is* the material world, our experience of subjectivity cannot be divorced from this world in all its ecological expanses. The temporal aspect of this expansion, however, assumes a postsecular form of historiography that both extends and overturns the critique of the Cartesian subject intrinsic to psychoanalytic theory and new materialist ecology. Put differently, animist critique further radicalizes new materialist critique: Since the intrinsically ecological subject also *is* the living ancestral nexus connecting the past, present, and future, our experience of subjectivity cannot be divorced from the ancestral in all of its expanse—the living, the dead, and the unborn.

Upon juxtaposing Soyinka's animist and Malabou's new materialist revisions of the Freudian death drive, I utilize this theoretical dialogue as a lens to analyze Soyinka's prison poetry as paradigmatic of the animist lyric as an aesthetic form. The cultural work of the animist lyric, I argue, is to ritualize animism's spatial-temporal expansion of subjectivity, and in doing so voice its expanded subject into existence, an existence emerging through the death of the individuated subject of colonial modernity. As a tactic of postcolonial subject formation, then, the animist lyric voices into being a cosmic personhood in response to its formal inheritance of this personhood's extirpation under colonization. Since this process restores colonized subjectivity to its ecological expanse, new materialist critique helps articulate the animist lyric's formal operations within the language of cultural criticism; but since this process is a dialectical response to colonized subjectivity, the animist lyric is inconceivable to criticism without a theory of trauma. From this lens, we can recognize the animist lyric as an aesthetic mechanism for a post-traumatic, ecological explosion of the colonized subject's ill-fitting, Cartesian borders.

This process is the impetus behind Soyinka's prison poetry's ritualization of Yoruba cosmology's creative-destructive principle, which is why I approach these poems as paradigmatic of the animist lyric. An understanding of this form not only adds to our understanding of animist poetics' widespread aesthetics, but also adds to the growing scholarship on what Walt Hunter calls "global poetics," the formal strategies intrinsic to the practices of global Anglophone poetry, which are often sidestepped by postcolonial studies' more frequent focus on narrative prose.[3] Operating as spells meant to be chanted, and through this chanting, meant to ritually conjure, in dialectical response to colonial modernity, a postcolonial subjectivity I describe as cosmic personhood, the prison poems I analyze in this chapter bear implications for lyric theory more broadly. In *Theory of the Lyric*, for example, Jonathan Culler places ritualistic logic at the core of lyric poetry from antiquity to the present. Through its doubling down on, and strategic use of, this ritualistic logic, the animist lyric, rather than depicting the subjective experience of a speaker, incants a postcolonial form through which to process subjective experience as such. Given that animist poetics is always a dialectical response to colonial modernity's extirpation of a perceived kinship between the living and the dead and the human and more-than-human world embodied in the colonized subject, the form of subjectivity the animist lyric voices must be irreducibly cosmic. The ecosystem of the Niger Delta in Gabriel Okara's poetry, the more-than-human incantatory visions of Christopher Okigbo's poetry, the repetitive warning to "Let no one / Uproot the Pumpkin" in Okot p'Bitek's *Song of Lawino* (56), and the polluted and diseased ecologies of Oswald Mtshali's and Uhuru Portia Phalafala's poems I analyzed in the previous chapter should all be contextualized within this formal logic, as should the more-than-human scope of postcolonial poetry beyond Africa: for example, the symbiosis between ecology, memory, and voice uniting figures as dissimilar as A. K. Ramanujan, Kamau Brathwaite, and Seamus Heaney.

Further, a more systematic understanding of this logic allows the postcolony's "lyric ecology," in Sonya Posmentier's terms, to speak to the growing discourse of postcolonial ecocriticism.[4] The poetry I examine in what follows is set in the constricted ecosystem of a prison—not the rivers, oceans, and forests more typically associated with ecopoetics. This isolated environment incarnates the Cartesian severance of internal subjectivity from external world. The prison thus signifies within this poetry the (anti)ecological structure of colonized subjectivity, the individuation that my animist lyric's incantation of cosmic personhood combats. Thus, as my analysis demonstrates, the animist lyric is intrinsically ecological, not due to lyrical depictions of specific environments, but as an outworking of its formal operations. By focusing on how Soyinka's prison poetry ritualizes postcolonial subject formation as the regeneration of post-ipseitic kinship, a cosmologically expanded form of what Cajetan Iheka calls "distributed agency" (50), I demonstrate that, from an animist viewpoint, a text's environmental depictions are not the locus of its ecopoetics. Instead, the formal logic of the animist lyric assumes a process of subject formation as intrinsically ecological in the most expansive, cosmic sense. Thus, for the animist, poetry of the colonized psyche, such as Soyinka's prison poems, are as ecocritical as any poetry of land- or seascapes. And since the animist logic I explicate from these poems is operative across so much of postcolonial poetry, including more explicit engagements with environmental content (e.g., Derek Walcott's depictions of the Caribbean ecosystem as a wounded subjectivity), my focus on formal process rather than environmental depiction suggests that postcolonial ecopoetics *is* postcolonial poetics.

New materialism's universalization of the ecological bears implications for trauma theory, especially theory approached through a lens of animist criticism I am modeling throughout this book. This claim is a starting point of my argument in this chapter, since, as I argued in the introduction and chapter 1, animist poetics addresses the more-than-human world as an aesthetic response to colonial modernity's wounding of this address. As critics seek to widen trauma theory's field of vision and revise the coordinates of its assumed subject, new materialism has become for some a resource to rethink trauma outside an overtly anthropocentric lens. Deniz Gundogan Ibrisim writes, "new materialist thinking" can help critics "recalibrate universalist and anthropocentric conceptions of Western trauma" (238). Such a recalibration would shift trauma theory to what Reza Negarestani describes as a "cosmologically deepened account of trauma": one that views "the particulate, the galactic, the stellar, the chemical, the biological, the socio-cultural and the neuropsychological" as intertwined (26). Such claims demonstrate a growing awareness in an era marked by mass environmental damage (trauma in the most collective form imaginable) that theorists must reimagine who or what is implicated in trauma studies' "implicated subject," as Michael Rothberg (borrowing a term central to Caruthian trauma theory) describes it. If for Caruth trauma awakens us to the fact that we are "implicated" in each other's histories (*Unclaimed* 24), for Rothberg the next step for theorists must be an increasing awareness of the various forms of our interconnectedness within these histories. Thus far, however, the discourse of trauma studies has not taken the implicated nature of subjectivity as far as new materialism has. While Freudian trauma theory imagines a subject implicated in the histories of other subjects, and post-Caruthian trauma studies seeks to expand whose history is included in this metahistorical implication, new materialism imagines a subject implicated in all of the eternally dynamic matter of the universe.

This post-anthropocentric recalibration of the subject is in some regards an ally of postcolonial critique. For many of the Indigenous populations subjected to the traumas of European colonization, subjectivity has always assumed a form infinitely implicated in the more-than-human world. To theorize trauma from such subaltern epistemologies thus necessitates theorizing the structure of personhood beyond the solely human. Hence the parallels between animist poetics and the ecological vitalism of new materialist critique. Central to my argument in this chapter, however, is that Soyinka's prison poetry exemplifies key distinctions between animist poetics and new materialism. First, Soyinka's animism does not reduce humans to an agent equal to all other agents (i.e., flat ontology), but is instead strategically focused on expanding human agency as a postcolonial act. As such, his animism does not lapse into the universalism characterizing much of new materialist philosophy, but is instead a self-consciously dialectical response to colonial modernity. Finally, and of most importance to this chapter, Soyinka's animism is fundamentally diachronic and thus offers a more radical expansion of subjectivity than new materialism. Although new materialism does sketch radically expansive subjective coordinates, thereby paralleling in key ways, within the discursive context of Euro-American theory, the forms of subjectivity intrinsic to the animist cosmologies operating throughout the colonized world, this expansion is purely spatial. It is focused on material interconnections across the more-than-human world, but envisions these interconnections within a nondiachronic spatial logic. As Soyinka's prison poetry demonstrates, animist poetics, on the other hand, expands the borders of the subject to include both the more-than-human world *and* the interpenetrating realms of living, dead, and unborn people. As I argue in this chapter, this temporal logic (intrinsic to the material world), which Soyinka appropriates from Yoruba cosmology, pushes his writing beyond the limits of new materialism and implicitly intervenes in psychoanalytic theory by reimagining the role of the death drive as regenerative.

Consider this passage from Soyinka's prison poetry:

Death
Embraces you and I
A twilight cone is
Meeting-place
The silent junction of the grey abyss (*Early Poems*, 157)

This stanza comes from "Animystic Spells," a cycle of lyric-spells Soyinka composed during his incarceration (and the central object of interpretation in this chapter). In this particular spell, Soyinka, who believes himself to be awaiting his imminent death sentence, casts death as intimate. It "Embraces" the speaker and addressee, "you and I." He also casts death as transitional, as the temporal flux of "twilight" and spatial flux of "junction" both suggest. Functioning as the apex of a "twilight cone," death in this spell is a locus of transition mutually informing subjects on either side of its geometry, a "Meeting-place" between all forms of life: past, present, and future. Composed and chanted to survive the trauma of solitary confinement, Soyinka's spell envisions death as generative of a radically expanded notion of subjective life.

Now consider this quote from Malabou's *The New Wounded: From Neurosis to Brain Damage*, her most extended critique of Freud: "The study of brain damage reveals that traumas and wounds have a new signification that psychoanalysis can only ignore at the price of failing to grasp present-day suffering. This new signification is linked to negative or destructive plasticity. Its result can be characterized as a metamorphosis unto death or as a form of death in life" (212). Like Soyinka, Malabou finds a symbiotic relationship between life and death revealed in the experience of trauma, a relationship Freud famously termed the death drive. In order to more accurately theorize contemporary trauma, however, psychoanalysis must be rethought in light of neuroscientific discoveries, she argues, which results in a new, post-Freudian theory of the death drive. More specifically, psychoanalysis must begin to theorize neuronal plasticity, the brain's material form of "signification" functioning as the catalyst of trauma as well as all subjective life, a form Freud was unable to recognize. What might it mean for psychoanalytic theory, she asks, if the "metamorphosis unto death" undergirding the subject's experience of trauma—the death drive—is a result of the same neuronal process that allows the subject to experience life itself? Soyinka blends Indigenous ritual and poetry, whereas Malabou blends neuroscience and psychoanalysis. While these projects may appear disparate, both are formulated in response to trauma, and through this response both discover an intertwinement between life and death structuring subjectivity.

Soyinka discovers this intertwinement in Yoruba cosmology and terms it the creative-destructive principle.[5] As I argue in this chapter, this principle reveals Soyinka's implicit animist alteration of Freud's death drive. To make this argument, I utilize Malabou's work as a bridge to apply Soyinka's writing to the forefront of Euro-American theory. As I demonstrate, through her signature theory of destructive plasticity, she proposes a new materialist critique of the humanism assumed by the Freudian death drive. As such, destructive plasticity bears striking congruity with the creative-destructive principle: Malabou's explicit revision of the death drive, like Soyinka's implicit revision, expands the borders of the Cartesian subject to include the more-than-human world. I therefore appropriate Malabou's psychoanalytic new materialism to articulate the theoretical relevance of the revision of the Freudian death drive I find intrinsic to Soyinka's animist poetics. Namely, decades before Malabou's new materialist recalibration of psychoanalytic trauma theory, Soyinka offered through his prison poetry a similarly "cosmologically deepened account of trauma" (Negarestani 26).

As I also argue, however, Soyinka's utilization of Yoruba cosmology's cyclic temporality challenges what I take to be Malabou's retainment of post-Enlightenment European humanism's linear, sequential temporality. As the stanza quoted above suggests, death is for Soyinka an intersection between the past, present, and future: a transitional moment in cyclic time. In contrast, for Malabou, time is resolutely linear (in fact, as I will demonstrate, her theory of destructive plasticity rests on time's linear form). Thus, while Soyinka's creative-destructive principle parallels Malabou's destructive plasticity insofar as it locates a revised death drive intrinsic to the material world, it contextualizes this dynamic within an alternative temporal structure. This structure assumes an animist form of subjectivity that operates beyond the coordinates of new materialist discourse. I therefore argue that through a spatial-temporal expansion of subjectivity, Soyinka's creative-destructive principle both precedes and critiques Malabou's new materialist revision of the Freudian death drive.

Since this expansion is central to the form of the animist lyric Soyinka's prison poetry epitomizes, my analysis in this chapter demonstrates how the animist lyric speaks to the state of contemporary theory at large. First, if theorizing trauma in the postcolony requires taking postcolonial conceptualizations of the psyche and memory systems seriously, then understanding non-Western philosophies of time is a necessary step. In addition to enabling an understanding of postcolonial trauma in more postcolonial terms, Soyinka's poetry demonstrates a simultaneously posthumanist and postsecular form of historiography he terms "active history" (*Myth* 110). I therefore conclude this chapter by juxtaposing this historiography, which Soyinka aligns with the creative-destructive principle, to that of psychoanalysis and new materialist ecology. By challenging the latent secularism of Euro-American theory's attachment to linear temporality, Soyinka's poetry demonstrates how animist poetics not only allows critics to theorize trauma in terms internal to African culture, but also to recognize the manner in which animism invests the colonized subject with political agency *through temporality*: the ability to recreate the historical conditions of the colonized present by imaginatively engaging with the interpenetrating worlds of the past and future—which, from an animist standpoint, is not separate from ecology. This animist philosophy of time adds a contingency to new materialist ecology often lacking. Rather than a universally flattened ontology of equally "vibrant" (Bennett), "intra-active" (Barad), or "trans-corporeal" (Alaimo) agents, animist poetics' regeneration of nonlinear philosophies of time intrinsic to the material cosmos casts its ecologically expansive subjectivity not as a universal form, but as a historically contingent process of appropriating Indigenous cosmologies: a dialectical response to colonization's rupturing of worlds.

Contextualizing Soyinkan Animism
(Historically and Theoretically)

Though almost two decades before winning the Nobel Prize (1986), Soyinka boasted at the time of his arrest a growing reputation in Anglophone letters as a dramatist, novelist, critic, and more recently a poet.[6] In Nigeria he was also well known as a public intellectual and political activist.[7] He had been an outspoken critic of the nationalist identity politics then fueling ethnic conflict in Nigeria, lamenting in particular the recent anti-Igbo pogroms of 1966, a precursor to the Biafran War.[8] After campaigning against the supply of weapons to both the secessionist Biafra and Nigeria's military government, he organized a clandestine meeting with secessionist leaders. His goal was the inauguration of what he terms a "Third Force" (*The Man Died* 178): a social energy that might emerge through an encounter between the oppositions structuring the civil war and, by exceeding the their antimonic structure, transform Nigerian politics.[9] Instead, he was arrested by Nigeria's federal military government for being a suspected Biafran sympathizer and detained without trial, mostly in solitary confinement.

His prison poetry demonstrates the historically contingent and pragmatic nature of his experimental use of animism. Often taking chantlike forms, such as curses and spells, these poems are instances of Soyinka's strategic appropriation of Yoruba cosmology. Rather than offering a lyrical representation of a precolonial worldview, he appropriates an Indigenous knowledge system for the purpose of processing and surviving, through literary writing, a postcolonial experience: his incarceration during his nation's civil war.[10] He describes his time in prison as his participation in a "two-year experiment on how to break down the human mind." Composing and chanting lyric-spells in solitary confinement was thus for him an incarceration survival tactic. Such spells, poetry as ritual mechanism to combat mental breakdown, "induced a state of self-hypnosis," he explains. "The result—a state of weightlessness . . . familiar enough to those who dabble in the more esoteric religions" (*Early Poems* 149). During this time he also "scribbled fragments of plays, poems, a novel," and his prison memoir, *The Man Died*, in between the lines of books smuggled in to him, including Paul Radin's *Primitive Religion* (*The Man* 9). A classic of comparative mythography, this monograph is an apt location for the autographs of Soyinka's prison poems.[11] In these poems Soyinka, like Radin, explores archetypes of the numinous, utilizing symbols from African cosmologies, Judeo-Christian monotheism, Hindu cosmology, and other traditions of world literature and religion to uncover a primal dynamic within the psyche, a dynamic Soyinka defines as animism.[12]

While these poems are only one portion of Soyinka's "civil war tetralogy" (Jeyifo 179), the most fertile period of his writing, I focus on them in this chapter for two reasons. First, while his interest in animism shapes his oeuvre, in his prison poetry (and in "Animystic Spells" in particular) we see his embrace of animism in its most explicit, and indeed abstruse, manner.[13] By the time of his imprisonment, Soyinka had already incorporated animism into his dramaturgy to much acclaim. *A Dance of the Forests* (1960) and *The Road* (1965), for example, both draw on Yoruba cosmology to stage the ritual dramaturgy that would find its culmination in *Death and the King's Horseman* (1975).[14] Yet even his most ritualized plays exist in a narratively ordered universe aimed at engaging an audience. In contrast, his prison poems, as he explains, were composed for the purpose of "sheer self-protection" (*Early Poems* 87). Since the poems are less representational than they are mystic, initiatory, and incantatory, they embrace more bluntly the animist poetics structurally influencing his more recognizable, representational works.[15] Second and consequently, while most of his writing explores the collective traumas of colonization and neocolonial rule in Africa, in these poems we see Soyinka's most immediate and concrete use of literary writing to survive a traumatic experience.[16] These two points are inseparable: Not only does Soyinka fully embrace an animist Weltanschauung within these poems, since he composed them for the specific function of aiding his psychic and spiritual survival amid the trauma of incarceration (and even solitary confinement), they distill the mutually informing animist poetics and trauma theory intrinsic to his writings to their most base level.[17]

This collection's eventual title, *A Shuttle in the Crypt*, condenses this animist trauma theory. The crypt signifies Soyinka's "Live Burial" (as the title of one poem puts it), culminating in his solitary confinement. The shuttle, on the other hand, is "a unique species of caged animal," he explains, "a restless bolt of energy, a trapped weaver-bird yet charged in repose with unspoken forms and designs." An ancient tool of weavers, a shuttle is used to create textiles, etymologically linked to Soyinka's vocation as a writer of texts.[18] His definition emphasizes movement, suggesting that a caged shuttle still harbors potential force, a "bolt of energy." His association of the shuttle with the "weaver-bird"[19] expands this kinetic imagery, signifying the simultaneous potentiality of imprisoned nest-weaving (the construction of a habitable space) and flight (the escape from an uninhabitable space). Yet this potential force is encrypted: both trapped in the crypt of prison and "charged" with "unspoken forms and designs" (such encrypted energy immediately raises animistic connotations). He continues: "In motion or at rest it is a secretive seed, shrine, kernel, phallus and well of creative mysteries." "Secretive" suggests both the harboring of secrets and the act of secreting—hence the seed, shrine, kernel, phallus, and well, all of which both contain and release "creative" energy. The shuttle and the crypt of the title thus exist in a dialectic.[20] The crypt is not antithetical to the shuttle, but rather that which harbors the shuttle's motion and always carries the possibility of its ecstatic release, what he describes as "the essence of innate repletion" (*Early Poems* 87). In short, the title signals Soyinka's animist approach to processing trauma in that survival is invoked through the subject's mystic engagement with their encrypted state of being, which harbors creative energy.

While it may be tempting for Western critics to interpret such an approach as a product of Soyinka's Yoruba heritage, he actually began studying animism as a way to combat his own severance from this heritage. Like many African intellectuals of his day, he was partially raised and educated within a colonial Christianity that separated itself from so-called pagan practices.[21] During his studies at the University of Leeds in the 1950s, however, he was struck by his English professors' curiosity about his people's spirituality. He began visiting an array of religious establishments, noticing similarities between European and African forms of spirituality. The carvings on church pews in Leeds, for example, reminded him of West African wood carving. Such similarities solidified his rejection of primitivist discourse on African traditions. This experience sparked what has become a lifelong interest in African Indigenous knowledge systems and in particular the Yoruba cosmology of his heritage.[22] Returning to Nigeria as a Rockefeller Research Fellow in 1960 (the year of independence from British rule), he embarked on a Land Rover purchased with his grant to study West African Indigenous theater. An understanding of local theater practices became for him inseparably linked to an understanding of animism. Throughout the sixties he would famously experiment with animism in his own drama, fiction, and poetry, and seven years after his study of West African theater he would compose "Animystic Spells" in solitary confinement. As his pun *animystic* suggests, he combines the animism he studied during his Rockefeller research project with the mysticism he studied in Greek and English literature through his colonial education—a hybrid lyric style that is "introspective, visionary, and metaphysical" (Maduakor 37). Although he writes of animism throughout his career, he only uses *animystic* in this title, marking the cycle as a tactical utilization of animism for the purpose of ecstatic experience in solitary confinement. Their style, moreover, embodies in exaggerated form the animist poetics found across his oeuvre, from his ritual drama to his esoteric essays to his self-fashioned devotion to the Yoruba god Ogun.

The germination of Soyinka's animist poetics utilized as a ritual mechanism for surviving incarceration is therefore not the "Yoruba world" as a precolonial Indigenous habitus. Rather, his strategic appropriation of animism is part of his fundamentally modern struggle for a model of subjectivity crafted in response to Africa's colonization and advanced by the post-independent neocolonialism he was imprisoned for attempting to stop. In other words, Soyinka's discovery and creative adaptation of animism is an aesthetic strategy of cultural trauma survival, which in prison was also an immediate strategy for his own psychic survival. Indeed, modern African writing for Soyinka is nearly always linked to "survival patterns" (*Art* 134), first and foremost from the material and spiritual ruptures constitutive of colonial modernity. "Cultural and spiritual violation," he writes, "has left indelible imprints on the collective psyche and sense of identity of the peoples, a process that was ensured through savage repressions of cohering traditions by successive waves of colonizing hordes (*The Burden* 41–42). "The black poet" (whom he describes as a latter-day griot) is thus "thrust into the heart of . . . hunger for closure" (20) from Africa's "yet unexpiated past" (19); this poet's duty is then to "appropriate . . . the voice of the people and the full burden of memory" (21) in order to activate "the healing of a bruised racial psyche" (23). In Soyinka's own writing, animism functions as a mechanism for this historical appropriation and healing of a "bruised racial psyche," a process demonstrated most explicitly in his prison poetry, but theorized more systematically upon his release from prison.

Four years after his release, in his lecture series at Churchill College, Cambridge University, in 1973 (later published as *Myth, Literature and the African World*), he philosophically systematizes his aforementioned theory of animism as a strategic response to cultural trauma. Here he presents an animist theory of the cosmos and directs this theory toward the process of collective subject formation. Collective subject formation in Africa must begin, he suggests, by recognizing the continent's "primal systems of apprehension" (xii), which for him are animist cosmologies. This process is by no means straightforward, since, as I argue in detail in chapter 1, the alienation of the African subject from such systems through what Frantz Fanon describes as "the settler's violence in the beginning" (*Wretched* 73) was an essential aspect of colonization. Given this constitutive alienation, the spiritual outworking of colonization I call ancestral trauma, the process Soyinka describes as "self-apprehension" is only possible through a reanimation of what he calls "the African self-apprehended world": a habitus his writings consistently portray as ruptured under European colonialism and African neocolonialism (ix). The double bind is clear: A subject must be formed so that the world needed to form this subject can enter the subject's consciousness. Soyinka finds a catalyst for this belated process of subject formation in "the simultaneous act of eliciting from history, mythology and literature . . . a continuing process of self-apprehension whose temporary dislocation [via colonization] appears to have persuaded many of its non-existence" (xi). His explication of cosmological frames of reference from African history, mythology, and literature therefore form part of his attempt to craft a critical theory of African subjectivity to combat the subjective residue of colonization, which sought to erase the very possibility of African "self-apprehension."[23] He sums up this unapologetically erudite approach to the problem of post-colonial subject formation via his ongoing hermeneutic of reading for the reanimation of lost frames of reference as the "process of apprehending my own world" (ix).

This process leads Soyinka to a form of subjectivity I conceptualize as cosmic personhood: a subject incarnating "the animist interfusion of all matter and consciousness" (*Myth* 145) he explicates from African literature, mythology, and history in response to his own severance from an Indigenous conceptualization of himself and the world. According to Soyinka, the totality of the cosmos exists in a perennial state of co-animation. Thus, unlike the self-authorizing, sovereign subject of post-Enlightenment Europe, Soyinka's African subject inhabits what Soyinka describes as a fundamental "inter-relation with Nature" (52) at large: "the infinite cosmos" (43). Against a Cartesian concept of subjective ipseity introduced to Africa through European imperialism, then, Soyinka's cosmic personhood aims to awaken the African subject to an apprehension of their inextricability from the more-than-human world.

He describes the agential force of this cosmic personhood as an outworking of the "creative-destructive principle" (28). In Yoruba cosmology, he suggests, all life emerges out of a dynamic of auto-destruction intrinsic to the material and spiritual makeup of the cosmos: an eternally recurrent "inchoate matrix of death and becoming" (142). This dynamic is prominent throughout Yoruba mythology, which he claims is best conceptualized as a "recurrent exercise in the experience of disintegration" continuously happening throughout the cosmos (151). What is more, aesthetic form in Africa operates by ritually participating in the process of this eternally recurrent, generative death, he argues. Drum craftsmanship serves as one example of this conceptualization of aesthetics through the lens of the creative-destructive principle, which is itself intrinsically tied to a form of cosmic personhood:

> What thoughts accompany the integrated African craftsman when he sets out to make a drum? He first of all recognizes the tree trunk as an organic member of his universe. He celebrates this awareness in various forms, the commonest of which is the ritual of appeasement. And he celebrates this awareness in the animal also whose skin is going to provide the membrane. So when the drum is completed, when he launches the new entity into its new existence, into its new function in the affective consciousness of society, he celebrates through a poetic evocation the transformed existence of these objective manifestations of Nature. (*Art* 54–55)

African drum craftsmanship operates under a reverence toward the interfusions of the human and more-than-human world, Soyinka suggests. These categories are interfused within the "affective consciousness" of Indigenous cosmologies, leading to what he calls the "organic totalism" of the African subject (55). Since this subject as "organic totalism" is inextricable from the cosmos's eternal process of "death and becoming," through the trunk of a fallen tree and the skin of a slaughtered animal the drum craftsman ritually creates "transformed existence." Drum craftsmanship thus allows a community to experience, much like Soyinka's description of witnessing ritual drama, "participating in the process of bringing to birth a new medium in the cosmic extension of man's physical existence" (*Myth* 13). Building a drum is an act of creating, through the death of particular forms of subjectivity, "an essential piece of the integrated reality of a functioning universe" (*Art* 55): a new subjective incarnation of "organic totalism." Aesthetics is therefore within this paradigm the science of ritually activating and strategically utilizing the "creative-destructive principle" to transform the subjective conditions of the world (i.e., instantiations of cosmic personhood).

We might describe this transformative process as a simultaneously postcolonial and posthumanist notion of agency revealing the theoretical proximity between Soyinkan animism and new materialism with which I began this chapter. Indeed, the similarities between the passage above and new materialist approaches to agency as ecology are striking. Karan Barad, for instance, influentially declares that "the universe is agential intra-activity in its becoming"—that is, everything emerges in a mutually constitutive, ongoing process. Thus, "Agency is not an attribute but the ongoing reconfiguring of the world" (818)—that is, agency is not owned by an individual subject, but is rather a congealing of the material world as and through the ecological process of intra-active subject formation. This process of intra-activity (which is different from interactivity in that it presupposes no independent subjects prior to such mutually informative action) functions as the central concept of what Barad describes as new materialism's "relational ontology" (822). Both Jane Bennett's "vital materialism" and Stacy Alaimo's "trans-corporeality," for instance, are ways of conceptualizing intra-active relations within various ecosystems. We might also say that the agential coordinates Soyinka explicates from Yoruba cosmology and applies to aesthetic creation in the passage above cast the African subject as dwelling in a "relational ontology" experienced as "the animist interfusion of all matter and consciousness" (Soyinka, *Myth* 145). Like new materialist ecology, Soyinka's organic totalism casts nonhuman matter as central to the cosmic personhood of the African subject; or, to blend theoretical lexicons, through the "vital" matter of bark and skin, the drum craftsman "intra-actively" participates in the "ongoing reconfiguring of the world," which necessarily reconfigures the African subject's experience of their "trans-corporeality."

Yet the passage also augments new materialist thinking. Soyinka connects the subject as an incarnation of cosmic personhood's ongoing process of becoming—what Barad calls the universe's "performative metaphysics" (818)—to the universe's ongoing process of death. The universe's intra-active reconfiguration, in other words, emerges through its intra-active experience of dying. In this sense we could say that Soyinkan animism reroutes new materialism back to psychoanalytic theory, a discourse far more fixated on the symbiotic relation between life and death, most notably in Freud's theory of the death drive. Unlike both psychoanalysis and new materialism, however, Soyinka envisions death as a transition, not an endpoint. This difference implies a different philosophy of time. Death in Yoruba cosmology is not the final moment of the subject's movement through linear time, but rather a transitional moment in the subject's engagement with cyclic time: a threshold connecting the world of the living to the world of the ancestors. In this temporal dynamic lies Soyinka's implicit revision of both new materialism and the death drive and thus the theoretical proximity between his animist poetics and Malabou's critique of Freudian psychoanalysis.

Destructive Plasticity as a Lens for Interpreting Soyinka's "Animystic" Perception of Death

Malabou places continental philosophy and neuroscience in dialogue, seeking to theorize trauma anew in light of her synthesis of these two discourses. This project's theoretical stakes are most apparent in the critique of Freud she posits in *The New Wounded*. She seeks to conceptualize trauma as a consequence of material brain damage rather than, as it is for Freud, a rupture in the structure of (nonmaterial) memory. Trauma is for Malabou, contra Freud, primarily somatic rather than psychic. What Freud does not fully take into account is, she argues, the material form through which all subjectivity (traumatized or not) emerges: the brain's neuronal plasticity. This plasticity operates outside the paradigm of Freud's Cartesian dualism, she further argues, which separates mind and brain and privileges the latter, replicating the spirit-matter binary of post-Enlightenment European humanism. Malabou sees "absolutely no justification for separating mind and brain," as Freud does, and instead operates from a "naturalist philosophy of mind" *as* brain (*New Wounded* xiii, xii). This difference demonstrates the new materialist bent of Malabou's work. Rejecting notions of human uniqueness, she casts human subjectivity as animated by that which animates everything else: matter, not spirit.[24]

It also demonstrates an implicit connection between her project and Soyinkan animism. To claim that the psyche is enforced by a vital dynamic intrinsic to our material embodiment attunes trauma theory to the shared focus of new materialism and animism: "matter's inherent creativity" (DeLanda 16). My account of Malabou's critique of the Freudian death drive in what follows therefore serves two functions. First, it highlights Soyinka's relevance to the state of contemporary theory. Since Malabou stakes her revision of the death drive to a critique of Freud's humanism (realized in his Cartesian inoculation of the human psyche from the external world), her synthesis of neuroscience and psychoanalysis aims to posthumanize trauma theory via new materialist critique. Reading Soyinka in dialogue with Malabou therefore not only helps us recognize the revised notion of the death drive implicit in his engagement with animism; more precisely, Malabou's "destructive plasticity" helps us recognize how the preemptively posthumanist bent of Soyinka's "creative-destructive principle" implicitly posits a death drive that breaks away from the humanism assumed in Freud's Cartesian separation of the human psyche from the external world. Second, my reading of Malabou lays conceptual scaffolding for the next section of this chapter, in which I argue that Soyinka's approach to time challenges the latent secularism of Malabou's project.

Malabou accepts Freud's metanarrative in *Beyond the Pleasure Principle* of the subject emerging from and returning to inorganic matter (a metanarrative central to my argument in chapter 1). However, she seeks to replace the spirit-matter binary that Freud's mind-brain dualism infuses into this metanarrative with a new materialist monism. Doing so requires a rejection of Freud's division of the internal and external spaces of the subject, a division that allows him to justify the death drive as a consequence of (spiritual) mind and not purely (material) brain. Further, this rejection necessitates a rejection of the temporality assumed in Freudian trauma theory. For Freud, in order for an event to become traumatic, it must reactivate an original "conflict between the ego and the sexual drives" (*New Wounded* 6), which means that trauma is a product of the mind's experience of time: a repetition of a trace of a primal sexual scene within the unconscious. Put somewhat daftly, one consequence of this logic is that the material brain does not ultimately matter for Freudian trauma theory. A blow to the head is only traumatic insofar as it reawakens a repressed memory. Thus, the locus of trauma is for Freud mind, not brain; spirit, not matter. The temporal implications of this logic, Malabou writes, is that "sexuality, understood as a specific causality and regime of events, will always triumph over the brute accident, the pure effraction, the wound without hermeneutic future" (7–8). In other words, Freud's separation of trauma from the material brain implies a certain temporality—more specifically, a sequential causality—outside of which Malabou claims the structure of traumatic brain damage actually operates.

In the trauma of brain damage, she argues, the past self is not a repressed memory whose trace can never be erased, as Freud would have it, but is rather fully destroyed. The survivor is severed from all past experiences, relationships, and beliefs, and is effectively a new person. Instead of a return of the repressed, trauma in this framework is a transformative "event, without cause or explanation," an event structured by a temporal logic irreconcilable with Freud's sequential causality (*Ontology* 57). Malabou's shift of the locus of trauma from mind to brain (or spirit to matter, in her view, a radicalization of Freud's materialism), thus raises the philosophical problem of the relation between time and subjectivity. She writes:

> The individual's history is cut definitively, breached by the meaningless accident, an accident that it is impossible to reappropriate through either speech or recollection. . . . These types of events are pure hits, tearing and piercing subjective continuity and allowing no justification or recall in the psyche. How do you internalize a cerebral lesion? How do you speak about emotional deficit since words must be carried by the affects whose very absence is precisely what is in question here? (29)

If trauma is an event that constitutes a new subjectivity, Malabou asks us to conceptualize a form of trauma in which this new subjectivity is thoroughly severed from one's past subjectivity, a temporal rupture tied to a subjective death and regeneration that Freud never conceived.

What is more, for Malabou, the philosophical problem facing contemporary psychoanalysis is to reconceptualize its subject as being preinscribed by the material building blocks of life itself with this possibility of auto-destructive regeneration. In the same way that Freud's late metapsychology universalizes the subject of trauma theory into the subject as such (casting life, culture, and history as traumatically structured in texts like *Beyond the Pleasure Principle*, *Civilization and Its Discontents*, and *Moses and Monotheism*), Malabou universalizes the subject of her trauma theory, "the new wounded." The route toward this materialization and universalization of a new subject of trauma is an understanding of what she terms the "destructive plasticity" of the brain. Destructive plasticity signifies the brain's neuronal capacity to *receive form* (like plaster), *give form* (like a plastic surgeon), and *destroy form* (like plastic explosives) (*New Wounded* 17): the simultaneous, paradoxical "reception, donation, and annihilation of form" (20). We perpetually craft our daily lives through neuronal plasticity, she reasons, the same phenomenon through which one's subjectivity can regenerate itself as a new form post-trauma; therefore, that which allows us to be ourselves also always places us at risk of becoming someone else. Such a theory represents auto-destruction as "potentially present as a threat in each one of us" (*Ontology* 38): a possibility pre-inscribed in the material basis for subjective life.

Freud actually opens the door for such a notion through his theory of the death drive, which casts auto-destruction as the driving force of subjectivity. For Malabou, however, Freud's mistake is to sever this force from materiality, representing it as a product of the internal mind, not external matter. This logic forms part of Freud's justification of psychoanalysis's humanism. As I note in chapter 1, Freud is wary of the challenges to humanism that the "mystical impression"(*Beyond* 328) of his belief that the subject is animated by a force resembling "some 'daemonic' power" (292) might make. If organic life evolved from inorganic matter, then the originary stuff of subjectivity is this matter, Freud reasons, but for him the subject cannot be enforced by an all-encompassing material vitality (à la animism or new materialism). To admit such would be to imply that the subject is externally animated (even if by the material world), which is the very "mystical impression" he wishes to disassociate from psychoanalysis. His demystification of psychoanalysis thus follows a decidedly idealist, and as Malabou argues Cartesian, logic. He represents the death drive as a consequence of mind/spirit, not brain/matter: a force purely internal to the subject that emerges to counteract forces from the external world. In this way, Freud erects resolutely humanist coordinates for the death drive, thereby separating it from a "primitive" worldview that locates the site of subjective dynamics outside the subject (an external, seemingly "daemonic" power).

The locus of Malabou's critique of Freud is in other words his attempt to ward off, by doubling down on a form of Cartesian humanism, the animist vision of subjectivity immanent in psychoanalytic trauma theory. Freud disavows not only psychoanalysis's sociohistoric relation to animism (its borrowing of the concept of the fetish, for example)[25], but also the animist structure undergirding the vision of subjectivity toward which his study of trauma leads him, most notably through his theory of the death drive. By rejecting the measures Freud takes to distance the death drive from this "mystical impression," Malabou's critique opens a conceptual window through which we can more clearly envision how a theorist and practitioner of animism such as Soyinka might reframe psychoanalysis. Like

Malabou's approach to the subject, Soyinka's vision of cosmic personhood obliterates Freud's attempt to demarcate internal and external spaces of subjectivity. This recalibration of the subject models an approach to the death drive tethered, like Malabou's recalibration, to an "interfusion of all matter and consciousness" (Soyinka, *Myth* 145). Thus, while for Freud, like Soyinka and Malabou, death plays a constitutive and impetuous role for the subject, for Freud the death drive is fundamentally conservative, meant to protect the human psyche's sovereignly bordered agency against the material forces of the external world. Soyinka's creative-destructive principle, on the other hand, is communal in a more-than-human sense, meant to tap into and even deepen the cosmic consanguinity both he and Malabou find at the core of the human psyche. For Soyinka and Malabou, then, the psyche can never be partitioned into clear spaces of internality and externality (which, as I detail in chapter 1, is precisely Fanon's critique of Freud). However, while this expansion of subjectivity is for Soyinka tied to his embrace of "animystic" spirituality, Malabou's goal is to further distance psychoanalysis from Freud's feared "mystical impression."

For Malabou, Freud's insistence on a division between mind and brain (and his privileging of the former) creates another, unintentional "mystical impression": a dualistic separation from and transcendence of spirit over matter, which is tied to his assumed temporality. He embeds the deepest internality of the subject, what he often calls the primitive, within an indestructible temporal form that blocks the possibility of a complete transformation of the subject. Even trauma for Freud only becomes trauma insofar as it triggers a primal scene constitutive of the subject, which is to say that at the core of the Freudian thought is a temporality of sequential causality that negates the possibility of the auto-destructive regeneration Malabou finds in traumatic brain damage. Taking Derrida's claim in *The Post Card* that Freud never truly ventures beyond the pleasure principle further (and in doing so decidedly breaking from Derrida's emphasis on the *à-venir* of such a break), Malabou argues that a death drive anchored to destructive plasticity would break away from the pleasure principle by reimagining the relationship between matter and time and therefore opening the possibility of auto-destructive regeneration. "If there is anything beyond the pleasure principle," she writes, "it can only be a certain category or concept of time": the originary moment or "time of materiality" before life to which the subject is driven to return ("Plasticity" 78). The existence of this prehuman, material time is indeed central to Freud's positing of the death drive, but he struggles to keep this time from enforcing the dynamics of subjectivity. The time of organic life emerges from the time of inorganic matter, but being enforced by this originary temporality would cast the catalyst of human action outside the human mind, Freud reasons; thus, he anchors the death drive to the indestructible time of the mind's most primitive, unconscious will. While this logic's goal is a humanist demystification of psychoanalysis's approach to subjectivity, Malabou argues that the primacy it gives to the purely internal space of the subject ultimately traps psychoanalysis in an idealist, Cartesian dualism—an unintentional mysticism irreconcilable with neurobiology. If mind *is* brain, she reasons, then psychoanalysis need not ward off the primacy of inorganic matter but rather recognize its material time as the external building blocks of the subject's internally facilitated drive toward auto-destruction.

This new materialist and fundamentally temporal revision of the death drive offers a productive lens through which to analyze how Soyinka's experiments with animism in his prison poetry envision subjectivity. His celebration of death as a "twilight cone" and "Meeting-place" "Embrac[ing] you and I" (*Early Poems* 157), for example, suggests that death in this poetry functions as, in Malabou's terms, the ur-space of auto-destructive regeneration: the locus of a collective subject's simultaneous "reception, donation, and annihilation of form" (*New Wounded* 20). "Recession (*Mahapralaya*)" similarly focuses on, in Soyinka's words, "the consoling experience of man in the moment of death" and takes its parenthetical subtitle from Hindu metaphysics, a cosmic dissolution resulting in "the return of the universe to its womb." Death brings the subject and the universe back to our arch-animacy, the "marsh-glow of origin," where life can be remade anew (*Early Poems* 139). Likewise, in "Space," through death the subject is "Thrust from the matrix of an ark" (144). The dying persona is figured here as a Noah, one who, on an "incense-boat inlaid / With currents of hope" (145) journeys through "flood cycles" (144). The poem concludes with astonishment at this journey's destination:

> Is it a wonder he will not return?
> He seeks his rest on crosswinds
> Emptying to one inchoate flux
> Eternal deluge of a Word's design! (145)

Through death, the subject enters a paradoxical rest—not stasis, as the Freudian death drive would have it, but instead the embrace of perpetual flux. The flood, an archetypal image of catastrophic flux, does not end.

Instead, as the subject enters death, deluge is revealed to be the eternal configuration of the universe: the "Word's design." Destructive plasticity is, in other words, the ontological mold of an existence propelled by a life-death symbiosis. Ultimately, though, Soyinka's approach to subjectivity in these poems departs from Malabou's, and the subject of new materialist critique more broadly, in regard to two interrelated concepts: the relation between spirit and matter and the structure of time, the latter of which highlights Soyinka's distinct relevance to the constellation of theoretical discourses I have set up in this chapter.

The Creative-Destructive Principle in Cyclic Time: Reading Regenerative Death beyond Destructive Plasticity's Secular Coordinates

Much like destructive plasticity, the creative-destructive principle casts life as emerging from a movement of auto-destruction inseparable from the material world and, like Malabou, Soyinka connects his revised death drive to a theory of the subject. Yet Soyinka embeds his creative-destructive principle within a cosmological framework that, contra new materialism, fully embraces a spirit-matter continuum: a perpetual negotiation between *aye* and *orun*—the distinct yet inseparable realms of matter and spirit in Yoruba cosmology (Henry Johan Drewal et al. 14). Contrasting this continuum to what he takes to be an inheritance of a European mindset among African intellectuals, he remains throughout his career a vocal critic of "superstitious marxism" (*Art* 66), by which he means a dialectical materialism that neglects recourse to spirit by superstitiously fetishizing a narrow concept of matter. Against such neocolonial epistemic residue, he proposes post-independent Africa's need for an "organic revolution." This revolution begins for Soyinka with the process toward which his animist poetics aims: the aforementioned "self-apprehension" of the African subject as an incarnation of cosmic personhood. As William McPheron writes:

> As he defines the concept, organic revolution is a process of communal renewal reached in moments of shared cultural self-apprehension—moments whose manner and content are particular to each society. Such revolution is inherently local and cyclical, qualities more appropriate to African culture, Soyinka argues, than the global teleologies of either Marxist

communism or capitalist nationalism. Indeed, Soyinka's mode of liberation ultimately displaces the logic of Western politics with the rhythms of native ritual. For the revolution he advocates rejects the abstractions of both dialectical materialism and market economics for the particularity of ceremonial healing—of the divisions that isolate individuals from society and sever both from their sustaining integration with nature.

By no means opposed to dialectical materialism outright (as Hegel, Benjamin, and Derrida all assert in their own ways, this tradition can be overtly spiritual), Soyinka is instead frustrated with the manner in which capitalist and Marxist forms of post-independent African politics perpetuate the severance between the individual, the collective, and the more-than-human world so foundational to the colonization of the African subject. Organic revolution, Soyinka suggests, must invest material liberation with a spiritual liberation by reanimating the colonized subject's severed ties to community and the cosmos. Viewed from this framework, Malabou's critique of what she takes to be Freud's idealism tied to his Cartesian dualism, inspiring her attempt to more fully materialize psychoanalysis (via new materialist monism), appears provincially Euro-American. If the (Euro-American) subject of psychoanalysis is for Malabou too invested with spirit and in need of recalibration from within an ontology of pure matter, the African subject for Soyinka has already been dislocated from the spiritual through the ancestral trauma of colonization. The crosscurrent between *aye* and *orun* in Soyinka's thought is therefore less a form of Cartesian dualism than a sociohistorically situated logic meant to align a theory of the subject with the project of organic revolution.

Furthermore, through organic revolution Soyinka tethers the "inter-relation with Nature" (*Myth* 52) in which he nests African subjectivity to the "cyclic consciousness of time" (2) he explicates from Yoruba cosmology's life-death symbiosis. Soyinka was in fact philosophically developing this temporal dimension to the creative-destructive principle while in prison. While the co-existence of a mutual interaction between material and spiritual realms and cyclic temporality's ritualized unfolding shape his writing from at least *A Dance of the Forests* (1960) onward, the latter took him longer to systematize into a coherent philosophy. As he writes in an unpublished manuscript note on "Idanre," "For a long time I could not accept why Ogun, the Creator God, should also be the agency of death. Interpretation of his domain, the road, proved particularly depressing and symbolically vexed especially inasmuch as the road is so obviously part of this same cyclic order. I know nothing more futile, more monotonous or boring than a circle" (qtd. in Robert Fraser, 231). As Soyinka drafted "Idanre," his experimental poem reinventing Ogun's origin myth, the concept of time as a circle, and therefore the perpetually negotiated connection between life and death, struck him as essential to the Ogun narrative, yet philosophically puzzling. As Biodun Jeyifo notes, it would take the years between "Idanre" (written in 1965, published in 1967) and his Cambridge lectures in 1973 for Soyinka to incorporate cyclic temporality into a systematic philosophy. Jeyifo writes, "The great spiritual and epistemological awakening implied here is the recognition, at last, that the monotony and repetitiousness inherent in the figure of the cycle . . . as a symbol of history and human existence subsists within a larger cosmic order which involves the duality of decay and renewal, destruction and creation" (226). In other words, between 1965 and 1973 Soyinka shifts from viewing the circle as "futile," "monotonous," and "boring" to placing it alongside the creative-destructive principle at the core of his poetics and cosmology. He first does so intuitively (as in "Idanre," *The Interpreters*, and his other experimental writing of the sixties) and then systematically (as in *Myth, Literature and the African World*, where he contextualizes cyclic temporality within an eternal, cosmic process of "death and becoming" [142]).

In between his intuitive embrace and systematizing of cyclic temporality, the principal event of Soyinka's life was his incarceration. And during his incarceration Soyinka became obsessed with what he describes in his prison memoir as his "demented Time-Space Research project" (*The Man Died* 251). Through "frantic obsessive scribbling at night and increasingly careless calculations in daytime," he plunged into a "dangerous fantasy" of "relating Time and Space, mathematically, within the concept of Infinity." This project led him to "greater and greater absurdities and plunged at some point over the brink of rational principles" (273). In the only surviving autograph from this short-lived project, his esoteric equations—for example, "$C = 2^{u-1}(m_1 m_2 m_3 \ldots \ldots m_m)$????"—coincide with labels such as "Time/Space Entities" and "matter in Time/Space" (Figure 1). After realizing the "frightening" psychological state in which these metaphysical-algebraic inscriptions were leading him, he destroyed most of them. Although he claims to have "no recollection" of writing most of these equations (*The Man Died* 274), his explanation of the projects' metaphysical stakes illuminates the manner in which it plays a role in his journey toward incorporating cyclic temporality into a holistic cosmology. He writes, "It began . . . with an idea that Time ought to be *integrally* related to its companion in Infinity—Space; it required only the discovery of the right mathematical principle. . . . I could not, alas, recall the formula for Einstein's Theory of Relativity but consoled myself with the thought that it dealt with too narrow an aspect of Time" (273). Soyinka's "demented" equations are attempts to construct a post-Einsteinian theory of time. If for Einstein the relativity of space and time is constituted in relation to the speed of light, Soyinka is here attempting to reconceptualize the constant through which space and time integrally emerge as relative categories. This constant is a reformulation of the infinite, a reformulation tethered to the cosmic personhood he discovers in Yoruba cosmology. His handwritten comments on his frenzied algebra gesture toward this interpretation: "We must reduce to a Time and Space Unit where only ONE Me can occupy a ts [time/space] unit" (Figure 1). What makes this declaration so enigmatic is the conflation of "We and "Me." In the first half a collective subject is reduced to a relation between time and space, while in the second half Soyinka alone occupies this relation. In other words, Soyinka attempts through animystic mathematics to become an incarnation of a relationship between time and space that is itself constituted within a concept of infinity—which, filtered through his utilization of Yoruba cosmology, is a product of the cyclic nexus of relations between the living, the dead, and the unborn, who themselves emerge through humanity's symbiotic relation to "the infinite cosmos" (*Myth* 43). His various prison experiments—from algebra to poetry—can in this sense be approached as transitional texts leading to the formulation of infinity he discovers in cycle time and maps out in his Cambridge lectures.

Time in the Yoruba world unfolds, Soyinka argues in these lectures, as the infinite interfusion between past, present, and future as incarnated by the relations between dead, living, and unborn people. The expression "the child is father of the man" (famously used by Wordsworth, though Soyinka dubs it a "proverb"),[26] demonstrates for Soyinka this temporal structure. He writes:

[T]he degree of integrated acceptance of this temporal sense in the life-rhythm, mores and social organisation of Yoruba society is certainly worth emphasising, being a reflection of that same reality which denies periodicity to the existences of the dead, the living and the unborn. The expression 'the

> child is father of the man' becomes, within the context of this time-structure, not merely a metaphor of development, one that is rooted in a system of representative individuation, but a proverb of human continuity which is not uni-directional. Neither 'child' nor 'father' is a closed or chronological concept. The world of the unborn, in the Yoruba world-view, is as evidently older than the world of the living as the world of the living is older than the ancestor-world. And, of course, the other way around. . . . (*Myth* 10)

The chronology assumed in the proverbial schema of children fathering men highlights a key dimension of the form of subjectivity Soyinka finds immanent in Africa's "organic totalism" (*Art* 55). By negating "periodicity"—borders between the worlds of "the dead, the living and the unborn" that cast the past, present, and future as "closed chronological concept[s]"—this time that is "not uni-directional" necessitates conceptualizing "human continuity" beyond "a system of representative individuation." In other words, a time open to the intra-animation of the past, present, and future via the perpetual intra-animation of dead, the living, and unborn people who inhabit these cross-penetrating temporal spheres necessarily recasts the structure of personhood as irreducibly cosmic in both spatial and temporal terms.[27]

Operating in tandem, Soyinka's two concepts I have thus far described, the spirit-matter continuum and time's cyclic structure, anticipate new materialism's *spatial* expansion of subjectivity (its opening the borders of the subject to include the more-than-human world), while also expanding the subject *temporally* to include past, present, and future life. And these two concepts demonstrate the formal proximity and distance between Soyinka's and Malabou's theories of the subject. For Soyinka, like Malabou, matter and consciousness (brain and mind in psychoanalytic terms, *aye* and *orun* in Yoruba terms) are inseparable. By tethering this inseparability to cyclic time, Soyinka implicitly posits a "time of materiality," in Malabou's terms ("Plasticity" 78), but one that breaks from her insistence on sequential causality's determinant position for the subject. To be sure, like Soyinka, Malabou argues that to properly theorize the subject we must think beyond linear chronology. For her, though, this need means recognizing a potential for auto-destructive regeneration (a break in sequential causality that necessarily creates a new subject) as intrinsic to subjectivity as such (a potential absent from Freud's logic). Through this critique, however, she ultimately solidifies sequential causality's determinacy, a determinacy against which Soyinka pins animist temporality. If Malabou conceptualizes the subject as always potentially ruptured from the past and henceforth determined by this rupture, Soyinka conceptualizes the subject as mutually animated by interwoven realms of temporal-material totality, the past always included. Malabou's critique of linear chronology, in other words, retains the sovereignty of its sequential causality (the past is past, the former subject dead), while Soyinka's critique of linear chronology posits instead a more radically nonsequential form of temporal continuity: The child is the father of man (and vice versa), the unborn precede the ancestors (and vice versa). Thus, while Malabou's revision of Freud follows Soyinka's logic insofar as it offers a material expansion of the subject, it also reinforces one of the predominant legacies of post-Enlightenment European humanism: a sequential, linear approach to time, which she casts as a rejection of the spiritual for a purer materialism, or "naturalist philosophy" (*New Wounded* xii). Alternatively, Soyinka's "organic totalism" (which he also takes to be a naturalist philosophy) contextualizes the subject within the material dynamics of spirit, or the spiritual dynamics of matter, and he contextualizes this more-than-human spirit-matter continuum within the perpetual interfusions between past, present, and future incarnations of human subjectivity.

This fundamental irreducibility between spirit, matter, time, and subjectivity—incarnated as cosmic personhood—is central to what he takes to be the metaphysical structure of African animism. To be clear, this animism does not operate through some nebulous form of conservative spiritualism, claiming to return the African subject to a precolonial habitus. Such a view would actually retain a linear chronology (in which the subject can move backward). The rupture between past and present constitutive of Malabou's new wounded is also constitutive of Soyinka's view of the modern African subject, who has been irreversibly severed from the precolonial past through the ancestral trauma of colonization. Although his writings in this manner implicitly accept the temporal conundrum of Malabou's trauma theory as conditioning African modernity, the goal of his engagement with animism is the process of post-traumatic mediation between Africa's past subject of Indigeneity and present subject of colonized modernity (a process whose impossibility is central to Malabou's logic). In other words, what Malabou takes to be the unbridgeable nature of traumatic rupture is that which Soyinka's animist poetics seeks to mediate within the modern African subject via the process of "self-apprehension."

In this sense, Soyinka accepts time's irreversibility (and thus colonization as having achieved irreversible effects on African modernity), but combats the structure of colonized modernity's "homogenous, empty time," to use Benjamin's oft-quoted phrase ("Theses" 261), by imaginatively reanimating a ruptured "time of materiality," in Malabou's words ("Plasticity" 78), as co-constituted by the perennially negotiated nexus connecting "the living, the dead, and the unborn" (Soyinka *DKH* 3).

Reading the Regenerative Death Drive in "Animystic Spells"

This mediation of time and subjectivity is at the core of Soyinka's approach to the aesthetic, casting his animist poetics as fundamentally concerned with resisting colonization's sequential determinacy. To be sure, Malabou's new materialist revision of psychoanalysis is most relevant to a postcolonial theory of trauma through her focus on sequential determinacy. Achille Mbembe's approach to subjectivity, for example, rests on a similar sequential determinacy. For him, colonized subjectivity is conditioned by an arbitrarily shifting and continuously fleeting temporality. This time as "entanglement" (*Postcolony* 14) casts the subject as constitutively wounded much like Malabou's new wounded, though the rupture through which postcolonial subjectivity emerges is for Mbembe an effect of a socially constructed form of political sovereignty produced through colonial history rather than an effect of cerebral materiality. Still, if for Malabou cerebral lesions abolish any sense of past self, for Mbembe political sovereignty in the postcolony functions similarly to "abolish . . . any debt with regard to the past" within the colonized subject ("African Modes" 269). Malabou and Mbembe, in other words, each diagnose the same formal conundrum: a subject constitutively ruptured from past subjectivity. As I argued in chapter 1, this rupture from the past emerging from what Fanon calls "the settler's violence in the beginning" (*Wretched* 73) casts colonization as an ancestral trauma that postcolonial African literature is tasked to mediate. If this rupture between the precolonial past and the neocolonial present conditioning African modernity (a rupture that Malabou's trauma theory helps elucidate) can (contra Malabou) be mediated by reactivating Indigenous cosmological frames of reference, this activation must be an impetus of modern African arts, Soyinka reasons. His animist poetics therefore elucidates the means through which the African artist can participate in a cosmological process of post-traumatic mediation—in his words, the "self-apprehension" of the postcolonial African subject.

"Animystic Spells" distinctly serves this purpose. The cycle is designed as an incantation of cosmic personhood through its activation of the creative-destructive principle, which the spells aim at ritually mediating the past, present, and future within the imprisoned speaker as an embodiment of a collective, transhistorical subject. Throughout all his prison poetry, Soyinka depicts himself as a manifestation of the hostile condition of his nation undergoing the Biafran War. As Msiska writes, for Soyinka:

> [T]he prison is merely an extension of the evil of the outer world, that of the totality of the public sphere. In this sense, then, the whole nation is itself imprisoned in a cell devoid of hope and renewal. This demonstrates that the postcolonial formation as a whole and its political imaginative capacity in particular have been incarcerated in a restless static space of history, from which only the assumption of the transformative kinetic energy of the shuttle of subjectivity and agency can extricate it. (144)

Soyinka conceptualizes himself as an incarnation of the modern Nigerian subject imprisoned first by colonial history and then by the neocolonial ideology undergirding the contemporaneous Biafran War, the latter of which pins itself against the emancipatory potential of a postcolonial imaginary.

The formal rigidity of the "Prisonnettes" (the section of *A Shuttle* including "Animystic Spells") emphasizes this imprisonment-as-allegory. On the one hand, as Soyinka writes, "The form was quite arbitrary, something short enough and as self-containing as possible to remain in the head until, at night-time or in a slack moment of surveillance I could transfer it to the inside of a cigarette packet or an equally precious scrap of salvage" (*Early* 149). Yet, on the other hand, as Jeyifo notes, the "Prisonnettes" uniform style is out of the norm for Soyinka. They each bear "two mutually self-cancelling features": "on the one hand, a rigid, unvarying stanzaic pattern in which, without exception, each poem is made up of five-line stanzas, the fifth line of each stanza being the only line with ten or eleven syllables, each of the remaining four lines comprising between two to six syllables; and on the other hand, uniformly sardonic sentiments and attitudes uncontainable, it seems, by the extreme formalism of the stanzaic pattern" (250).[28] For Jeyifo, this rigid form defamiliarizes the agony and protest of the content, which leaves "Animystic Spells" too opaque and thereby the least successful of Soyinka's prison poetry. In my interpretation, however, this rigid form and combative content work together as a dialectic mirroring the shuttle and crypt of the collection's title. This dialectic formalizes Soyinka's predicament of attempting to chant life into a postcolonial subjectivity he incarnates while stuck in solitary confinement. That the fifth line of each stanza is significantly longer than the first four, moreover, formalizes Soyinka's political goal of incanting a "Third Force" (*The Man Died* 178) from the Nigeria/Biafra opposition to transform his public sphere. The first four lines form a constricted dualism, and from this constriction bursts the fifth line's energetic declaration—visually and sonically functioning as a sonnet's volta, yet refusing the traditional sonnet's formal and philosophical resolution.

Death thus becomes a resolution. Consistently, death throughout these poems harbors "transformative kinetic energy" for the stuck subject: the imprisoned Soyinka and, by extension, the Nigerian public sphere, both of whose conditions are formalized in the poetry's stanzaic rigidity. In an overtly constricting form, these poems suggest, death is the space of ritual regeneration. In the first stanza of the first poem, for example, the speaker leads the addressee through the first step of surviving solitary confinement:

> First you must
> Walk among the faceless
> Their feet are shod in earth
> And dung
> Caryatids in anterooms of night's inbirth. (*Early Poems* 156)

"First" (the opening line casts the stanza as both instruction and genesis) comes the loss of ipseity, trading an individuated subjectivity to instead "walk among the faceless." Thus begins the recurrent imagery of subjective dismemberment and decay (immediately associated with becoming) that fills the spells: for example, "Shards strewn," "discarding," "dissolves," "rust," "Fragments," "withered," "broken," "skull," "stubbed," "mangled" (156–61). As such necrotic terms suggest, regeneration begins with the self dying. As Soyinka chants this spell to himself in solitary confinement, he functions as both the poem's speaker and addressee: a pragmatic intertwinement of lyric and dramatic monologue into an incantation. He instructs himself (as a prisoner and incarnation of the *polis*) to "walk" toward the experience of dying to oneself, thereby becoming a depersonalized subject "among the faceless." By embracing such facelessness, the mystic experience dictated in the spells combats the sectarianist logic undergirding the Biafran War with a universal lack, a deactivation of all identitarian and nationalist binds (be they Nigerian or Biafran).

This death, moreover, operates throughout the spells as an experience essential to "The quest" (156) through which the speaker leads both himself and the addressee: "Death / Embraces you and I" (157). A Freudian reading of this death might emphasize the universality of its rule over human life, death's affirmative function as that which drives "you and I" toward survival. Such a reading connects to Tanure Ojaide's interpretation of the "you and I" whom death is said to embrace. The "I" is Soyinka, and the "you," the poem's immediate addressees, Ojaide argues, are the prison guards as well as General Yakubu Gowon, who led the Nigerian federal government in the Biafran War and oversaw Soyinka's imprisonment (90).[29] Death renders Soyinka's tormentors his equals (all will eventually die), and this equalizing vision of humanity's shared mortality, Ojaide suggests, aids Soyinka's psychological survival, his will to live until he can die on his own terms, as Freud would have it.

A new materialist, Malabouvian reading would highlight, however, that death functions throughout the spells as a transitioning force, the space of the subject's material regeneration. The feet of the opening stanza's "faceless," post-ipseitic subject are in the third line earth and dung-shod. This terrestrial and fertilizing imagery (the inverse of "shod" feet dividing humanity from earth in Gerard Manley Hopkins's "God's Grandeur") suggests that the subject instructed to die to themselves will become inseparable from the material world and by doing so will enter a state of germination. Thus begins the spells' recurrent imagery of the natural world (e.g., "dew," "star," "pines," "bough," "hill," "valleys," "sea," "wind," "sands," "forest," "mineral," "lakes," "cavern," "sky," "weeds") and reproduction, notably by surrounding natal terms (e.g., "birth," "crib") within more abundant agrarian terms (e.g., "pollen," "stamens," "seed," "sieve"). Such terms tether the cycle to reproductive processes across the material world, suggesting a consanguinity between the subject and the universe, which becomes increasingly intensified as images of height (e.g., "sky," "sun") and depth (e.g., "abyss," "Buried lakes") begin to mingle (157–60). In the first spell the speaker compares the skin of this subject-in-transformation to "star-wells" (156), for example, a compound unifying the galactic and subterranean. And in the twelfth spell "caverns of the mind" lead the addressee to "skyscapes of the mind" (160), much like the dream vision of Samuel Taylor Coleridge's "Kubla Khan." The first stanza's final word, "inbirth," highlights the mystic and regenerative nature of this subject-universe symbiosis. The cycle's goal is self-induced union with life across the cosmos, a union that necessitates a death of the individual, human subject, which functions as the catalyst for a new, posthumanist form of collective, ecological subjectivity. That this collective, ecological form is incanted within the individuating architecture of a prison cell emphasizes through juxtaposition its expanse. Such a reading revises the humanist coordinates assumed by a Freudian reading of the spells' death drive through a new materialist emphasis on the vitality of the more-than-human world in which Soyinka's poetry embeds death. Destructive plasticity thus helps elucidate in the terms of new materialist ecology death's function throughout the cycle as the harbinger of, in its own language, "earth's own regenerate need" (159).[30]

Soyinka, we should note, dedicates his "Prisonnettes," including "Animystic Spells," to "all who participated" in his imprisonment, including "those who gave the orders" (149). Considering the poetry's ritual form alongside its dedication, "Animystic Spells" casts Soyinka's incarceration as a communal rite he undergoes alongside his tormentors. Rather than equalizing the tormented and tormentors by embracing their inevitable end in death, then, the spells' embrace of death recasts the tormented and tormentors as mutually constitutive actors within a cosmological drama of "death and becoming" (*Myth* 142). By placing death's embrace of "You and I" (*Early Poems* 157) in the service of "earth's own regenerate need" (159), the spells combat the ethnopolitical stratification sustaining the Biafran War with a resolutely more-than-human death drive. Working against the act of demarcating ethnic claims to land and its extractable resources (an impetus of the Biafran War), the cycle revitalizes through ritualized death networks of life that render all demarcations between the land and its inheritors obsolete. Whether the ritual participant is Igbo, Hausa-Fulani, or Yoruba, a military dictator or a persecuted activist, ceases to matter as the cycle ushers the subject into the "ongoing reconfiguring of the world" (Barad 818) taking place within the Crypt (as a space of intra-active subject formation) in which the spells are chanted.

The temporality of this death drive is, however, distinctly postsecular in a manner that ultimately breaks away from the hermeneutic reference points of such a new materialist reading. That the spells' ritualized "inbirth" is connected with night inaugurates their continual references to natural cycles of time (e.g., "sun," "moon," "tides") (157–60). Such references suggest that death, in addition to commencing a material, spatial expansion of the subject, ushers the subject into an experience of nonlinear temporality connected to natural cycles. These two shifts are interrelated. Time throughout the spells is an outworking of the subject's "inter-relation with Nature" Soyinka views as foundational to African metaphysics (*Myth* 52). The experience of cyclic time is thus not separate from the material expansion of the subject; for Soyinka cyclic time is an outworking of "the animist interfusion of all matter and consciousness" and vice versa (*Myth* 145). It is, in Malabou's words, a "naturalist philosophy," but one that refuses to sever nature from spirit (*New Wounded* xii). In the poem "A Cobweb's Touch in the Dark," for example, a cobweb brushing up against Soyinka's body in solitary confinement becomes an "ancestral web": a thread connecting living, dead, and unborn subjects (104). This spiritual gateway is the product of raw material, a spider's web, in the same way that death, an event intrinsic to material vitality, becomes throughout "Animystic Spells" a portal to spiritual connection.

This threshold function of death is a consequence of cyclic time. As the third spell declares, death functions as a "Meeting-place" between the living, dead, and unborn, shifting the subject in the fifth spell "Across a thousand years to a bygone sage" (157). For the ancestrally informed subject produced within this temporal intersection, "The past / Dissolves" (157) among "discarding / Weights of time" (156). In place of a linearly demarcated past partitioned from the present, the self from a bygone sage, the "secret passages of night" (156) ritually birthed through the spells carry the speaker and addressee to an eternal cyclic now incorporating all past, present, and future life: "The quest / Is all, endless" (156). The loss of ipseity for an expanded form of subjectivity dictated in the opening stanza of "Animystic Spells" is thus both spatial and temporal (which in Soyinka's philosophy also means both material and spiritual): a facelessness that incorporates all life, the ancestors and unborn, the human and more-than-human. Through this spatial-temporal expansion, the subject functions as "Caryatids": sculptures of women used as pillars in classical Greek architecture. This line recasts the "anteroom" in which Soyinka chants these spells from prison cell to temple, from solitary confinement to a space of ritualized communion, from technology of neocolonial punishment to a sacralized complex of "secret passages" leading to spiritual "home-coming" (156).

This sacralized continuum between the human subject and the cosmos as well as material embodiment and temporal interpenetration leads the spells' "You and I" to become, by the end of the cycle, a ritual sacrifice. Within the sacred space of the "Crypt," the subject of the cycle becomes by the penultimate spell "Offerings": an "Altar-vessel" through which "Multitudes / Shall dance on flesh remains of a cosmic dare" (160). By ritually chanting such lines, the incarcerated Soyinka frames what appears to be his death sentence as a sacrificial rite. He recasts his corporeal punishment by the Nigerian federal government as a "vessel" through which a collective "dance" might emerge, thereby investing his immediate reality with political meaning. By casting capital punishment as the outworking of a "cosmic dare," Soyinka also places Gowon's military leadership within the same cosmological matrix as himself, further enmeshing the spells' "You and I." In other words, the cycle expands the agential borders of the sovereign and the subjugated simultaneously, contextualizing each within a mythopoetic framework that envisions all borders between selves and the cosmos as porous. This framework robs Gowon and the federal government of power in the eyes of the chanter: Soyinka becomes a sacrifice for a cosmic force, not the decisions of a political persona or party.

By emphasizing the cycle's agrarian imagery, the concluding spell casts this sacrifice as part of a larger harvest ritual:

> Three millet
> Stalks. A tasseled crown
> On a broken glass horizon
> Weeds clogged
> Their feet, winds came and blew them down
>
> New ears arose
> Lean lances through
> A stubbed and mangled mound—
> And this I saw—
> Their grains were ripened closer to the ground. (161)

In the first stanza three millet stalks are choked by weeds and blown down by the wind. In the second stanza new ears arise through this death. If the penultimate spell casts Soyinka and his tormentors as becoming together a vessel of ritual sacrifice, in the final spell they are becoming through this sacrifice a future sacrament. The "crown" and "lance" (reified power and political struggle) together become the bread toward which the cycle's agrarian imagery points[31]—a coming unification emphasized by the concluding rhythmic rhyme of *crown*, *down*, *mound*, and *ground*.

As Ojaide argues, farming in Soyinka's early poetry is nearly always about sex (9).[32] In his poems on the anti-Igbo pogroms of 1966,[33] however, Soyinka utilizes agrarian imagery to symbolize the hatred and violence preceding the Biafran War, which led to his eventual imprisonment. In "Harvest of Hate," for example, Nigeria's post-independent generation reaps its "father's seeds in the form of an unnatural harvest" (Ojaide 60). In the two stanzas above, both of these themes, sexual reproduction and ethnic violence, merge in agrarian symbolism. As in "Harvest of Hate" (published the year of Soyinka's arrest), the farming motif in this spell functions to condemn the sectarian divisions undergirding the Biafran War as a perverted harvest: The stalks are clogged by weeds, the farmland's horizon resembles broken glass, and the dying stalks resemble a crown (suggesting Gowon's militarized power is built upon extermination and, moreover, the desecration of natural order). Inversely, the next stanza invests this death-harvest with a regenerative force resembling the function of agrarian imagery in Soyinka's erotic poems (emphasized by phallic "lances").[34]

This death and regeneration encapsulate the ritual journey of the cycle's subject, and by concluding with a harvest scene, the cycle contextualizes this journey within Ogun's ritual axis. Ogun, the god Soyinka believes most intimately embodies the creative-destructive principle,[35] is celebrated through annual harvest festivals in Ondo State, the setting of "Idanre," Soyinka's poetic revision of Ogun's origin narrative. The final section of "Idanre," "Harvest," contrasts the perverted harvest imagery of the preceding "October '66" section with images of a sanctified harvest banquet in celebration of Ogun.[36] Much like "Idanre"'s conclusion, in which the speaker describes "our vision" of the moment a true "Harvest came" to a world of perverse harvests (80), "Animystic Spells"'s final stanza concludes with a prophetic vision connected to Ogun worship through harvest imagery: Ears of corn grow, grain ripens. Of Ogun, Soyinka writes in "Idanre," "He comes, who scrapes no earthdung from his feet / He comes again in Harvest" (58). That "Animystic Spells" begins by instructing the addressee to "shod" their feet in "dung" (mimicking Ogun in "Idanre") and concludes with harvesting casts the entire cycle as a ritual conjuring of Ogun through a catastrophic metamorphosis of the colonized subject.

Given Ogun's symbolic role in Soyinka's oeuvre as the deistic embodiment of the creative-destructive principle, I interpret this conjuring as the incarcerated poet's strategic activation of the creative-destructive principle. By enveloping the cycle with images of loss and recalibration of the subject's face, Soyinka connects Ogun's advent with a prophecy of the creative-destructive principle's coming historical repercussions. The final stanza's emphasis on sound and vision—"ears arose," "I saw"—reinvest the "faceless" subject of the first spell with ears and eyes more attuned to reality and thus able to perceive this prophecy. "And this I saw," declares the ritually transfigured prophet of Ogun: "Their grains were ripened closer to the ground." Against the Christian metanarrative alluded to in the final spell's first stanza (three stalks dying and rising anew), which rests on theological abstraction and sublimation of the divine from the earth, the final prophecy foresees of a bounty closer to the ground, the stuff of ritual sacrament regenerating in terrestrialized form. Yoruba cosmology's creative-destructive principle thus replaces the Christian theology of resurrection. Ogun's ritual practice swallows the spell's Christian symbolism, reanimating monotheism by placing a harvest ritual (a communal performance of cyclic time) at the apex of "Animystic Spells." In this way, the spells' animism combats the political-theological root of Africa's colonial history and Nigeria's neocolonial present, dialectically extirpating the very mythos that, at the advent of colonial modernity, extirpated animism.[37]

In the end, then, these rigidly formalized spells operate together as a cyclic, incantatory narrative of fragmented images (far more modernist than criticism has recognized). Through this cycle, Soyinka, in solitary confinement awaiting death, chants himself into becoming ritually sacrificed and harvested by his tormentors. And through this harvest ritual, Soyinka chants, he and his tormentors will connect their culture more closely to the ground from which they have been estranged under European colonial and African neocolonial rule. This sacrifice as subjective metamorphosis is simultaneously an auto- and extra-destructive regeneration of the subject, an outworking of the subject's will aligned with "earth's own regenerate need" (*Early Poems* 159). Through this process, "Animystic Spells" ritualizes Soyinka's philosophy of the African subject's irreducible "inter-relation with Nature" (*Myth* 52) to enter a cosmic "matrix of death and becoming" (142) in order to survive the traumas of colonial and neocolonial modernity. Through its vision of regenerative death, the cycle responds to the neocolonial *polis* occasioning Soyinka's incarceration by creating an ancestral rite in which the prisoner-poet and his tormentors participate:

a becoming-harvest festival in which divisions between people, earth, the living, the dead, and the gods give way to a posthumous, postcolonial form of collective subjectivity.

While composing this poetry, Soyinka also drew sketches envisioning this form of collectivity. One surviving sketch represents the subject as an arachnid-humanoid in a pose reminiscent of the Hindu god Brahma (Figure 2). Brahma is in Hindu cosmology associated with creativity, much like Ogun in Yoruba cosmology. Moreover, spiderwebs are in Soyinka's early poetry associated with ancestral connection (as in "A Cobweb's Touch in the Dark") and creative vision (as in the opening line of *Idanre and Other Poems*: "Such webs as these we build our dreams upon" [*Early Poems* 3]). In Soyinka's sketch, the arachnid-humanoid's Brahmaesque arms spin in a cycle around the subject's body, personifying the philosophy of time Soyinka was concurrently exploring through his experiments in mathematics and poetry. A weaver of ancestral webs, the subject of this sketch is, much like the subject of "Animystic Spells," conjuring through a cyclic philosophy of time a visionary connection between the living, the dead, and the unborn. This process is further personified through the subject's third eye, or *ajna*, the locus of clairvoyant vision in Hindu cosmology, located on the arachnid-humanoid's forehead. This sketch is in other words a self-portrait of Soyinka's visionary journey toward becoming, by aesthetically ritualizing his incarceration (and, in his mind, his impending death), a collective subject. That the bottom-right arm appears to be engaged in masturbation further casts the self-portrait as a depiction of both Soyinka's animystic experiments in prison and, more holistically, the cultural work of African literature's animist poetics. Soyinka is in solitary confinement and must therefore generate the collective subjectivity he envisions alone. Much like his act of composing and chanting lyric-spells, this sketch is aimed at the imaginative secretion of collective life in a context predicated on such life's political capture. Like Fanon's vision of the colonized subject estranged from their ancestral tradition, the incarcerated poet responds to the prison of colonized modernity by imaginatively impregnating a renewed relation between the past, present, and future.

To be sure, this auto/extra-destructive regeneration of the self on behalf of a colonized collective, "You and I," extends beyond Soyinka's prison experiments in mathematics, poetry, and visual art. It is a dominant theme throughout his oeuvre. He pulls this sacrificial process from Ogun's role in the Yoruba pantheon as the god who bridges through his subjective dissolution and reassembly in the "fourth stage" of existence the "transitional gulf" between the humanity and the gods (*Myth* 143). This sacrificial, mediatory dynamic intrinsic to the creative-destructive principle is central to Soyinka's tragic drama, the subject of my next chapter. While his drama is written to be performed communally, however, his prison poetry was composed and vocalized in isolation for the sheer purpose of processing and surviving the trauma of his incarceration. In this manner, "Animystic Spells" distills the work of African literature's animist poetics at its most base level: This literature is less a mode of representing history than of ritually processing and surviving it. And through this ritual process, a speaker alienated from ancestral connection incants a new form of collective life emerging through death.

Conclusion: On Active History, Becoming-Ancestral, and the Historiographic Horizon of Theory

Soyinka terms the historiography assumed by this transformational process "active history" (*Myth* 110). Active history is the historiographic framework operative in the creative-destructive principle, the view of history his animist poetics seeks to activate. It is a mode of historical imagination committed to the recreation of the present through creative engagement with the perpetually interpenetrating spheres of the past and the future. And active history demonstrates the apex of the manner in which Soyinka's creative-destructive principle both preemptively extends and overturns Malabou's extension and overturning of the Freudian death drive. Malabou casts destructive plasticity as a new materialist death drive operating outside the parameters of Freudian temporality: a "death of the drive" (*New Wounded* 20) as a determining causality that opens a "new freedom" (*What Should We Do* 13) for the subject. But her trauma theory anchored to this destructive plasticity ultimately retains a form of sequential determinacy: The new wounded subject's past and present cannot be mediated. Soyinka's creative-destructive principle is also a dynamic of auto-destruction immanent in the material world, but he argues that this dynamic harbors for the African subject the possibility of post-traumatic/postcolonial mediation. This possibility of mediation takes place through the African artist's ritual reanimation of a cosmo-temporal axis undergirding the intra-animation of a subjectivity in which the dead, the living, and the unborn participate. The ritual activation of active history through aesthetic creation thus rejuvenates a living relation between the past, present, and future extirpated by the advent of colonial modernity. In this way Soyinka's animist poetics offers a postcolonial, posthumanist, and postsecular challenge to the sequential determinacy Malabou, following Freud, assumes.

This temporal shift demonstrates the stakes of the approach to reading Soyinka's animist poetics I have modeled in this chapter. If new materialism is concerned with a spatial expansion of subjectivity (beyond the coordinates of the solely human), Soyinka goes further: He also expands subjectivity temporally by claiming that the dead and the unborn can participate with the living in the intra-animation of subjective life. He describes this ancestrally informed subjectivity as emerging from the link between a "cyclic concept of time and the animist interfusion of all matter and consciousness" (*Myth* 145). As the latter half of this phrase suggests, consciousness is inseparable from all matter, as the new materialists would have it, casting subjectivity as inextricable from the entire cosmos. Yet, as the first half of the phrase suggests, Soyinka links this matter-spirit inextricability to time's cyclic unfolding: the interfusion between the past, present, and future as incarnated in relations between dead, living, and unborn people. This temporal interfusion marks both Soyinka's departure from new materialism and the intervention within theory at large I find implicit in his practice of animist poetics.

Like new materialism, trauma studies is currently attempting to expand its assumed subject beyond post-Enlightenment European humanism, yet the discourse retains the linear, sequential form of this tradition's philosophy of time. To be sure, for Caruth, Freudian trauma theory posits a deconstruction of the subjective ipseity assumed in the psychological experience of being an individual sequentially progressing through linear time. Trauma is a shock inaugurated by a "break in the mind's experience of time," she writes, summarizing Freud (*Unclaimed* 61). Since the subject cannot integrate the traumatic experience *in time*, they experience it belatedly, through the repetition compulsion, which ushers the subject into Freud's infamous temporality of *Nachträglichkeit*. This "deferred action," in James Strachey's translation, or perpetual "afterwardsness" in Jean Laplanche's terms,[38] deactivates the sequential determinacy of time's linear flow within the subject's psyche. The eternal return of post-traumatic memory in this way deconstructs ipseity by way of rupturing linear temporality: Trauma awakens the Cartesian subject to the fact that they are not an individual perpetually moving forward in a straight temporal line. Yet this metanarrative on the subject of trauma assumes time's linear form as a starting point to be deconstructed. Other philosophies of time, such as those experienced by the many Indigenous populations subjected to the traumas of European imperialism and its afterlives, are largely ignored by psychoanalytic theory (and its critiques). Even radical interventions within the discourse, such as Malabou's, assume in the end time's linear unfolding. If theory in the wake of posthumanism seeks to open wider the borders of subjectivity, and if new materialism's ecological vision of subjectivity promises to assist this project through its material expansion of these borders, animist poetics radicalizes this expansion with an alternative philosophy of time. Thus far, no critic has taken the "implicated" nature of subjectivity as far as Soyinka does. The result is a subject constitutively implicated not only in human history and global politics, as Caruth and Rothberg each convincingly argue, but also (and more fundamentally) in the intertwinement of the material and temporal movement of the cosmos.

By preemptively approaching the new materialist critique of ipseity from a more radically diachronic and explicitly postcolonial angle, animist poetics offers contemporary theory an alternative form of historiography, which is anchored to an alternative philosophy of time, which is anchored to an alternative philosophy of the subject. Through his fundamentally modern, experimental appropriation of Yoruba cosmology, Soyinka's paradigmatic use of the animist lyric chants into being a cosmic personhood moving in cyclic time, activating through the creative-destructive principle at work throughout the cosmos the active history he believes endows the colonized subject with postcolonial agency. In the most constrictive conditions of the postcolony, animist poetics emerges as an aesthetic tactic aimed at the continual reshaping of present historical conditions.

In the introduction to his edited collection *Poems of Black Africa* (1975), Soyinka suggests that Tchicaya U Tam'si's "Fragile" (1962) models this animist vision of political agency uniting so many of the continent's modern writers:

> Endlessly I decalcify my joy
> And lo its hands become islands
> They surpass the Antilles!
> Child I cling no longer to the Zaïre
> I am no more master of my tears
> Master of this patchwork of time

> What flowers to dress
> for Emmett Till
> Child whose soul is bleeding in my own! (13)

The poem's speaker emerges through the "nature-saturation" of the animist subject, Soyinka interprets, and this saturation is "inseparable from recognition and assertion of a political self, constantly expanding in its humane concerns." Thus, the joyous "transcendentalism" of the speaker no longer clinging to the Zaïre and instead becoming-cosmos—a relinquishing of nationalist identity for a cosmopolitan animism—quickly becomes "infiltrated by political anguish" (13). The presence of Emmett Till, an African American boy who at the age of fourteen was lynched in Mississippi in 1955, interrupts the speaker's ecstatic movement with a memory of the violence foundational to the colonized, racialized, global modernity in which the poet speaks. Joining what the poem calls the "patchwork of time" alongside the speaker—indeed, infusing with the speaker's ecstatic movement—Till at the end of this passage is becoming-ancestral.

For Soyinka, the creative-destructive principle casts Till's death as a potential source of regenerative life, a portal to activate, as U Tam'si's speaker discovers, an active history connecting all who have been subjugated under the weight of colonial history. If for Freud death is the ontological stasis at the end of linear time, for Soyinka and U Tam'si the animist lyric can recast death as a transitional experience into a new form of collective life. As the speaker wonders how to mourn Till's death, then, the question U Tam'si raises is less how to *remember* Till than how to *ritually join Till's ecstatic anguish in the memory of the cosmos*. This interpretive shift leads us by way of trauma theory into animist ecology, and by way of ecology into the more fundamental relation between poetics and subject formation. To posit a theory is to assume a subject. To assume a subject is to assume a poetics: a theory of creative formation through which subjectivity can become an embodied, culturally meaningful experience. It is in the service of this core process of poetics as subject formation that the animist lyric operates. Functioning beyond the parameters of literary and cultural theory's post-Cartesian, secular field of vision, the animist lyric voices cosmic personhood into the colonized world; through incantation, this form lays the poetic groundwork for a coming, postcolonial community. In the next chapter, I shift focus to the dramaturgy of animist tragedy, which stages the communal bonds formed through the regeneration of cosmic personhood voiced by the animist lyric.

Chapter 4

Animist Tragedy's Biopolitical Mediation
Staging Human Sacrifice in Wole Soyinka's *Death and the King's Horseman*

Wole Soyinka's *Death and the King's Horseman* was first titled *Death and the District Officer*. This title places antagonist Simon Pilkings, British district officer in colonial Nigeria, in striking parallel with protagonist Elesin Oba, horseman of the king of Oyo. A scene deleted from *Horseman* demonstrates this proximity. Simon complains to his wife, Jane, that he is stationed away from then-raging World War II. "I just can't go through the war sitting at an outpost of empire while my old school chums are all doing their bit and getting killed," he declares. "Oh Simon do stop being silly," she responds, "[a]nd anyway, why do you want to commit suicide?" Simon is confused, but Jane persists: "Why are you so anxious to be a dead hero?" (*Death and the D.O.* II.10). Jane's questions reveal a will to die on behalf of the community, which unites the horseman and the district officer and their respective communities. In the published version of the play, Soyinka extrapolates this scene's rhetorical function into a passage in which Elesin's son, Olunde, extols the self-sacrifice of a British sea captain who kills himself to save a coastal community (41–42). The explicit nature of the deleted scene, focalized around the desire of the colonizing antagonist rather than a Brit outside the plot, however, poses a narratological unity complicating the plot as well as the interpretive framework through which most critics approach the play.

Later, Simon arrests Elesin before he completes a death rite on behalf of the Oyo Kingdom. Elesin calls himself a "traveller" to the "navel of the world" (13), conceptualizing his death not as, in Simon's view, the stasis at the horizon of sequential time, but a transition into another form of life within the "cyclic consciousness of time" I explained in the previous chapter (Soyinka *Myth* 2). Simon and Elesin thus embody the different conceptions of death, tied to different philosophies of time, I have detailed throughout this book. Like Freud, and like most of Euro-American theory, Simon interprets death through a framework of linear temporality. The Yoruba characters in *Horseman*, by contrast, interpret death through the animist approach to nonlinear temporality that, as I detailed in the previous chapter, Soyinka creatively appropriates from Yoruba cosmology: a time conditioned by the interpenetrating realms of the living, the dead, and the unborn. What Simon deems suicide is thus, from an animist perspective, sacrifice leading to renewed communal life.

Speaking candidly with Jane, however, Simon reveals the hypocrisy of his judgment against Elesin by wishing he too could die for his empire, or as Jane puts it, commit suicide. Despite Simon's aversion to the Oyo Kingdom's practice of human sacrifice, the British Empire—and its incarnation central to the plot, himself, the deleted scene implies—bears the same sacrificial structure. Soyinka places the political communities his plot seems to juxtapose, European and African, in mimetic relation by hinging both on the willed sacrifice of their subjects. Put simply, the play plots a shift from Indigenous monarchy to British colony, but as the desire uniting Simon and Elesin demonstrates, these political structures are not essentially differentiable because willed sacrifice is essential to each. *Horseman*'s tragedy—the Yoruba people's severance from the sacrificial structure of the Oyo Kingdom—is both contingent and universal, symbolizing through a crisis in the Oyo *polis* a crisis central to the political as such: what Jacques Derrida calls the "sacrificial structure" of culture ("'Eating Well'" 112).

Taking this scene as a point of departure, in this chapter I analyze the role of human sacrifice[1] in *Horseman*'s dramatization of colonization as the process I theorize in chapter 1 as ancestral trauma. By staging the loss of a Yoruba sacrificial rite coinciding with the desacralization of a communal experience of time—the cyclic time of Yoruba cosmology—Soyinka dramatizes colonization as a cosmological rupture resulting in an entanglement between the Indigenous temporality on which I focused the previous chapter and the sequential time of European modernity I have been critiquing throughout this book. But the crux of my argument is a seeming paradox: *Horseman* depicts this desacralization, the Yoruba world's loss of a sacrificial rite, as in reality a transition into a new grammar of the sacred, which, like the Indigenous order, depends on ritualized sacrifice. What critics conceptualize as the process of secularization staged is, I will therefore demonstrate, a misnomer. On the one hand, *Horseman*'s Yoruba world becomes sacrificially severed from its form of ancestral mediation; on the other, being sacrificed implies a sacred structure remains. Although what is staged as the "modern" time of the nation-state may appear to be at odds with the "primitive" time of Indigenous monarchy, Soyinka suggests that we moderns, much like *Horseman*'s colonized Oyo Kingdom, "*do not sacrifice sacrifice*" (Derrida, "Eating Well" 113).

Hence Soyinka's preference of the term *transition* over *clash*. As he infamously writes in his author's note, "The confrontation in the play is largely metaphysical, contained in the human vehicle which is Elesin and the universe of the Yoruba mind—the world of the living, the dead and the unborn, and the numinous passage which links all: transition." Soyinka pins this phrase against what he terms the "clash of cultures" interpretation critics of African literature often assume (3). Deeper than a culture clash, Soyinka claims, *Horseman* stages a metaphysical transition. In this chapter, I specify this transition's form: through colonization, the Indigenous order of the sacred conditioning the drama is transfigured, somewhat paradoxically, into the collective experience of desacralization conditioning its tragic force. In short, the desacralization of Yoruba cosmology central to *Horseman*'s tragedy functions within the drama as the sacrificial and sacralized foundation of its vision of colonial modernity.

Soyinka theorizes the cultural outworking of this process as a form of collective trauma in his *Myth, Literature and the African World* lectures, which he delivered as a visiting scholar at Cambridge University while writing *Horseman* (a few years after his release from prison, the context of the previous chapter). My argument in this chapter, like the previous, is informed by *Myth*. Here, though, I recast the animist theory of tragedy as ritual sacrifice that Soyinka proposes in these lectures as a postcolonial prefiguration of the sacrificial politics framing the critiques of sovereignty in the intersecting theoretical discourses of biopolitics, political theology, and Afropessimism. Like the previous chapter, my goal in constellating these theoretical discourses is to apply Soyinka's experimental animism to the forefront of cultural theory, highlighting another aspect of animist poetics' relevance to contemporary literary and cultural criticism. First, I place Soyinka in dialogue with the post-Foucauldian critique of Carl Schmitt's theory of sovereignty, mapped most influentially by Derrida in his *The Beast and the Sovereign* lectures (2001–03) and Giorgio Agamben in his *Homo Sacer* series (1998–2016). Frank B. Wilderson III's *Afropessimism* (2020) builds on a growing corpus of Black biopolitical critique, I then argue, to offer an explicitly racialized form of Derrida's and Agamben's shared critique of the modern nation-state. This revised biopolitical theology partially resonates with Soyinka's animist approach to colonial modernity's sacrificial politics.

But there is a stark difference between Soyinka and the aforementioned theorists. Soyinka's animist approach to the generative process of sacrifice, epitomized for him in the aesthetic form of Yoruba tragedy, operates outside the secularized, European coordinates of Derrida's and Agamben's biopolitical theology. Moreover, Soyinka offers a similar critique of colonial modernity as Wilderson's racialized biopolitical critique, but he does not accept Wilderson's pessimistic conclusions. Instead, Soyinka responds to the sacrifice of African subjectivity at the foundation of modernity with an affirmative aesthetic only graspable beyond the epistemic confines of the post-Enlightenment secular rationalism retained in the Wildersonian model of racialized sacrifice. As I argue in this chapter, the animist theory of tragedy Soyinka proposes in *Myth* and stages in *Horseman* invests the form with the ability to ritually transform that which it stages, the erasure of Indigenous subjectivity under the pressures of colonial modernity, into the sacrificial foundation of a new community. In other words, animist tragedy, by ritualizing the ancestral trauma that biopolitical theology and its racialized revision diagnose, makes its wounding politically generative. *Horseman* is paradigmatic of this process, demonstrating an affirmative political aesthetic unavailable to contemporary theory's critics of sovereignty without recourse to animism.

Biopolitical Theology in the Postcolony

In *Horseman*, West African communal life is ruptured under the sovereignty of the European nation-state. Michel Foucault influentially terms the regime inaugurated by this sovereignty biopolitics. Under modernity, he claims, life itself becomes the target of a power no longer incarnated by monarchy, a claim relevant to *Horseman*. Foucauldian biopower is inaugurated through the transition of sovereignty from the body of the king (or Alafin of Oyo) to the body politic of the nation-state, the life of "the people" (or British Empire). As I will argue, Elesin incarnates this transition during his ritual performance of his sacrificial rite. Although unacknowledged within *Horseman*'s extensive body of criticism, this Indigenous death rite transfigures, I will argue, into an imperial possession rite. As he loses connection to Alafin, he incarnates what I will articulate, by placing Soyinka in dialogue with the constellation of theory I have been setting up, the biopolitical theology of colonized, African life—a biopolitical theology taking the form of ancestral trauma, as I define this process in chapter 1.

As my use of the term *theology* implies, Foucauldian biopolitics is less important to my argument than the post-Foucauldian critique of Schmitt influentially posed by Derrida and Agamben, among others. According to Schmitt's *Political Theology*, sovereignty—the locus of that which constitutes the political—operates within modernity as an "aftereffect of the idea of God" animating state authority (49). Political theology—the ideology of the sacred informing sovereignty—does not for Schmitt necessitate religious belief. Rather, it names the theological form inherent to the constitution of authority, despite religious or sociohistoric context. As the deleted scene with which I began this chapter implies, Soyinka conceptualizes this form as sacrifice. Likewise, in his *The Beast and the Sovereign* lectures, Derrida filters Foucauldian biopolitics through Schmittian political theology, stressing sovereignty's sacrificial foundation. In agreement with Schmitt, the allegedly secular "sovereignty of the people or of the nation merely inaugurates a new form of the same fundamental structure" of the sacred, he claims, and in this structure "man is caught, evanescent, disappearing, . . . a hyphen between the sovereign and the beast" (282, 13). According to this framework, during European modernity's transition of sovereignty from the king to the people, all that changes is content. The nation-state, rather than the monarch, now functions as the site of the numinous, that which hails "bare life," as Agamben famously puts it, into the domain of the political through the sacrifice of its subjects. Against Schmitt's infamous celebration of state sovereignty, Derrida critiques its sacrificial logic, dreaming instead of a future biopolitics divorced from theological authority, a new form of collective life after the sacrifice of sacrifice.

This critique and hope together offer a framework for grasping what I take to be the politics of animist tragedy. While Schmitt celebrates the inescapability of the numinous, Soyinka, like Derrida, recognizes the structural necessity of political theology (hence Simon and Elesin's mimetic relation), yet combats the perversity of its sacrificial logic. As he writes in his prison memoir, *The Man Died*, for instance, the structure of the European nation-state oversees African modernity with "divine authority": "What God (white man) has put together, let no black man put asunder. The complications of neo-colonial politics of interference compel one to accept such a damnable catechism for now, as a pragmatic necessity. Later perhaps, the black nations will themselves sit down together, and, by agreement, set compass and square rule to paper and reformulate the life-expending, stultifying, constrictive imposition of this divine authority" (181). His immediate point is that as long as the Biafran War, and by implication any post-independent African conflict, is waged without fighting the structural problem of nationality, people will continue to be sacrificed on behalf of the nation-state—which is precisely Simon's desire in *Horseman*. Thus, the political theology introduced to Africa through European imperial expansion (and dramatized in *Horseman*) will continue to inform African cultural dynamics. As Elesin and Simon, one a so-called primitive African, the other a so-called modern European, are united by sacrificial desire, and as post-independent Africa in the passage above inherits Simon's fastening of this desire to the nation-state, what Derrida and Agamben construe as biopolitical theology provides a philosophical entry point for articulating Soyinka's dramatization of modernity as an entanglement of sacrificial rites.

This discourse is, however, notoriously Eurocentric. In *Homo Sacer: Sovereign Power and Bare Life*, for instance, Agamben traces the discursive formation of sovereignty from ancient Greece to the Holocaust, but largely ignores its presence in the Global South. The Nazi concentration camp, he famously claims, is the "*nomos* of the modern" because it demonstrates the sovereign-subject relation in its most raw form: human sacrifice (166). Yet, as Achille Mbembe argues in "Necropolitics," published soon after Derrida's post-Foucauldian, theological reframing of biopower, the barring of particular life from the political, which sacrificially constitutes the political Agamben discovers in Auschwitz, is the fundamental technique of European imperial expansion. As I will demonstrate in my analysis of *Horseman*, Mbembe's recasting of the slave plantation as, prior to Agamben's Auschwitz, the *nomos* of the modern, provides a fruitful framework for interpreting Elesin's incarnation of his people's ancestral trauma via his desecrated ritual performance and imprisonment.

Since Mbembe's postcolonial intervention in this discourse, a growing body of Black biopolitical critique has emerged, anchoring what Derrida and Agamben diagnose as the sacrificial structure of politics to colonial modernity's constitutive barring of African subjectivity from its vision of a universalized humanity. To be sure, theorists such as Sylvia Wynter, Hortense Spillers, and Saidiya Hartman were analyzing the constitutive function of the sacrifice of African subjectivity in a global *polis* carved out by European imperial expansion before Derrida's and Agamben's biopolitical theologies or Mbembe's postcolonial reformulation. As Hartman memorably puts it in *Scenes of Subjection* (1997), "The slave is the object or the ground that makes possible the existence of the bourgeois subject and, by negation or contradistinction, defines liberty, citizenship, and the enclosures of the social body" (62). The more recent work of Black biopolitics draws heavily on such theorists, especially Wynter's consistent claim that the concept of a universal "Man" rests on the strategic barring of non-Western people from a Eurocentric vision of life itself. In fact, Wynter frequently uses theological terminology in her critiques of this "sociogenic" construct she simply calls "Man." For her, this form of sovereign subjectivity, emerging only through its sacrifice of others, is an outworking of "a *theocentric* view of the relation between God and man" (255) intrinsic to monotheism. In this way, Wynter's theoretical writings have always been doing what would later be conceptualized as biopolitical theology, but in a mode more attuned to racialization as modernity's primary technology of the sacrifice conditioning the very concept of collective human life.

Anchoring the critiques of sovereignty exemplified by Derrida and Agamben back to theorists such as Wynter therefore enables critics such as Zakiyyah Iman Jackson to refocalize biopolitical theology around the cultural processes through which Black life is barred from the category of the human. As she writes, "The current conceptualization of universal humanity does not move beyond a Western, secularized cultural mode and thus misrecognizes and occludes African subjectivity" (32). For Alexander G. Weheliye, this barring of African subjectivity from the human domain undergirding modern philosophies and practices of collective life suggests that thinking "beyond the genocidal shackles of Man" must be the first principle of Black studies—a claim that resonates with the work of Fred Moten, Christina Sharpe, and many others in this field (4). As Tendayi Sithole argues, moreover, this refocalization of biopolitical theology requires not only widening the corpus of Agamben's model, but also thinking beyond its limits, which "cannot account for the ontology of the black subject" (222). For him, the sacrifice of African subjectivity is even more primary than the sacrifice of "bare life" on behalf of the state that Agamben takes to be the genesis of political community. The concept of life, even in its most bare form, hinges on the cultural process of annexing African subjectivity in the position of "social death" (238), he argues, utilizing Orlando Patterson's term to signify the structural position sacrificially constituting Agamben's philosophical categories.

This concept of Black social death as sacrificially necessary to conceptualizing human life itself, even life in its most "bare" form, is central to the most famous recent text to offer an explicitly racialized critique of the sacrificial politics informing the modern *polis*: Wilderson's *Afropessimism* (2020). As he sums up his argument, "Human life is dependent on Black death for its existence and for its coherence" (41–42). While Wynter, Spillers, Hartman, and others have made similar claims, Wilderson's approach is distinct in his application of this biopolitical theology to an inescapable negative ontology that forecloses hope for the future. For him, "[I]f Blacks were completely genocided, Humanity would find itself in the same quandary that would occur if Black people were recognized and incorporated as Human beings. Humanity would cease to exist; because it would lose its conceptual coherence. . . . The Black is needed to mark the border of Human subjectivity" (164). For Wilderson, Black subjectivity is, in Derrida's terms, the beast sacrificed to the sovereign, which is human life. Since these structural positions are mutually constitutive, as Derrida argues, there is no escape, Wilderson claims. As a "prelogical phenomenon" (92), the sacrifice of Black subjectivity is for him the process conditioning all human life and thought; thus, there can be no humanly imaginable way to sacrifice the violent necessity of sacrifice, as Derrida dreams. Instead, according to Wilderson, all the critic can do is critique the racial politics of this sacrificial structure of collective life. Afropessimism names for Wilderson "critique without redemption or vision of redress except 'the end of the world' ": the death of life as we know it (174).[2]

But what if this death is not "the end," but rather a transition, a threshold for a polity's posthumous transfiguration into a new form of collective life? Put differently, what if the discourse of biopolitical theology took up Jackson's call to "move beyond a Western, secularized cultural mode" that "misrecognizes and occludes African subjectivity" and began taking Indigenous cosmologies seriously as modes of philosophy and critique (32)? My reading of *Horseman* as animist tragedy makes precisely this move. Through its formal use of Yoruba cosmology, *Horseman*, I argue, stages the structural conundrum Wilderson critiques but models an affirmative, dialectical response, inconceivable to Wilderson's secularized logic.

Before I lay out this argument in more detail, I wish to note that this animist alternative to Wilderson's negative ontology also challenges the secular aesthetic framework assumed across most of the body of criticism on *Horseman*, which predominantly tethers literature to aesthetic representation rather than ritual transformation. In one of the most influential interpretive approaches to *Horseman* in the past few decades, for example, Olakunle George concludes that the ultimate lesson the play bestows on cultural theory is an awakening to the unbridgeable abyss that separates the literary and the political. "[A]cts of language are no more than acts of language," he writes, and "literary structures cannot be conflated with social structures." He continues, "[T]he fine deconstruction of imperialism achieved in the play cannot in itself reorder the phenomenality of imperialism itself. This merely tells us something we all know but too often repress in the inner logic of contemporary theory, namely, that criticism cannot solve or stop political traumas; it can only witness and give voice to the witnessing" ("Cultural" 88). For George, *Horseman* bears witness to the trauma of colonization by representing its historical reality. As I argued in chapter 2, this representational aesthetic is emblematic of debates on trauma within literary and cultural criticism over the past few decades. Yet this approach crucially misses the way animist poetics engages with historical trauma: "art as a ritual process," as Soyinka puts it ("Ritual" 7). For him, literary signification operates beyond the secularized field of representation to which his critics remain anchored, and his alternative, animist approach to aesthetics as ritual mending on behalf of a cosmic collective is central to his theory of Yoruba tragedy.

In the previous chapter I argued that the animist lyric incants a form of cosmic personhood as a modernist response to its own erasure via colonization; in this chapter, I argue that animist tragedy stages the communal bonds formed through such incantations. In *Tragedy and Postcolonial Literature*, Ato Quayson utilizes the Akan concept of *musuo*, "harms to the soul" (11), to conceptualize the "fluid and interacting contours" of tragic suffering on "self and society" (12). Soyinka radicalizes this fluidity by taking an animist approach to tragic form, thereby conceptualizing the polity this form addresses as more-than-living, more-than-human: in a word, cosmic. Staging this cosmic polity is, for Soyinka, central to Indigenous African dramaturgy. Against what he calls the "compartmentalising habit" (*Myth* 37) of European theater criticism, he links African theater to a cosmic form of "communal presence": "Where such theatre is encountered in its purest form . . . we will find no compass points, no horizontal or vertical definitions. There are no reserved spaces for the protagonists, for his very act of representational being is defined in turn by nothing less than the infinite cosmos within which the origin of the community and its contemporaneous experience of being is firmly embedded" (43). As tragedy, *Horseman* dramatizes the loss of this kinship with "the infinite cosmos" functioning as the dramaturgical principle of African theater. In other words, what marks *Horseman* as tragedy is its staging of the process I theorize in chapter 1 as the ancestral trauma of colonization: the cultural inheritance of the extirpation of the African subject's perceived kinship between the living, dead, and unborn and the human and more-than-human world.

Sam Durrant and David Scott have each noted the intrinsic connection between postcolonial tragedy, trauma, and time to which I am pointing. For Scott, "tragic vision" enables postcolonial critique to reformulate its notions of how the relationship between past and present shapes political futures, which therefore endows tragedy with an affirmative politics. For Durrant, this affirmative mode is possible because postcolonial tragedy's most basic function is to perform the cultural work of the traditional epic, conjuring a collective, in response to colonial trauma ("Surviving"). My understanding of animist tragedy builds on these definitions, but more specifically situates the form as a mode of processing ancestral trauma through the operations of the regenerative death drive—two terms central to my argument throughout this book. As I will demonstrate, *Horseman* stages a modernity in which the colonized subject must inherit a ruptured temporality, a severed kinship between the living, the ancestors, and the unborn central to the Yoruba concept of nature. But it is precisely by dramatizing this inheritance in the form of animist tragedy that the play aesthetically mediates the loss it represents. Paradoxically, it gifts its audience a passage into modernity by ritually regenerating, through its performance, the Indigenous temporality it laments as being irrevocably ruptured.

In this sense, through its animism, *Horseman* is properly postcolonial: It dialectically reenacts colonization as immanently part of African culture—that is, colonial trauma is dramatized as emerging through the Indigenous metaphysics it extirpated. Critics may take offense to the idea of reenacting the historic subjugation of Africans under European imperialism as unfolding from an Indigenous metaphysics, but in this chapter I justify what I take to be the politics of Soyinka's tragic mythopoetics.

My analysis is thus not a biopolitical-theological reading of *Horseman*'s depiction of colonial trauma. Instead, I offer an explication, informed by Soyinka's scholarship, of the biopolitical cosmology intrinsic to *Horseman*, framed by my argument that Soyinka's utilization of animist tragedy offers biopolitical theology (including its Black studies critique) an affirmative aesthetic. By ritually staging a political community emerging through yet pointing beyond the sacrificial foundation of colonial modernity, *Horseman* passes on through the political subjugation dramatized a vision of what Derrida calls "an other politicization . . . and therefore another concept of the political" (*Beast* 75). Soyinka exegetes this regenerative process—operating through the creative-destructive principle I detailed in the previous chapter—from Yoruba cosmology, thereby recasting *Horseman*'s dramatization of the death of the Yoruba world under the pressures of colonial modernity into its posthumous survival. The force of animist tragedy is therefore its ritualization of the regenerative death drive I have throughout this book placed at the core of animist poetics.

"A Stranger Force of Violence"

Dramaturgically, the "radically anti-Manichean" (*Myth* 127) nature of the deleted scene with which I began this chapter means that, as Soyinka tells Martin Banham in an interview on drama in West Africa, the "Greek classics" informing the Western *polis* can transfer to Africa "without any problem" ("Theatre" 3). Hence *Horseman*'s classically tragic form. Philosophically, it means the play addresses, through its tragic form, the trauma of colonization as, transtemporally, the generative structure of the precolonial *polis*. Soyinka describes this contingent universality in his author's note. "The Colonial Factor is an incident, a catalytic incident merely," he writes (3). Following Anthony Appiah, most critics interpret this claim as a rhetorical rejection of political reality through which Soyinka attempts to write an "African world" without reference to Europe. This interpretation remains rooted in a juxtaposition between Europe and Africa, however, which the sacrificial desire uniting Simon and Elesin challenges. As Soyinka explains in an interview with Alby James, "I wanted to pick at this word *juxtaposition*. Juxtaposition of the colonial culture and the traditional experience of peoples. You see, for any kind of drama . . . there is always a circumstance that triggers . . . abnormality. . . . In this case it was, indeed, the colonized set of values, but I always insist that *this kind of tragedy could have taken place without external intrusion*" (1; emphasis added). By staging the historically contingent trauma of colonization as a universal tragedy, the play addresses a generative rupture arising from yet also preceding colonization. Critics are thus right that the play places psychoanalytic trauma theory and postcolonial theory in dialogue. Using the Freudian concepts *Angstbereitschaft* (preparedness for anxiety) and *Nachträglichkeit* (deferred action), for example, Ogaga Ifowodo and Andrew Barnaby trace within the play a structural relation between the traumatized psyche and the colonized *polis*. But critics largely miss the structural trauma Soyinka stages as generative of colonial history and human history: sacrifice. For Soyinka, the sacrifice of Indigeneity at the foundation of colonialism is a repetition of the sacrificial foundation of all forms of political community—a political philosophy that mirrors Freud's theory of the primal horde.

The horseman ritual of the Oyo Kingdom incarnates this foundation and moreover hinges the meaningful passing of time on it. The Alafin has died. After nearly a month of ceremonies, Elesin must sacrifice himself. Characters describe this ritual in threshold terms such as *gateway* because, according the dramatic rendering of the ritual, Elesin must enter what Soyinka describes in his author's note as the numinous passage of transition between the living, the dead, and the unborn (3). This passage arises as what Soyinka terms "the fourth stage." If the ancestors, the living, and the unborn (and thus the past, present, and future) exist simultaneously, Soyinka reasons, the fourth stage is the abyss between them, through which they mutually animate one another. Meeting Alafin's spirit at this ontological threshold, Elesin must utter a sacred message at the precise moment consecrated by the elders to conjure Alafin into "the land of the ancestors" (34, 60, 53). According to the logic implied by the play, only when Alafin becomes an ancestral spirit can the link between the Yoruba cosmological and Oyo political orders continue. During Elesin's death, then, his body, which mediates the body politic of the Oyo Kingdom, becomes an *orita meta*—a threshold between *aye* and *orun*, the distinct, inseparable realms of matter and spirit in Yoruba cosmology—through which the Oyo monarchy and Yoruba cosmos remain intertwined (Drewal et al. 14).

This political-theological ritual exemplifies the sacrificial drive Soyinka takes to be central to Yoruba tragedy, which narratively functions as a "recurrent exercise in the experience of disintegration" central to Yoruba mythology as a whole (*Myth* 151). Soyinka recalls Orisa-nla, the first deity, whose slave rolled a stone on him, shattering him into thousands of pieces and thereby creating, through his disintegration, the Yoruba pantheon (152). Ogun, arising from this destruction, was the first deity to bridge the abyss between the gods and humanity, thereby becoming the first king of Ife, yet tragically killing his subjects and himself in a repetition of Orisa-nla's primal disintegration. The Yoruba "tragic actor," Soyinka argues, repeats Ogun's repetition of Orisa-nla's sacrifice by ritually regenerating, through his or her willful disintegration and reassemblage in the fourth stage, the intertwinement between life that was, is, and will be (142–43). Soyinka's concept of Yoruba tragedy is, then, a performance of the creative-destructive principle I detailed in the previous chapter, his Yoruba instantiation of animist poetics' regenerative death drive. The tragic actor's function is to incarnate the polity in its cosmic totality, and, by ritually crossing the fourth stage of existence on behalf of the polity, regenerate life through death. In short, Soyinka's animist approach to tragedy casts it as a form of generative sacrifice.

His concept of the fourth stage is therefore a cosmological and aesthetic term. Unlike the fourth wall—the imagined gulf between the audience and the actors rooted in the tradition of the proscenium arch—Soyinka's onto-dramaturgical fourth stage names the "immeasurable gulf of transition" between subjective life and cosmic totality, implicating all ritual participants, the audience included (148). In *Horseman*, as Elesin prepares to sacrifice himself on behalf of the Oyo Kingdom under British colonization, he also functions as a sacrificial mediator for the audience witnessing the drama in the present. His mediatory act is, like the tragedy itself, both contingent and universal; by interceding on behalf of the Oyo Kingdom, he becomes, as Iyaloja (mother of the market) words it, "intercessor to the world" (16).

But Elesin fails to fully reach the fourth stage. Since the sacred message that conjures Alafin's spirit into the ancestral realm is patrimonially passed on among the horsemen, nobody beyond Elesin's son, Olunde, knows the words (60). Thus, after Simon arrests Elesin, Olunde sacrifices himself in his father's place. Horrified and ashamed that "the son has proved the father," Elesin strangles himself with his colonizer's chains (62). As Elesin's response to Olunde's death suggests, although Olunde's name, *my lord has come*, implies a messianic role, his substitutionary death does not carry the redemptive force of the Christian doctrine of substitutionary atonement. Rather than mediating human and divine life, or even ancestral, living, and unborn as the horseman ritual is meant to do, Olunde's death symbolizes a crisis in which sacrificial mediation must—but may no longer—carry ontological efficacy. With both Olunde and Elesin dead, the horseman ritual itself dies because nobody else knows the sacred message. The ancestors, the living, and the unborn have no intercessor to ritually bridge the numinous passage between them, and the intertwinement of these multiple planes of existence enters a mode of crisis.

Most critics assume Elesin performs his ritual correctly until he is arrested (e.g., Izevbaye [120]; Hepburn [597–98]; and McLuckie [154]). Soyinka, however, does not stage the arrest, which raises a question regarding the play's crisis in transtemporal mediation. Act 3 contains the performance of the death rite, but the act closes before the interruption—lights fading as the drums beat, women chant a dirge, and Elesin dances entranced. As Tanure Ojaide observes, the consecrated moment of Elesin's death is never revealed to the audience, which means it is impossible to know if he is arrested before or after he is meant to sacrifice himself (214). This narrative absence complicates the question of Elesin's and Simon's roles in the desecration, making it impossible to say with assurance that Simon's intervention causes the tragedy. By not staging the disruption of the ritual on which the play's tragic force hinges, Soyinka depicts the moment as what Jacques Lacan would call a "missed encounter" (55). Constitutively missed within the collective frame of reference Elesin incarnates, the disruption of the ritual emerges in the drama indirectly—as trauma—through its impact on his performance of the ritual.

As Elesin's performance transfigures from a traditional death rite into an unknown possession rite, the language of this scene suggests that his performance becomes what Ato Quayson calls a "maimed rite" before Simon's arrival, recasting it as both a maimed rite and a prophetic incarnation of colonial modernity. When Alafin's spirit enters Elesin's Praise-Singer's body to perform ritual exhortations, he recognizes the danger signified by the "drowsy as palm oil" movements composing what the stage directions label Elesin's "trance-dance" (36, 35). Praise-Singer fears his companion may be anchored to the earth by "evil minds who mean to part us at the last" (34). This fear proves true. "Strange voices guide my feet," Elesin admits (35). Guided by these voices, Elesin rejects the rhythm of the death rite for a new, unrecognizable rhythm, which cannot be heard by his companions or the audience. As Praise-Singer asks, "Are there sounds there I cannot hear . . . ?" (36). This alien rhythm places the ritual in jeopardy. He continues: "[D]o footsteps surround you which pound the earth like *gbedu*, roll like thunder round the dome of the world?" (36). Elesin must sacrifice himself at the moment deemed sacred by the *gbedu* drums.³ The *gbedu* is a "deep-timbred royal drum," as Soyinka defines it, used by the *Osugbo*, which he defines as both the "secret 'executive' cult of the Yoruba" and "its meeting place" (63).⁴ Soyinka leaves both the members and location of the *Osugbo* off-stage, yet asserts their presence through the sound of the *gbedu* drums, providing a rhythm for Elesin's sacrifice. But Alafin's spirit contrasts the rhythm of Elesin's dance to that of the afterlife—that is, the tempo of the ancestral realm and thus the horizon of Elesin's death rite. Only the *Osugbo* sages recognize this spiritual tempo, and they inscribe it within the material world through their drumming. But Elesin, channeling the strange voices, begins to dance out of sync with the *gbedu* rhythm. "The drums are changing now but you have gone far ahead of the world," Alafin's spirit exclaims. "It is not yet noon in heaven. . . . So why must you rush like an impatient bride: why do you race to desert your Olohun-iyo [Praise-Singer]?" (35). It is not that a polyrhythm arises from the death rite, constituting a cross-rhythm among the ritual participants, but rather that a rhythm purely external to the pattern of the ritual arises within Elesin alone. Strange voices replace the sacred role of the *gbedu* drums by asserting a tempo alien to that through which the *Osugbo* sages transpose the intertwinement between ancestral, living, and unborn time into the material world.

Elesin's skin—that which, under a racialized polity, marks him as African—begins to mark the presence of the voices now animating his body: "Is your flesh lightened Elesin[?]," asks Praise-Singer (36). Most critics recognize that Elesin's lightening skin signals his spiritual journey into the fourth stage (e.g., Katrak [98]). But I would add that if we are attentive to the play's staging of colonial modernity as a sacrificial ritual, the "strange voices" should be interpreted as voices of the British Empire, which possesses and is transfiguring not only Elesin's body (the Yoruba tragic actor, in Soyinka's dramaturgical terms), but the body politic he is currently mediating: the Oyo Kingdom in the drama, the colonized African subject in its performance. *Lightened* thus simultaneously signals a dematerialization of Elesin's body as he approaches the fourth stage, as critics have recognized, but also the internalization of white supremacy foundational to colonial subject formation. As Elesin later laments while rethinking his performance, "[W]hite skin covered our future, preventing us from seeing the death our enemies had prepared for us" (51). White skin refers to Elesin, whose lightening/whitening embodies the colonial process Frantz Fanon terms "epidermalization," and the *gbedu* drums, whose skins resonate prior to Elesin's possession, casting the maiming of this ritual performance as collective and transtemporal (*Black Skin* 11).

The stage directions describe Elesin's consequential loss of agency: "Elesin is now sunk fully deep in his trance, there is no longer sign of any awareness of his surroundings" (35).[5] Although his companions cry out, "Elesin dances on," the directions explain, "completely in a trance" (36).[6] Praise-Singer, in contrast, maintains awareness and poise in his possession rite. While channeling Alafin's spirit, he participates in the animation of his body. This reciprocal enforcement is denoted by the two proper names Praise-Singer uses in ritual calls: Elesin *Oba* and Elesin *Alafin*, both of which translate as horseman of the king. The latter title signifies Alafin's spirit in Praise-Singer's body calling his servant, while *Oba* signifies Praise-Singer calling his lord. Embodying the voices of the British Empire, on the other hand, Elesin, as he later confesses, experiences a sapping of the will through the "power of the stranger" (54):

> It is when the alien hand pollutes the source of will, when a stranger force of violence shatters the mind's calm resolution, this is when a man is made to commit the awful treachery of relief, commit in his thought the unspeakable blasphemy of seeing the hand of the gods in this alien rupture of his world.... My will was squelched in the spittle of an alien race, and all because I had committed this blasphemy of thought—that there might be the hand of the gods in a stranger's intervention. (56–57)

Elesin gives his will to imperial voices interpreted as gods, figuring what Soyinka laments in his prison memoir as the "disposal of African peoples into nationalities" as theologically structured (*The Man* 175). Becoming possessed by an alien hand through his own will, Elesin dances himself into estrangement from both his consciousness and his ritual participants. Praise-Singer, for instance, asks if the *gbedu* drums have "blocked the passage to [Elesin's] ears" (36). Severed from the calls of his companions—"Elesin Oba, can you hear me at all?"—the possessed Elesin transfigures from consecrated mediator to a stranger to his own death rite, thereby desecrating his intercessory role before his arrest (36). This desecration does not locate the source of the ritual's maiming within solely Elesin, but rather stages the transtemporal effects of the maiming that will soon arrive: The ritual's rupture reverberates across time, even the past, thereby maiming the ritual's enactment before the rupture takes place.

This possession challenges what is perhaps the most common assumption within *Horseman* criticism: The trauma of colonization is, within the play, a Weberian secularization of Africa under modern, European rule. This assumption unites decades of debate. Many early critics praised Soyinka's fusing of Yoruba and Greek mythic and tragic poetics to craft a "drama of existence" for modern Africa (e.g., Gibbs; Moore; Izevbaye; Gates; and Katrak); the "Ibadan-Ife" critics, on the other hand, opposed this mythopoetic technique as a glorification of a lost culture as steeped in inequality as the colonial order. Casting Soyinka as either "archetypical African writer" or nativist ideologue, both sides assumed *Horseman* to be a tragic rendering of the traumatic loss of a sacralized, Indigenous culture under the rise of the secularized, modern colony (Appiah 78). Critics such as George, Adebayo Williams, and Mpalive-Hangson Msiska have fruitfully moved *Horseman* criticism beyond this battle between myth criticism and ideology critique, but have retained the Weberian assumption. The play represents the intersection of traditional logic and scientific-secular rationalization (George 75–76, 82–83), feudalism and capitalism (Williams 73–75), or tradition and modernity (Msiska 77) as the constitutive trauma of contemporary Africa, they argue.

These interpretations are partially correct. As Simon's death wish suggests, however, for Soyinka—much like the critics of biopower with which I framed this analysis—modernity is not a triumph of the secular over the sacred, but a transition into a sacrificial and sacralized order in which life becomes subject to the sovereignty of the nation-state. When Elesin embodies this transition as both an enforced and willed possession rite, he performs Soyinka's vision of the sacred structure (both sacrificial and sacralized) of African modernity in which the colonized subject is caught, thereby staging the collective need of a regenerated animist sacrality. This regeneration of an animistic sacred structure in dialectical response to its sacrifice on behalf of the British Empire (and its continued extirpation under global capitalism in the present of the play's performance) is the political horizon of the play's form of animist tragedy.

Biodun Jeyifo gestures toward this process, yet ultimately falls short of articulating Soyinka's animist critique of the modern when he claims that *Horseman* plots René Girard's "sacrificial crisis" (124). Girard famously argues that the loss of explicit sacrificial rites has infected the modern

West with chaotic violence (51). Soyinka includes Africa in this cultural anxiety, Jeyifo claims, which, apart from defining modernity by a certain relation to sacrifice, is otherwise incorrect. Unlike Soyinka's aesthetics of sacrifice, which embraces the cosmological vibrancy of animist modes of thought, Girard's *Violence and the Sacred* is divorced from the cosmos. Girardian sacrifice is instead a purely social logic: a ritual through which a given culture represses and controls the ceaseless propensity for reciprocal violence inherent to the human condition by channeling it toward a scapegoat.

Soyinka's vision of modernity is also more regimented—indeed, ritualized—than Girard's rite-less chaos. As Adélékè Adéèkó claims, throughout *Horseman*, the Oyo Kingdom's and the British Empire's surveillance of human sacrifice "directly figures culture as law, something that has to be followed and obeyed and cannot be violated without incurring a violent reprisal": death (79). According to this logic, human sacrifice is never lost because a meaningful experience of collective life, culture, depends on it. The question then becomes not whether or not a culture still performs sacrificial rites (all do), but *who is being sacrificed and on behalf of whom?*[7] Indeed, the *nomos* of the colony is within the drama predicated on the British administration's right to "*take* life or *let* live," to use Foucault's formulation of sovereignty (136). Iyaloja mocks this *nomos* as Simon threatens to shoot anyone who may help Elesin complete his ritual. "To prevent one death you will actually make other deaths?" she asks. "Ah, great is the wisdom of the white race" (59). Such "wisdom" casts colonial modernity as, contra Girardian chaos, a tactical, calculated sacrificial regime.

As I have previously suggested, this postsecular conception of modern biopolitics partially aligns with Schmitt's *Political Theology*. Delineating the nation-state's sovereign-subject relation within Christian doctrine, Schmitt writes, "All significant concepts in the modern theory of the state are secularized theological concepts" (36). This departure from the Weberian narrative of "disenchantment" provides a useful framework through which to recognize Soyinka's critique of the modern, which entails not a loss of the sacred, as most critics believe, but its transfiguration. Yet Schmitt's framework is still lacking. As his retainment of the term *secularized* implies, for Schmitt, political theology is rhetorical, divorced from the movement of the cosmos. The sacred operates for him as what Louis Althusser terms an "ideological state apparatus"—more accurately, it is that which animates any ideological state apparatus's aura of authority.

In this way, despite Schmitt's departure from Weber, he retains his former teacher's secular assumptions. As I will demonstrate in the next section, in Soyinka's *Myth* lectures, he appropriates the word *secular* to theorize the cosmological praxis of the Yoruba world. In doing so, he offers a framework through which to read *Horseman*'s staging of sacrifice outside the secular parameters of continental theory, from Schmitt to Foucault, Agamben to Derrida—though the latter two come closest to Soyinka's project insofar as they take (monotheistic) theology seriously, apart from its sociohistoric importance. Overall, however, for such thinkers, sacrifice is a discursive formation, not a cosmological reality. For Soyinka—decidedly embracing an animist poetics and political philosophy—society, divinity, and the cosmos cannot be separated. And this animist logic means that *Horseman* is able to stage the sacrificial structure Wilderson diagnoses as Afropessimism's political impasse, while also modeling a future-oriented, affirmative response to this sacrificial structure. This affirmative response is an outworking of the more-than-human life/death symbiosis embedded in the cosmos that, as I detailed in the previous chapter, Soyinka appropriates from Yoruba cosmology.

While this argument will become clearer as my analysis unfolds, for now I wish to emphasize the point that an animist approach to Elesin's possession is, in contrast to the theoretical discourse of biopolitical theology, irreducibly social and cosmological—discursive, yet bearing layers of ontological potency. Socially, he incarnates the necropolitical theology of colonized life, to return to Mbembe's reconstruing of biopower. As Mbembe argues in "Necropolitics," modernity hinges on biopolitics as a racialized, territorialized technique, which the African subject experiences as social death. The post-Foucauldian discourse on the political capture of modern life under sovereign power (the biopolitical theology epitomized by Derrida and Agamben) largely neglects the historical fact that modern (European) life has been premised on the colonization of other (African) life as what Mbembe calls the "living dead." African life is thus sacrificed for the (European) *bios* fully hailed into the *polis*, which is sustained through the sacrificial function of what he calls "death-worlds": the habitus of slavery, colonization, and genocide. For Mbembe, then (in agreement with foundational arguments offered by Wynter, Spillers, Hartman, and others), the transatlantic slave trade reveals the "*nomos* of the modern," to appropriate Agamben's term, long before Auschwitz. Consequently, after Elesin's death rite transfigures into an unknown possession rite, when he is arrested and locked in a former holding cell for slaves, dramaturgically, he enters *Horseman*'s new locus of the numinous. He incarnates African subjectivity as a form of social death generative of the modern *polis*, the African's "inclusive exclusion" (in Agamben's term) from political life.[8]

Mbembe's utilization of biopolitical theology to analyze sovereignty's territorialized and racialized logic illuminates how the discursive formation of European sovereignty emerges within African literary forms. In the case of *Horseman*, its structure incarnates itself as a strange god animating Elesin's possession rite. With his agency disappearing, Elesin performs the sovereignty of the European nation-state over the colonized, sacrificial African subject, dancing the political-theological structure of modernity as an unknown ritual leading to a social death constitutive of colonial authority. Channeling a "stranger force of violence," Elesin gives his will to the voices of "unnamable strangers" appearing as "the hand of the gods" (56–57). Given Elesin's intercessory role, the audience witnessing this willed, theological submission in the post-independent present must ask the fundamental question of their own political stratification: *To whom am I a living sacrifice?* As I will suggest in the next section, this social submission sanctions cosmological consequences. Only a nondualist approach to nature and culture, an approach central to animism, can recognize this consequential relationship. This aspect of *Horseman*, its imbrication of discursive formations of sovereignty and the state of the cosmos itself, thus marks its formal departure from the discourse of biopolitical theology, its "move[ment] beyond a Western, secularized cultural mode" that "occludes African subjectivity" (Z. Jackson 32) and into an animist mode of tragedy. While Mbembe's necropolitical paradigm helps us recognize Elesin's maimed rite as a social text, we must filter this paradigm through the theory of animist poetics I have been proposing throughout this book to recognize the extirpation of cosmic kinship this maiming ritualizes.

Sacrificing Time

Horseman dramatizes this capture of African life as founded on a sacrifice of the Yoruba philosophy of time undergirding Soyinka's animism, as explained in the previous chapter. *Horseman*'s tragedy is not that Elesin does not kill himself (he does), not that Olunde must die (as the next Elesin he is prepared to die with the next Alafin), but that both die at the wrong time, which ruptures the Yoruba world's ontological continuum of time itself. As Iyaloja declares while Pilkings attempts to resuscitate Elesin's corpse, "He is gone at last into the passage but oh, *how late it all is*" (62; emphasis added). She scorns Elesin for his role in introducing not just this belatedness, but with it a temporal disjunction to the cosmos. This disjunction is substantiated by Olunde's suicide, which reverses the life cycle symbolized by the plantain: "Elesin Oba, tell me, you who know so well the cycle of the plantain: is it the parent shoot which withers to give sap to the younger or, does your wisdom see it running the other way?" (57). Again: "The pith is gone in the parent stem, so how will it prove with the new shoot? How will it go with that earth that bears it? Who are you to bring this abomination on us!" (55). This temporal crisis constitutes an epistemic crisis. As the horseman ritual transfigures from sacrifice to abomination, the temporal intertwinement regenerated in the fourth stage—the apex of Yoruba tragedy's communal function, according to Soyinka—degenerates. This degeneration enforces a "blind future" on the Oyo Kingdom, to use Praise-Singer's term for his people's loss of prophetic insight (62). This phrase suggests a loss of knowledge and time, becoming blind to the unfolding of history as a consequence of being severed from its ancestral, living, and unborn continuum. To summarize *Horseman*'s plot, Yoruba ritual sacrifice transfigures into substitutionary suicide detached from sacrificial mediation, twice, which functions as the sacrificial (and as I will soon demonstrate, sacralized) foundation of British colonial authority. Soyinka therefore plots two antagonistic cosmologies (European and African), Simon's desacralizing Elesin's. Dramaturgically, this process functions as a sacrificial act undergirding the colonized subject's severance from Indigenous experiences of time and thus Indigenous experiences of historical unfolding. *Horseman* thus stages the time of colonial modernity as a phenomenology of de(re)sacralization: On the one hand, Indigenous time is desacralized; on the other, this process itself is the sacrifice constituting the colonized experience of time, which paradoxically recasts desacralization as modernity's form of sacralization. The drama thus nests what Wynter calls the "theocratic and arbitrary model of divine creation" (257) undergirding the modern conception of collective humanity—European Man declaring Himself sovereign over the world—on a temporal rupture.

Soyinka describes the temporal discordance between Europe and Africa in *Myth*, beginning by explaining the normality of what he calls the "cyclic consciousness of time" in Yoruba life (2), illustrated by the Wordsworthian expression "the child is the father of man" (10) I noted in the previous chapter. In addition to explicating from this "proverb," in Soyinka's words, a non-unidirectional continuity implicating the living, the dead, and the unborn, he goes on to theorize its political-theological implications. He writes:

> And, of course, the other way around: we can insist that the world of the unborn is older than the world of the ancestor in the same breath as we declare that the deities preceded humanity into the universe. But there again we come up against the Yoruba proverb: *Bi o s'enia, imale o si* (if humanity were not, the gods would not be). Hardly a companionable idea to the Judeo-Christian theology of 'In the beginning, God *was*,' and of course its implications go beyond the mere question of sequential time. Whatever semantic evasion we employ—the godness, the beingness of god, the otherness of, or assimilate oneness with god—they remain abstractions of man-emanating concepts or experiences which presuppose the human medium. No philosophy or ontological fanaticism can wish that away, and it is formulative of Yoruba cosmogonic wisdom. It is also an affective social principle which intertwines multiple existences. . . . (10–11)

In accordance with this passage, the horseman ritual Elesin is meant to perform assumes a nonsequential, non-unidirectional time and, by extension, subjectivity that distinguishes Yoruba cosmology from the Judeo-Christian theology of God as sovereign subject and, by extension, author of sequential, teleologic time.[9] This infinitely implicated time and subjectivity rooted in the intertwinement of multiple existences—living, dead, and unborn; human and divine—implies an "affective social principle": in other words, a political theology. Thus, as the horseman ritual's desacralization, embodied by Elesin's maimed rite, degenerates its temporal structure, it also throws a vision of the social into crisis.

This principle is the "secular social vision" immanent in African cosmologies, Soyinka goes on to argue (xii). Much like Walter Benjamin's appropriation of the term "natural history" to propose a historiography undermining post-Enlightenment concepts of both nature and history, Soyinka appropriates the word *secular* in a manner that undermines post-Enlightenment concepts of both the secular and the sacred (Benjamin, *Origin*). This appropriation further challenges the Weberian assumption I have noted in *Horseman* criticism. In Africa, Soyinka claims, "the gods themselves, unlike the gods of Islam and Christianity are already prone to secularism; they cannot escape their history" (87). This statement implies that Soyinka's secularism is not so much a "suspicion of totalizing concepts," as Edward Said defines his "secular criticism," but rather a theological framework in which the sacred is implicated in, rather than sovereign over, historical time (*The World* 29). This immanence of the deities means the concept of "impurities or 'foreign' matter" in a "god's digestive system"—the cultural taboos that, according to Frazerian anthropology, define the sacred—can paradoxically be digested and thus sacralized by these gods. "Experiences," he writes, "which, until the event, lie outside the tribe's cognition are absorbed through the god's agency, are converted into yet another piece of the social armoury in its struggle for existence, and enter the lore of the tribe" (54). If the monotheistic God authors history, which leads humanity toward Him, African gods, Soyinka argues, can digest the very history that births them, allowing their followers to survive the passing of time by perennially ritualizing, and thus sacralizing, historical experience.[10]

In a call-and-response performance prior to Elesin's death rite, Praise-Singer recounts this sacralization of history Soyinka deems secular, celebrating the ritual construction of cosmological continuity despite the numerous catastrophes throughout Yoruba history. The performance uses the ancestors as a reference point:

> PRAISE-SINGER: In their time the world was never tilted from its groove, it shall not be in yours.
>
> ELESIN: The gods have said No.
>
> PRAISE-SINGER: In their time the great wars came and went, the little wars came and went; the white slavers came and went, they took away the heart of our race, they bore away the mind and muscle of our race. The city fell and was rebuilt; the city fell and our people trudged through mountain and forest to found a new home but—Elesin Oba do you hear me?
>
> ELESIN: I hear your voice Olohun-iyo
>
> PRAISE-SINGER: Our world was never wrenched from its true course.

ELESIN: The gods have said No.

PRAISE-SINGER: There is only one home to the life of a river-mussel; there is only one home to the life of a tortoise; there is only one shell to the soul of man; there is only one world to the spirit of our race. If that world leaves its course and smashes on boulders of the great void, whose world will give us shelter?

ELESIN: It did not in the time of my forebears, it shall not in mine. (6)

The Yoruba wars, the slave trade, the rebuilding of the capital city: Through these historical events, the horseman ritual has continued to mediate between the historically located Yoruba people and the cyclic time of the cosmos, Praise-Singer maintains, ensuring collective survival despite catastrophe by ritually regenerating a transhistorical Yoruba subject. However, the disruption of the call-and-response immediately prior to the celebration of this "true course" of the world—"Elesin Oba do you hear me?"—foreshadows the tragic outcome of the drama.

For Soyinka, this ritual construction of community in cyclic time is in fact intrinsic to the structure of classical tragedy. George Steiner famously argues that tragic drama's prolonged collapse, beginning in the seventeenth century, reached a point of no return with the modern "triumph of rationalism and secular metaphysics" over Europe's "organic world view" composed of "mythological, symbolic and ritual reference" (193, 292). Responding to Steiner's diagnosis, Soyinka declares in *Myth*, "The implication of this, a strange one to the African world-view, is that, to expand Steiner's own metaphor, the world in which lightning was a cornice in the cosmic architecture of man collapsed at that moment when Benjamin Franklin tapped its power with a kite. . . . For cultures which pay more than lip-service to the protean complexity of the universe of which man is himself a reflection, this European habit of world re-definition appears both wasteful and truth-defeating" (48–49). According to Soyinka, the "assimilative wisdom of African metaphysics" protects Indigenous cosmologies from the collapse of ritual frames of reference coinciding with European modernity (49). Thus, the discovery of electricity symbolized in the Franklin legend does not in Africa coincide with a disenchanted framework of teleologic discovery and progress, as the Weberian narrative would have it.[11] Rather than sequential "world re-definition," modernity enlarges the potential for ritual within cyclic time. Unlike Steiner's Europe, then, the mythic, symbolic, and ritual framework of tragedy coincides with Soyinka's Africa.

More specifically, tragedy survives African modernity, Soyinka argues, because of what he terms "the metaphysics of the irreducible" central to animism. Rather than the self-authorizing, sovereign subject of post-Enlightenment Europe (the subject of biopolitical theology's critique and the form of subjectivity Simon assumes in *Horseman*), Soyinka's theory of the African subject, as I argued in the previous chapter, is implicated within the forces of the cosmos. Consider the broader context of Soyinka's claim, quoted in the previous chapter, that the animist subject dwells within an "inter-relation with Nature":

> Where society lives in a close inter-relation with Nature, regulates its existence by natural phenomena within the observable process of continuity—ebb and tide, waxing and waning of the moon, rain and drought, planting and harvest—the highest moral order is seen as that which guarantees a parallel continuity of the species. We must try to understand this as operating with a framework which can conveniently be termed *the metaphysics of the irreducible*: knowledge of birth and death as the human cycle; the wind as a moving, felling, cleansing, destroying, winnowing force; the duality of the knife as blood-letter and creative implement; earth and sun as life-sustaining verities, and so on. These serve as matrices within which mores, personal relationships, even communal economics are formulated and reviewed. (52–53; my emphasis)

Against ipseity, Soyinka's African subject is cosmically enforced. This fundamental irreducibility is why he pairs cyclic time with what he calls "the animist interfusion of all matter and consciousness" (145). In the previous chapter, I discussed in more detail how this interfusion led to Soyinka's embrace of animist poetics as a mode of postcolonial subject formation. Here I wish to emphasize that its logic of perennial interdependence, or co-animation amid the entirety of the cosmos, raises for Soyinka a formal relation between African life and tragic form. "The profound experience of tragic drama is comprehensible within such irreducible hermeticism," he writes. "Because of the visceral intertwining of each individual with the fate of the entire community, a rupture in his normal functioning not only endangers this shared reality but threatens existence itself" (53). Africa's "metaphysics of the irreducible"—that is, the coexistence of cyclic time and animist consciousness (which endows a sacralized community with a "secular," historically implicated vision of the social)—suggests a tragic aesthetic lost in modern Europe, Soyinka argues, because of a cosmological difference.

Horseman's transitions between acts emphasize this difference. Acts shift between an Indigenous and colonial setting: a Yoruba market and a British residency. While the Yoruba scenes assume a ritual aesthetic and consist largely of verse, the British scenes shift to a representational aesthetic and consist largely of prose. Act 1, for example, introduces Elesin's death with proverbs, prophecies, incantations, and call-and-response performances, which seek to actualize the ritual in cyclic time. In act 2 the British (and Anglicized) characters simply explain the ritual in sequential time. This difference coincides with conceptions of the relation between language and the world. Praise-Singer and the market Women use language to prepare Elesin for his death, cast as his entrance to the "one river" and "great market," symbolic locations of the cyclic movement of the cosmos:

> PRAISE-SINGER: The gourd you bear is not for shirking.
> The gourd is not for setting down
> At the first crossroad or wayside grove.
> Only one river may know its contents
>
> WOMEN: We shall all meet at the great market
> We shall all meet at the great market
> He who goes early takes the best bargains
> But we shall meet, and resume our banter. (12)

Alternatively, the Pilkingses and their houseboy, Joseph, use language to describe Elesin's death and its social function. Unlike the cyclic, non-unidirectional continuity of the "great market," in which the living (present), the dead (past), and the unborn (future) meet, barter, and banter, this dialogue casts Elesin's death as a sequential event in an empty, linear narrative:

> PILKINGS: [W]hat is supposed to be going on in town tonight?
>
> JOSEPH: Tonight sir? You mean the chief who is going to kill himself?

PILKINGS: What?

JANE: What do you mean, kill himself?

PILKINGS: You mean he is going to kill somebody don't you?

JOSEPH: No master. He will not kill anybody and no one will kill him. He will simply die.

JANE: But why Joseph?

JOSEPH: It is native law and custom. The King died last month. Tonight is his burial. But before they can bury him, the Elesin must die so as to accompany him to heaven. (21–22)

With the British prose representing sequential time and Yoruba verse conjuring cyclic time, the play's stylistic shift contrasts two temporal structures coinciding with two cosmological frames of reference coinciding with two forms of political community: the British colony and the Oyo Kingdom.

As the tragedy unfolds, Elesin distills the colonization of the Oyo Kingdom in his use of language. The arrested Elesin's words molder from elevated verse—his usual mode of articulating the cosmological import of his actions—to metaphysical abstractions, as David Richards asserts (268). This stylistic shift away from what Jane calls the Yoruba people's "long-winded, roundabout way of making conversation" should be considered in relation to Martin Rohmer's observation that Soyinka pairs "words, music, and dance" together to "constitute the fundamental pattern of communication throughout the play" (Soyinka 44; Rohmer 69, 57). As the drums' silence in the final act coincides with a shift in Elesin's language, the "enormous vitality" of his marketplace dancing and singing in the opening scene is replaced by his handcuffed, dead body in the closing scene (5). The simultaneous staging of silent drums, devalued language, and a lifeless body in the final act therefore signify a larger shift in the play's frame of reference.[12] What Henry Gates, Jr., terms the play's "semantics of death" thus arises from the intertwinement of two semiotic systems: Yoruba cosmology and post-Enlightenment European modernity.

The law dramaturgically functions as the site in which this intertwinement emerges as a cosmological trauma. While Yoruba characters refer to Elesin's fate as ritual *death*, the colonial administration renders it ritual *murder* (20). The cleavage between these biological and jurisprudential referents demonstrates what Soyinka means when he claims in his author's note that the play's confrontation is "largely metaphysical" (3). As Eugene McNulty observes, *Horseman* more specifically stages the "metaphysics of Law" (2). Elesin's sacrifice assumes a law based on ontological transition in cyclic time, but before he completes his rite, he is forced before a law based on the sequential subordination of life itself under the sovereignty of the nation-state, as Derrida and Agamben would have it. As he sits chained in a former holding cell for slaves, now the Pilkingses' "disused annexe" holding broken furniture, the past, present, and future of the Oyo Kingdom mediated by Elesin's (now imprisoned) body is revealed to be captured by a legal structure that forms/enslaves its subjects through the process Derrida (following Fanon) calls the "becoming-thing of the person" (*Horseman* 47–48; *Beast* 199). What the stage directions describe as Elesin's "animal bellow" resounding from off-stage during his arrest signifies his entry into this process of dehumanization under the law—the necropolitical foundation of biopolitical modernity (49). That this bellow is heard, but not staged, emphasizes its constitutive function. That it is "animal" emphasizes the extirpation of kinship with the more-than-human world taking place in Elesin's body—who, as the "tragic actor," incarnates the state of Yoruba community in its cosmic form. As Elesin laments his loss of incantatory power, then, he incarnates an Oyo body politic being severed from his people's temporal consciousness, which is tied to his people's praxis of animism. "My powers deserted me," he cries, "My charms, my spells, even my voice lacked strength when I made to summon the powers that would lead me over the last measure of earth into the land of the fleshless" (55). By incarnating the desacralization of the horseman ritual and thus the degeneration of cyclic time and its coinciding political theology (more accurately, political cosmology), Elesin's possession, arrest, and lamentation signifies the structural sacrifice of what Soyinka terms Africa's "metaphysics of the irreducible" under the metaphysical structure of colonial law.

Severed from his consecrated mediator, Alafin's spirit is condemned to "roaming restlessly on the surface of the earth," in Iyaloja's words, while the Yoruba "world leaves its course and smashes on the boulders of the great void"—that is, the British Empire—in Praise-Singer's words (58, 6). *Void* suggests a temporality akin to what Benjamin terms the "homogenous, empty time" of modernity: a teleologic succession of distinct moments

("Theses" 261). The Yoruba characters continue to believe in the presence of ancestral spirits and ritual efficacy, implying that the drama's collective consciousness is not fully submerged within the temporality of the great void. But its Oyo Kingdom is plagued with a certain blindness, or demediated relation to the cyclic time that, according to Yoruba cosmology, is natural to the cosmos. As Praise-Singer laments to Elesin, "Your heir has taken the burden on himself. What the end will be, we are not gods to tell. But this young shoot has poured its sap into the parent stalk, and we know this is not the way of life. Our world is tumbling in the void of strangers, Elesin" (62). The play's Yoruba consciousness encounters, through its dramatization of the agonism between Indigenous time and "void" time, what Mbembe describes as African modernity's temporality of entanglement (*Postcolony* 14). Cosmologically entangled between cyclic and sequential time through a process of desacralization (which actually functions as colonial modernity's constitutive process of sacralization), Soyinka's characters embody a "social vision" (*Myth* xii) rooted in an infinitely implicated subjectivity being grafted into the sovereign-subject continuum functioning as the genesis of the modern nation-state.[13]

Conjured Communities and the Creative-Destructive Principle

Amusa, sergeant in the colonial army, comically incarnates this entanglement. He inhabits a state of interpellation arrested at the threshold between the political-theological structures of the Oyo Kingdom and the British Empire. This threshold leaves him shocked by and unable to assimilate within the logic of each community. Amusa is filled with "disbelief and horror," for example, by the Pilkingses' use of *egungun* costumes. While such costumes, like the one on this book's cover, incarnate ancestral spirits, the Pilkingses don them as "fancy-dress" to accompany their tango (18). Yet Amusa is equally frightened by threats from Yoruba schoolgirls. "Off with his knickers!" they taunt, expelling the "eater of white left-overs" from the market (31). Neither British nor Yoruba (Yoruba characters describe Amusa as a castrated son of the white man who can no longer recognize his own mother), *Horseman*'s "inarticulate, obsequious fool," as George dubs him, plays the role of the colonial mimic man (Soyinka 27–29; George, *Cultural* 74).[14] Amusa is, however, a fool of a Shakespearean mold. What

George terms his "logic of immediate transparency" both constitutes the play's humor and reveals most clearly what I have been describing throughout my analysis as the process of sacralization undergirding the play's staging of community formation (82).

George contrasts Amusa's logic with Olunde's. The latter returns to Nigeria from medical training in England on the day of Elesin's death rite, planning to bury his father before returning to England. Donning what the stage directions call a "sober Western suit," he represents a less foolish form of the Anglicized native than Amusa (40). He is also alienated from his Yoruba culture, though, unlike Amusa, at the level of epistemology. In contrast to Amusa's horror as he witnesses the Pilkingses in *egungun*, for example, Olunde asks "mildly," as the stage directions dictate, the reason Jane must "desecrate an ancestral mask" (41). While Amusa assumes the immediate transparency of ancestral spirits in the Pilkingses' tango, George claims the "secularized" Olunde (George's use of the term does not follow Soyinka's appropriative use) recognizes the significance of authorial intention. Thus, Olunde is able to confront Jane, whom he does not believe to be channeling ancestral spirits, but rather "desecrating" his culture.

Amusa, on the other hand, refusing to relay information of Elesin's impending death rite to Simon in *egungun*, nervously asks him, "How can man talk against death to person in uniform of death? Is like talking against government to person in uniform of police" (19). By associating the police uniform with *egungun*, this line, I would suggest, implies not simply Indigenous panic at a broken taboo, but a theory of reference through which Amusa interprets the symbols of both the Oyo Kingdom and the British Empire. Amusa would be equally frightened of speaking against the government to a man in a police uniform as he is speaking against death to the Pilkingses in *egungun*. For him, sacred symbols channel the presence of the signified. They ritually conjure, rather than represent, the power of that which they reference. As he explains *egungun* to Simon, "This dress get power of dead" (40).

That Amusa views the police uniform as sacred like *egungun* baffles both British and Yoruba characters. The market women, for example, mock Amusa and the Constables, but by dubbing their batons and hats phallic symbols—fetishes for the "white man's eunuch" to mediate imperial power—the women agree with Amusa more than they recognize (27). The schoolgirls snatch the batons and hats and model the fetishes as they mimic the British and by implication Amusa (29). They banter in English accents, finally calling for Amusa's service:

GIRL: . . .
—You've kept the flag flying.
—We do our best for the old country.
—It's a pleasure to serve.
—Another whisky old chap?
—You are indeed too kind.
—Not at all sir, Where is that boy? [*With a sudden bellow.*] Sergeant!

AMUSA: [*snaps to attention*] Yessir!

[*The Women collapse with laughter.*] (31)

For Amusa, the girls in police uniform, like the Pilkingses in *egungun*, channel the spirit of that to which they refer. Witnessing the girls' mimicry, he sees not acting like, but a channeling of, the colonizers. What makes Amusa laughable to both the British and Yoruba characters is not his "non-modern" belief in spirit possession, but rather his refusal to structurally differentiate the Indigenous and the modern, the sacred and the secular, animism and capitalism. For Amusa, symbols of the British Empire, such as the police uniform, as well as its language, such as the girls' imperial bellow (an inverse of Elesin's animal bellow), hold sacred, incantatory power.

Crucially, in act 4's opening stage directions, British characters reveal their community to be, as Amusa believes, ritually conjured. The setting is a masque at the residency in honor of the Prince of Wales's visit: "At last, the entrance of Royalty. The band plays 'Rule Britannia,' badly, beginning long before he is visible. The couples bow and curtsey as he passes by them. Both he and his companions are dressed in seventeenth-century European costume. . . . The Prince bows to the guests. The band strikes up a Viennese waltz and the Prince formally opens the floor. . . . The orchestra's waltz rendition is not of the highest musical standard" (37). The poor quality of the music contrasts the scene to the Yoruba characters' vibrant singing and dancing. Yet much like Simon's death wish in the deleted scene, the use of seventeenth-century costume places a stale, European "tradition" in mimetic relation with the Yoruba characters' "rituals," exposing European tradition as ritual.[15] More specifically, this scene's ritual "costume" signals the epoch of England's rise to prominence within global capitalism, an epoch of the transatlantic slave trade (Elesin's capture in a former holding cell for slaves should be interpreted in relation to this scene), and thus an epoch crucial to the discursive *nomos* of European sovereignty as critiqued by theorists of racialized biopower such as Mbembe and Wynter.

Rather than independently functioning as a ritual artifact, the seventeenth-century costume obtains its numinous function through its ritualized relation to Yoruba costume as performed within the masque. The Pilkingses, for instance, appropriate *egungun* into their dance: "The Prince is quite fascinated by their costume and they demonstrate how the *egungun* normally appears, then showing the various press-button controls they have innovated for the face flaps, the sleeves, etc. They demonstrate the dance steps and the guttural sounds made by the *egungun*, harass other dancers in the hall, Mrs Pilkings playing the 'restrainer' to Pilkings' manic darts. Everyone is highly entertained, the Royal Party especially who lead the applause" (37). Like *egungun*'s incarnation of ancestral spirits in masks, the British conjure through their masque a European past onto the African present, incanting without words (but rather poor music) that "Britannia rules the waves." The Pilkingses, meanwhile, have "innovated" *egungun* costumes with mechanical controls. As the audience becomes captivated by their tango—part anthropology, part celebration of Europe's techno-scientific imaginary—the masque becomes a parodic mise-en-scène of colonization. It dramatizes a formal proximity between Indigenous African culture and European modernity's own sacralized economy of which the Pilkingses, the guests, and the Prince remain unaware.[16]

Olunde recognizes this repression of the sacred at the core of European modernity, which Soyinka elsewhere describes as a "world of ritual repression" ("Ritual" 8). Despite Olunde's interpretation of *egungun* filtered through perceived authorial intention, his interpretation of the masque demonstrates a fundamental agreement with Amusa. Challenging Jane's assumed superiority, he contends that the British Empire is equally "feudalistic," "barbaric," and "savage," in Jane's words, as the Oyo Kingdom (43, 45). Olunde in this way concurs with Max Horkheimer and Theodor Adorno: The so-called secular world assumes its own mythos, and this "mutual implication of enlightenment and myth" renders modernity "the new barbarism" of the West (46, 32). The aristocratic "decadence" of the Prince of Wales's current "tour of colonial possessions" amid the "mass suicide" of World War II, Olunde claims, parallels the Oyo monarchy and the sacrifice his father must undergo, blurring the Pilkingses' distinction between death and murder and leaving them with no "right to pass judgement on other peoples" (43, 44).

Like the fool to which he is juxtaposed, then, Olunde rejects the Pilkingses' differentiation between the Indigenous and the modern, arguing that the colony is, like the Oyo Kingdom, conjured through sacred rituals mistakingly taken to be, in Jane's words, "the preservation of sanity in the midst of chaos" (43). As Iyaloja approaches the arrested Elesin, Simon proves both Olunde and Amusa correct by imagining a border between the two neither can cross, inscribing colonial law on the earth itself (55). When Iyaloja crosses this border, transgressing Simon's spoken law, whistles blow and guards leap forward to confine her (57). She berates Elesin for this new world in which the district officer's voice (not Alafin's) can speak a law into existence, redefining her agential movement as sacrilege (58). That Simon wears a police uniform in this scene reinforces Amusa's association between it and *egungun* and, more expansively, the Oyo Kingdom and British Empire's interrelated structures of the sacred (50).

At the height of the Pilkingses' *egungun* performance, moreover, a prophetic interruption casts Indigenous desacralization as, through the cosmological entanglement of the two communities staged, a form of ritual sacrifice. The Resident interrupts the dance with news that Elesin's death rite is impending. With the Prince of Wales visiting, what the stage directions call Pilkings's "far-flung but key imperial frontier" must appear a "secure colony of His majesty" (37, 39). As news of Elesin's impending death halts the Pilkingses' *egungun* performance, Simon decides, because of the British ritual of the royal visit, to halt the Yoruba ritual. This scene intertwines the two halted rituals tied to the cosmological differentiation enforcing the play's tragic plot. The Pilkingses' dance prophesizes, through its interruption, the interruption of Elesin's death rite and thus the loss of the temporal continuum through which the *egungun* the Pilkingses appropriate incarnates for the Yoruba ancestral life. Despite the Pilkingses' authorial intention in performing an *egungun* ritual, then, their dance incarnates not ancestral spirits, as Amusa believes, but ancestral trauma: the desacralization of the horseman ritual on which the temporality of ancestral mediation depends. Furthermore, unbeknownst to the Pilkingses, Elesin performs his death rite during the masque, which means the death rite transfigures into a possession rite as the Pilkingses tango. It is thus impossible to say which maimed rite conjures the other's maiming. Rather, the Pilkingses and Elesin together prophetically dance the theological structure of biopolitical modernity's African advent. And their synchronized performance places Elesin in the position of the sacrificial surrogate (i.e., the necropolitical, African subject barred from political life) for the Pilkingses' "secure colony." By prophesying the transfiguration of the horseman's sacrifice into suicide (and thus a sacrifice on behalf of the colony), the Pilkingses' and Elesin's transsubjective dance casts Indigenous desacralization as the drama's form of ritual sacrifice, revealing the Pilkingses as the drama's pillager-kings.[17]

This performance reveals the culmination of my theoretical approach to *Horseman*. Thus far, I have built on the previous chapter's explanation of Soyinka's appropriation of Yoruba cosmology to trace his crafting of a dramaturgy of animist tragedy. And I have used this experiment in animist poetics via Yoruba tragic drama to nuance the intersecting discourses of European biopolitical theology and Black biopolitical critique. Soyinka's theory and practice of animist tragedy is a critical response to the same discursive formation of sovereignty critiqued by these discourses. Soyinka's appropriation of Yoruba cosmology, however, allows his dramaturgy to operate beyond the post-Enlightenment secular rationality conditioning European theory's prominent critiques of biopower, a break from Eurocentrism that many theorists in Black biopolitical critique have articulated as necessary for conceptualizing "the world of the humanity to come" (Sithole 61). By using the interpretive framework produced by this meta-critical dialogue to approach *Horseman*, and by building on the theoretical terms I have defined in this book's previous chapters, I have explicated from the play a theory of colonial trauma as cosmological rupture incarnated by Elesin's maimed rite as an ancestral trauma the Yoruba world must inherit. This trauma, I have argued, coincides with the play's dramatization of an epochal transition from an Indigenous to a European political theology of sacrifice, both of which are tied to sacralized cosmologies assuming competing temporalities: cyclic and sequential time. In making these claims, I have posed a postsecular critique of the modern as hinging on a racialized, territorialized process of sacrifice, but the affordances of Soyinka's use of animist tragedy are more powerful than this critique.

I now conclude my analysis by more explicitly moving beyond the representational aesthetic assumed within *Horseman* criticism and the theoretical discourses with which I have placed Soyinka in dialogue, arguing that *Horseman*'s ritual aesthetic carries a radical political vision for a postcolonial future. This vision, I will now suggest, overturns the pessimism Wilderson emblematizes, demonstrating the theoretical stakes of my placement of animism and biopolitical theology in dialogue. By dramatizing a Yoruba death rite transfigured into an imperial possession rite as what he theorizes in *Myth* as Yoruba tragedy, Soyinka crafts this transfiguration into a new ritual. As ritual, the play generates within the transition dramatized a vision of collective life emerging through the social death reenacted. This modernist act of hubristically inventing cultural survival by performing its extirpation is the affirmative function of animist tragedy. As a distinctly animist tragedy, *Horseman* is not a representation of sequential events implying a moral lesson gathered from the failure of a high-ranking individual, as many critics assume (e.g., Booth; Ogundele; and Losambe), but a performance in which the actors and audience witness themselves universally addressed by the failures staged.[18] During Elesin's maimed rite, a vision of new life addresses the audience as the cosmological severance witnessed is aesthetically mediated as tragedy. This ritual mediation and the communal bonds formed through its regenerative process distill what I take to be the politics of animist tragedy as an aesthetic form.

During his possession, Elesin is unable to recognize the consecrated moment of his death. "I cannot tell where is that gateway through which I must pass," he confesses as he searches the sky, attempting to interpret the position of the moon (33). The *gbedu* drums are meant to relay to him the consecrated moment as signified by the placement of the moon. By attempting unsuccessfully to interpret the moon himself, Elesin performs the collapse of the *Osugbo* hermeneutic process central to the horseman ritual. The audience becomes addressed by this collapse through Elesin's dramaturgical role as interpretive mediator during the ritual. The moon is visible to Elesin, but not the audience, yet its significance is hidden from both; the *Osugbo* is hidden from everyone, yet their presence resonates across the stage through the sound of their *gbedu* drums. Elesin can only comprehend the visible (moon) by listening to the invisible (drums), while the audience can only comprehend the invisible (moon) by watching the visible (Elesin) interpret the invisible (drums). This dramaturgical structure stages inheritance as communal interpretation. Elesin must pass on, through his voice, a sacred vision he can only witness by hearing himself called within the drumbeat, and the audience must make sense of this calling. But through his inability to interpret the drums, the moon, and therefore his position within the rhythm of the cosmos, Elesin passes on the collapse of the horseman ritual and, furthermore, its cosmological frame of reference. The audience is thus tasked with the problem of inheriting the ancestral trauma conditioning colonial modernity.

Performing the maimed inheritance of that which he is condemned to incarnate—the Oyo *polis* becoming a "colonial possession," in Olunde's words—Elesin passes to the audience the sacrifice of his own Indigenous meaning, thereby mediating, through the hermeneutic conundrum he performs, the loss of sacrificial mediation dramatized throughout the play. As Elesin later tells the Pilkingses, "[T]he honour of my people you have taken already; it is tied together with those papers of treachery which make you masters in this land" (55). Since the Oyo Kingdom is legally conscripted into the British Empire through these papers before the play begins, Elesin embodies that which is most intimate to his companions precisely when he becomes ritually estranged from them. Elesin and Olunde thus become "enabling agents" for the Yoruba world's transition into modernity, in Lokangaka Losambe's words, but not due to their rejection of their people's "unproductive cultural essentialism," as he argues (21, 28). Rather, their failed sacrifices become productive through the mediatory function of their dramatic reenactment (that is, through their paradoxical function as generative sacrifice). Giving aesthetic form to the psychic, political, ecological, and, for Soyinka, spiritual death constitutive of the modern African nation-state, *Horseman* regenerates mediation by ritualizing its deactivation. Through its scripted performance, the plot ultimately subjects the advent of European sequential time it represents to the cyclic time of Yoruba ritual it mourns, a process Soyinka terms the play's "threnodic essence" (3). Ritual sacrifice transfigures into substitutionary suicide detached from sacred mediation, twice (through Elesin's death, then Olunde's), which paradoxically ritualizes the loss of ritual. By staging this sacrifice of sacrifice as animist tragedy, thereby charging Elesin and Olunde with the task of mediating the cosmic community intrinsic to the Yoruba worldview, the aesthetic process itself becomes a sacrifice meant to regenerate a kinship between the colonized subject and cosmic totality the play dramatizes as extirpated.

Soyinka conceptualizes this regenerative process as an outworking of "the creative-destructive principle" (28) I described in the previous chapter, his Yoruba instantiation of the regenerative death drive undergirding African literature's animist poetics as broader aesthetic logic. Consider his justification of tragedy through this principle:

> [T]here is knowledge from within the corpus of Ifa oracular wisdoms that a rupture is often simply one aspect of the destructive-creative unity, that offences even against nature may be part of the exaction by deeper nature from humanity of acts which alone can open up the deeper springs of man and bring about a constant rejuvenation of the human spirit.

Nature in turn benefits by such broken taboos, just as the cosmos does by demands made upon its will by man's cosmic affronts. Such acts of hubris compel the cosmos to delve deeper into its essence to meet the human challenge. . . . Tragic fate is the repetitive cycle of the taboo in nature, the karmic act of hubris witting or unwitting, into which the demonic will within man constantly compels him. (156)

In sum, cosmological rupture is generative and its tragic occurrence in human hands natural, that which through the creative-destructive principle mutually compels human history and the cosmos. This animist approach to tragedy is, from an Aristotelian view, comic: This form affirms that the human spirit and the cosmos are rejuvenated precisely when their interfusion is ruptured. Thus, when Elesin's and Olunde's suicides are performed and witnessed as tragedy, they shift, through literary performance, from a representation of the colonial sacralization of Indigenous desacralization to the postcolonial sacralization of desacralization itself. As animist tragedy, *Horseman* de(re)sacralizes the Yoruba world otherwise than colonially, thereby passing on, through the audience's inheritance of the ancestral trauma dramatized, communal bonds regenerated through the death of Indigenous community.

Through this process, Soyinka conceptualizes Yoruba tragedy as the form most paradigmatic of the creative-destructive principle, and thus a form through which the politics of postcolonial African aesthetics in general can be articulated. Taking the Yoruba sculptor as symbolic of the modern African writer, he claims, "When gods die—that is, fall to pieces—the carver is summoned and a new god comes to life. The old is discarded, left to rot in the bush and be eaten by termites. The new is invested with the powers of the old and may acquire new powers. In literature the writer aids the process of desuetude by acting as a termite or by ignoring the old deity and creating new ones" (86). Like Friedrich Nietzsche, Soyinka takes the death of a god to be an affirmative, ritual process.[19] The task of the postcolonial African writer, he claims, is to strategically utilize theological desuetude. That is, the writer must become the termite to what Soyinka calls in his prison memoir the European nation-state's "divine authority" in order to craft a postcolonial future out of the rotting colonial history animating African modernity.

Animist tragedy offers precisely this radical, cosmo-dialectic vision of the aesthetic: what I have been describing throughout this book as the work of animist poetics. As Soyinka dramatizes the death of a sacred way of life under colonization, he transforms this death into a generative rupture. Rather than resurrecting a lost sense of Indigenous community, *Horseman*, according to this logic, stages the possibility of a new community rooted in the simultaneous rescripting of Yoruba cosmology within colonized modernity and (perhaps more importantly) vice versa. As Iyaloja stands before Olunde's and Elesin's corpses—symbolic of the breathless body politic of the Oyo Kingdom—she declares in the final, choric line of the play, "Now forget the dead, forget even the living. Turn your mind only to the unborn" (63). Her direct reference is Elesin's unborn heir, conceived immediately before the transfiguration of his death rite. This "seed," Iyaloja asserts, carries the promise of a coming *polis* birthed through its father's unconsecrated death. By imagining the racialized, territorialized sacrifice constitutive of biopolitical modernity as leaving behind a seed, *Horseman* points the colonized subject toward an "affirmative biopolitics of community" to come (Lemm 10). That is, the play does more than critique the modern by representing a pessimistic or utopian vision of its *polis*. Soyinka ventures beyond the representational framework truncating so much of literary and cultural criticism, emblematizing an animist path for literature and criticism anchored in an affirmative approach to the aesthetic open to its ritual and cosmological resonance.

This openness returns us to the limits of Wilderson's style of Afropessimist critique. My analysis of *Horseman* in this chapter does not undermine his point that the sacrifice of Black subjectivity functions as that which enables the modern conceptualization of human life. This point is precisely what makes the play a tragedy. However, Soyinka models for Black biopolitical critique an animist response to this impasse that remains invisible to Wilderson due to the latter's retention of the logic of post-Enlightenment European humanism. Wilderson's designation of anti-Black violence as a "prelogical phenomenon" (92), for example, assumes (much like colonial anthropology) that Indigenous logic does not exist, that the only solution must take teleological form (hence his non-solution: all must die). In a certain sense, *Horseman* agrees: Indigenous logic is irrevocably ruptured by colonial modernity. Yet—and this yet, the affirmative dialectic of animist tragedy, is the crux of my argument—the "end of the world" that Wilderson claims to be the only solution to the racial politics of sovereignty is recast by animist tragedy as the very means of Indigenous regeneration: death is the ritual passage into a coming "planetary humanism," in Wynter's terms. Let me be clear: I am not proposing a supernatural alternative to a biopolitical impasse—magical thinking to combat racism. On the contrary, the life-death symbiosis intrinsic to *Horseman*'s ritualization of Indigenous temporality is not supernatural, but instead intrinsic to the material world: Death always generates life. This post-anthropocentric naturalism is why Soyinka is resolute in claiming that the process I have been describing throughout this book as the regenerative death drive is part of African animism's "secular social vision" (xii). From an animist perspective, Wilderson's mistake is his supernatural inoculation of the human from the rest of nature—a repetition of Freud's humanist, unnatural inoculation of the internal psyche from the external world critiqued extensively in chapters 1 and 3. By contrasting Wildersonian pessimism to the "secular social vision" intrinsic to *Horseman*'s animism, we can recognize Wilderson's response to modernity's biopolitical conundrum as a discursive outworking of this conundrum's post-Enlightenment rationality.

The form of animist tragedy I have theorized in this chapter challenges such supernatural pessimism with an affirmative logic immanent in nature, a logic from which we subjects of biopolitical modernity have been severed, and thus a logic requiring a posthumanist and postsecular paradigm shift to appreciate. This form operates in variegated modes across postcolonial culture requiring further study: for example, Chinua Achebe's *Things Fall Apart*, Haile Gerima's *Sankofa*, or Arundhati Roy's *The God of Small Things*. As tragedy, this form points its audience "not to politics as a question of representation but to that political possibility that emerges when the limits to representation and representability are exposed" (Butler, *Antigone* 2). And as animist tragedy more specifically, this form stages a "paradigm for the coming politics" rooted in the regenerative death drive, which allows, through its ritual (rather than purely representative) aesthetic, the nonlinear time of animism to swallow the history of colonization that extirpated it (Agamben, *Coming* 93). Animist tragedy dramatizes the ancestral trauma of colonization as a biopolitical impasse, but—more radically than diagnostic critique—by ritualizing its dramatization of animism's extirpation, this form enables a postcolonial model of kinship-as-survival. Animist tragedy fuses the aesthetic and the sacred, pointing an audience sacrificially severed from sacrificial mediation toward a future birthed on the altar of such a process. As the silent body of Elesin's pregnant bride signifies in *Horseman*'s final scene, much like the rest of the natural world, new life is arising through this death; the seed of the animist polity is here.

Chapter 5

Multidimensional Memory

Environmental Wounds and the Architecture of Animism in Yvonne Vera's *The Stone Virgins*

In the previous two chapters I analyzed the aesthetic logics of the animist lyric and animist tragedy. The animist lyric incants a form of cosmic personhood in response to its extirpation under colonial modernity, I argued, while animist tragedy stages the communal bonds emerging through the ritualization of this extirpation-incantation dialectic. Operating on the ritual side of the realism-ritual spectrum I proposed in chapter 2, these forms are marked by their ritual activation of the regenerative death drive—a process, as I have been arguing, undergirding animist poetics' multifaceted attempts to mend the ancestral trauma conditioning its historical emergence. As I argued in the introduction and chapter 1, if ancestral trauma is the cultural inheritance of colonial modernity's wreckage of the perceived kinship between the living and the dead as well as the human and more-than-human world, then our inherited paradigms of interpreting cultural memory cannot adequately apply to animist modes of memorialization. This problem is the starting point of my argument in this chapter.

As my analyses of the animist lyric and animist tragedy both demonstrated, the politics of their regenerative processes hinge on a dialectical departure from the discursive logic of sovereignty. I have analyzed these departures at the level of the psyche: The animist rejects the self-presencing sovereign subject of Cartesian dualism for a form of cosmic personhood. I have analyzed them at the level of the *polis*: The animist combats political sovereignty's claims on the subject by ritualizing its enforced sacrifice into the foundation of a community otherwise. In this chapter, I use this post-sovereign logic to reframe the question of cultural memory from an animist standpoint. Animist poetics, as I have demonstrated throughout this book, is a dialectical response to the discursive formation of European sovereignty—in particular the historical processes through which this discursive formation wrecked Indigenous modes of conceptualizing the subject's consanguinity with the cosmos. It follows that a cultural memory studies informed by animism must articulate an explicitly post-sovereign theory of memory, a theory tracing how animist poetics aims the process of memorialization at the regeneration of subjectivity extirpated by European imperial expansion's violent enactments of a perceived sovereignty.

In this chapter I propose a theory of multidimensional memory: an animist practice of memorialization dialectically aimed at combating the architectural dimensions framing colonized subjectivity, dimensions that are intrinsically ecological. Colonial modernity is founded on material damage with spiritual consequences: The material wreckage to Indigenous ecosystems and economies is what produces the ancestral trauma to which animist poetics responds. Thus, the extirpation of Indigenous memory frameworks is an outworking of the enforcement of European dimensions on the environmental-political habitus of the colonized subject. Since animist poetics' primary work is the reinvention of Indigenous cosmologies as strategic responses to their erasure, the form of memorialization intrinsic to animist poetics is a process of regenerating Indigenous dimensions through which the colonized subject can remember their animist kinship with their environment. Since this kinship was extirpated by the linearly demarcated architecture of colonial subject formation—mirrored in the psyche by Cartesian borders between internal and external that, as I detail in chapter 1, Frantz Fanon critiques in Freud—multidimensional memory dialectically responds to the linear architecture of the colonized subject's habitus. An animist form of cultural memorialization is not satisfied with remembering a particular event in the past. Rather, its goal is to open new dimensions through which a postcolonial subject can emerge precisely by remembering the lost architecture of their own animism.

Zimbabwean novelist, scholar, and public intellectual Yvonne Vera is a paradigmatic figure of this animist approach to cultural memory. In this chapter I therefore analyze her practice of multidimensional memory in her scholarly and literary writings. In particular, I trace how her doctoral dissertation, "The Prison of Colonial Space: Narratives of Resistance" (1995), and public writing on Zimbabwean culture shape her narration of Zimbabwean cultural memory in her final novel, *The Stone Virgins* (2002). More specifically, upon explaining Vera's political-philosophical project in "The Prison of Colonial Space" and situating this project within the theoretical paradigm of animist poetics I have been constructing throughout this book, I trace how the *The Stone Virgins*' frame narrative and protagonist constellation (the interrelated character arcs of the four protagonists) together formalize her theory of colonization's environmental wounding as well as her belief in the possibility of postcolonial resistance through animist practices of cultural memory.[1]

In her dissertation, Vera argues that colonialism fundamentally ruptured and reshaped African subjectivity by inaugurating a spatial architecture based on linear demarcation and violently inscribing this architecture on the earth itself. This eco-architecture is embodied most explicitly, she argues, in the colonial prison.[2] But it also constitutes the underlying structure of the colony more broadly and, consequently, the colonized subject. Drawing on Frantz Fanon's conception of "literature of combat" (*Wretched* 193), she concludes her argument by claiming that African literature should open spatial dimensions obliterated by colonialism's spatial ideology by dialectically resisting its paradigm of linear demarcation. The more-than-human political horizon of such an opening (after all, colonial demarcation is inscribed on the earth itself) is the formation of new subjectivities no longer created in the image of the colonial prison, but instead in the image of a subject-environment co-animacy lost in the wake of colonial history.

As I demonstrate in this chapter, this political horizon—the construction of new dimensions for a postcolonial, more-than-human subject—is the impetus behind Vera's novels of cultural memory. Throughout her fiction, I argue, she narrates Zimbabwean cultural memory as a strategy of combat against what she takes to be the spatial ideology of colonialism functioning as the eco-architecture of contemporary African subjectivity. And this combat strategy hinges on Vera's filtering of Wole Soyinka's animist poetics through Fanonian dialectical materialism. Her practice of multidimensional memory thus approaches cultural memorialization as an act of postcolonial animism through which the colonized subject resists colonialism's demarcations of subjectivity and remaps more expansive forms of collective life.

This practice of multidimensional memory offers a posthumanist and postsecular intervention in cultural memory studies. In using the term *multidimensional*, I allude to what has become an ur-text for literary criticism's approaches to cultural memory in postcolonial contexts: Michael Rothberg's *Multidirectional Memory: Remembering the Holocaust in the Age of Decolonization* (2009).[3] Rothberg's blending of Holocaust studies and postcolonial studies is indeed useful for approaching a novel such as *The Stone Virgins*. Like Rothberg, Vera utilizes cross-cultural aesthetic engagement (finding inspiration in Anglophone modernism and cinema, for example)[4] to depict life during a genocide that to this day remains under-examined: the *Gukurahundi* massacres in Matabeleland, Zimbabwe (1982–87).[5] Similarly, like Rothberg Vera challenges the liberal identity politics undergirding so much of today's public debates on cultural memories of trauma. For Rothberg, criticism must challenge our public sphere's current framework of "competitive memory," which pins collective identities against one another in an endless battle for cultural recognition. Against this identitarian approach, his vision of multidirectional memory casts all acts of post-traumatic memorialization as potentially generative of a multiplicity of collective identities. Since cultural memory, he suggests, moves in multiple directions—back-and-forth between various subjects and cultures—no collective identity owns it; rather, all collective identities are founded upon its constant movement. As I will demonstrate, *The Stone Virgins*' frame narrative and protagonist constellation together offer a similar challenge to "competitive memory" by casting all identitarian boundaries as too porous to foster any sustained attachment.[6] Considering the ethnic cleansing surrounding the novel's setting makes this "multidirectional" approach to cultural memory all the more poignant.[7]

To recognize the political work toward which Vera aims her writing, however, Rothberg's paradigm must be expanded beyond its fundamentally secular, humanist scope. This scope, representative of cultural memory studies at large, misses what is at stake in Vera's scholarship on the genealogy of the colonial prison and consequently the political bent of her literary writing. For her, the spatial architecture exemplified by the colonial prison ruptured the coherence of Indigenous African modes of being-in-the-world. In other words, what I have been describing throughout this book as ancestral trauma—the severance, operating at the core of colonial modernity, from a co-animacy with the more-than-human world intrinsic to so many Indigenous African cosmologies—is both revealed and enforced through the European introduction of the prison in colonial Africa. By interpreting Vera's literary writing as a response to this political problem she examines in her scholarly writing, I demonstrate in this chapter the manner in which her fiction challenges Rothberg's theoretical framework. How does one remember the loss of collective co-animacy—in Vera's schema, the African world before the advent of the colonial prison? Can this memory be recovered via "multidirectional" debate in the public sphere, à la Rothberg's paradigm? For Vera, the answer is no; the public sphere itself has been so reshaped by colonization that, as the title of her dissertation suggests, colonized space is itself a prison. Consequently, if for Rothberg the writing of postcolonial memory should be aimed at the ongoing construction of cosmopolitan identities, for Vera it should be aimed at the creative reconstruction of a co-animacy with the world whose damage via colonial trauma has erased the very possibility of Rothberg's desired cosmopolitanism.

To be sure, I am not arguing against Rothberg's project, but rather suggesting that Vera's writing demonstrates the ways in which cultural memories of trauma in postcolonial literature often require an expansion of what is meant by multidirectionality. Just as I have suggested in previous chapters that Caruthian trauma theory's vision of implicated subjectivity must be expanded to include the more-than-human world, so too I argue here that literary criticism's working theories of post-traumatic cultural memory, Rothberg's included, must be expanded beyond their fundamentally secular, anthropocentric axis. If, as Caruth writes, "history is precisely the way we are implicated in each other's traumas" (*Unclaimed* 24), Vera's writing (much like Soyinka's) requires a rethinking of who is included in this "we" (e.g., the human and more-than-human, the living, the dead, and the unborn). Similarly, Rothberg's vision of cross-cultural memorialization is not ill-suited for interpreting Vera's writing; as I argue, however, *The Stone Virgins*' incorporation of the human and more-than-human as well as the living and dead into its production of cultural memory necessarily expands Rothberg's framework to include posthumanist, postsecular dimensions.

Throughout Vera's oeuvre, she continuously experiments with animist poetics. Her first novel, *Nehanda* (1993), for example, narrates the life of a historical spirit medium who was executed in 1898 for inspiring a failed insurrection against the British South Africa Company. But after *Nehanda*, Vera's animism is often less explicit than Soyinka's; nevertheless, as I demonstrate in this chapter, Soyinka is a direct influence on her utilization of "poetic fiction" to create a "new spiritual and psychological cartography" (Muponde and Taruvinga xi–xii). Unlike the ethnophilosophical particularities upon which Soyinka's appropriation of animism insists, however, Vera's animist poetics largely sidesteps the question of cosmology's ethnic context, not out of ignorance, but out of aesthetic strategy. She draws on Soyinka's creative-destructive principle to formulate her mythopoetic approach to historical writing, but she departs from his focus on theology proper, developing instead a mode of literary animism independent of any systematic theology. Whereas Soyinka systematizes distinct Yoruba principles and then universalizes them into a postcolonial hermeneutic, Vera crafts an animist poetics in which cosmology is divorced from ethnicity from the beginning.[8] If colonial spatial ideology has transfigured Indigenous cosmologies throughout Africa, as she argues in her dissertation, the task of the postcolonial African writer is not to re-craft the cosmology of their heritage, but rather to invest colonized space with what she terms a "new mythology" ("The Prison" 12). Her animist poetics thus appears as a spiritual form of dialectical materialism (Soyinka filtered through Fanon, as I will demonstrate)[9]. Explicating a theory of post-traumatic cultural memory from Vera's writing, then, necessitates approaching the problem of cultural memory from an animist vantage point partially akin to what I have mapped out through Soyinka's writing in the previous two chapters, yet more focused on spatial form than cosmological principles. Since she believes spatial forms assume their own cosmologies, and that the eco-architecture exemplified by the colonial prison operates to reshape the colonized land and thus Indigenous conceptualizations of the subject and the cosmos, Vera is more interested in systematizing a resolutely combative, postcolonial exegesis of colonial spatiality (thereby opening new cosmological potentials for the inherited space of the postcolony) than systematizing cosmological principles from her Shona heritage.

Approached from such a vantage point, I further argue in this chapter, it becomes clear that Rothberg's spatial conception of directional movement falls short of recognizing the politics of Vera's writing. For Rothberg, although cultural memory is discursive and always moving between subjects and cultures in a manner that challenges identitarian claims to its ownership, it is nonetheless negotiated in a linear line, back-and-forth. As will become clear as I analyze Vera's genealogy of the colonial prison, one consequence of her theory of colonialism's spatial ideology is that conceptualizing memory as moving in a linear motion—a straight line between the present and the past, or between disparate subjects standing in various directions—reproduces the spatial ideology of colonialism (even if a specific act of memorialization sheds light on histories repressed by colonial and neocolonial political orders). Thinking memory as movement between a linearly demarcated present and past based on the actions of similarly demarcated subjects in the present (an approach often assumed natural within cultural memory studies) presupposes that memory as such coincides with what Vera takes to be the architecture of colonial modernity. Ignoring a priori the ways in which Indigenous memory systems include dimensions of the living, the dead, and the unborn as well as the human and more-than-human in the process of memorialization, this approach not only fails to account for cultural memory's various forms in the colonized world, but also actively reproduces the spatial ideology that, according to Vera, colonized such forms.

What I am calling Vera's paradigmatic practice of multi*dimensional* memory, on the other hand, strategically sediments not only collective memory, but also competing ideological architectures of memory: the social, ecological, and even cosmological dimensions, always for Vera anchored to spatial forms, shaping how historically conditioned subjects remember. And it does so with the purpose of forming, in dialectical response to colonial spatiality, a new subject. Here, I am extending and redefining what Ranka Primorac terms Vera's "space-time of memory": the fundamental chronotrope of her oeuvre. As Primorac explains, in all of Vera's fiction "memory represents non-physical movement into the past, against the flow of chronological time. . . . [S]uch movement is not conceptualized as going back, but as an act of *advancing* into another *dimension*, only describable in terms of space. In all of Vera's novels, such movement is somehow linked to physical trauma" ("Crossing" 87, my emphasis). As Primorac intuits, the tendency of Vera's characters to enter elevated dimensions through "non-physical," temporal movement that is nonetheless only describable in spatial terms is the primary trope through which Vera depicts trauma (embodied by individual characters, yet always linked to the cultural traumas of Zimbabwean history). What Primorac (along with most Vera criticism) misses, however, is that this chronotrope is an outworking of Vera's animist approach to combating colonial spatial ideology, which Vera takes to be the underlying logic of colonial trauma. One way of categorizing Vera's practice of multidimensional memory is, then, as a revision of Primorac's insight on Vera's poetics of post-traumatic memory, which implies a revision of Rothberg's theory of cultural memory, each revision hinging on a recognition of Vera's animist poetics as a strategic response to her theory of colonial spatial ideology. Not content with shedding light on the repressed traumas of history, Vera's multidimensional memory combats what she takes to be the underlying trauma shaping the colonized African subject by investing the spatial form fostering this subject (the colony's rectilinear architecture epitomized by the prison) with a mythopoetics operating to remap new dimensions for a postcolonial subject.

My polemic springboard for what follows is therefore that Rothberg's theory of multidirectional memory assumes a post-Enlightenment liberal subject whose ongoing process of cross-cultural identity formation is both the horizon of Rothberg's politics and the pre-given form determining his practice of literary and cultural criticism. This problem is not Rothberg's alone, but is rather a consequence of the fundamentally secular, anthropocentric rationality overseeing cultural memory studies. Intrinsic to Vera's writing is, I argue, a mode of theorizing post-traumatic cultural memory beyond this framework's limits. The stakes of this theoretical juxtaposition become clear when considering the question of how to respond to the aftereffects of the ancestral trauma I have theorized in this book, which Vera takes seriously and Rothberg's framework does not—or rather cannot. If colonial modernity is founded on the extirpation of the cosmologies undergirding Indigenous memory systems, then Rothberg's framework for reading and writing cultural memory in postcolonial contexts is severely limited. In fact, it is unable to produce the "multidirectionality" he seeks. By championing a cosmopolitan process of cross-cultural memory while sidestepping the question of what cosmological forms undergird given memory systems, Rothberg's attempt to place Holocaust studies and postcolonial studies in dialogue becomes, against his intention, a utilization of Holocaust studies' post-Enlightenment European epistemology to interpret cultural memory in postcolonial contexts. In sum, while Vera's writing demonstrates the cross-cultural fertilization of cultural memory upheld by Rothberg's schema (Vera, much like Soyinka, draws on European as well as African forms throughout all of her writing), I argue in this chapter that her fiction's process of memorialization hinges upon a theory of ancestral trauma (as demonstrated in her genealogy of colonial imprisonment) and a practice, in response to this trauma, of animist poetics (demonstrated in her fiction's reanimation of spiritual dimensions eclipsed by colonial modernity), both of which operate beyond the secular, anthropocentric dimension of cultural memory studies' coordinates.

Contextualizing Vera's Approach to Narrating Cultural Memory

Vera defines the goal of all her writing as the "transformation of consciousness" ("Shaping" 76). This transformative goal lies behind *The Stone*

Virgins' narrative depiction of the *Gukurahundi*. To provide some context, it is estimated that this genocide left somewhere between 10,000 and 30,000 people dead. A numeric count remains impossible because of the ways victims were disappeared—for example, buried in mass graves or dropped in abandoned mine shafts (Alexander et al.; Catholic Commission; Ranger, *Voices*). When Vera, two decades later, chose this genocide as the setting to her final novel, she placed herself in undeniable risk because the *Gukurahundi* existed outside of Zimbabwe's strategically curated national memory. Robert Mugabe's government actively suppressed cultural memory of the *Gukurahundi* through what Terence Ranger, historian and close friend of Vera, terms the widespread movement of "patriotic history" throughout the 1980s and 1990s.[10] Functioning as an ideological state apparatus in the newly independent Zimbabwe's media, education, and the public sphere at large, patriotic history is "different from and more narrow than the old nationalist historiography," Ranger writes, "which celebrated aspiration and modernization as well as resistance. It resents the 'disloyal' questions raised by historians of nationalism. It regards as irrelevant any history which is not political. And it is explicitly antagonistic to academic historiography" ("Nationalist" 220). What Ranger diagnoses is one strategy through which the Mugabe regime curated a cultural memory aimed at forgetting the massacres the newly formed Zimbabwean state sanctioned upon its transition from Rhodesian white minority rule into ZANU-PF's single-party rule. When the Catholic Commission for Justice and Peace in Zimbabwe released their official report on the *Gukurahundi*, for example, Mugabe publicly responded by warning, "If we dig up history, then we wreck the nation" (qtd. in Alexander et al., 258). His response not only suppresses cultural memory of the genocide, but grants the victims' absence from history a constitutional status: Their erasure, he declares, sustains the nation.

By simply depicting the *Gukurahundi*, then, *The Stone Virgins* threatened Zimbabwe's concurrent cultural memory by challenging "patriotic history" with what Mugabe describes as "digging up" history. As Vera writes in a letter to her ex-husband in Canada four months before *The Stone Virgins*' release, "I am not sure what the response to *The Stone Virgins* will be in April, government wise as it involves the government violence of the 80's, but I am making plans with people in Stockholm to get asylum there should that be necessary, and in Germany. I have a few friends on alert. Zimbabwe is unpredictable in terms of its politics" ("Letter to John Jose"). As director of the National Gallery of Zimbabwe in her hometown of Bulawayo from 1997 to 2003, Vera was no stranger to the politics surrounding the construction of cultural memory under a dictatorship. In the end, though, Vera's novel was not censored, and she was not harassed by the government. Surely, one reason is that *The Stone Virgins* narrates life in Matabeleland during the genocide while bypassing important names and explicit historical markers (Mugabe and the *Gukurahundi*, for instance, are never mentioned). More importantly, the most horrific act in the novel—the rape of two sisters followed by one's murder and the other's mutilation—is committed not by a member of Mugabe's Fifth Brigade, but by a "dissident" (see note 5). These aspects of the novel warrant for some critics the objection that Vera is complicit in the state's official forgetting of the *Gukurahundi*.[11] What such critiques miss, however, is how the novel's form—notably the symbiosis between its frame narrative and protagonist constellation—critiques post-independent Zimbabwean cultural politics by contextualizing the newly independent nation within the genealogy of colonial spatial ideology Vera examines in her dissertation.

As I therefore argue in the following sections, analyzing *The Stone Virgins'* narrative form through an interpretive lens influenced by her scholarship on how colonial spatial ideology shapes modern African subjectivity through its architectural restructuring of African environments, as well as her public writing on Zimbabwean culture, illuminates the novel's politically charged historiography. This historiography, what I am calling multidimensional memory, challenges, in her context, Mugabe's "patriotic history" and, in our context of literary theory and criticism, commonly held assumptions in the discourse of cultural memory studies. More specifically, I utilize the theoretical approach Vera models in her genealogy of the colonial prison as an interpretive lens for analyzing how *The Stone Virgins* employs animist poetics to construct cultural memory as what Vera takes to be anti-colonial "combat literature" against what she takes to be the ancestral trauma inflicted by colonial architecture.

Before I elucidate this argument, however, I wish to summarize Rothberg's justification of multidirectional memory's stakes for cultural politics, noting this framework's limits for theorizing post-traumatic cultural memory in the postcolony, especially if the goal of such theory is Vera's "transformation of consciousness." Rothberg's fundamental political claim is that multidirectional memory challenges what he diagnoses as the problem intrinsic to competitive memory's real estate development model: contemporary liberalism's compulsion to imagine collective memorialization of trauma as a "zero-sum struggle over scarce resources" with which to construct a publicly recognized identity (3). More specifically, competitive memory, claims Rothberg, assumes that boundaries of collective memories of trauma equate to boundaries of identity, the public sphere is a pregiven space on which to demarcate these boundaries, and this act of demarcation results in winners and losers in the aforementioned "zero-sum struggle" for identity recognition. This approach, to be sure, functions as contemporary liberalism's hegemonic model of how post-traumatic cultural memorialization operates. And I concur with Rothberg's sharp critique of its limits. His solution, however, is where I wish to focus my critique. In contrast to competitive memory, Rothberg argues, multidirectional memory imagines that collective memories of trauma are "subject to ongoing negotiation, cross-referencing, and borrowing" (3), the public sphere is a discursive space upon which this negotiation mutually produces memory and identity, and this process fosters a theoretical reframing of justice in light of late capitalist globalization (20). This final point is where his argument becomes explicitly postcolonial and thus correlated to the work of someone like Vera (whose entire oeuvre explores the dynamics of post-traumatic cultural memory in Zimbabwe).

To arrive at this final point, Rothberg uses Richard Terdiman's polemic that cultural memory is not the past but the past made present as a pathway through which to realize Nancy Fraser's political project of three-dimensional social justice for a post-national, globalized world. In *Scales of Justice*, Fraser argues that although contemporary capitalism's global economy casts the nation-state as a severely limited frame for theorizing the political, the contemporary left's calls for cultural recognition and economic redistribution remain rooted in a vision of the public sphere framed by the nation-state. Effective social justice must therefore incorporate a representational dimension of framing that, much like Judith Butler's *Frames of War*, shifts the problem of justice from how to equalize subject positions to who in the first place counts as a subject in the global *polis*. Rothberg's political gambit is that Fraser's notion of globalized justice can be theorized (via Terdiman) as a question of cultural memory. Conceptualizing memory as an ongoing negotiation outside the boundaries of territorially bordered representation, Rothberg argues, lays the groundwork for a politics operating beyond the limits of multicultural nationhood. More specifically, taking seriously Hannah Arendt's depiction of the nation-state as the synergist between the entangled histories of colonialism and totalitarianism means, Rothberg suggests, recognizing the nation-state as the catalyst for its own undoing as a foundation for collective representation in a globalized world. Consequently, he argues, decolonizing our understanding of how post-traumatic cultural memory produces collective identities necessitates critiquing the representational tactics of the Keynesian-Westphalian nation-state to which interlocutors in competitive memory debates so often cling. Structural multidirectionality is Rothberg's escape map out of liberal multiculturalism, and a post-nationalist theory of social justice is his payoff.

Despite this project's theoretical sophistication, Rothberg's resolute focus on the representation of cultural memory necessarily tethers his project to the form of the competitive politics of identity and difference he seeks to transgress. He seeks a postcolonial, structural transformation of the public sphere, yet roots this transformation in the identitarian claims that structure competitive memory debates, albeit through an ongoing, globalized, productive struggle. His alternative to the liberal identity politics informing public debates on cultural memories of trauma is consequently another identitarian struggle within a self-consciously global public sphere in which participating subjects are critically aware of the contingent and productive nature of their struggle. But just because we are conscious of our discursive contingency does not mean the construction of the "we" through which we arrive at this consciousness is not still structured by Keynesian-Westphalian tactics of collective representation—even if mediated by Fraser's and Arendt's illuminating critiques of such tactics or Rothberg's equally illuminating anchoring of such critiques to the dynamics of memory. Put differently, Rothberg effectively replaces the identity politics undergirding popular discourse on post-traumatic cultural memory with a certain neopragmatism (identity politics robbed of faith in identity) and therefore unconsciously traps himself within the liberal pluralism he seeks to transgress. I agree that representations of cultural memory can function as useful barometers for the political, but I would add that imagining a postcolonial *polis*—the utopian goal of Vera's writing (what she terms the "transformation of consciousness")—requires a conception of the political operating beyond the process of identity-formation-via-memory-representation (even if we are aware of the contingent nature of this process). In light of this goal, I now turn to Vera's scholarship on the colonial prison, which reveals the manner in which her animist approach to cultural memory assumes a posthumanist and postsecular rationality that challenges even the most prescient interventions in the discourse of cultural memory studies.

Tree-Prisons: The Geographical Violence Constitutive of Modern African Subjectivity

Vera's approach to writing cultural memory in her fiction is a direct response to the problem of colonial spatiality she analyzes in her dissertation. Here, she makes the historically controversial claim that "[t]here is no pre-colonial equivalent of the prison within Southern Africa." Thus, the introduction by colonizers of the "architectural apparatus of the prison" (9), she argues, "introduces transformation and reorganization in the African configuration of space" (38). This spatial transformation functions for Vera as the groundwork for the trauma of colonization. Put simply, "Colonialism is the interruption of a spatial universe and its autonomy" (52), an interruption that produces an ongoing chain of "geographical violence," a phrase Vera takes from Edward Said to signify African land undergoing a "metamorphosis" into imperial space (2). Of course, this enforced "metamorphosis of space" (53) at the core of the colonial encounter exceeds the effects of the prison proper. It is a process co-constituted by various colonial apparatuses alongside which the prison functions: for example, "the system of thumb-print identity passes, the introduction of hut-tax, registration of births and marriages," and so on (14). For her, though, the prison in colonial Africa (her study is not limited to Southern Africa, though her birthplace of Rhodesia features prominently) is the most revealing "metaphor" (9) of the process of colonization. This metaphoric nature is due to the fact that "colonialism reproduces space as alienation" (9) so that the entirety of the colonies become "geographical prisons" (54) for the colonized. The architecture of the colonial prison, then, reveals the holistic transformation of African space (and consequently, as will become clear, subjectivity) toward which it contributes.

According to Vera, a paradigmatic example of this transformative power is a baobab tree near the police station in Kasane, Botswana, dubbed The Historic Baobab. Before constructing brick prisons, Vera explains, colonizers created "tree-prisons" by hollowing out trunks of baobab trees such as this one, where they could lock up to six people at a time (44–46). Now standing near a brick prison built during the colonial epoch (which is still in operation), The Historic Baobab, Vera claims, "constantly reflects and traces the evolution of that colonial prison" and, by extension, colonial history as such (45). A baobab old enough for colonizers to hollow out, Vera reasons, would have years of precolonial growth, and now, in the post-independent era, the "apertures" carved by colonizers for doorways and windows have compressed into slits as such trees heal. In this way, "[h]istory is grafted on the body of the tree" (46), enmeshing nature and culture by incarnating in arboreal form "a precolonial, a colonial, and a neo-colonial identity for which [such trees] have become 'living' relics or artifacts" (45). Like Freud's reading of Tasso's *Jerusalem Liberated* analyzed in chapter 1, Vera here interprets wounds carved into a tree as "apertures" testifying to a trauma incorporating the living and the dead as well as the human and the more-than-human world. The baobab jail is a "living," animate archive of colonial trauma, she argues, suggesting that a theory of how colonial trauma has reshaped African subjectivity must necessarily also be a theory of how this trauma has reshaped African environments.

Incorporating Vera's logic into a criticism aimed at conceptualizing cultural trauma and memory thus necessitates expanding Caruth's and Rothberg's notions of the "implicated subject" to include entire ecosystems; but it also necessitates anchoring postcolonial environmentalism to a theory of colonial trauma and postcolonial memory—a theoretical orientation critics in the environmental humanities too often neglect when examining postcolonial ecologies.[12] Vera's approach to Zimbabwean history, in other words, combines the focal points of cultural trauma and memory studies with ecocriticism, yet her theoretical orientation implicitly revises each of these discourses by anchoring them to a notion of environmental wounding requiring a posthumanist and postsecular lens to appreciate.

Although Vera posits a posthumanist approach to reading the history imprinted in the baobab jail insofar as she claims the tree embodies a colonial order that begins by wounding the earth, her focus remains on how the colonized human subject inherits this trauma. She writes:

> The baobab prison, a space which held different indices and registers prior to occupation, is gorged, transformed . . . for the sake of punishment and detention. It is this violation of space and its enforced transfiguration that has to be assimilated by the indigenous people. . . . The baobab jail offers an instance of the mutation of space, and the significant influence on symbolic meaning that occurs with the onset of colonial government. The baobab jail impacts on a perception of the physical environment that preceded colonial contact. Out of the baobab tree space becomes relativized and institutionalized as it becomes the concrete manifestation of a particular

knowledge, power and control—the baobab becomes the space of surveillance though still echoing its antecedent historical and political configuration. (46–47)

Although colonial trauma, Vera here argues, begins as an act of ecological shape-shifting, land is only experienced as space (and consequently "mutated" space) by a subject. Hence her focus on how Indigenous people "assimilate" the "symbolic meaning" of the land's "mutation" into an apparatus of colonial spatiality. Baobab trunks (which she suggests may have been used as burial sites in the precolonial era) are "gorged" by colonizers to manifest the colony's social logic of "knowledge, power, and control." Despite being "transformed" into a "space of surveillance," however, the baobab continuous to "echo" the "historical and political configuration" it lost through its colonial "transfiguration." Like Freud's reading of Tasso's magical forest, the traumatized tree harboring the dead testifies to an animism extirpated by the advent of colonial modernity.

A hermeneutic problem that accordingly arises is, then, how to read these "echoes" when the "enforced transfiguration" of the tree coinciding with a holistic "geographical violence" constitutive of the colony as a social space has so thoroughly "mutated" the foundation of African subjectivity. This problem of post-traumatic interpretation of a transfigured archive, or the inheritance of precolonial configurations in the wake of colonial modernity (a postcolonial framing of what Nicolas Abraham and Mária Török call cryptonymy) is where Vera's analysis of The Historic Baobab coincides with the theory of ancestral trauma I have been proposing throughout this book. She writes, "The prison banishes and makes irrelevant Indigenous systems of punishment and cultural autonomy by appropriating and controlling that specific geography. The purpose of the European prison is to empty the colonized of their history, to reduce that culture and tradition to a murmur, to the level of gossip and hearsay" (269). Alluding to Fanon's claim in *The Wretched of the Earth* that colonialism "turns to the past of the oppressed people, and distorts, disfigures and destroys it" (169), Vera writes that the fundamental purpose of the colonial prison is to "empty the colonized of their history": in other words, to inflict an ancestral trauma that must be continuously "assimilated by the indigenous people" (46–47). This assimilation of a severance from the past is, to be sure, a severance from a cosmological framework. Since Indigenous settlements, Vera argues, "express the cosmology of the group" (47), by introducing new architecture, colonial powers implicitly introduce new "cognitive structural mapping" (47) to "interrupt the autonomy of previously held belief systems" (41) and forever distort a preexisting cosmology.

Citing a study of the Bororo of South America, for example, Vera describes how Salesia missionaries converted a village to Christianity simply by reorganizing it in a "rectilinear plan" (48). In this example colonizers graft post-Enlightenment European notions of teleological cohesion upon the land itself, producing ideological ripple effects within a village. Colonial modernity, this example illustrates, displaces through rectilinear architecture and thus the naturalization of linear demarcation and all its epistemological, political, and cosmological insinuations Indigenous social structures and all their epistemological, political, and cosmological assumptions.[13] The colonial construction of prison buildings—rectilinear architecture par excellence—is for Vera nothing less than the extirpation of Indigenous cosmologies through ideologically charged architecture. Linear demarcation and consequently the enforcement of a bordered, ipseitic subjectivity first shifts the everyday geography of Indigenous life and then its cosmological assumptions: for example, animist notions of the subject's infinite relationality, which do not coincide with a rectilinear universe. As Indigenous populations are forced to "assimilate" the "symbolic meaning" of this "geographical violence" (to use Vera's terms), ancestral trauma becomes the foundation of African modernity (to use mine).

How can one remember a culture whose extirpation constitutes the conditions of cultural memory in the present? Due to this conundrum (unrecognizable in Rothberg's schema), the trauma emblematized by The Historic Baobab necessitates that the postcolonial critic take a postsecular approach to reading colonial history. Rather than positing a model of precolonial rationality that can be explicated from the baobab tree-as-archive, for example, Vera claims that what is passed on through the baobab's "echoes" is a silence. This notion of a silent echo, the past's erasure haunting the present, is for Vera also central to the function of the prison in modern African literature. Quoting an officer working in the prison adjacent to The Historic Baobab, then interpreting his comments in dialogue with African literature, she writes:

> [T]he locking of people within the tree was a constant humiliation: "The treatment was bad . . . there was no African who had a mouth to ask why this was so". . . . The silence indicated on this occasion coincides with the silence described among the imprisoned men of Umuofia on their homecoming in Things

> Fall Apart. If language and speech indicate a whole symbolic universe, the experience of prison, in its strangeness and violence, radically alters epistemological certainties. The transformation of the baobab into a prison, and the phenomenon of the prison itself, interrupts the scale of understanding of the local people of Kasane to the extent that to this day they are still fascinated with the event of this history. (46)

Vera here identifies a connection between contemporary Kasane culture and the conclusion of African literature's most famous novel, a connection implying a critique of secularist approaches to reading colonial trauma in culture and literature. When Okonkwo and his fellow inmates return to Umuofia from their punishment under the District Commissioner's orders, *Things Fall Apart*'s narrator notes their humiliating silence and its spread throughout the entire village, which becomes "astir in a silent, suppressed way" (112). It is soon after this return that Okonkwo kills a court messenger sent to halt a village gathering. During this incident the narrator describes the messenger's "uniformed body" (116) (suggesting that the imprisoning authority's transformation of Umuofia's social space is also a transformation of the African subject) as well as the village's "utter silence" (115) in response to the messenger's orders. Like Achebe's novel, Vera claims above, the colonized prisoners of Kasane were humiliated into silence as their "epistemological certainties" became "radically altered," a shift that spread through the village as the colonial prison's larger transfiguration of Kasane's spatiality "interrupt[ed] the scale of understanding" assumed by Kasane's locals. In using such phrases, Vera casts the emergence of the colonial prison as a trauma in the Freudian sense: the breakdown of a frame of reference (which, to be sure, is a central theme of Achebe's novel). Thus, by highlighting the silences of the precolonial world that "echo" from the baobab as it heals, Vera not only casts colonial trauma as a posthumanist phenomenon (the colonized subject is imprisoned within a transfigured ecology), but also a postsecular one. The postcolonial critic, Vera (alongside Achebe) suggests, must learn to read that which echoes as silence, an erasure of the Indigenous "mouth," as the prison officer describes it, which necessitates severing hermeneutics from the positivism of secular interpretation.

Hence the motifs of spiritual signification (be it the voicing of prophetic utterances or, as I will later analyze, the explication of ancient cavern art) across Vera's oeuvre. In fact, she suggests in her dissertation that one way the corpus of modern African literature has inherited such silences as explicable to the subject of colonized modernity is by reinscribing "the prison of colonial space" with new mythologies. And this dialectic response to colonial imprisonment throughout postcolonial writing, what I have been describing throughout this book as the structural dynamic of animist poetics, is modeled by what she takes to be Rhodesia's first prison narrative, voiced in 1897. She writes:

> The hanging of Nehanda in Rhodesia may be seen to have produced the first prison narrative in that country. Nehanda's pronounced cry against the settlers following imprisonment and just before being hanged was: "My bones will rise." Brief though this narrative was, it inspired the second revolutionary struggle against the British which led to independence in 1980. This second struggle was conceived of as the rising of Nehanda's bones. . . . The hanging of Nehanda rather than induce subservience only empowers the colonized by providing them an opportunity for a new mythology. (12)

As Nehanda's dying words demonstrate, the colonial infliction of ancestral trauma lays the groundwork for the postcolonial crafting of animist poetics: in this case a prophecy that spurred an anti-colonial revolution culminating in the dissolution of Rhodesia. Nehanda's prophecy thus exemplifies what Vera takes to be the political drive that should undergird all postcolonial African writing: the crafting of what she, drawing on Fanon, terms "combat literature." Such literature, Vera concludes, must aim at "the continuous negation of a limit, the freeing and recovery of space" previously transfigured into forms of imprisonment (272) and in doing so fosters an "insistence on agency" against, yet through the social architecture constitutive of colonial modernity (286). Combat literature is, then, for Vera, a form of dialectical materialism (Nehanda's anti-colonial prophecy emerges through her colonial punishment, thereby laying the ideological groundwork for the latter's undoing) that is resolutely spiritual (Nehanda's prophecy is precisely that, a prophecy).

Like Nehanda's prophecy, African literature written in the wake of colonization is filled with the creation of new mythologies combating the trauma structuring their emergence, Vera argues. Citing novels such as Amos Tutuola's *The Palm-Wine Drinkard* (1952), Gabriel Okara's *The*

Voice (1964), and Ngũgĩ wa Thiong'o's *Matigari* (1986), she claims that in modern African fiction,

> [T]he threat of prison is also the threat of death. Each text argues that if imprisonment also means death then it cannot achieve the kind of silence it desires. In traditional belief death is wisdom, confers understanding, elevates, grants speech, determines the unique utterance, the uncontested judgment. To imprison is to conjoin with the departed and their telling and their seeing. It is to gather words from beyond the boundary, to return with seeing eyes, to enshrine. . . . The space between life and death is an in between space, but it is not silence. It is the place of narration. (74–75)

Just as Nehanda's prophecy transforms her death sentence into the conditions for a new, postcolonial form of collective life, writers like Tutuola, Okara, and Ngũgĩ narrate death as a form of "conjoining" between what Soyinkan animism, as I argued in this book's previous two chapters, figures as the living, the dead, and the unborn and thus the past, present, and future. That which rectilinearly transfigures African space and in doing so extirpates Indigenous cosmologies, forcing Indigenous people to assimilate silence, becomes, through its narration via animist poetics, that which enables the regeneration of ancestral ties through the production of new mythologies. In other words, for Vera, African "combat literature" responds to the infliction of ancestral trauma with a logic of animist poetics structured by a regenerative death drive and in doing so transfigures "silence" into "narration."

It should come as no surprise, then, that Vera alludes to Soyinka on multiple occasions when discussing this combative, ecopolitical, cosmodialectic, regenerative dynamic of the literary. She does so, for example, in her oft-quoted description of the goal of all African women's writing: "opening spaces" previously unavailable to African women ("Preface"). Considering the fact that Vera's vision of combat literature is a response to her theory of colonial spatiality, this phrase takes on an ideological specificity, a political form, which Vera criticism has not yet acknowledged. To open spaces, the woman writer, Vera here claims, must "invent new gods and banish ineffectual ones" (1), a process by which such writers "swallow history" (2). This description recalls Soyinka's in *Myth, Literature and the*

African World of the Yoruba sculptor who participates in the destruction and creation of new gods, thereby becoming a symbol for the process by which the modern African writer participates in the creative-destructive principle (86). It also recalls his use of digestive metaphors to describe how animist cosmologies incorporate symbols of colonial modernity into systems of sacralization, thereby swallowing the history meant to crush them (54). This application of Soyinkan animism can be traced as far back as 1992, the year Vera's first book (*Why Don't You Carve Other Animals?*) was published. She claims in an interview on Canadian public television that her correlation of feminist critique and Indigenous spirituality

> has to do with new models of history, of writing history, where in fact myth is a legitimate form of looking at events, of recording and reinventing history. . . . There's no pretense that it is anything other than a construct and that it can be refashioned to suit whatever political needs the community has, which is the way in which most societies have dealt with events. . . . There are some societies, for example, that have been able to invent new gods and goddesses according to a catastrophe that has occurred. ("Yvonne")

As Vera explains, there is no paradigm outside of myth from which to view a demystified history. Myth is instead the lifeworld of historical unfolding and vice versa. Colonial spatiality, for example, extirpates the social functioning of Indigenous myth by inscribing its own mythography onto the land, as Vera demonstrates through the example of rectilinear architecture. Alluding again to Soyinka's paradigm of the Yoruba sculptor as well as his theory of tragedy I espoused in the previous chapter, Vera in this interview anchors Soyinkan animism to "catastrophe," casting it as a strategy for responding to cultural trauma. This use of animist mythopoetics to transform a collective wound into a locus of regeneration (we should note that she defines her oft-cited goal of "opening spaces" as a "seemingly impossible birth" ["Preface" 5]) structurally mirrors her definition of combat literature. In an interview conducted nearly a decade later, while Vera was writing *The Stone Virgins*, she makes a similar claim, this time referencing Soyinka's home country: "In Nigeria, they can create new gods, isn't it? That's how we were as well. The legend, the history, is created in the mouth, and therefore survival is in the mouth." The context of this claim is her explanation of her process of writing *Nehanda*. She wrote, she claims, "as though I were myself a spirit medium. . . . I wrote it from remembrance, as a witness to my own spiritual history. . . . I felt I had an internal, intimate knowledge of our ancestors, and how they impact on our relationship to ourselves, to death, to life, to time, to sky, to rock" (Reading Frantz Fanon). Drawing on Soyinka, Vera represents her writing process as an animist process, noting the postsecular and posthumanist bent of her practice (her role as a medium of spiritual history and intercessor between the subject and the cosmos). Read in relation to her call for a literature to combat colonial spatiality, what each of these references to Soyinka demonstrates is that throughout Vera's oeuvre she strategically places Soyinkan animism in the service of a Fanonian dialectic. This dialectic (which begins "in the mouth," the locus of African silence in Vera's analysis of *Things Fall Apart* and *The Historic Baobab*) is aimed at "opening spaces" that have been "transfigured" by colonialism's ongoing "geographical violence."

Ekoneni: Movement as Combat in *The Stone Virgins*' Frame Narrative

This dialectical response to colonial trauma motivates *The Stone Virgins*' frame narrative, which depicts a process of more-than-human, collective subject formation taking place throughout Matabeleland. Before introducing the protagonists, the novel introduces Matabeleland's environment, offering glimpses of how its people alongside its flora navigate its architecture. The first two chapters, which function together as a frame narrative, consist entirely of vignettes describing movement throughout Bulawayo and Kezi (a township south of Bulawayo) connecting colonized people with each other and the colonized land. In these chapters kwela[14] musicians perform in an abandoned storage room, lovers cram into a broken telephone booth, and children play near a river with beach balls made from trash; all the while various flowers bloom, tree roots curl, and thatch roofs release their scent. This list is not exhaustive, but it reveals the frame narrative's function: Matabeleland's human and nonhuman inhabitants are depicted less as individuals (no character is named) than as participants in a choreographed[15] movement through which dispersive sites of "anonymity" (6) function to form a collective subject.

Reading this process through a lens informed by Vera's scholarship reveals the frame narrative as a form of architectural criticism functioning to place the novel in dialectical combat against the colonial spatial ideology its frame depicts. Combat literature operates, Vera explains, by "reordering cultural expression within . . . inherited colonial space" ("The Prison" 275). Such a "reordering" cannot be inaugurated by critically representing and thus revealing the ideological nature of the "architectural elements that order the lived world of post-colonial subjects" (273). Such a representation is only the first step. The postcolonial African writer must go further, Vera believes, by offering an alternative poetics that both dialectically emerges from "inherited colonial space" and aims resolutely at its "reordering." In *The Stone Virgins*, Vera's vernacular model for the novel's combative form is Bulawayo's many sites of *ekoneni*: the street corners where strangers serendipitously meet. She writes, "*Ekoneni* is a rendezvous. . . . You cannot meet inside any of the buildings because this city is divided; entry is forbidden to black men and women. . . . Here, you linger, ambivalent, permanent as time. You are in transit. The corner is a camouflage, a place of instancy and style; a place of protest" (*Virgins* 11–12). The right angles at the edges of Bulawayo's buildings are products of the rectilinear plan informing the colonial city's layout, a spatial form Vera associates in her dissertation with the extirpation of Indigenous cosmologies. These angles hide strangers walking on both sides until corners are crossed, making *ekoneni* a place of subjective co-transition in the proper sense, a shift in which subjects on either side of the corner cannot foresee with whom they will merge. This transitional nature is why Vera associates *ekoneni* with "style" and "protest." By meeting at an *ekoneni* the colonized craft together a subjectivity in agonistic relation to the colonial architecture denying their entrance into the *polis*. That plants join this agonistic movement (blooming jacarandas "bulge off the earth where they meet rock, climb over, then plunge under the ground" [3]) casts *ekoneni* meetings as analogous to the choreographed more-than-human movement central to the frame narrative.

Consequently, *The Stone Virgins*' framing depiction of a simultaneously postcolonial and posthumanist subject emerging through Matabeleland's colonial architecture functions like an *ekoneni*: It both represents and combats this architecture's claim on African subjectivity. More specifically, as my analysis will demonstrate, the pedestrian movement through Bulawayo depicted in the novel's first sentence navigates the form of spatial imprisonment foundational to Vera's understanding of colonial trauma. And the process of subject formation the frame depicts as emerging through this movement threatens the architecture informing it with a postcolonial "reordering." By framing *The Stone Virgins* this way, Vera contextualizes her narration of life in Matabeleland during the *Gukurahundi* and thus her act of writing post-traumatic cultural memory in early twenty-first-century Zimbabwe within her project of dialectically combating the geographical violence she believes informs the modern African subject.

The novel's opening sentence, set in Rhodesia sometime prior to Zimbabwean liberation and thus framing the post-independence political violence the novel later depicts within Rhodesian colonial history, narrates pedestrian movement: "Selborne Avenue in Bulawayo cuts from Fort Street (at Charter House), across to Jameson Road (of the Jameson Raid), through to Main Street, to Grey Street, to Abercorn Street, to Fife Street, to Rhodes Street, to Borrow Street, out into the lush Centenary Gardens with their fusion of dahlias, petunias, asters, red salvia, and mauve petrea bushes, onward to the National Museum, on the left side" (3). Functioning like a film's opening sequence, this sentence, though narrated in third person, depicts anonymous first-person movement through one of Bulawayo's major streets during an epoch of institutionalized white supremacy. Rather than offering a particular character's view, it focalizes the subjectivity produced by Bulawayo's urban architecture, which is itself a product of colonial history (as each of the proper names implies). This colonial architecture reflects, as Sarah Nuttall argues, the colonial paradigm evoked in its street names, becoming a "metaphor for the colonial gaze itself" ("Inside" 188). Consider, for instance, the way Selborne Avenue shapes pedestrians' field of vision. The "straight and unbending" (*Virgins* 5) street, "proud of its magnificence" (3), offers a "single solid view, undisturbed" (5). Interpreted in dialogue with Vera's scholarship on the colonial prison, it is easy to recognize how this gaze is a projection of colonial spatiality as imprisonment, the vantage point from a world in which "[a]ll colonized people are in one mode or another, restricted persons" ("The Prison" 271). Such an interpretation casts the first sentence's anonymous focalizing subject as the subject of, to quote the title of Vera's dissertation, "The Prison of Colonial Space."

Moreover, by highlighting Bulawayo's rectilinear architecture—for example, the city is "built on a grid" (10), "revolves in sharp edges," and its "roads cut at right angles" (11)—the novel's frame narrative exposes how the naturalization of linear demarcation intrinsic to colonial space informs the opening sentence's focalization. That the movement depicted in this sentence is not embodied by an individual character, but instead operates as depersonalized subjective movement, emphasizes the connection between colonial spatial ideology and colonial subject formation as trauma Vera theorizes in her scholarship: The sentence's focalizing subject is erased by the social space informing them. Here arises an ambivalence central to Vera's genealogy of the colonial prison. The geographical violence it enforces both erases Indigenous individuality and produces it. In fact, it realizes the latter through the former. "While Fanon . . . and Albert Memmi . . . each argue that colonizers refuse to grant individual identity to the native but constantly refer to an amorphous 'they,'" Vera writes, "it is equally true that 'criminalizing' the colonized consists in significant degrees of individualization" ("The Prison" 14). For Vera, what Fanon and Memmi each downplay is the process by which the British penological system, which relies on a model of individual responsibility, displaces Indigenous penological systems, which typically rely on kinship models of responsibility. The colonial fantasy of an Indigenous "they" Fanon and Memmi critique thus hinges on an erasure of an Indigenous "they" via the systematization of processes of individuation to which the prison contributes.[16] The extent to which the prison building epitomizes the rectilinear architecture Vera associates with colonial modernity is the extent to which it erases Indigenous subjectivity by transfiguring it into a population: a body of individual subjects to be linearly demarcated and policed.[17] Ironically, then, by depicting movement focalized not by an individual character, but by an unnamed subject-as-historical/architectural/ideological by-product, *The Stone Virgins*' opening sentence both reveals the violence of colonial spatial ideology and plants the seeds to combat it. The opening sentence's de-individuated focalizing subject incarnates the African subject transfigured by the architecture of colonial modernity and, precisely through this de-individuation, challenges the process through which the colony's structure of linear demarcation forms subjects as bordered individuals.

This combative response to colonial spatial ideology motivates Vera's interest throughout *The Stone Virgins* in walking. Walking in the novel is a postcolonial act: movement through space designed to restrict movement.[18] The last chapter also begins with pedestrian movement through Bulawayo, yet this time the focalizing subject is one of the novel's protagonists, Nonceba Gumede, and Bulawayo is now part of the newly liberated Zimbabwe. Nonceba, recovering from rape and mutilation and thus incarnating a wounded body politic entering a new epoch, walks, like the anonymous focalizing subject of the novel's opening sentence, on pavement. While such an assertion may seem mundane, the role of pavement in Vera's dissertation endows *The Stone Virgins*' scenes of pedestrian movement with historical and political significance. Focusing on a 1904 debate in Southern Rhodesia's legislative council, Vera cites a law proposed by Colonel William Napier[19] that led to Rhodesia's infamous banning of Indigenous Africans from using its public footpaths. She writes:

> Napier moved that "it is desirable that Municipalities and sanitary boards be empowered to make the necessary bye-laws to restrain natives of Africa from making use of such parts of streets and roads as are set aside for public footpaths". . . . Napier argues that it is imperative to "regulate the natives" in these built public spaces since the natives, with bundles on their heads, "obstructed the thoroughfares to the detriment of the general traffic on the pavement". . . . He adds that Maholis who are the principal traders, are a particular nuisance, and they do not recognize the short stage they are from barbarism: "They thought they were on equality with the white man, and they could go further than the law permitted". . . . (33–34)

Vera's reading of Napier's motion emphasizes the dehumanizing logic informing Rhodesia's pavement law, which utilizes the neutral rhetoric of jurisprudence to halt Indigenous economies by restricting Indigenous movement. The rectilinear structure of public pavement thus provides a space of teleological movement for settlers deemed fully human (the colonizing subject walks straight to his destination) while eliminating access to the emerging colonial economy (which depends upon pavement for trade) for those deemed too close to barbarism. Vera therefore contextualizes this law within the genealogy of the colonial prison guiding her study. Much like the creation of tree-prisons, "Space has been produced, appropriated from the local authority, then made to speak the interests of the settler" (34). Through the pouring of pavement, then, African "land acquires new horizons" (31), and these horizons coincide with the colonial prison's use of "confinement as a means of social control" in order to reformulate the colonized subject as constitutively immobile (25).[20] Despite their "contrasting architectural forms," then, Vera argues that pavement functions alongside the prison to sustain the "spatial transformation" (270) upon which its "entrenched colonialism" (44) rests.[21]

Vera's reading of Napier's law provides historical-architectural-ideological backdrop to *The Stone Virgins*' first and last chapters. It casts the movement the first sentence depicts as illegal and thus an act of anti-colonial resistance. It also contextualizes Nonceba's walking at the end of the novel within a legal history of pavement, implicitly making a political claim in Vera's present. The legacy of Rhodesia's pavement law was reproduced, as Dorothy Driver and Meg Samuelson suggest, via Zimbabwe's "Operation Clean-Up," through which the newly independent nation banned single women from walking on Bulawayo's sidewalks (193). Through its mirroring of the opening sentence, then, Nonceba's walking draws a historical-ideological line between Rhodesian and Zimbabwean politics marked by their shared architecture. By returning the narrative to its opening, Nonceba's walking suggests that part of the frame narrative's function is to claim Zimbabwe has inherited Rhodesia's colonial spatial ideology. Thus, the novel's framing casts the novel as combating both colonial history and the post-independent political structures concurrent to Vera's writing. Ultimately, then, by depicting a process of more-than-human, collective subject formation, the frame narrative casts the opening sentence (read in relation to Nonceba's walking) as a depiction of a subject emerging in dialectical relation to its own incarnation of the colonial spatial ideology structuring the colonial modernity uniting the Rhodesian and Zimbabwean *polis*.

The first sentence's allusions to Bulawayo's colonial history, paired with the route it depicts, further solidifies this dual nature of the novel's act of combat—that is, its critique of Rhodesian and Zimbabwean politics. The route takes place on Selborne Avenue, a name memorializing Lord Selborne's 1906 visit to the region. It was on this visit that Selborne, then high commissioner for Southern Africa, met with Indigenous leaders in Bulawayo and the Matapos Hills, leading to the 1907 publication of the Selborne Memorandum, which proposed formally integrating the region into British South Africa. The novel's opening word therefore marks the colonial history of its setting, while the rest of the sentence depicts movement informed by this history, beginning at Charter House and ending at the National Museum. These titles cast the route depicted in the sentence as analogous to Rhodesian/Zimbabwean national history: the transition from a charter (a manuscript penned by a sovereign power to found and define its rule) to a national community, or from a house (Zimbabwe means "House of Stone" in Shona) to a museum (a space of strategically curated collective memory). Writing an explicit critique of Zimbabwean politics under Mugabe's ZANU-PF would place Vera in immediate danger, but her opening sentence nevertheless implies the route from Rhodesia's institutionalized white supremacy to post-independent Zimbabwean politics is a straight line. That this sentence's destination is the National Museum suggests, moreover, that the narrative that follows is moving toward the construction of a cultural memory; yet the memorialization Vera hopes the novel can perform, this sentence also suggests, must combat the very history that defines its subjective gaze: cultural memory as curated by the Rhodesian and Zimbabwean states.

This history, the novel's first sentence suggests, begins with the British South Africa Company (BSAC). Thanks in large part to the efforts of Cecil Rhodes (after whom Rhodesia was named), this company received a royal charter (modeled on the British East India Company's) in 1889 to bolster mining in the region and lay groundwork for its legal colonization under the British Empire. Nearly all of the proper names in *The Stone Virgins*' first sentence hearken back to the BSAC. Charter House was its administrative offices. Leander Starr Jameson was a doctor, colonial administrator, and close friend and confidant of Rhodes, who led (under Rhodes's employment) a paramilitary unit of the BSAC in a failed attempt to overthrow the South African Republic. Albert Grey (4th Earl Grey) was administrator of Rhodesia from 1896 to 1897 and in 1898 became one of the BSAC's first directors. James Hamilton (2nd Duke of Abercorn) was also on the BSAC's first board of directors, as was Alexander Duff (1st Duke of Fife) and Rhodes himself. Finally, Barrow Street was named after an officer in the Pioneer Column, a paramilitary force designed by Rhodes to annex Mashonaland for the BSAC in 1890. Crucially, Vera misnames this street as *Borrow*. If the novel's opening sentence depicts subjective movement through Bulawayo as analogous to the historical movement of Rhodesia/Zimbabwe from a charter to a nation, from a house to a museum, this movement is enforced by the historical misnaming and borrowing (or misnaming through borrowing) of land inaugurated by the BSAC.

The word *Borrow* stands between the list of BSAC officials (the region's arch-borrowers) and Centenary Gardens, home of the 1953 Central African Rhodes Centenary Exhibition. Opened by the Queen Mother to celebrate the centenary of Rhodes's birth, this exhibition featured artifacts from various African cultures alongside demonstrations of the BSAC's role in bolstering the region's industry, agriculture, transportation, and overall modernization. In other words, this exhibition functioned to produce Rhodesian cultural memory through settler colonial ideology rooted in the pioneering work of BSAC. Ironically, it is on these grounds that the National Museum, the space of cultural memory toward which *The Stone*

Virgins' opening sentence moves, is located. This location further suggests that the act of memorialization the novel is working toward is predetermined by colonial history's restructuring of African space, the ground upon which the anonymous focalizing subject of the opening sentence moves. What is more, this museum opened in 1902 under Rhodes's direction as a space to house Rhodesia Scientific Board's extracted minerals and opened to the public in 1964 as a museum of the region's "economic geology." Rhodesian national memory, the disconnect between this building's title and contents suggests, is founded on an extractive relationship to the land.

The opening sentence's constellation of historical markers, culminating in a symbol of national memory curated around an ideology of land as property to be extracted, supports James Graham's argument that critics should pay more attention to the "socio-ecological imaginary" framing Vera criticism's typical focus: the "aestheticization of pain, trauma, and the body" (358).[22] Given that the novel was published while Zimbabwe's Fast-Track Land Reform Program (FTLRP) (the seizing of white-owned farmland, beginning in 2000, by the Mugabe-backed Zimbabwe National Liberation War Veterans Association, then legalized by parliament in 2005) was under way, I agree. In such a context, the novel's opening sentence makes a resolutely political claim: FTLRP's ideology of land as human property is a continuation of a historical arc beginning with the BSAC in the late nineteenth century (an arc mirroring the novel's association of Rhodesia's and Zimbabwe's pavement laws). The sentence's depicted movement toward a symbolic space of collective memorialization thus combats not only the colonial history framing its vision, but also Mugabe and the ZANU-PF's ideology of land as human property to be reseized and nationalized. As Vera writes to her friends in a 2003 email update, upon describing the National Gallery she had directed for five years being robbed, "We must abandon all sense of property and of ownership. It is a good lesson all in all, indeed, an old idea for enlightened communities everywhere" ("A Blue"). It is worth noting that the movement depicted in *The Stone Virgins'* first sentence begins in front of the National Gallery (at the intersection of Selborne and Fort). The movement I have been analyzing therefore begins and ends at two spaces of collective memorialization: the art gallery Vera directed (until the government withdrew funding in 2003) and a museum that places human sovereignty over the earth at the core of national memory, thereby symbolically uniting the BSAC of the past and the ZANU-PF of the present. Vera's opposition to property and ownership articulated in her email quoted above thus permeates *The Stone Virgins* from its opening sentence.

This opposition reveals the stakes of the more-than-human form of the frame narrative's process of collective subject formation. In contrast to the idea of land as property and thus subject to human ownership, Vera depicts throughout all of her fiction, and especially in *The Stone Virgins*, what she takes to be vitality of the earth, a vitality in which human characters participate. Arlene Elder describes this aspect of Vera's fiction as her ecofeminism (95), and I would further highlight its ideologically combative position in relation to both Rhodesia's colonial history and the politics of land ownership contemporaneous to the novel. In fact, a dialectical relationship between land as human property and land as living subject, as animate, appears as early as the opening sentence I have been analyzing. In Centenary Gardens (a space associated via the centenary celebration of Rhodes's birth with collective memorialization through a framework of Rhodesian settler ideology) and just before the National Museum (a space associated with the region's history of "economic geology") blooms an array of flowers. The list of proper names—"dahlias, petunias, asters, red salvia, and mauve petrea bushes"—stands in contrast to the sentence's list of BSAC officials (visually marking the dialectic the sentence introduces). In response to these officials' acts of "borrowing," the flowers enact together a "fusion" of life (3). Alongside this list of flowers eucalyptus emit their aroma while the blooming cassias and jacarandas contrast the "concrete and sandstone cityscape" in which they thrive (*Virgins* 4). This "fusion" of non-native flora, planted to beautify colonial infrastructure, constitutes an agonistic relation between the life envisioned by Bulawayo's colonial design and the form of life asserted by the colonized land. Throughout the frame narrative that follows, all of Matabeleland participates in this dialectical formation of collective life.

Such reclaiming of the land, not as property to be owned by individuated subjects, but as a participant in the multidimensional formation of postcolonial subjectivity, is also present throughout Vera's work as a public intellectual for her hometown of Bulawayo. In an article she wrote on revolutionary Joshua Nkomo's burial published in the *Bulawayo Chronicle* on July 7, 1999, for example, she describes the military ceremony overseen by the Mugabe regime in a manner similar to the way she frames colonial space in *The Stone Virgins*.[23] To offer some context for the following quote, viewing Nkomo's Ndebele ethnicity as a challenge to ZANU-PF's

Shona-based single-party ideology, Mugabe oversaw the *Gukurahundi* massacres in Nkomo's home of Matabeleland largely to stamp out support for the revolutionary figure.[24] Here, Vera reports on Nkomo's military burial a decade after the genocide (while she was drafting *The Stone Virgins*): "[T]he police and military covered the hill to its zenith in their hundreds. They forged a picturesque entourage, a grand and impressive spectacle of order, quilted like cloth against the steep slope, their hats and uniform in patterned series throughout, all of them so still that after staring long and hard you had the charmed feeling that the hill was swaying. There was no movement. Each body choreographed to stillness" ("Nkomo"). Vera contrasts the troops' "spectacle of order" and "stillness" to the "charmed feeling that the hill was swaying." While Mugabe's military spectacle seeks to impose what Vera describes as a "choreographed . . . stillness" on the landscape, transfiguring it much like former colonial powers, the hill asserts a movement that cannot quite be stilled. This passage thus reveals a similar dialectic as *The Stone Virgins*' frame narrative. This connection becomes even more clear as Vera contrasts Mugabe's inheritance of colonial order with the crowd's collective movement: "Sweeping down from this hill, into the valley, then climbing up directly ahead, along the entire flank of an opposite hill, were the crowds in their motley colours, swaying and singing revolutionary songs, blending their own fate with that of the departed. . . . They sang in unison, their arms raised to meet the sun" ("Nkomo"). This collective movement, a symbiosis between a human crowd and the landscape, mirrors the process of postcolonial subject formation depicted in *The Stone Virgins*' frame narrative. This passage reveals a unison between her scholarly, literary, and public writings, all of which she places in combat against the imprisonment of African space and thus subjectivity. More importantly, though, it further solidifies the fact that *The Stone Virgins*' architectural critique of Rhodesia is also a critique of the Zimbabwean politics contextualizing the novel's publication: These states, Vera implies, operate through a shared ideological architecture.

In sum, the enmeshment of human and nonhuman vitality intrinsic to the frame narrative's depiction of anonymous movement through colonial space casts this movement as a dialectic of postcolonial subject formation. Like *ekoneni*, a collective subject is formed by movement through architecture designed to reproduce African subjectivity as constitutively individuated and motionless. This dialectic is a response to Vera's understanding of colonial trauma. The spatial metamorphosis foundational to colonization, she argues throughout her dissertation, is a transfiguration of

African land and consequently African subjectivity—a more-than-human trauma requiring a posthumanist response. In *The Stone Virgins*' frame narrative colonized humans and the colonized earth thus move together in an animist choreography anchored less to ethnophilosophy (e.g., notions of nonhuman agency in Shona cosmology) than to the historical materialist dialectic Vera, drawing on Fanon, defines as combat literature's operative mode. Further, by tracing a pathway toward a location of strategically curated cultural memory hinging on an ideology of land as fundamentally human property, the opening sentence contextualizes the Zimbabwean politics conditioning the novel's publication (e.g., the state's filtering of the *Gukurahundi*'s memory through "patriotic history" and reclaiming of colonized land via the FTLRP) as an outworking of the colonial spatial ideology first brought to the region by the BSAC. The frame narrative thus depicts a postcolonial process of subject formation emerging in dialectical combat to both colonial and post-independent political structures. It critiques the spatial dimensions through which these structures inform African subjectivity and depicts the ongoing opening of new dimensions for a postcolonial subject perpetually in formation. The frame narrative thus not only sediments agonistic cultural memories into its construction of cultural identity (the political horizon of Rothberg's multidirectional memory), but more fundamentally sediments agonistic architectures of such memories in order to create the conditions for what Vera elsewhere calls "that seemingly impossible birth" ("Preface" 5) to which literature must contribute: the birth of a liberated, postcolonial subjectivity. The genesis of colonial memory is, the novel reveals, the colony's linear demarcation and thus its individuated subjectivity. But through the work of multidimensional memory the novel also reveals the ways in which this very architecture provides the groundwork for a process of postcolonial subject formation that, undermining the spatial ideology from which it emerges, opens new dimensions for a postcolonial *polis*.

The Protagonist-Constellation's Ritualized Self-Burial

The intertwining character arcs of the novel's four protagonists (Thenjiwe, Nonceba, Cephas, and Sibaso) cast them as operating together as a constellation investing the frame narrative's posthumanist dynamics with postsecular dynamics. In doing so they allegorize the process by which subjects shaped by colonial trauma might rekindle a connection between subjectivity and ecology ruptured by this trauma's "geographical violence." This arc begins with Thenjiwe Gumede and Cephas Dube's romance plot. Immediately after the frame narrative the two meet in Kezi. The scene begins as Thenjiwe walks into the bustle of a crowd spilling out of the "Kezi-Bulawayo-Kezi" bus (39). She "absorb[s] the melody, if not the dance" of this crowd (31), then notices Cephas "swinging, swinging" (32). She joins him with a "swing in her walk" (35), and in response he whistles a tune and taps his feet while she, still swinging, "takes the stranger home" (36). By emphasizing the choreography of their encounter as well as its location, a crowded space of flux between Bulawayo and Kezi, the novel casts their romance as an outworking of the frame narrative's collective movement taking place across Matabeleland. Further, through numerous allusions to the biblical narrative of the Garden of Eden (e.g., Thenjiwe "feels naked" near Kezi's central marula tree, Cephas praises Thenjiwe's bones "as though she is a new creation" [37], alluding to Adam's "bone of my bone" poem[25]), the novel casts Thenjiwe and Cephas as an "originary couple"[26] (Driver and Samuelson 114). Both of these points (the romance plot's narrative placement and biblical allusions) function together to depict Thenjiwe and Cephas's sexual encounter as potentially generative of a new beginning: a human incarnation of the frame narrative's more-than-human process of collective subject formation. That Cephas's infatuation with Thenjiwe's bones also alludes to Nehanda's prophecy of her bones rising (thus enabling an anti-colonial revolution), and that Vera takes this prophecy to be Rhodesia's first example of "combat literature" voiced against colonial imprisonment, further suggests that what is at stake in Thenjiwe and Cephas's relationship is the insemination of a postcolonial dispensation. Like Adam and Eve, however, Thenjiwe and Cephas soon lapse from the utopian horizon promised by their symbolic roles. As I argue in this section, this lapse, culminating in Cephas leaving town, casts their brief relationship as plotting the politics of post-traumatic cultural memory in Zimbabwe, thereby setting up a problem to which the novel responds by way of the intertwined character arcs of the novel's two male protagonists: Cephas the lover and Sibaso the rapist.

The generative potential of Thenjiwe and Cephas's relationship is immediately associated with the psychodynamics of memory: "She walks by and takes over the corner in his mind where some thought is trapped, some useless remembrance about fences with NO TRESPASS signs and NO WORK signs" (32). The sight of Thenjiwe's flirtatious dance awakens in Cephas's psyche memories of the spatial ideology Vera analyzes in her dissertation. Memories emerge of prohibitive markers on linear borders—"fences with NO TRESPASS signs and NO WORK signs"—and thus, as Vera argues, rectilinear architecture's function of reconstituting the colonized subject, through enforced individuation, as immobile. Yet Thenjiwe's swinging hips replace these memories, deeming them "useless." Insofar as Thenjiwe walks in choreographed synchronicity with the frame narrative's depiction of Matabeleland's collective, more-than-human movement dialectically emerging in response to its colonial architecture, her hips swing through the space they replace in Cephas's psyche. Thenjiwe and Cephas's encounter is therefore at the level of form another *ekoneni*, this time operating within the architecture of the colonial psyche (inseparable from the architecture of colonial space), thereby threatening to dialectically invest this psyche (the subjective experience of space) with new coordinates. The romance plot, in other words, traces the dynamics of the novel's work of multidimensional memory.

The couple, however, begins desiring an understanding of each other's past through a form of memory coinciding with the architecture of colonial spatiality, and this desire quenches the liberatory potential of their relationship. For Cephas, this desire sparks while following Thenjiwe home: "[H]e places his foot where she has left her imprint on the soil, wanting to possess, already, each part of her, her weight on soft soil, her shape. He wants to preserve her in his own body, gathering her presence from the soil" (38). Thenjiwe's imprint signifies for Cephas a bordered other made of separate parts to be "gather[ed] and "preserve[d]" within himself. Since the frame narrative's vision of postcolonial subject formation introduces and structures Thenjiwe and Cephas's encounter, his desire to "possess" her is a rejection of the collective movement in which they "swing" for the colonial fantasy of an individuated subjectivity operating within an economy of ownership. This quenching of dialectically combative subject formation is, moreover, played out as a process of memory. Cephas covers Thenjiwe's footprint (a sign of Thenjiwe's presence) with his, desiring to possess the other by controlling the signs through which she is remembered. In this way, Cephas's desire is produced by the retention of the colonial spatial ideology that, according to Vera, extirpates through the construction of individuated subjects Indigenous conceptions of relational subjectivity. And through its articulation via memory, this retention becomes a metaphor for post-independent Zimbabwe's retention of colonial ideology through its discourse of cultural memory. Just as Mugabe and the ZANU-PF's "patriotic history" anchors Zimbabwean cultural identity to a strategically curated history of the nation's origins, which decidedly forgets the victims of the *Gukurahundi*, Cephas (who we later learn is a government archivist) attempts to cover Thenjiwe's imprint with his own, an act of self-fashioning dependent on the erasure of another's memory.

Thenjiwe, too, embodies Zimbabwean cultural politics concurrent with Vera's writing of the novel by anchoring the romance plot to the ideology of ethnicity. This anchoring informs Thenjiwe's obsession with a mazhanje seed Cephas gifts her. She keeps the seed in her mouth at all times, which sparks in her a desire to become impregnated by Cephas. Yet the seed quickly becomes a barrier between the couple. Since Cephas carried the seed from his hometown of Chimanimani,[27] it marks for Thenjiwe their cultural difference and consequently, in her mind, the fragility of their bond. She thus begins to constantly question him about the mazhanje, fearing he might leave her to return to "his own tree" (46–47), and wishes she knew more about the roots of "her" marula tree to share with him and thus secure their attachment. "She knows that if she finds the shape of these roots," writes Vera, "he would know a deep truth about her land" (46). As this sentence implies, Thenjiwe fixates on her and Cephas's geographically demarcated ethnic identities, culminating in the interethnic couple's separation. The symbolic nature of the mazhanje tree associates this demarcation, operating entirely in Thenjiwe's mind, with the Zimbabwean cultural politics informing the novel. The mazhanje tree is indigenous to Southern Africa and is a dioecious species, two facts that contrast themes introduced in the novel's frame narrative and therefore complicate the obvious symbolism of fertility intrinsic to a seed inside of a woman's orifice. First, the indigenous origins of the plant contrast the frame narrative's global flora. Bulawayo's jacarandas and eucalyptus (plants cosmopolitanized through colonial history) symbolize constant movement, the mazhanje rootedness. Second, the mazhanje's dioecious nature (an individual plant produces either male or female gametes) casts it also as a symbol of the sexual difference separating Thenjiwe and Cephas. In fact, "dioecy" derives from the Greek *dioikía*, "two households," suggesting the plant is a symbol of differentiated subjectivity as such—and in a narrative set during a state-sanctioned ethnic cleansing, this symbolism is especially potent. The seed in Thenjiwe's mouth thus comes to symbolize her attachment to a sense of rootedness dependent on individuated subjectivities mapped onto disparate claims to land—a holistic antithesis to the frame narrative's process of collective subject formation.

Thus, just as Cephas incarnates the ZANU-PF body politic by attempting to "preserve" Thenjiwe's memory "in his own body," so too does Thenjiwe by figuring their split as a metaphor of Zimbabwean ethnic division.[28] That Cephas's projection of memory ownership takes place on the "soil" and Thenjiwe's via a fantasy of roots, moreover, associates their romance plot with the ZANU-PF's ideology of land as fundamentally human property (an ideology Vera vehemently rejects). The fact that the soil upon which they "swing" boasts "color like buried bone" (47) deepens this metaphor by alluding to the thousands of corpses of the *Gukurahundi*'s victims hidden in mass graves throughout Matabeleland, a region whose Ndebele population was targeted to ensure a Shona majority and thus secure Mugabe's dictatorial power. Through Thenjiwe and Cephas's romance, then, Vera draws an ideological line between ethnic identitarian division and land ownership by attaching both categories, embodied in two protagonists, to the form of individuated subjectivity she takes to be a product of colonial spatial ideology. The novel's postcolonial Adam and Eve thus lapse into dialectical combat against the frame narrative's dialectical combat: They counter the collective subject formation taking place throughout Matabeleland with a reinscription of the individuated subjectivity Vera associates with colonial modernity. In doing so they cast the Zimbabwean politics of cultural memory they incarnate (politics undergirding the *Gukurahundi*) as structured by the colonial spatial ideology with which the novel begins. Much like its opening sentence, the novel's romance plot implies that post-independent Zimbabwe retains the ideological architecture the liberation struggle fought to dismantle.

This genealogical conundrum becomes the problem to which Sibaso and Cephas together model a response through their interconnected character arcs. Sibaso is the dissident soldier who rapes the Gumede sisters after Cephas's departure, decapitating Thenjiwe and leaving Nonceba mutilated. Through narrative structure and recurrent symbols, though, the novel places Cephas and Sibaso in mimetic relation. Both have sexual encounters with the Gumede sisters: Sibaso as their rapist and murderer and Cephas as Thenjiwe's lover and, by the end of the novel, Nonceba's companion. Much like Cephas, who is not named until the penultimate chapter, during the narration of the rape and murder Sibaso is not named, but referred to as "the man." Their mimetic incarnations of "man" become even more intimately connected as Sibaso and Cephas harbor the same desire for ownership of their shared lover/victim. The narrator describes

Sibaso's rape, for example, with the same possessive language framing Cephas's adoration of Thenjiwe. Sibaso possesses Nonceba's body, reaching toward the "pit of her being" (68) until she "feels him inside her body. . . . [H]is breathing is her breathing. She is breathing in. His sweat is in her nostrils. His perspiration" (70). As he refashions her into a "receptacle for his dreaming," he "owns her like a memory" (71). Through this projection of ownership figured as memory, the lover and rapist become increasingly difficult to separate.

Thus, when Sibaso decapitates Thenjiwe and "bone-bright white flashes, neck bone pure" (75), or when he rapes Nonceba and the narrator describes him holding her "dark bone" (70), this language solidifies the connection between his attack with Cephas's professions of love via the latter's adoration of Thenjiwe's bones. More specifically, it grafts Sibaso into Cephas's symbolic function as a postcolonial Adam and thus his narrative arc of lapsing from Nehanda's liberatory promise of her bones rising to enable decolonization back into the colonial spatial ideology commencing the novel. Hence each character's association with the environment: Sibaso's "blood brown" (67) shoes anchor him to bloodied soil of Matabeleland during the *Gukurahundi*, while Cephas appears to "link rock and sky together, grass and pathway" (146), embodying the totalizing shift in the subjective experience of space Vera claims functions as a "pathway" to colonial modernity.

If Cephas and Thenjiwe's romance plot casts the politics of cultural memory contextualizing the novel as an outworking of colonial spatial ideology's formation of individuated subjects, Cephas and Sibaso's mimetic relation attaches this process to a desire for ownership that corrupts relations between these subjects and their environment. In sum, the novel's protagonist-constellation of the Gumede sisters and their men (a constellation emerging from and quenching the collective movement of the frame narrative's environmental protagonist) rotates around a problem of colonial desire: the force coinciding with the colonial spatial ideology the frame narrative combats and the protagonist-constellation reinscribes. And it is the abandonment of this desire that therefore comes to function as the horizon of Sibaso and Cephas's mimetic character arcs.

Sibaso, despite being the perpetrator of the novel's most horrific scene, performs most radically this abandonment of colonial desire and with it the individuated subjectivity operating as its mutually constitutive form. Sibaso lives in a cave in the Matapos Hills, referred to as Gulati throughout the novel. Deriving from a Karanga term meaning "The Voice from the Rock," *Gulati* associates this region with its many cavern shrines, thought to be the mouth of Mwali[29]: the creator-god who speaks through spirit mediums living in these caves.[30] Through his cavern dwelling, Vera casts the novel's rapist as also its prophet,[31] and his prophecy begins as a symbolic rebirth. After his attack of the Gumede sisters, he climbs into the Mbelele cave, the most sacred shrine in Gulati. The cave functions as a "womb" protecting Sibaso from the widespread violence of the newly liberated Zimbabwe. "Mbelele has its own seasons" despite the season of genocide taking place across Matabeleland, with its overhanging rock shielding the cave from "the rain that heals" (100)—a reference to the so-called cleansing rains of *Gukurahundi*.[32] Through such language, Sibaso's entrance into the cave functions as a symbolic reentrance into the womb of prehistory. "In Gulati," he declares, "I travel four hundred years, then ten thousand years, twenty more. The rocks split open, time shifts, and I confess that I am among the travelers who steal shelter from the dead" (104). This "shelter" necessitates that Sibaso give up his individuated identity. Thus, wedged between an "ancient parting" in the rocks flows the stream of Simude, a stream "so pure that you can hardly see your own reflection in it," which creates a "strange sensation of being invisible" (102). In psychoanalytic terms, the prehistoric cavern-womb fosters, through its stream's lack of reflection, a deformation of the ego originally produced, through reflection, in the mirror stage. Sibaso's symbolic rebirth thus plots an anti-mirror stage, the dissolution of the bordered subjectivity created when one recognizes one's external reflection mirrored back as distinct. To filter this psychoanalytic scenography through Vera's genealogy of the colonial prison, if the architecture of the colony mirrors an individuated subjectivity to the psyche of the colonized (the colonized subject recognizes themselves as constitutively bordered and motionless by way of this subjective form being reflected throughout the spatial architecture of the colony), Sibaso's anti-mirror stage is performed in dialectical combat to colonial spatial ideology's psychosocial function. Thus, he claims that in Gulati "[e]verything is infinite; it is there, not you" (102). In this sense Sibaso replaces the mazhanje seed. Like the seed, he is here cradled in an oracular orifice functioning as a locale damaged by colonial trauma. If the seed, cradled in the mouth of a colonized body, comes to symbolize the quenching of the frame narrative's liberatory movement through a lapse back into individuated subjectivity, Sibaso, cradled in the mouth of a damaged ecology, comes to symbolize this subject's potential to be reborn. Sibaso's symbolic rebirth is in this way a reconnection of the protagonist constellation to the frame narrative's process of collective subject formation and therefore a rekindling of the dialectical combat against colonial spatial ideology with which the narrative begins.

Consequently, the novel's titular passage incorporates the narrative as a whole into Sibaso's cavern rebirth. Here, Sibaso beholds an ancient cave painting[33] depicting "virgins who walk into their own graves before the burial of a king" (103). These virgins form a circle like "wavering strokes of blood-lit tendrils on the rock" (104), a description recalling Nonceba, who during her rape bends like "tendril on a hard rock" (68). That the stone virgins have "legs that branch from their bodies like roots" (103), moreover, associates them with Thenjiwe's desire to understand the roots of her and Cephas's trees. The clearest connection between the stone virgins and the Gumede sisters, however, comes in a passage immediately after the rape and murder, as Sibaso gazes at his victims: "He sees her dancing heels, her hands chaste dead bone, porously thin, painted on a rock. . . . She is a woman from very far, from long ago, from the naked caves in the hills of Gulati. She does not belong here. She bears the single solitude of a flame, the shape and form of a painted memory" (78). Just as the narrative grafts Sibaso into Cephas's symbolic function, Sibaso's focalization here grafts the Gumede sisters into the cavern painting's symbolic function. If Sibaso the rapist is he who sacrifices the Gumede sisters on behalf of the colonial desire he (like Cephas) incarnates, in the sacred cave he becomes a prophet who interprets this sacrifice through a "painted memory" of an archaic sacrifice. Given the function of rectilinear architecture in Vera's scholarship and the novel's frame narrative, the fact that stone virgins are memorialized in a circle at the moment before their death is key. On the one hand, the painting depicts an archetypal sacrifice (women ritually slaughtered for a patriarch), yet their choreographic architecture casts this process as the sacrifice of a circular form of subjectivity: a subject composed of women infinitely entwined with each other and, as the arboreal terms suggest, the more-than-human world. The memory of an archetypical sacrifice thus becomes, as Sibaso witnesses the painting, a memory of the "geographical violence" informing colonial modernity's advent. The sovereign of the painting is by implication not only a primal patriarch, but also the social logic of the colonial *polis* (a logic in which spatial ideology functions as a primal patriarch) and, moreover, post-independent Zimbabwe. Under Mugabe's leadership, the latter is (while Sibaso gazes at this painting) sacrificing thousands of

Ndebele and Kalanga throughout the novel's setting of Matabeleland in order to ensure an ethnically defined single-party state.[34]

Much like the frame narrative's dialectic of colonial imprisonment and postcolonial liberation, however, Sibaso explicates not just social critique from this painting, but more importantly hope. "Perhaps they have been saved from life's embrace. Not dead," he speculates of the virgins (104). Indeed, he observes the "women float, moving away from the stone" (103). Given the frame narrative's more-than-human movement (to which Sibaso is reconnecting via his cavern rebirth out of his individuation), Sibaso witnesses in this "painted memory" what the novel casts as an underlying structure of reality: a process of postcolonial subject formation emerging precisely through the traumas structuring colonial modernity. The death of the virgins (which is the death of an infinitely implicated subjectivity intrinsic to animist cosmologies) produces not only the bordered and imprisoned subject Vera places at the heart of colonial modernity, but also the conditions through which the postcolonial reanimation of extirpated subjectivity becomes possible. Sibaso, in other words, reads the regenerative death drive I have been theorizing throughout this book in the painting of the stone virgins. And he joins this death drive: While interpreting the painting, he is cloaked in grass, "odor severe, like a carcass, dead things" (102). While recognizing the virgins' assertion of life emanating through the "painted memory" of their death, Sibaso is adorned as a decomposing carcass while seeking shelter in the womblike space of a cave, thereby casting his symbolic rebirth as also a regenerative death. By giving up his individuated subjectivity and with it the colonial desire he and Cephas incarnate, Sibaso's regenerative death becomes the condition of reanimating animism's infinitely implicated subjectivity sacrificed at the advent of colonial modernity and memorialized in the painting by the virgins' circle.

This interpretation explains why immediately after viewing the painting Sibaso dives into a mine crater full of cadavers: His symbolic rebirth necessitates a ritualized self-burial. He joins victims of the mass violence taking place across post-independent Zimbabwe, people sacrificed (like the ancient virgins) on behalf of a newly formed nation-state. He narrates: "I lie among the arms, legs, the torso of an already-forgotten man. This is a resting place, this singed place, this shrine of powdered stars. I enter the lives of the dead. The soil is chaos and ash. I enter into its burning. The soil is warm like a liquid. I am among the dead voices. I inhale their last breath. I share their last memory, this sight of thundering perfume. I hear their last sounds, charred voices" (105). Sibaso joins a collective body (arms, legs, and torso) of people killed in the *Gukurahundi*. By declaring this mass grave (resembling the many left behind during the genocide) a "shrine" (indeed, the "burning" soil of this "singed place" suggests the crater is an altar)[35], he memorializes this mass death as, like the painting of the stone virgins, a sacrifice. And by inhaling their breath, reanimating this sacrificed collective, he hears their "forgotten" voices. Through his inscription of himself as part of a collective subject dead and forgotten, Sibaso, in giving up his own individuated subjectivity, re-members[36] the subject functioning as that which is constitutively extirpated on behalf of an emerging *polis*. He thus places the state of Zimbabwe in a genealogy of sacrifice, connecting the new nation to the colonial *polis* from which it revolted, yet also combats this sacrifice by regenerating a co-animacy between the living, the dead, and their ecosystem lost in the wake of colonial history.

Sibaso thus invests the frame narrative's posthumanist movement with the grammar of postsecular ritual. In fact, the novel's depiction of a symbiosis between the human and more-than-human world is in Sibaso's rite inseparable from a connection between the living and the dead: "I nestle into the warm soil, as close to the dead as I can travel, as far away from the claims of the living, far from myself. Here, in this soil, there is something I can trust, someone. . . . Geographies are my only matter, my absolute concern. *Umhlaba*. This earth. The darkness falls close to my skin, like skin" (106–07). As Sibaso continues to leave his "self," soil and darkness become his skin (an environmental skin-ego, in Didier Anzieu's terms); in his becoming-dead, Sibaso is also becoming-earth (*Umhlaba* means earth in Zulu). The soil gains personhood ("someone"), while Sibaso, losing the last vestiges of his individuated personhood, concentrates only on geography: the ideological foundation, according to Vera, of colonial modernity. What began as Sibaso's symbolic rebirth in a cave thus culminates in his ritualized self-burial in a mass grave, which Vera casts as a belated burial rite for the victims of the *Gukurahundi*. Sibaso grabs a whistle from a dead man's pocket: "I hold the whistle with my thumb and forefinger. This is how he must have held it, the man before me. I know I have erased his last touch, the impress of his fingers. I have lost him. I blow a soft tune, which I can hardly hear. It is the only way to bury man—with a sound lighter than his own ashes" (106). The last finger "impress" on the whistle—left, presumably, during the mine explosion—is forever erased, replaced by the impress of Sibaso's finger, but it is during this act of erasure that the dead man's last breath—his last blow of the whistle and thus the breath signifying his own death—is finally heard, yet through Sibaso's breath as a medium. The word "impress" places this belated burial rite in contrast to Cephas's desire to possess Thenjiwe's "imprint" on the soil, the former emerging from an individuated desire to own the other, the latter a signal of the former's dissolution.

As the individuated subject of colonial modernity is buried alongside the victims of the *Gukurahundi*, the environment—the original site of colonial trauma, according to Vera—joins the rite: "In the darkness, a wind builds, whipping through the trees. It moves against my cheek and throws wild dust into my eyes, hard and sharp grains like bits of ground bone. . . . [I]t is a merciful burial. . . . My eyes are open to the breath of a wind. I hold the rough grains between my fingers. The sensation is not unpleasant. I sleep" (107). The frame narrative's more-than-human movement reenters the narrative as Sibaso reconnects the protagonist constellation to it through his giving up his individuated life. The wind (personified as breathing) shakes the trees (recalling the tree-prisons of her dissertation and thus the arch-space of colonial trauma) and offers Sibaso a "merciful burial" under "wild dust." The phrase "bits of ground bone" implies a culmination of the Cephas-Sibaso mimetic character arc by grinding the recurrent Adamic symbol back into dust as Sibaso fully gives up the colonial desire to which it points. The phrase also associates this burial with Nehanda's prophecy, suggesting that a true anti-colonial revolution must begin by reanimating a lost transsubjectivity in which the living and the dead as well as the human and nonhuman participate, a reanimation that can only come through the death of colonial modernity's individuated subject. Considering the colonial history of this scene's setting deepens this point. Sibaso's burial rite takes place not only among victims of the *Gukurahundi*, but also beside the burial site of Rhodes, who dictated in his will that he be buried in the Matapos Hills beside a monument to the BSAC soldiers who died fighting the first Matabele War.[37] Sibaso's self-burial (an antithesis of Rhodes's self-aggrandizing funeral) thus, like the rest of the novel, combats the violence at the origins of both post-independent Zimbabwe and colonial Rhodesia. This combat allows the more-than-human collective movement of the frame narrative to reenter the novel: hence Nonceba's walking through Bulawayo's streets while Cephas, reappearing for the first time since his departure from Thenjiwe, appears "surrounded by a burst of hibiscus blooms" (146–47).

"A More Fertile Ground"

The novel concludes with Cephas modeling a form of cultural memory enabled by Sibaso's ritualized self-burial and thus, to return to the theoretical polemic framing my analysis, the work of multidimensional memory beyond the boundaries of multidirectional memory. Now living with Nonceba in Bulawayo, Cephas works as an archivist for the National Museums and Monuments of Zimbabwe (182), a job associating him with the end point of the novel's opening sentence and thus its work of constructing post-traumatic cultural memory. The novel's final paragraph describes his current assignment in terms that cast it as a symbol of the novel's immanent theory of multidimensional memory:

> He must retreat from Nonceba; perhaps he has become too involved in replicating histories. He should stick to restorations of ancient kingdoms, circular structures, beehive huts, stone knives, broken pottery, herringbone walls, the vanished pillars in an old world. A new nation needs to restore the past. His focus, the beehive hut, to be installed at Lobengula's ancient kraal, kwoBulawayo, the following year. His task is to learn to re-create the manner in which the tenderest branches bend, meet, and dry, the way grass folds smoothly over this frame and weaves a nest, the way it protects the cool, livable places within—deliverance. (184)

First, Sibaso must forgo "replicating histories" (a problem uniting his love life and job) and instead focus on "restorations of ancient kingdoms." This alternative framing of cultural memory shifts focus to the renewal of space: the same goal, according to Vera, of literature penned to combat colonial spatial ideology. Hence this paragraph's focus on "circular structures" (resembling the stone virgins' formation): Indigenous forms replaced by the colony's rectilinear architecture. In a world transfigured by colonial trauma, the novel concludes, what the "new nation" of Zimbabwe needs is the restoration of African space and thus the regeneration of an African subject. This regenerative process is the goal of Cephas's current assignment. King Lobengula's kraal is the very space in which Lobengula was tricked into signing the Rudd Concession in 1888 and is thus the space of the contractual genesis of Rhodesia.[38] By installing in this historical kraal a beehive hut (a "circular structure" that, in form and title, reblends the human and the more-than-human world into a single domestic space and thus combats colonization's "geographical violence"), Cephas is given the chance to "re-create" African subjectivity by restoring an arch-space of colonial trauma. Thus, as the avicultural terms in the final sentence suggest, Cephas's task is to regenerate a habitat, to weave a nest in which a postcolonial subject might emerge from the very site of colonial trauma. His restoration of the past is thus future oriented: He must restore "memories of the future" (*Nehanda* 3), as Vera puts it in her first novel. This task—both posthumanist and postsecular (and as such, intrinsically ecological)—operates beyond the purveyance of cultural memory studies' post-Enlightenment European epistemology. As *The Stone Virgins'* final paragraph suggests, restoring the possibility of the future embedded in the past (in a word, prophecy) is what is at stake in Vera's writing of multidimensional memory.

In conclusion, consider how Vera explains to a Zimbabwean reading public in *The Bulawayo Chronicle* the difficulties facing an African writer who attempts to depict Indigenous culture:

> Our culture is not transparent; it is living. It has been shaken, violently, like certain kinds of trees which when shaken repeatedly lose their leaves and drop some of their fruit and their many seeds to the ground. Beneath the ground, their roots remain breathing and able, then the seeds grow and sometimes are even stronger than the tree from which they have fallen. On such an occasion it is clear then that sometimes it takes a violent wind to find new roots from which to begin or to discover a more fertile ground. ("The Writer's World")

Colonization, Vera argues, has "shaken" African culture so violently that the postcolonial writer is unable to depict it through "transparent" signification. A positivist, secular hermeneutics will not suffice for the writer who seeks to memorialize that which has been extirpated by the advent of colonial modernity. Rothberg's model of multidirectional memory, as productive as its challenge to competitive memory is, assumes culture to be "transparent": readable through cross-cultural analysis. In contrast, in the passage above, like in her fiction, Vera implicitly rejects Rothberg's vision of collective memorialization, not because it is false, but because it cannot adequately conceptualize the way colonial trauma structures African modernity. Motivated by a recognition of what I have been describing throughout this book as ancestral trauma, Vera's scholarship and fiction alike render impossible the debates within the public sphere imagined by Rothberg as a pathway to global justice.

Importantly, though, Vera proposes an affirmative aesthetics in response to her claim that her culture has been "shaken . . . violently" to the point of an apparent unreadability. She does so by describing another process I have described throughout this book: the regenerative death drive. Extending her arboreal metaphor, she explains that the fallen fruit of a shaken tree releases seeds, which produce new, sometimes stronger, trees. In this way a "violent wind" enables, through the death it inflicts, new life. While the wind in this passage functions as a metaphor of colonial trauma, the erasure of Indigenous culture to which the postcolonial African writer must respond, it also makes a more specific address to the Zimbabwean reading public to whom she writes. *Gukurahundi* roughly translates to the wind that separates the chaff from the grain. What this allusion suggests is that central to *The Stone Virgins'* depiction of the genocide is an attempt to transfigure its memory into a site of collective regeneration, an act of renewal akin to Cephas's kraal restoration. We could filter Vera's metaphor through Rothberg's framework, claiming that cultural traumas are always sites of collective identity formation through processes of memorialization. But such an interpretation ignores Vera's insistence on the extirpation of culture and thus the damage done to the mechanisms of cultural memory undergirding the postcolonial African writer's condition. In fact, this insistence recasts Rothberg's oft-quoted real estate development metaphor. For Vera, postcolonial African literature must combat the spatial forms through which Indigenous cultural memory has been transfigured by colonialism's "zero-sum struggle over scarce recourses" (*Multidirectional* 3). Her animist poetics, developed as a strategic response to this historical-political nexus, is an attempt to "discover more fertile ground."

Conclusion

Principles of Animist Criticism

In this book I theorized three interrelated concepts: ancestral trauma, animist poetics, and the regenerative death drive. I analyzed their presence in postcolonial African literature in English, all the while considering how literary and cultural criticism might benefit from the paradigm shifts they enable. This brief conclusion distills the main points developed across this book. It is my hope that this abstraction will help those who study the postcolonial condition from different linguistic, racial, historical, and geographic contexts apply the mode of animist criticism I have modeled, then nuance, revise, or challenge this critical lens to account for alternative structures of the psyche, culture, ecology, and subjectivity occluded from this study.

Ancestral trauma is the spiritual outworking of colonization's material damage: the problem of cultural inheritance after Indigenous cosmologies are wrecked alongside the economies and ecosystems in which they operate. This natural and cultural mutilation results in the extirpation of the perceived kinship between the living and the dead and the human and more-than-human world embodied in the colonized subject: an "extirpation of animism" that Max Horkheimer and Theodor Adorno cast as the genesis of modernity (2). This extirpation is inherited by the colonized subject as an erasure of ancestral ties and thus the erasure of the psychosocial mechanisms through which Indigenous cultural memory operates.

Animist poetics is the appropriation and reinvention of Indigenous cosmologies as strategic responses to their erasure under colonial modernity—a widespread and variegated aesthetic practice across the postcolonial social imaginary. Since colonial modernity only emerges through the ancestral trauma it inflicts, animist poetics is always an aesthetic response to this trauma. Since ancestral trauma is the cultural outworking of animism's extirpation, animist poetics is always an aesthetic of dialectical regeneration. As such, it is an explicitly modernist logic, a postcolonial enactment of Ezra Pound's slogan "Make It New!" The utopian horizon of this remaking is a renewed kinship between the subject and the cosmos in its more-than-human, more-than-living, cosmic totality. Not all texts within the aesthetic logic of animist poetics are equally suited for this task. Conceptualizing a realism-ritual spectrum within animist poetics helps criticism differentiate between texts that re-enchant modernity through representational aesthetics and texts that mend modernity through ritual aesthetics—a dialectical processing of history at the level of form that mirrors many practices of postcolonial spirit possession.

The regenerative death drive is the logic conditioning animist poetics' symbiotic relationship to ancestral trauma, the force undergirding its multifarious attempts to mend the wounding constitutive of its historical emergence. Since the goal of animist poetics is to regenerate Indigenous cosmologies in response to their erasure—not a precolonial return, but a postcolonial remaking—the dynamic of regenerative death is intrinsic to animist poetics' aesthetic operations. By naming this immanent dynamic "the regenerative death drive," however, I emphasize the manner in which it implicitly extends and overturns the Freudian death drive. While Freud claimed that the aim of all life is death, animist poetics casts the aim of death as a new form of collective life—which is the ultimate goal of Frantz Fanon's appropriation of psychoanalytic theory. This revision of the death drive functions as an entry point for a more holistic revision of psychoanalytic theory's retainment of post-Enlightenment secular humanism—a contrapuntal reading of Freud that undermines his attempts to distance his most radical discoveries from the animism he perceives as "primitive," "neurotic," and "childish."

Operating together, these three concepts provincialize Euro-American trauma theory as well as its postcolonial critique, which tends to critique Eurocentrism's blind spots without taking the next step to theorize trauma from Indigenous epistemological frameworks. If we move beyond this debate, we can productively juxtapose canonical and animist trauma theories. Canonical trauma theory tends to focus on the individual, the human, and the living. Freudian and deconstructive trauma theory productively critique and undermine each of these categories, but do not venture beyond their logic as radically as many Indigenous cosmologies do. In contrast to canonical trauma theory, many Indigenous cosmologies understand trauma as transpersonal, transspecies, and transtemporal. This juxtaposition contrasts the ipseitic subject with the animist subject. The latter categories—transpersonal, transspecies, and transtemporal—cast the animist subject as a form of collectivity intertwining the living and the dead as well as and the human and more-than-human world. This is because subjectivity, according to animism, is not an individuated experience, but is instead an ongoing environmental process. Consequently, theorizing trauma throughout the colonized world requires a posthumanist, postsecular, and ecocritical framework. In fact, according to animism, theorizing anything requires this framework.

It follows that discourses frequently employing aspects of this framework (e.g., the environmental humanities) can help articulate the assumed subject of animist poetics, which means that interpreting trauma across the colonized world should not solely rely on the coordinates and lexicon of trauma theory proper. However, since animism in the modern epoch is always a response to ancestral trauma, a critical understanding of animism requires a theory of trauma as a starting point. An ecocriticism with no interest in trauma, for instance, misses the fact that in the modern epoch, animist ecologies are always conceived in response to a form of trauma that is intrinsically environmental. At the same time, a study of animist poetics should not be content with fully defining its logic as a logic of trauma. Since the goal of animist poetics is the regeneration of an extirpated subject, a critical understanding of animism should move through trauma theory into a broader theory of postcolonial subject formation as the regeneration of cosmic kinship.

This process is dialectical. Just like animist poetics is a response to colonial modernity, its envisioned subject is a response to the ipseitic subject that was violently imposed upon Indigenous cultures and ecosystems through colonization. All forms of animist poetics are therefore aesthetic strategies of dialectical subject formation emerging in combative response to the individuated, sovereignly bordered subject of post-Enlightenment European rationality. The animist lyric, for example, incants a form of cosmic personhood as a dialectical departure from this individuated subject, while animist tragedy stages the communal bonds enabled by this departure. Moreover, an animist process of cultural memorialization—which is central to the problem of ancestral trauma and is thus intrinsic to all modern practices of animism—must be approached as a dialectical response to the constricting dimensions of an individuated subjectivity that the academic discourse of cultural memory studies typically assumes as natural.

It follows that theoretical discourses set on critiquing the myth of the sovereign subject, such as new materialist ecology and biopolitical theology, can help critics articulate the phenomenon of ancestral trauma and the cultural work of animist poetics. But we must recognize the aspects of animism that venture beyond Euro-American theory's post-Cartesian framework. New materialism, for example, often unconsciously perceives the Cartesian subject it critiques as the only viable subject and therefore casts its utopian horizon as a universally flattened ontology of nonsubjects. This horizon separates new materialism from animist poetics' historically contingent act of postcolonial subject formation, even if both seek the radical expansion of agency. Animist poetics' most striking departure from contemporary theory, however, is its nonlinear forms of temporality: its incorporation not only of atoms, but also of the ancestors, into its expansion of agency. Comparing animist temporalities to the temporalities assumed in contemporary theory highlights the ways in which theory, even during its sharpest critiques of the post-Enlightenment European *polis*, retains an attachment to this *polis*'s secular rationality. The pessimism that often plagues biopolitical critique, for example, is a consequence of its inability to conceive of death as a threshold leading to new communal vitality rather than vitality's teleological end point. Theory, it seems, is still catching up with African literature.

Notes

Introduction

1. One influence on my approach to animism as postcolonial rather than precolonial is the anthropological study of spirit possession exemplified by Michael Taussig's and Paul Stoller's studies of shamanic healing rituals. For them, such rituals are less examples of precolonial religion than modes of postcolonial critique. Similarly, while the examples of poetry, drama, and fiction I analyze in this book attempt to produce Indigenous modes of healing, none proposes a return to the precolonial, Indigenous past. Instead, they take for granted that Indigenous cosmologies are necessarily implicated in colonial modernity. Fritz Kramer's *The Red Fez: Art and Spirit Possession in Africa*; Jocelyn Alexander, JoAnn McGregor, and Terence Ranger's *Violence and Memory: One Hundred Years in the Dark Forests of Matabeleland, Zimbabwe*; Donald Cosentino's *Defiant Maids and Stubborn Farmers: Tradition and Invention in Mende Story Performance*; and Jean and John Comaroff's edited *Modernity and Its Malcontents: Ritual and Power in Postcolonial Africa* and their "Occult Economies and the Violence of Abstraction: Notes from the South African Postcolony" are a few examples of other helpful socio-anthropological approaches to possession rituals. Other anthropological studies, not focused specifically on such rituals, but useful in contextualizing and illuminating them, are the Comaroffs' *Of Revelation and Revolution: Christianity, Colonialism and Consciousness in South Africa*, William Bascom's *Ifa Divination: Communication Between Gods and Men in West Africa*, and Andrew Apter's *Black Critics and Kings: The Hermeneutics of Power in Yoruba Society*.

2. By *posthumanist*, I do not mean anti-humanist, but rather theory assuming a critical disposition toward anthropocentrism. This disposition reconsiders cultural semiotics outside the purely human domain overseeing most of the theoretical humanities, approaching the nature/culture relationship in a non-dualist manner. For the preeminent introduction to posthumanism, see Cary Wolfe's *What Is Posthumanism?* For examples of how this discourse relates to

African, Black, and postcolonial literatures, see Evan Mwangi's *The Postcolonial Animal: African Literature and Posthuman Ethics*, Alexander Ghedi Weheliye's *Habeas Viscus: Racializing Assemblages, Biopolitics, and Black Feminist Theories of the Human*, Zakiyyah Iman Jackson's *Becoming Human: Matter and Meaning in an Antiblack World*, and Dominic O'Key's *Creaturely Forms in Contemporary Literature: Narrating the War on Animals*.

3. By *postsecular* I mean an approach to the sacred/secular divide as porous, mutually constitutive, and always in the process of renegotiation. For an introduction to postsecular critique, see Jürgen Habermas's "Religion in the Public Sphere," Talal Asad's *Formations of the Secular*, Charles Taylor's *A Secular Age*, John D. Caputo's *On Religion*, Saba Mahmood's "Secularism, Hermeneutics, and Empire: The Politics of Islamic Reformation," and Asad, Wendy Brown, Judith Butler, and Mahmood's *Is Critique Secular?* For an introduction to how this discourse relates to postcolonial and African literature, see Graham Huggan's "Is the 'Post' in 'Postsecular' the 'Post' in 'Postcolonial'?" Jeanne-Marie Jackson and Nathan Suhr-Sytsma's "Introduction: Religion, Secularity, and African Writing," Manav Ratti's *The Postsecular Imagination: Postcolonialism, Religion, and Literature*, and Rebekah Cumpsty's *Postsecular Poetics: Negotiating the Sacred and Secular in Contemporary African Fiction*.

4. *Ecopoetics* signifies an approach to cultural form attentive to the ecologies in which such forms are produced. For examples of ecocritical approaches to African and postcolonial literatures, see Rob Nixon's *Slow Violence and the Environmentalism of the Poor*; Cajetan Iheka's *Naturalizing Africa: Ecological Violence, Agency, and Postcolonial Resistance* and *African Ecomedia: Network Forms, Planetary Politics*; Elizabeth de Loughery's *Allegories of the Anthropocene*; Jennifer Wenzel's *The Disposition of Nature: Environmental Crisis and World Literature*; Emily McGiffin's *Of Land, Bones, and Money: Toward a South African Ecopoetics*; Louise Green's *Fragments from the History of Loss: The Nature Industry and the Postcolony*; Lesley Green's *Rock/Water/Life: Ecology and Humanities for a Decolonial South Africa*; and Byron Caminero-Santangelo's *Different Shades of Green: African Literature, Environmental Justice, and Political Ecology*.

5. While anthropologists such as Michael Taussig and Eduardo Viveiros de Castro have long been promoting the ontological insights intrinsic to Indigenous knowledge systems, as well as the postcolonial critique such insights enable, postcolonial literary scholarship has been slower to make such an "ontological turn" away from the particular vision of historical materialism overseeing the field. While a focus on the material forces of history is undoubtedly important for literary criticism, it also strikes me that critics should take more seriously the overwhelming presence of spiritual concerns in African literature—which, as I will demonstrate, is by no means antithetical to historical materialism, but is instead an expansion of its critique of global capitalism.

6. See also Adéléke Adéèkọ́'s "The Spell That Fails Lacks an Essential Term: Poetry, Animism, and Ideophones" and *Arts of Being Yoruba: Divination, Allegory, Tragedy, Proverb, Panegyric*.

7. For Pumla Gobodo-Madikizela, the practice of psychoanalysis in postcolonial contexts demands such a paradigm shift. Justifying her use of psychanalysis to conceptualize traumatic memory in postapartheid South Africa, she writes, "The intersubjective epistemological model has broadened the notion of the intrapsychic realm beyond its individualistic confines. Going beyond this idea of the 'internal unconscious/intrapsychic' as a concept that refers *exclusively* to what is happening inside the mind of the subject, contemporary psychoanalytic thought now views the development of the self as occurring in relation to the other" (1100).

8. *Oxford English Dictionary*'s initial definition of *cosmology* reads "The science or theory of the universe as an ordered whole, and of the general laws which govern it. Also, a particular account or system of the universe and its laws." Its second definition, focused on philosophy, reads "That branch of metaphysics which deals with the idea of the world as a totality of all phenomena in space and time." I use the term with both definitions in mind. The Indigenous knowledge systems informing so much of African literature assume theories of the universe and metaphysical systematization of such theories, which often differ from the cosmological frameworks literary critics assume. Indeed, most literary criticism sidesteps questions of cosmology, focusing instead on a totalizing binary of epistemology and ontology through which all acts of critical interpretation are filtered. Cosmology, however, deals not only with knowledge (epistemology) or being (ontology), but more fundamentally contextualizes each of these categories within the movement of the cosmos itself. By framing animism as a cosmology operating through coordinates that do not always coincide with the metaphysical tradition of Western philosophy, I am influenced by the effort of many modern Africanist philosophers to take Indigenous knowledge systems seriously as coherent philosophical orders. See, for example, Emmanuel Chukwudi Eze's edited *African Philosophy: An Anthology*, Placide Tempels's *Bantu Philosophy*, Paulin Hountondji's *African Philosophy: Myth and Reality*, Kwasi Wiredu's *Philosophy and an African Culture*, V. Y. Mudimbe's *The Invention of Africa: Gnosis, Philosophy, and the Order of Knowledge*, Kwame Anthony Appiah's *In My Father's House: Africa in the Philosophy of Culture*, and Kwame Gyekye's *An Essay on African Philosophical Thought: The Akan Conceptual Scheme*. I am also influenced by scholars who likewise take Indigenous knowledge systems seriously within the framework of religious studies. For introductory explorations of animism in this vein, see John Mbiti's *Introduction to African Religion*, Philip M. Peek's edited *African Divination Systems: Ways of Knowing*, Jacob Olupona's *African Religions: A Very Short Introduction*, and his edited *Beyond Primitivism: Indigenous Religious Traditions and Modernity*. In this book I take a more aesthetic approach to animism than

the aforementioned scholars, analyzing how animist cosmologies shape and become reshaped by literary experimentation. In this sense I am most influenced by Soyinka's touchstone theorization of African cosmologies in *Myth, Literature and the African World*.

9. By casting African writers' engagements with animism as *strategic* responses to a trauma foundational to modernity, I am redeploying Ato Quayson's concept of "strategic transformations"—that is, the process by which African writers transform their traditions through literary representation. Quayson quotes Claude Lévi-Strauss as articulating such a process as part and parcel with all myth: "[A] mythic system can only be in a *process of becoming*; not as something inert and stable but in a process of perpetual transformation" (67).

10. As F. Abiola Irele memorably puts it, in postcolonial African literature "the archaic imagination" functions as a "collective resource from which to derive a new relation to the world" (60–61). By framing animist poetics as thoroughly modern in this way, my study implicitly casts postcolonial African literature as a salient corpus for "the new modernism"—that is, modernism with a global scope. See, for example, Douglas Mao and Rebecca Walkowitz's "The New Modernist Studies" and, for a more postcolonial perspective, Simon Gikandi's "Preface: Modernism in the World." While it might be tempting to consequently cast animist poetics as one example of what S. N. Eisenstadt labels "multiple modernities," I am wary of the manner in which an overly relativistic approach to modernity risks ignoring the historical fact that all modernist logics are responses to a single, world-shaping modernity: global capitalism. In this sense I am influenced by the Warwick Research Collective's *Combined and Uneven Development: Towards a New Theory of World-Literature*. While such an approach rightly casts animist poetics as implicated in the same modernity as, say, that of Freud, it also risks diluting non-Western logic until it resembles a bootlegged version of Marxist economics. As Charles Taylor reminds us in "Two Theories of Modernity," a theory focused on the universal advent of capitalist modernity should still be attentive to the epistemic coordinates framing disparate subjects' experiences of modernity:

> The belief that modernity comes from one single universally applicable operation imposes a falsely uniform pattern on the multiple encounters of non-Western cultures with the exigencies of science, technology, and industrialization. As long as we are bemused by the Enlightenment package, we will believe that they all *have* to undergo a range of cultural changes drawn from our experience—such as "secularization" or the growth of atomistic forms of self-identification. As long as we leave our own notions of identity unexamined, so long will we fail to see how theirs differ, and how this difference crucially conditions the way in which they integrate the truly universal feature of "modernity." (28)

11. We might therefore interpret Mntambo's composite as a postcolonial response to W. B. Yeats's poem "Leda and the Swan," which also casts a mythic rape as generative of the European world.

12. Colonial anthropology of animism (a major source for Freudian psychanalysis) in this sense envisions what Saidiya Hartman calls a "reductive metaphysics of Africanity that produces Africa as the temporal other of the West and the values of Africanity as little more than a shorthand for sensuousness, instinct, rhythm, superstition, improvisation, naturalness, and physical prowess" (*Scenes* 74). A postcolonial approach, by contrast, "does not bifurcate animism and magic from science," Delali Kumavie writes, "but rather positions them as simultaneous and interwoven" (39).

13. See Harvey's *Animism: Respecting the Living World* and *The Handbook of Contemporary Animism*; in a similar vein, see David Abram's *The Spell of the Sensuous: Perception and Language in a More-Than-Human World*. For anthropological studies at the forefront of this new animism, see Eduardo Viveiros de Castro's "Cosmological Deixis and Amerindian Perspectivism" and *Cannibal Metaphysics*; Nurit Bird-David's "'Animism' Revisited: Personhood, Environment, and Relational Epistemology"; Tim Ingold's "Rethinking the Animate, Re-animating Thought"; and Alf Hornborg's "Animism, Fetishism, and Objectivism as Strategies for Knowing (or not Knowing) the World." For introductions to how literary and cultural theorists are currently utilizing animism, see Christopher Bracken's *Magical Criticism: The Recourse of Savage Philosophy*, Anselm Franke's edited "Animism" special issue of *e-flux*, Mischa Twitchin and Carl Lavery's "On Animism" special issue of *Performance Research*, Rosemary Jolly and Alexander Fyfe's edited "Reflections on Postcolonial Animations of the Material" special issue of *Cambridge Journal of Postcolonial Literary Inquiry*, and Sam Durrant and Philip Dickinson's edited "Animism in a Planetary Frame" special issue of *New Formations*.

14. Abram, a major figure for the environmental humanities, bases his ecological philosophy in animistic modes of thought. The consequential connections between his approach to ecology and my approach to colonial trauma and postcolonial literary form demonstrate that this book, though focalized around trauma theory, intrinsically speaks to discourses outside the fields of psychoanalysis, trauma studies, and postcolonial literature—perhaps most pertinently the environmental humanities. Since the global climate disaster cannot be separated from colonial modernity and the collective ruptures of Indigenous cosmologies it has inflicted (and continues to inflict) across the world, it is my hope that this book will help ecocritics outside of postcolonial and African studies recuperate a trauma theory more adequate to the task of conceptualizing the more-than-human crisis in which we live.

15. For a recent grappling with individualism in African philosophy and literature, see Jeanne-Marie Jackson's *The African Novel of Ideas: Philosophy and Individualism in the Age of Global Writing*.

16. In this sense animist poetics resonates with Arne Naess's approach to "deep ecology," an ecology that stresses kinship across life forms, place, and time,

what he calls a total-field model. This model, he argues, "dissolves not only the man-in-environment concept but every compact thing-in-milieu concept" (28).

17. My interpretive act of locating subjective coordinates in these poems builds upon Olakunle George's argument in *Relocating Agency: Modernity and African Letters* that African literature offers an articulation of a form of agency crafted in response to modernity. Just as D. O. Fagunwa's fiction carries for George "at once a principle of interpretation and a vision of history and agency," so do all of African literature's instantiations of animist poetics (108).

18. Placide Tempels's *Bantu Philosophy* influentially places being-as-force (or being-enforced) at the core of ontology for Bantu-speaking cultures. For an insightful response to Tempels's project, see V. Y. Mudimbe's *The Invention of Africa*.

19. Louise Green therefore uses animism as a corrective to new materialist approaches to the material body. "The vital materialist project," she writes, "wishes to displace the human, divide consciousness from the materiality of the body. Within the animist tradition, thinking outside the body or inhabiting another's materiality is possible, but it is always precarious undertaking fraught with danger and difficulty" ("Thinking" 314).

20. Hence my insistence that animist poetics begins with trauma. Although the theoretical humanities have largely moved beyond the influence of the "trauma studies" of the 1990s and 2000s, it is my contention that more current theoretical discourses (such as the environmental humanities) would benefit from taking seriously the way animist poetics envisions its expansion of subjectivity in dialectical response to the cosmological trauma intrinsic to colonial modernity. Since the environmental crises of our epoch cannot be separated from the rupture of living connections across the cosmos systematically perpetuated by European imperial expansion via global capitalism, the emerging use of animism in the environmental humanities (for example, the "ecological animism" Thom van Dooren and Deborah Bird Rose champion as the logic of "lively ethnography") would greatly benefit by returning to trauma theory in light of the critique of anthropocentrism central to the field. Such a return would help the environmental humanities shift its conception of animism—a term increasingly used within this discourse to describe a feeling of interspecies connectivity—away from the affect of empathy and toward the collective dialectical movement intrinsic to my postcolonial use of the term.

21. The legal-theological notion of a covenant derives from the Latin *convenire*, to assemble or come together. The intimate connection in Judaic theology between the Abrahamic *covenant*, the *binding* of Isaac, and the *formation* of the Jewish people is thus a useful analogy for my distinction between animist poetics and new materialism. Unlike new materialism, the animism revealed in these poems is aimed at binding together the living and dead through a covenant rooted in the natural symbiosis between life and death perceived in so many Indigenous knowledge systems. This covenant (quite different, to be sure, from

the Judeo-Christian understanding of a human-divine covenant abstracted from nature) aims to form a collective subject beyond the philosophical parameters of subjectivity erected through European imperialism.

22. This ontological reframing of metaphysics around life force (espoused most famously by Placide Tempels's study of African Indigenous knowledge systems), I would add, casts animism as cosmological before it is ontological. This priority alone—the cosmos is before being is—has the potential to reframe much of theory after deconstruction.

Chapter 1

1. I borrow the term "historiographic perversion" from Marc Nichanian, who sees it as fundamental to modern genocide.

2. Mbembe states this problem poignantly: "Various factors have prevented the full development of conceptions that might have explained the meaning of the African past and present by reference to the future, but chief among them may be named historicism" (238).

3. An analysis of the symbiotic relationship between ancestral trauma and animist poetics from, in Paul Gilroy's terms, a Black Atlantic framework, would in this sense be a pertinent addition to scholarship. Toni Morrison, Derek Walcott, Robert Hayden, M. NourbeSe Philip, and many other writers across the African diaspora have formed their own styles of animist poetics in response to variegated historical experiences of ancestral trauma. Similarly, given that Indigenous populations across Asia, Oceania, and the Americas have experienced colonization and have creatively utilized Indigenous cosmologies in response, a comparative analysis of ancestral trauma and animist poetics from disparate postcolonial perspectives—not limited to Africa or the Anglophone world—would likewise be a welcome addition to scholarship. I hope that my focus on African writing, which is too often ignored in US academia, will be useful for critics in other fields concerned with the historical legacies of imperialism, racism, and the uneven conditions of the capitalist world system.

4. Mbembe does not define "witchcraft." I prefer the term animism as to avoid conflation with the European figure of the witch.

5. My argument in this chapter thus resonates with Uzoma Esonwanne's call to "bring both psychoanalysis and African literatures into a mutually productive dialogue" (142).

6. In *Culture and Imperialism*, Said defines contrapuntal interpretation as reading the canon "with a simultaneous awareness both of the metropolitan history that is narrated and those of other histories against which (and together with which) the dominating discourse acts" (51). His most famous example of reading contrapuntally is his focus on Thomas Bertram's Antiguan plantation

in Jane Austen's *Mansfield Park*. Like Said arguing that the colonial plantation economy made possible the nineteenth-century English novel even as this form repressed it, I am claiming that psychoanalysis's repressed animism, revealed by reading African literature and psychoanalytic theory contrapuntally, is central to understanding psychoanalysis as a discourse of colonial modernity.

7. For an early example of an inquiry into the relation between psychoanalysis and colonialism (and the first work of psychoanalysis to be published in South Africa), see Wulf Sachs's *Black Hamlet*.

8. See also Shoshana Felman and Dori Laub, Geoffrey Hartman, and Dominick LaCapra. For an introduction to the impact of this tradition within literary and cultural studies, see Mary Jacobus's edited "Trauma and Psychoanalysis" in *Diacritics*; Karyn Ball's edited "Trauma and Its Cultural Aftereffects" in *Cultural Critique*; and Linda Belau and Petar Ramadanovic's edited "Trauma: Essays on the Limit of Knowledge and Experience" in *Postmodern Culture*.

9. As Freud goes on to argue, this process challenges his previous theory of dreams as wish fulfillment and necessitates a restructuring of psychoanalysis from the pleasure principle to the repetition compulsion, out of which emerges his theory of the death drive.

10. For a detailed articulation of Levinasian ethics, see Simon Critchley's *The Ethics of Deconstruction: Derrida and Levinas*.

11. Berlant writes that while "trauma theory conventionally focuses on exceptional shock and data loss in the memory and experience of catastrophe, implicitly suggesting that subjects ordinarily archive the intensities neatly and efficiently with an eye toward easy access," in reality the experience of "[c]risis is not exceptional to history or consciousness but a process embedded in the ordinary that unfolds in stories about navigating what's overwhelming" (10).

12. Two indicative and relatively early examples of this formula—from a believer and a skeptic—are Eleanor Kaufman's "Falling from the Sky," one of the first employments of Caruthian trauma theory, and Greg Forter's "Freud, Faulkner, Caruth," an influential critique of Caruthian trauma theory. Kaufman perceptively reads Caruth, but does so in order to interpret a literary text as a diagnostic representation of a sociohistorically situated trauma. The motif of falling in Georges Perec's *W*, she argues, functions as "a particular emblem for one form of postwar trauma—and here specifically post-Holocaust trauma" (45). Forter perceptively reads William Faulkner, and does so to demonstrate the failure of what he calls Caruth's "punctual" theory of trauma to account for the mundane traumas of patriarchy and racism (260, 281).

13. Michelle Balaev takes this productive nature of trauma to be central to the form of the novel. A "traumatic experience disrupts the previous framework of reality and the protagonist must reorganize the self in relation to this new view of reality," she writes, which necessitates a departure from considering trauma

simply as fragmentation but rather as a reorganization of the modern subject as decentered (*The Nature* 40).

14. For Stephen Frosh, psychoanalysis perceives two forms of haunting. The subject is haunted vertically (temporally), as in the intergenerational transmission of trauma (e.g., the work of Nicolas Abraham and Maria Torok) as well as horizontally (spatially), as in transference or projective identification (5).

15. Throughout his series of encounters with strange forms of life—"Invisible Pawn" and "half-bodied baby," for instance—the protagonist and first-person narrator of *The Palm-Wine Drinkard* and *My Life in the Bush of Ghosts* morphs into elements, natural phenomena, and creatures: air, rain, a stick, a bird, a fish, to name a few examples. Sometimes the narrator quickly morphs back into human form—for instance, by his boss: "In the presence of these guests, my boss was changing me to some kinds of creatures," the narrator describes. "First of all he changed me to a monkey, then I began to climb fruit trees and pluck fruits down for them. After that he changed me to a lion, then to a horse, to a camel, to a cow or bull with horns on its head and at last to my former form" (36).

16. The centrality of "mechanical" and "railway" accidents to Freud's trauma theory, we should note, situates it both as a response to modernity and, by implication, the imperialist economy that made possible European modernization by fueling (literally) such accidents.

17. Freud himself recognizes the more-than-human, cosmological aspect of the death drive when, in *Beyond the Pleasure Principle*, he interprets human embryo development in conjunction with fish and bird migratory cycles, a comparison demonstrating for Freud that the instinct to return to a previous state is shared across the natural world.

18. See note 4 of the introduction.

19. This structure of subjectivity is also central to the materialism mapped out by Louis Althusser, whose theory of interpellation casts the subject as hailed into being by the external force of ideology, itself always tied to materiality, yet internal to human subjectivity.

20. For a germinal contextualization of Freudian, Marxist, and West African theories of the fetish within the history of colonialism, see William Pietz's article series on "The Problem of the Fetish." For Pietz, Freud's focus on the fetish object as a representation of a "singular personal event" structuring the subject's desire as well as Marx's focus on commodity fetishism as "the institutional structuring . . . of constructed value consciousness" both ignore the genealogy of the fetish as a modern concept (9). This genealogy is rooted in the long history of European and West African economic exchange and slave trade. Crucially, for Pietz, Indigenous theories of the fetish are also rooted in this history. "Akan goldweights," for example, "were a direct cultural response to the impact of gold-seeking European (and Arab) traders" (16). Just as Freud and Marx utilize a concept that emerged

through a "cross-cultural situation formed by the ongoing encounter of the value codes of radically different social orders" in order to theorize the subject of capitalist modernity, so do African Indigenous knowledge systems, Pietz argues (10). One consequence of Pietz's argument is that psychoanalysis, Marxism, and African Indigenous knowledge systems are each constitutively global and modern.

21. Edward Said's reading of *Moses and Monotheism* in *Freud and the Non-European* allows us to see Freud's late text not as a mere repetition of his earlier plot of the primal patricide and thus the constitution of sovereign authority (as René Girard, among others, has influentially argued), but rather the undoing of this sovereignty and thus the emergence of the possibility of a new form of community. For Said, this undoing and possibility result from Freud's argument that Moses was an Egyptian, which implies that Jewish identity—and more broadly the monotheistic structure of the Western *polis*—begins with an Arab. I will briefly return to this argument in the next chapter.

22. See Benjamin's "Critique of Violence" for an example of what I am calling his digressive use of Schmitt—that is, his utilization of the structure of Schmitt's jurisprudential theory in order to subvert jurisprudence itself. See also Nancy's "Deconstruction of Monotheism," Agamben's *Homo Sacer: Sovereign Power and Bare Life*, and Derrida's *The Beast and the Sovereign Volume 1*.

23. As Derrida writes in *The Beast and the Sovereign*, "The sovereignty of the people or of the nation merely inaugurates a new form of the same fundamental structure. The walls are destroyed, but the architectural model is not deconstructed—and will . . . continue to serve as a model and even as an international model" (282).

Chapter 2

1. In this sense, in terms of practical criticism, Garuba's animist realism is best applied in dialogue with Brenda Cooper's germinal study, *Magical Realism in West African Fiction* (1998).

2. The civil war (1991–2002), which left more than fifty thousand people dead and 2.5 million displaced, was mainly waged between the Sierra Leone Army and the rebels, the Revolutionary United Front.

3. Such critiques tend to ignore the fact that Derrida explicitly pins *Of Grammatology* against the West's "most original and powerful ethnocentrism" (3).

4. For examples of postcolonial trauma studies in this vein, see Abigail Ward's edited *Postcolonial Traumas: Memory, Narrative, Resistance*, Sonya Andermahr's edited *Decolonizing Trauma Studies: Trauma and Postcolonialism*, and Jay Rajiva's *Postcolonial Parabola: Literature, Tactility, and the Ethics of Representing Trauma*. Ogaga Ifowodo's *History, Trauma, and Healing in Postcolonial Narratives: Reconstructing Identities* and Roger Kurtz's *Trauma and Transformation in African*

Literature both productively resist the Manichaeism through which such critics often separate psychoanalytic trauma theory and postcolonial literature (Ifowodo's use of Fanon is exemplary in this manner). Zoe Norridge's *Perceiving Pain in African Literature* and Omar Chérif Diop's *Violence and Trauma in Selected African Literature* both focus on trauma in African literature but sidestep psychoanalytic trauma theory for examinations of personal pain and systemic violence, respectively.

    5. For a more extended analysis of this process focused on the rehabilitation of child soldiers, see Shepler's *Childhood Deployed: Remaking Child Soldiers in Sierra Leone.*

    6. For a posthumanist analysis of Forna's *Happiness* that resonates with the limits of her approach to animism I am addressing, see Dominic O'Key's "Aminatta Forna's Postcolonial Romance."

    7. Rothberg uses this phrase to mark his intervention in cultural trauma and memory studies, but, as I demonstrate in more detail in chapter 1, awakening to implicated subjectivity is the fundamental logic of Caruthian trauma theory. In chapter 5, I offer a more extensive engagement with Rothberg's paradigm for cultural memory.

    8. Zulu conceptions of the ancestral do saturate *Sounds of a Cowhide Drum*, the collection in which "An Abandon Bundle" was published. The speaker of the title poem, for example, is a drum incarnating the voice of ancestral spirits residing within the poem's addressee:

> Boom! Boom! Boom!
> I am the drum on your dormant soul,
> cut from the black hide of a sacrificial cow. (170)

"An Abandoned Bundle"'s focus on material economy should therefore be contextualized within the collection's more explicit engagements with animist content.

    9. Arthur Rose's use of Paul Ricoeur's narratology to conceptualize how literature formalizes the environmental and bodily damage inflicted by the asbestos mining industry offers a productive theoretical entry point for a more extended analysis of *Mine Mine Mine*'s engagement with silicosis and the South African mining economy.

Chapter 3

    1. For a preliminary definition of new materialism and its theoretical correlations with animism, see the introduction.

    2. For exceptional studies of time in Yoruba cosmology and culture, see J. A. Ayoada, Fayemi Ademola Kazeem, Sophie Oluwole, and J. D. Y. Peel. While

there are productive overlaps between Soyinka's theory of cyclic time and these scholars' attempts to map out Yoruba time's "labyrinth" form, to use Oluwole's formulation, for the purposes of this chapter I focus on Soyinka's self-consciously idiosyncratic and creative adaptation of its coordinates. As Andrew Apter argues in *Black Critics and Kings: The Hermeneutics of Power in Yoruba Society*, such creative adaptation is part and parcel of Yoruba culture, which approaches its cosmology as perpetually adaptable to sociopolitical context and ideology.

3. See, for example, Jahan Ramazani's *The Hybrid Muse: Postcolonial Poetry in English*, Nathan Suhr-Sytsma's *Poetry, Print and the Making of Postcolonial Literature*, Rajeev Patke's *Postcolonial Poetry in English*, Omaar Hena's *Global Anglophone Poetry: Literary Form and Social Critique*, and Sonya Posmentier's *Cultivation and Catastrophe: The Lyric Ecology of Modern Black Literature*.

4. See note 4 of the introduction.

5. He first espouses this principle in his celebrated essay "The Fourth Stage" (1967), written just prior to his imprisonment, and further elaborates it in *Myth, Literature and the African World* (1976).

6. Although he had published individual poems since the fifties, his first poetry collection, *Idanre and Other Poems* (1967), was published the year of his arrest.

7. He was first arrested in 1965 for holding up an Ibadan radio station at gunpoint in order to broadcast a protest against election fraud. Although he was acquitted, the spectacle placed him under national attention. He would continue to use this attention for political purposes, ranging from road safety to anti-war efforts.

8. An estimated 8,000 to 30,000 Igbos were killed in the pogroms, while an estimated 1 million fled to the Eastern region, which would become a secessionist state (the Republic of Biafra) the following year, spurring the Biafran War. This civil war, waged from 1967 to 1970, left a death toll estimated anywhere from 500,000 to 3 million ("Biafra"). While sectarian divisions (e.g., the anti-Igbo pogroms) spurred this conflict, political-economic control over the Niger Delta, the center of Nigeria's oil production, also played a vital role.

9. Mpalive-Hangson Msiska notes how similar Soyinka's Third Force is to Homi Bhabha's more influential theory of Third Space, the main difference being that Soyinka's term prioritizes subjective agency as opposed to Bhabha's prioritization of subjective location (76). This difference, I would add, emphasizes Soyinka's confidence in the always possible transformation of the social through subjective action, what he elsewhere defines as "the Will" (*Myth* 150).

10. The question of the extent to which Soyinka ever believed in specific theological attributes of Yoruba cosmology or conceptions of the afterlife, or became during his incarceration an authentic practitioner of Indigenous religion, is irrelevant to my argument. While Soyinka becomes increasingly critical of organized religion throughout his career—proposing in 2015, for example, to make

raising children in any religion illegal across Nigeria ("Narcissus")—philosophical engagement with animism remains a through line across his oeuvre, despite his claims of being agnostic and even atheist (*Climate* 119). While his own religious outlook might be described as neopragmatic, animistic agnosticism, I do not wish to propose a doctrinal approach to postcolonial exegesis, but rather to model a hermeneutic practice of tracing the ways in which postcolonial African writers strategically appropriate Indigenous cosmologies to process, survive, and ultimately reshape the historical forces of colonial modernity.

11. These poems were first published as *Poems from Prison* in 1969, then expanded as *A Shuttle in the Crypt* in 1972.

12. For Tanure Ojaide, this collection's "Christian tone is markedly different from *Idanre*," Soyinka's first poetry collection, which is seeped in Yoruba cosmology. This shift in the prison poems' "spirituality is appropriate to the poet's solitary confinement and the occasional inward nature of its concerns" (68). While I agree that Soyinka pulls more from Christianity in his prison poetry than any of his other work, I would hesitate describing the poetry's tone as Christian. Rather, Soyinka, in his idiosyncratic construction of a perennial spirituality contextually suited for his survival of solitary confinement, discovers an animist structure at the origins of Judeo-Christian monotheism, connecting "Western" theology with "African" cosmology. Thus, images of Christ and Ogun coexist within the collection less as oppositions than as archetypal incarnations of a universal, numinal core of psychic life and thus allies in Soyinka's struggle to retain his sanity in solitary confinement.

13. Since its primary audience is Soyinka himself scribbling and ritually vocalizing lyrics in his cell, "Animystic Spells" is perhaps the most esoteric writing of his oeuvre. I partially concur with C. Tighe that since Soyinka is "creating a language" through this cycle to articulate the trauma he is experiencing, its incoherence to readers is a necessary part of its form (10). That the poetry "had a definite function makes it difficult for us to come to grips with it. . . . These poems are literally incantations understood only by Soyinka" (14). As I demonstrate throughout this chapter, however, I believe productive interpretation of these incantations is still possible for readers, especially if the cycle is approached as a strategy of trauma survival informed by Soyinka's theoretical writings on animism.

14. *A Dance*, moreover, famously headlined the Nigerian independence celebrations of 1960, casting postcolonial experience as originating in ritual.

15. His earliest published poetry, published in *Black Orpheus* (1959) and *Modern Poetry from Africa* (1963), has few to no animistic qualities and instead utilizes psychological realism to offer social critique, especially of racism (e.g., "The Immigrant" or "Telephone Conversation"). His first poetry collection, *Idanre and Other Poems* (1967), demonstrates a drastic shift to the cosmological and the ritualistic and introduces into his poetry the animism he had throughout the sixties more fully incorporated into his drama. He composed his prison poetry,

a more extreme application of *Idanre*'s animism, just months after the former's publication. Mainly due to the animistic experimentalism fundamental to Soyinka's poetry of this era, critics often judge this poetry as too arcane for systematic criticism. The "wild and Wole idiom" (Lindfors 30) that propels his drama and prose is often thought to infect such poems with "knotty, elusive style," leaving them "metaphorically irresponsible and syntactically messy" (Booth 57, 70) or "deficient in clear statement" (Goodwin 114). Frustrated by Soyinka's frequent "parade of verbal fireworks" (Wilson 73), critics often note that he is "more of a dramatist" (Irele 7). Some critics train interpretive attention to his pre-animist poems, which are less "craggy, lumpy, full of obstructions, [and] unnecessarily and artificially difficult" (Chinweizu et al. 29): e.g., the clear social critique of "Telephone Conversation." Alternatively, many critics claim Soyinka's lyrical complexity can be resolved by turning to the "primal source of [Soyinka's] being," Yoruba cosmology (Macebuh 203). While I am partially sympathetic to such an approach, I am wary of the manner in which mythographic approaches tend to utilize essentialist notions of precolonial African culture to resolve interpretive difficulty. Soyinka's engagement with Yoruba cosmology is indeed fundamental to my argument in this chapter, but I take his relationship with this cosmology to be dynamic, creative, and resolutely modernist—a catalyst for interpretive complexity rather than a key to interpretive closure. For a detailed summary of how early critics approached one of Soyinka's most famous poetic experiments with animism, "Dawn," see James Booth.

16. As Biodun Jeyifo writes, Soyinka's prison poetry is at its core a "regress into the innermost recesses of a psyche under stress—a psyche on the brink of dissolution" (241–42).

17. This distillation is also why the modernist aesthetics of fragmentation so frequent in Soyinka's animist poetics reaches its most exaggerated form in his prison poetry. As Jeyifo notes, Soyinka's "relentless emphasis on fragmentation, disjuncture, and alienation, as themes and techniques, places his mythopoesis solidly in post-Romantic, *modernist* framework. For it is in the cracks and disjunctures generated by this "fragmentation" that Soyinka both locates the necessity and efficacy of ritual and justifies his great investment in actions and expressions of the Will that attempt to bridge the chasms that separate different spheres and orders of reality" (81).

18. In "Procession" Soyinka associates his prison poetry with Yoruba weavers, "[o]ur old women of the loom" (*Early Poems* 134). As Jeff Thompson notes, the role of Yoruba tapestries in archiving communal history and upholding ancestral worship suggests that Soyinka is here casting himself as "the new weaver," one who creates texts to both archive and resist the neocolonial rule that has displaced such traditions (99). As Lucy Hayden notes, the shuttle is also an allusion to Job's archetypal lament: "My days are swifter than a weaver's shuttle, and are spent without hope" (549).

19. The village-weaver, or *ega* in Yoruba, is known for intricately woven nests, a natural example of the creative process toward which Soyinka directs his poetry. That the bird is "trapped" suggests Soyinka is drawing on Paul Laurence Dunbar's 1899 poem "Sympathy," whose refrain "I know why the caged bird sings" also influenced Maya Angelou's autobiography, published in 1969, the year of Soyinka's release from prison. Given Soyinka's interest in Greek mythology, he is no doubt also drawing on the myth of Philomela. After King Tereus rapes Philomela and chops off her tongue, she weaves her experience into a tapestry and is later transformed into a nightingale.

20. As Msiska convincingly argues, "What Soyinka enacts in all his works is a postcolonial dialectic" (164), which constitutes a mode of "reading the global from below" (xxxvii) outside any vulgar antimonies.

21. As clear in his memoir *Aké: The Years of Childhood* (1981), he was by no means raised separated from Yoruba culture. As Bola Dauda and Toyin Falola write:

> Soyinka grew up within what Odia Ofeimun has described as . . . a mix of strong Christian upbringing and European values, and an equally strong induction into dialectics of the Yoruba culture and anticolonial nationalism. For example, just as his mother, alias Wild Christian, regularly prayed to exorcize *emi esu* (evil spirit) from Wole's boisterous mind, so also did Pa Akiode, Wole's grandfather, name Wole as Maren, a shortened form of *maren nijo ebi pona* (may you not be on the road on days when the vampire spirits of Ogun are famished and hungry for blood), and religiously made the necessary offerings to the Yoruba pantheon gods, especially Ogun and Sango, to protect Wole from the machinations of evil spirits. (115)

Despite Soyinka's grandfather's practice of Yoruba rituals, as Msiska notes, Soyinka's formal education and maternal side of the family regarded nearly all African Indigenous traditions as barbaric; in fact, his mother's great-grandfather preached at London's St. Paul's Cathedral in 1905 (xvi). This Europeanized side of Soyinka's heritage would greatly mold his formal understanding of culture and theology until his university studies.

22. I am grateful to Soyinka for narrating this history to me before his Leeds University Centre of African Studies Annual Lecture on 8 October 2015.

23. For further analysis of this process of self-apprehension in Soyinka's thought, especially as it relates to what Soyinka describes as "race retrieval," see Tejumola Olaniyan.

24. As she writes, "The time has come to elaborate a new materialism, which would determine a new position of Continental philosophy vis-á-vis neurobiology" ("Go Wonder" 72).

25. See note 20 in chapter 1.

26. By paraphrasing one of Wordsworth's most famous lines, Soyinka raises a comparison between his philosophy of African animism and Romantic poetry's immanent critique of post-Enlightenment rationality. Yet by decidedly not mentioning Wordsworth, and instead defining this phrase as a proverb, he also undermines the tendency of Euro-American literary criticism to ascribe value to "non-Western" literature through its kinship with the Western canon.

27. As Msiska argues, Soyinka's view of the dead and living co-constituting existence offers a "multiple ontology of being" (14) that fits into his larger aesthetic project: "an imaginative retrieval of African myth from the domain of a static ontology to that of a non-essentialist and dynamic *multiple political ontology*" (15).

28. The syllabic lineation varies more than Jeyifo admits, but he is nevertheless correct that the formal rigidity of these poems is striking.

29. Jeyifo likewise takes "Animystic Spells" to be directed at Gowon (250–51).

30. This reading concurs with Ojaide's emphasis on death's equalizing power but expands this equalization beyond the solely human domain. The thought of General Gowon's destructive plasticity, however, his ability to regenerate through death, is hardly a comfort to aid Soyinka's psychological survival in solitary confinement, which is a core purpose of "Animystic Spells." This problem returns us to the question of whom the spells' "You and I" references. As Ojaide notes, in "Flowers for My Land" (also written in prison and immediately preceding "Animystic Spells" in *A Shuttle in the Crypt*), Soyinka draws on T. S. Eliot's *The Waste Land* by "mythologizing the national tragedy as a garden" turned wasteland under Gowon's military rule (90). Through the Biafran War, such a reading contends, Gowon contorts Nigeria into a "garden of decay" (*Early Poems* 152). The phrase "You and I" in "Animystic Spells," I would add, evokes the opening line of another Eliot poem: "The Love Song of J. Alfred Prufrock." Read alongside "Flowers for My Land," the third spell's vision of death embracing "You and I" conjures a distinctly modern, Prufrockian speaker's experience of suffering while seeking in death repose—and, as in *The Waste Land*, regeneration. Prufrock finds mundanities symbolically imprisoning: discussing art over "tea and cakes and ices" leaves him "pinned and wriggling on the wall." He seeks escape from this imprisonment in death (the poem's final word is "drown") and transfiguration into the more-than-human world (e.g., his wish to become a crab: "I should have been a pair of ragged claws / Scuttling across the floors of silent seas" [5]). Soyinka (who is literally imprisoned) voices a "You and I" that seeks to ritually realize Prufrock's desire for catastrophic metamorphosis. *The Waste Land*, moreover, weaves together disparate rituals, famously concluding with the elemental form of the mantra ("Shantih Shantih Shantih" [50]); "Animystic Spells" begins where *The Waste Land* leaves off, employing the elemental form of the chanted spell to survive an imprisonment in which Soyinka views himself as incarnating the state of his nation as a wasteland of civil war. Such ritualized modernism clarifies Gowon's position within the spells' "You and I." He and the prison guards are

certainly included in this "You," as Ojaide claims, but Soyinka undoubtedly also functions as an addressee, as do all implicated in the Biafran War.

31. That a trinitarian, crowned subject is in this stanza dying suggests a biblical parallel. Indeed, the image of three dying stalks resembles a crucifixion scene through which the new ears sprouting in the second stanza might be interpreted as a resurrection. In the second spell, however, the speaker urges the addressee to "Shun / Visions / Of the unleavened" (157). Given unleavened bread's ritual use during Passover and the Eucharist, this shunning suggests a rejection of a Judeo-Christian ritual paradigm, embracing instead "bread as breath," as the first spell puts it (156). If unleavened bread points the participant of Judeo-Christian ritual to the need for a transcendent God to function as a leavening agent, Soyinka's spells embrace instead a radical immanence, a subject leavened by the "yeast of pollen" (157) coinciding with "earth's own regenerate need" (159). Rather than pointing a deprived subject to a transcendent spiritual being, then, bread and breath (the carnate and the spiritual) are in this paradigm one and the same. Consequently, the life that emerges through death in the second stanza of the final spell offers an explicitly animist vision of afterlife—less a resurrection than the subject's ritual participation in the cosmos's perennial dynamic of creation and destruction. In this way the final spell nests imagery associated with Judeo-Christian ritual within the framework of a harvest ritual, archetypal coordinates preceding the historical advent of monotheism. Much like Soyinka's revision of capital punishment as an outworking of cosmic movement, here signs of the religious paradigm coinciding with Africa's colonization under European imperialism are contextualized within a larger cosmological process coinciding with Africa's "primal systems of apprehension" (*Myth* xii). In sum, animism throughout the cycle of spells ritually resignifies both the political structure of African neocolonialism and the theological structure of Judeo-Christian monotheism, structures Soyinka envisions as interconnected.

32. In *Idanre and Other Poems* (1967), Soyinka "employs language of farming to represent love as fruitful. In poem after poem the sexual act is likened to the watering of a farm in which seeds are planted; the seeds grow and are later harvested in child-birth" (Ojaide 36). In "Season," Soyinka connects this reproductive imagery to death: "Rust is ripeness," the poem begins, and it concludes with farmers garnering "wilted" cornstalks, recognizing in "germ's decay" this "promise of rust"—that is, life (*Early Poems* 41). Ojaide interprets: "Corn, an aspect of nature, is the dominant symbol of the human condition to affirm that man, like corn, is natural; and therefore will obey the natural laws of birth and death, of seasons. Death is part of the cycle since the 'germ's decay' will produce new stalks" (42).

33. See the "October '66" section of *Idanre and Other Poems*.

34. "Psalm," for instance (a lyrical celebration of a sexual encounter between the speaker and an unnamed woman, also published the year of Soyinka's arrest),

begins by utilizing agrarian imagery to describe the speaker's erection: "the seeds have ripened fast my love / and the milk is straining at the pods." It ends by utilizing such imagery to describe the speaker's orgasm:

> of pulses and the stranger life
> comes to harvest and release
> the germ and life exegesis
> inspiration of your genesis. (*Early Poems* 30)

That this sex-as-harvest is also connected to interpretation (exegesis) and origins (genesis) contextualizes Soyinka's erotic poetry within his larger project of the "self-apprehension" of African subjectivity through animist poetics.

35. He writes, "The practitioners of *Ijala* [traditional Yoruba chants performed by hunters], the supreme lyrical form of Yoruba poetic art, are followers of Ogun the hunter. Ijala celebrates not only the deity but animal and plant life, seeks to capture the essence and relationships of growing things and the insights of man into the secrets of the universe. With creativity, however, went its complementary aspect, and Ogun came to symbolise the creative-destructive principle" (*Myth* 28).

36. "The first fruits rose from subterranean hoards," the speaker declares, as participants enjoy

> . . . domes of eggs and flesh
> Of palm fruit, red, oil black, froth flew in sun bubbles
> Burst over throngs of golden gourds. (*Early Poems* 81)

37. Gowon, we should note, was and remains a Christian nationalist. This political-theological aspect of "Animystic Spells" should be read in dialogue with the animist revision of Freud's reading of Tancred and Clorinda I detail in chapter 1.

38. For a detailed analysis of this temporal structure in Freud's and Laplanche's trauma theories, see John Fletcher.

Chapter 4

1. The anachronistic nature of the play's staging the Oyo Kingdom's practice of human sacrifice is worth noting. The Oyo Kingdom had been declining, as Ato Quayson notes, since the eighteenth century, and in the colonial period in which the drama is set, it had been "completely superseded by fresh realities that called for reassessment of its former glory" (*Strategic* 97). The same is true of the horseman ritual centered in the play. As James Booth writes, "By the time the Rev. Samuel Johnson was completing his *History of the Yorubas* in the 1890s, he could assert that the practice was dying out at Oyo: 'With the exception of

the women, all the men now refuse to die and they are never forced to do so'" ("Self-Sacrifice" 140). *Horseman* is thus not a historical representation of the Oyo Kingdom's practice of human sacrifice, but a "strategic transformation" of history, to use Quayson's term, into a myth of modernity. For the historical narrative the play transforms, see James Gibbs (117–18).

2. He lifts the phrase "the end of the world" from Frantz Fanon, who uses it to mean the colonial world. Its end, for Fanon, opens the possibility of a "new man" no longer in the image of the European concept of humanity. For Wilderson, however, the racialized, sacrificial structure of the human as a category casts Fanon's hope as an impossibility.

3. "Human eyes are useless for a search of this nature," Elesin explains, "[b]ut in the house of *osugbo*, those who keep watch through the spirit recognised the moment, they sent word to me through the voice of our sacred drums to prepare myself" (51).

4. Also called *Ogboni*, the *Osugbo* is "the traditional society of elders that historically formed the judiciary in communities throughout southern Yorubaland" (M. Drewal 33).

5. The Norton Critical Edition italicizes stage directions. To differentiate them from rhetorical emphases, I de-italicize them. In quotations that contain both dialogue and stage directions, I leave directions italicized.

6. What Quayson terms the "dialectic of stasis and mobility" tied to the play's "dynamic of ethical choice" should be interpreted in relation to this loss of agential mobility ("'All of the People, Some of the Time'" 68).

7. This question is central to Walter Benjamin's "Critique of Violence" and Derrida's interpretation in "Force of Law."

8. Msiska thus writes that like Paul Gilroy, Soyinka "reminds us of the importance of the Slave Triangle in the production of the concept and materiality of modernity, but unlike him, he locates its fundamental structures further in time, in the domain of ancient myth as well as history" (35).

9. As Soyinka writes, eternity for the Yoruba does not carry the "remoteness" or "exclusiveness" of Christian eschatology because "life, present life, contains within it manifestations of the ancestral, the living and the unborn" (*Myth* 143, 144). Derrida makes a similar claim in *Specters of Marx*. Turning like Soyinka to Shakespearean tragedy, Derrida finds this temporal and social structure haunting the West. While Hamlet laments that time is "out of joint," discovering the living's implication with the dead, such a recognition is natural, not "disjointed," in Soyinka's Yoruba cosmology, assuming its own form of continuity.

10. This process should be interpreted in dialogue with Michael Taussig's and Paul Stoller's anthropological studies of postcolonial spirit possession from chapter 2.

11. As Harry Garuba argues in "Explorations in Animist Materialism," the statue of Sango (Yoruba god of lightning) in front of the National Electric Power

Authority of Nigeria's headquarters illustrates this "assimilative wisdom" operating at the level of the cultural unconscious: Under industrialized capitalism, Sango becomes the god of the mass generation and distribution of electrical power.

12. Soyinka describes this shift as dramaturgy in the conclusion of his author's note: "*Horseman* can be fully realised only through an evocation of music from the abyss of transition" (3).

13. To be clear, I am not interpreting any particular character as Soyinka's mouthpiece, but rather the dramatic movement of the character constellation, or the logic through which each character becomes implicated in the tragedy, as aligning with Soyinka's scholarship.

14. George rightly casts Amusa alongside Joseph, the Pilkingses' houseboy, as the two fools, both serving the colonial administration. Since both perform a similar dramaturgical function, I narrow my focus to Amusa, whose role is more pertinent to my focus in this chapter.

15. The stage directions refer to this scene as a "ritual of introductions" (37).

16. In the *District Officer* draft, the band plays a Charleston while guests dance "like a speeded-up film," framing their obliviousness in a Chaplinesque, comic image of modernity (IV.1).

17. As the Anglican legal category *simony* denotes the corrupt instantiation of religious authority, Simon's name further suggests the structural violence through which he obtains his authority.

18. In *Myth*, Soyinka universalizes this animist aspect of Yoruba tragedy to read classical tragedy. Rejecting the concept of the tragic flaw, he asserts that "Oedipus the Innocent remained the ethical archetype" through his failure (14).

19. Soyinka places his theory of Yoruba tragedy in dialogue with Nietzsche's *The Birth of Tragedy*. If, for Nietzsche, "it is an act of hubris to be born," the Yoruba response, Soyinka writes, is that "it is no less an act of hubris to die" (158). But Soyinka departs from Nietzsche's focus on "illusion" by theorizing Yoruba tragedy as "essential" (141). Contra Nietzsche's celebration of illusion over reality, Yoruba tragedy ritualizes a "celebration of the cosmic struggle" that is the essence of being—the creative-destructive principle—and passes on in the performance of this essence an "aesthetic joy" operating outside the real/illusion binary (143).

Chapter 5

1. Much like chapter 3's focus on the incantatory voice and chapter 4's on ritual dramaturgy (concepts foundational to lyric poetry and tragic drama, respectively), the narratological focus of this chapter's analysis suggests that my argument bears implications for literary criticism's understanding of the formal conventions of the modernist novel in Africa. Incorporating a greater appreciation

for such conventions into a practical criticism is necessary if "the new modernist studies" (Mao and Walkowitz) is to achieve the globalization of novel studies for which it hopes.

2. Though focused on a different geographical context, Madhu Krishnan's study of French and British colonial spatial planning in relation to West African literary expression, *Writing Spatiality in West Africa*, is one example of how contemporary criticism is beginning to appreciate the type of spatial focus Vera models in her dissertation.

3. I focus my polemic on *Multidirectional Memory* (2009) rather than Rothberg's more recent *The Implicated Subject* (2019) because the former lays out the theoretical lens that the latter extends without significantly revising.

4. See, for example, Lizzy Attree's "Language, Kwela Music and Modernity in *Butterfly Burning*" and Jane Bryce's "Imaginary Snapshots: Cinematic Techniques in the Writing of Yvonne Vera."

5. In 1980, under Robert Mugabe's leadership, the Zimbabwe African National Union (ZANU) won Zimbabwe's first democratic election. Mugabe sensed an imminent threat of resistance, however, especially from Zimbabwe People's Revolutionary Army (ZIPRA), the armed wing of Zimbabwe African People's Union (ZAPRA), led by Joshua Nkomo. This threat motivated Mugabe to sign an agreement (that same year) with North Korean President Kim Il-Sung to train a special brigade for ZANU's armed wing, Zimbabwe National Army (ZANLA). Organized groups of so-called dissidents, former ZIPRA guerrilla warriors disillusioned to Mugabe's post-independence Zimbabwe, camped throughout Matabeleland and parts of the Midlands—a region boasting a largely Ndebele-speaking population. Since Nkomo was Ndebele, the region marked itself as an area of potential resistance, posing a threat to Mugabe's dream of a single-party state. In 1982 Mugabe sent the Fifth Brigade to combat the "dissidents" in Matabeleland and parts of the Midlands, and throughout this unofficial civil war the rural population was subjected to genocide. For years, the Fifth Brigade—which bypassed military command structures, answering directly to Mugabe—enforced curfew and surveillance and perpetrated mass tortures and killings throughout Matabeleland; concurrently, "dissidents," while combating the Fifth Brigade, regularly raped and killed civilians. This state-sanctioned genocide formally ended in 1987 with the Unity Accord signed by Mugabe and Nkomo, which dissolved Nkomo's ZAPRA into Mugabe's ZANU (renamed ZANU-PF). For the authoritative report on the genocide, see the Catholic Commission for Justice and Peace in Zimbabwe's *Breaking the Silence, Building True Peace: A Report on the Disturbances in Matabeleland and the Midlands 1980–1988*. For the genocide's historical context, see Terence Ranger's vast work on the subject, particularly *Voices from the Rocks: Nature, Culture and History in the Matopos Hills of Zimbabwe* and his coauthored (alongside Jocelyn Alexander and JoAnn McGregor) *Violence and Memory: One Hundred Years in the Dark Forests of Matabeleland, Zimbabwe*.

6. Through such dissolutions of individuated identities, Vera's fiction, Caroline Rooney writes, "constantly makes us aware of the incommensurability of self-referential identity and liquid life" (*Decolonising Gender* 153).

7. See note 5. Mugabe's single-party ideology was anchored to a rhetoric of Shona ethnic unity, against which Matabeleland's Ndebele (and Kalanga) population was marked as a threat.

8. Critics who focus on her use of Shona cosmology underappreciate the crucial role her strategic detachment from ethnic identity plays in her writing and politics. See, for example, Dorothée Boulanger's otherwise illuminating " 'In the Centre of Our Circle': Gender, Selfhood and Non-Linear Time in Yvonne Vera's *Nehanda*."

9. As I have suggested in the previous two chapters, Soyinkan animism is already consciously dialectic and thus interrelated with Fanon's theory of colonial trauma. The difference I am articulating is a matter of emphasis: Soyinka begins with animism and systematizes it into a cosmo-dialectic resonating with historical materialist critique, whereas Vera begins with historical materialism and crafts an animist poetics operating within its logic.

10. Ranger greatly shaped Vera's approach to Zimbabwean history, and vice versa, so much so that Vera's novel *Butterfly Burning* is dedicated to him. For more on Vera's challenge to the political ideology of her time, see Primorac's "The Poetics of State Terror in Twenty-First Century Zimbabwe" and Sofia Kostelac's "The Voices of Drowned Men Cannot Be Heard": Writing Subalternity in Yvonne Vera's *Butterfly Burning* and *The Stone Virgins*."

11. Maurice Vambe, for example, claims Vera's writing follows a dehistoricizing aestheticism that, through its mythologizing impulse (what Kizito Muchemwa likewise charges as Vera's essentialism), unintentionally fuels tribalist, ethnic division and thus fails to venture beyond the nationalism she attempts to critique.

12. See notes 4, 14, and 20 in the introduction.

13. Vera concurs with Soyinka's belief that African Indigenous cosmologies are anchored to circular forms. Consider, for example, the motif of circular architecture throughout Vera's fiction (most obvious in her first novel, *Nehanda*), which Boulanger recognizes as related to Vera's interest in nonlinear time.

14. Kwela is a form of Southern African street jazz played with pennywhistles and often makeshift instruments. For Vera's interest in kwela, see Meg Samuelson's "Yvonne Vera's Bulawayo: Modernity, (Im)mobility, Music, and Memory" and Attree's "Language, Kwela Music and Modernity in *Butterfly Burning*." Samuelson's introduction to the musical form's influence on Vera is especially helpful in light of my interpretation of *The Stone Virgins*' architectural criticism:

> Kwela takes its name from the injunction to 'climb up' into the police van, an injunction often consequent on infringements of pass laws

and influx control regulations—in short, of restrictions of mobility; it suggests . . . the desire for mobility born of, and partially contained within, prohibition and geographical violence. . . . Fashioned out of the debris of modern, urban life (children playing in the streets of Makokoba produce its melodies out of abandoned bottles and cartons), kwela speaks of the acquisitive force of African urban modernities. (25–26)

15. See Ashleigh Harris's "'An Ingenious Tenderness': The Choreography of Violence in Yvonne Vera's *The Stone Virgins*."

16. A prominent example, she claims, is hut-tax. This tax introduces a new crime into the social order, reconstituting the act of entering a hut a crime necessitating that an individual must be imprisoned. Hut-tax is thus "a system of surveillance consisting in knowing the dwelling place of individuals, then introducing a strategic alienation into that space. For the native to enter the hut is no longer a neutral act. The hut too has become a prison" (15).

17. To formulate this argument Vera relies on Foucault's canonical genealogy of the European prison in *Discipline and Punish*. Like Foucault, Vera argues that the colonial prison enables "the creation of a new subjectivity" by naturalizing biopolitical surveillance of Indigenous populations. Colonial prisons, however, become "abstracted" from "the humanitarian ideals of punishment recorded as evolving in Europe at the time" (11). Foucault famously traces European penology's historical transition from the public spectacle of torture to the hidden system of reformation it had become by the nineteenth century. Yet in this same period, Vera adds, "British colonialists . . . made the punishment of the indigene public" (12). That European penology's humanitarian reform culminates while this same penological system relies on public torture, hanging, and the exaggerated "spectacle of the body" (12) in the colonies, Vera claims, "introduce[s] reversals that modify the manner in which Foucault's observations on the question of the formation of subjectivity can be articulated" (13).

18. Walking is in this way an example of the leitmotif of combative movement throughout Vera's fiction. As Primorac puts it in another context, "In a Vera novel, movement is synonymous with resistance" (91).

19. Napier was a captain in the Shangani Patrol, a unit of the British South Africa Company that in 1893 ambushed and slaughtered over three thousand Matabele warriors before being defeated in "Wilson's Last Stand," which is memorialized by a plaque mentioned in *The Stone Virgins*' opening paragraph.

20. According to Vera, Fanon, more than any other theorist, diagnosed this universal dimension of colonial spatial ideology as imprisonment via its operations as an apparatus of colonized subject formation influencing every inch of the colony. Quoting from *The Wretched of the Earth*, she writes:

Fanon's description that colonialism engages a "strategy of encirclement" is focused on this radical appropriation of geography. . . . Fanon describes how the land is "parcelled out" in a radical separation which banishes any conciliatory discourse. In describing the colonized as being "without spaciousness" Fanon describes colonial domination as an imprisoning ideology. . . . The violence engaged in the separation, then final enclosure of the native is obvious—this is a world "cut in two". . . . The prison is defined by the imposition of immobility upon the inmate, a restriction already in play in the rapid proliferation of boundaries that accompanies colonial occupation. (30–32)

21. She writes, "Where the pavement suggests flamboyance, motion, light, the prison conjures contrition and surrender. Each of these spaces is produced to participate in meeting the demands of a governing power. In the discourse for self-rule that ensues in Southern Rhodesia, the Africans clamour for freedom on the pavements, and freedom from imprisonment" (36).

22. For an introduction to the critical discourse around Vera's writing of trauma, see Sofia Kostelac's "'The Body Is His, Pulse and Motion': Violence and Desire in Yvonne Vera's *The Stone Virgins*"; Stephen Chan's "The Memory of Violence: Trauma in the Writings of Alexander Kanengoni and Yvonne Vera and the Idea of Unreconciled Citizenship in Zimbabwe"; Martina Kopf's "Narratives of Wounded Time: Yvonne Vera's Poetics of Trauma"; Jessica Murray's "A Post-colonial and Feminist Reading of Selected Testimonies to Trauma in Post-liberation South Africa and Zimbabwe"; Ashleigh Harris's "Toni Morrison and Yvonne Vera: An Associative Fugue"; Régine Michelle Jean-Charles's "Toward a Victim-Survivor Narrative: Rape and Form in Yvonne Vera's *Under the Tongue* and Calixthe Beyala's *Tu t'appelleras Tanga*"; Anna-Leena Toivanen's "Remembering the Nation's Aching Spots: Yvonne Vera's Authorial Position of a Witness and Healer"; Robert Muponde's "Reading Girlhood Under the Tongue"; and Annie Gagiano's "Reading *The Stone Virgins* as Vera's Study of the Katabolism of War."

23. Vera frequently wrote op-eds on art, culture, and politics for local papers while directing the National Gallery in Bulawayo.

24. See note 5.

25. "And Adam said, This is now bone of my bones, and flesh of my flesh: she shall be called Woman, because she was taken out of Man" (Gen 2:23).

26. That they are the first traditional protagonists introduced further solidifies this symbolism.

27. Their homes suggest Cephas is most likely Ndau, while Thenjiwe is Ndebele.

28. Vera is influenced by Ranger's critique of the ideology of ethnicity in Zimbabwe. As he argues, a unified Shona ethnic identity (a concept Mugabe consistently utilized) is a construct of colonial missiology and statecraft. This construct, Ranger suggests, underlies much of the tribal politics plaguing the

region after independence, such as the "allegedly 'traditional' hostility between the 'Ndebele' and the 'Shona'" ("Missionaries" 118), a hostility that fueled the *Gukurahundi*. This critique of ethnicity further elucidates Vera's aforementioned detachment of animist poetics from ethnophilosophical particularities.

29. Also called Musikavanhu, Musiki, Tenzi, Ishe, or Inkhosi, this deity is typically framed as the high god of Shona cosmology, but he is worshiped across ethnicities (by the Ndebele, for example, who Mugabe and the ZANU-PF pinned against the Shona in order to justify *Gukurahundi*). This cosmopolitan nature is surely one reason for Vera's interest in Mwali.

30. See Ranger's *Voices from the Rocks*.

31. It is no surprise, then, that he seeks protection from the spirit of Nehanda (117).

32. The term refers to the wind or rain that washes away the chaff.

33. The Matopos Hills boast one of Southern Africa's highest concentrations of rock art.

34. Thus, Sibaso notices the painted women "spread their legs outward to the sun" (103), a phrase recalling Vera's description of the crowd at Nkomo's burial, who, in contrast to the military's motionless silence, sing "in unison, their arms raised to meet the sun" ("Nkomo").

35. Sibaso's name means "a flint to start a flame" (73).

36. See Samuelson's "Re-membering the Body: Rape and Recovery in *Without a Name* and *Under the Tongue*" and Harris's "Toni Morrison and Yvonne Vera: An Associative Fugue."

37. In fact, Rudyard Kipling wrote a poem titled "The Burial" to be read at Rhodes's funeral in the Matapos Hills. The poem celebrates Rhodes's choice of burial grounds:

> It is his will that he look forth
> Across the world he won—
> The granite of the ancient North—
> Great spaces washed with sun. (220)

Gulati, Kipling claims, provides Rhodes's remains with a view of the land he colonized and in doing so transforms its granite rock formations into a mirror image of England. What is more, the poem ends by claiming Rhodes's spirit has united with the landscape: "Living he was the land, and dead / His soul shall be her soul" (221). Ironically, this line articulates Vera's theory of colonization's "geographical violence": Rhodes, according to Kipling and Vera, transfigures African land into colonial space.

38. The Rudd Concession (negotiated by Charles Rudd, James Rochfort Maguire, and Francis Thompson on behalf of Rhodes) gave exclusive mining rights to BSAC. The concession functioned as the foundation for BSAC's royal charter and the legal justification of white settlement and imperial annexing.

Works Cited

Abani, Chris. *Hands Washing Water*. Port Townsend, Copper Canyon Press, 2006.
Abraham, Nicolas, and Maria Torok. *The Wolf Man's Magic Word: A Cryptonomy*. Translated by Nicholas Rand, U of Minnesota P, 2005.
Abram, David. *The Spell of the Sensuous: Perception and Language in a More-Than-Human World*. Vintage, 1996.
Achebe, Chinua. *Morning Yet on Creation Day: Essays*. Anchor, 1975.
———. *Things Fall Apart*. Heinemann, 1958.
Adéèkó, Adélékè. *Arts of Being Yoruba: Divination, Allegory, Tragedy, Proverb, Panegyric*. Indiana UP, 2017.
———. "Okonkwo, Textual Closure, Colonial Conquest." *Research in African Literatures*, vol. 42, no. 2, 2011, pp. 72–86.
———. "The Spell That Fails Lacks an Essential Term: Poetry, Animism, and Ideophones." *English Language Notes*, vol. 51, no. 1, 2013, pp. 185–89.
Agamben, Giorgio. *The Coming Community*. Translated by Michael Hardt, U of Minnesota P, 1993.
———. *Homo Sacer: Sovereign Power and Bare Life*. Translated by Daniel Heller-Roazen, Stanford UP, 1998.
Alaimo, Stacy. *Bodily Natures: Science, Environment, and the Material Self*. Indiana UP, 2010.
Alexander, Jeffrey. "Toward a Theory of Cultural Trauma." *Cultural Trauma and Collective Identity*, edited by Jeffrey Alexander et al., U of California P, 2004, pp. 1–30.
Alexander, Jocelyn, et al. *Violence and Memory: One Hundred Years in the Dark Forests of Matabeleland, Zimbabwe*. Martlesham: James Currey, 2000.
Allen-Paisant, Jason. "Animist Time in the White Anthropocene." *New Formations*, vol. 104, 2021, pp. 30–49.
Althusser, Louis. *Lenin and Philosophy, and Other Essays*. Translated by Ben Brewster, Monthly Review, 1972.
Andermahr, Sonya, editor. *Decolonizing Trauma Studies: Trauma and Postcolonialism*. MDPI, 2016.

Angira, Jared. "A Look in the Past." *Poems of Black Africa*, edited by Wole Soyinka, Heinemann, 1975, pp. 61–62.

Anzaldúa, Gloria. *Borderland/La Frontera: The New Mestiza*. Aunt Lute, 1987.

Anzieu, Didier. *The Skin-Ego*. Translated by Naomi Segal, Routledge, 2018.

Appiah, Kwame Anthony. *In My Father's House: Africa in the Philosophy of Culture*. Oxford UP, 1992.

Apter, Andrew. *Black Critics and Kings: The Hermeneutics of Power in Yoruba Society*. U of Chicago P, 1992.

Arendt, Hannah. *The Origins of Totalitarianism*. 1951. Schocken, 2004.

Asad, Talal. *Formations of the Secular: Christianity, Islam, Modernity*. Stanford UP, 2003.

——. and Wendy Brown et al. *Is Critique Secular? Blasphemy, Injury and Free Speech*. Fordham UP, 2013.

Attree, Lizzy. "Language, Kwela Music and Modernity in *Butterfly Burning*." *Sign and Taboo: Perspectives on the Poetic Fiction of Yvonne Vera*, edited by Robert Muponde and Mandi Taruvinga, Weaver, 2002, pp. 63–80.

Ayoade, J. A. "Time in Yoruba Thought." *African Philosophy: An Introduction*, edited by Richard Wright, UP of America, 1984, pp. 93–111.

Balaev, Michelle, editor. *Contemporary Approaches in Literary Trauma Theory*. Palgrave Macmillan, 2014.

——. *The Nature of Trauma in American Novels*. Northwestern UP, 2012.

Ball, Karyn, editor. *Trauma and Its Cultural Aftereffects*, special issue of *Cultural Critique*, no. 46, 2000.

Barad, Karen. "Posthumanist Performativity: Toward an Understanding of How Matter Comes to Matter. *Signs: Journal of Women in Culture and Society*, vol. 28, no. 3, 2003, pp. 801–31.

Barnaby, Andrew. "'The Purest Mode of Looking': (Post)Colonial Trauma in Wole Soyinka's *Death and the King's Horseman*." *Research in African Literatures*, vol. 45, no. 1, 2014, pp. 125–49.

Bascom, William. *Ifa Divination: Communication Between Gods and Men in West Africa*. Indiana UP, 1991.

Belau, Linda, and Petar Ramadanovic, editors. *Trauma: Essays on the Limit of Knowledge and Experience*, special issue of *Postmodern Culture*, vol. 11, no. 2, 2001.

Benjamin, Walter. "Critique of Violence." *One Way Street and Other Writings*, translated by Edmund Jephcott and Kingsley Shorter, NLB, 1978, pp. 132–54.

——. *The Origin of German Tragic Drama*. Translated by John Osborne, Verso, 1998.

——. "Theses on the Philosophy of History." *Illuminations*, translated by Harry Zohn, edited by Hannah Arendt, Schocken, 1969, pp. 253–64.

Bennett, Jane. *Vibrant Matter: A Political Ecology of Things*. Duke UP, 2010.

Bennett, Jill, and R. Kennedy, editors. *World Memory: Personal Trajectories in Global Time*. Palgrave Macmillan, 2003.

Berlant, Lauren. *Cruel Optimism*. Duke UP, 2011.

Bhabha, Homi. *The Location of Culture*. Routledge, 1994.

"Biafra." *Encyclopedia Britannica*, britannica/com/place/Biafra. Accessed 9 Sept. 2022.

Bird-David, Nurit. "'Animism' Revisited: Personhood, Environment, and Relational Epistemology." *Current Anthopology*, vol. 40, no. 1, 1999, pp. 67–91.

Boehmer, Elleke. "Tropes of Yearning and Dissent: The Troping of Desire in Yvonne Vera and Tsitsi Dangarembga." *Journal of Commonwealth Literature*, vol. 38, no. 1, 2003, pp. 135–48.

Booth, James. "Myth, Metaphor, and Syntax in Soyinka's Poetry." *Research in African Literatures*, vol. 17, no. 1, 1986, pp. 53–72.

———. "Self-Sacrifice and Human Sacrifice in Soyinka's *Death and the King's Horseman*." *Research on Wole Soyinka*, edited by James Gibbs and Bernth Lindfors, Africa World Press, 1993, pp. 127–47.

Boulanger, Dorothée. "In the Centre of Our Circle": Gender, Selfhood and Non-Linear Time in Yvonne Vera's *Nehanda*." *Angelaki: Journal of the Theoretical Humanities*, vol. 27, no. 3-4, 2022, pp. 223–35.

Bracken, Christopher. *Magical Criticism: The Recourse of Savage Philosophy*. U of Chicago P, 2007.

Braidotti, Rosi. *The Posthuman*. Polity, 2013.

Brew, Kwesi. "Ancestral Faces." *Poems of Black Africa*, edited by Wole Soyinka, Heinemann, 1975, p. 43.

Brown, Laura. *Cultural Competence in Trauma Therapy: Beyond the Flashback*. American Psychological Association, 2008.

———. "Not Outside the Range: One Feminist Perspective on Psychic Trauma." *Trauma: Explorations in Memory*, edited by Cathy Caruth, Johns Hopkins UP, 1995, pp. 100–12.

Brown, Wendy. *States of Injury: Power and Freedom in Late Modernity*. Princeton UP, 1995.

Bryce, Jane. "Imaginary Snapshots: Cinematic Techniques in the Writing of Yvonne Vera." *Sign and Taboo: Perspectives on the Poetic Fiction of Yvonne Vera*, edited by Robert Muponde and Mandi Taruvinga, Weaver, 2002, pp. 39–56.

———. "'Survival Is in the Mouth'": Interview with Yvonne Vera." *Sign and Taboo: Perspectives on the Poetic Fiction of Yvonne Vera*, edited by Robert Muponde and Mandi Taruvinga, Weaver, 2002, pp. 217–26.

Buelens, Gert, et al., editors. *The Future of Trauma Theory: Contemporary Literary and Cultural Criticism*. Routledge, 2013.

Butler, Judith. *Antigone's Claim: Kinship Between Life and Death*. Columbia UP, 2000.

———. *Frames of War: When Is Life Grievable?* Verso, 2009.

———. *Precarious Life: The Powers of Mourning and Violence*. 2nd ed., Verso, 2006.
Caminero-Santangelo, Byron. *Different Shades of Green: African Literature, Environmental Justice, and Political Ecology*. UVA P, 2014.
Caputo, John D. *On Religion*. Routledge, 2019.
Caruth, Cathy. *Literature in the Ashes of History*. Johns Hopkins UP, 2013.
———. *Unclaimed Experience: Trauma, Narrative, and History*. Johns Hopkins UP, 1996.
Catholic Commission for Justice and Peace in Zimbabwe. *Breaking the Silence, Building True Peace: A Report on the Disturbances in Matabeleland and the Midlands 1980–1988*. Harare: Catholic Commission for Justice and Peace in Zimbabwe/Legal Resources Foundation, 1997, https://archive.org/stream/BreakingTheSilenceBuildingTruePeace/MatabelelandReport_djvu.txt.
Caulker, Tcho Mbaimba. "Shakespeare's *Julius Caesar* in Sierra Leone: Thomas Decker's *Juliohs Siza*, Roman Politics, and the Emergence of a Postcolonial African State." *Research in African Literatures*, vol. 40, no. 2, 2009, pp. 208–27.
Chan, Stephen. "The Memory of Violence: Trauma in the Writings of Alexander Kanengoni and Yvonne Vera and the Idea of Unreconciled Citizenship in Zimbabwe." *Third World Quarterly*, vol. 26, no. 2, 2005, pp. 369–82.
Chinweizu, Onwuchewka Jemie, and Ihechukwu Madubuike. "Towards the Decolonization of African Literature." *Transition*, no. 48, 1975, pp. 29–57.
Coetzee, J. M. *The Life and Times of Michael K*. 1983. Vintage, 2004.
Coleridge, Samuel Taylor. "Kubla Khan." *The Norton Anthology of Poetry*, sixth edition, edited by Margaret Ferguson et al., 2018, pp. 848–49.
Comaroff, Jean, and John Comaroff, editors. *Modernity and Its Malcontents: Ritual and Power in Postcolonial Africa*. U of Chicago P, 1993.
———. "Occult Economies and the Violence of Abstraction: Notes from the South African Postcolony." *American Ethnologist*, vol. 26, no. 2, 1999, pp. 279–303.
———. *Of Revelation and Revolution: Christianity, Colonialism, and Consciousness in South Africa*. U of Chicago P, 1991.
Coole, Diana, and Samantha Frost. "Introducing the New Materialisms." *The New Materialisms: Ontology, Agency, and Politics*. Duke UP, 2010, pp. 1–46.
Cooper, Brenda. *Magical Realism in West African Fiction: Seeing with a Third Eye*. Routledge, 1998.
Cosentino, Donald. *Defiant Maids and Stubborn Farmers: Tradition and Invention in Mende Story Performance*. Cambridge UP, 1982.
"cosmology, n." *OED Online*, Oxford UP, December 2022. https://www.oed.com/dictionary/cosmology_n?tab=meaning_and_use#8239105. Accessed 1 July 2024.
Couto, Mia. *Sleepwalking Land*. Translated by David Brookshaw, Serpent's Tail, 2006.
Craps, Stef. "Beyond Eurocentrism: Trauma Theory in a Global Age." *The Future of Trauma Theory: Contemporary Literary and Cultural Criticism*, edited by Gert Buelens et al., Routledge, 2013, pp. 45–61.

---. *Postcolonial Witnessing: Trauma Out of Bounds*. Palgrave Macmillan, 2013.
---. and Gert Buelens, editors. *Postcolonial Trauma Novels*, special issue of *Studies in the Novel*, vol. 40, no. 1-2, 2008.
Critchley, Simon. *The Ethics of Deconstruction: Derrida and Levinas*. Edinburgh UP, 1992.
Crownshaw, Richard, et al., editors. *The Future of Memory*. Berghahn, 2010.
Culler, Jonathan. *Theory of the Lyric*. Harvard UP, 2015.
Cumpsty, Rebekah. *Postsecular Poetics: Negotiating the Sacred and Secular in Contemporary African Fiction*. Routledge, 2023.
Cvetkovich, Ann. *An Archive of Feelings: Trauma, Sexuality, and Lesbian Public Cultures*. Duke UP, 2003.
Dangarembga, Tsitsi. *Nervous Conditions*. 1988. Ayebia Clarke, 2004.
Dauda, Bola, and Toyin Falola. *Wole Soyinka: Literature, Activism, and African Transformation*. Bloomsbury, 2022.
de Castro, Eduardo Viveiros. *Cannibal Metaphysics*. Translated by Peter Skafish, U of Minnesota P, 2014.
---. "Cosmological Deixis and Amerindian Perspectivism." *The Journal of the Royal Anthropological Institute*, vol. 4, no. 3, 1998, pp. 469-88.
Delanda, Manuel. *A Thousand Years of Nonlinear History*. Princeton UP, 1997.
De Loughery, Elizabeth. *Allegories of the Anthropocene*. Duke UP, 2019.
de Man, Paul. *Blindness and Insight: Essays in the Rhetoric of Contemporary Criticism*. U of Minnesota P, 1983.
---. *The Rhetoric of Romanticism*. Columbia UP, 1984.
Derrida, Jacques. "Autoimmunity: Real and Symbolic Suicides." *Philosophy in a Time of Terror: Dialogues with Jürgen Habermas and Jacques Derrida*, translated by Pascale-Anne Brault et al., edited by Giovanna Borradori, U of Chicago P, 2003, pp. 85-136.
---. *The Beast and the Sovereign Volume 1*. Translated by Geoffrey Bennington, edited by Michel Lisse et al., U of Chicago P, 2009.
---. "'Eating Well,' or The Calculation of the Subject: An Interview with Jacques Derrida." *Who Comes after the Subject?* edited by Eduardo Cadava et al., Routledge, 1991, pp. 96-119.
---. "Force of Law: The 'Mystical Foundation of Authority.'" *Cordozo Law Review*, vol. 11, 1989-90, pp. 920-1045.
---. "Geopsychoanalysis: '. . . and the rest of the world.'" *The Psychoanalysis of Race*, translated by Donald Nicholson-Smith, edited by Christopher Lane, Columbia UP, pp. 65-90.
---. *Of Grammatology*. Translated by Gayatri Spivak, Johns Hopkins UP, 1976.
---. *The Post Card: From Socrates to Freud and Beyond*. Translated by Alan Bass, U of Chicago P, 1979.
---. *Specters of Marx: The State of Debt, the Work of Mourning, and the New International*. Translated by Peggy Kamuf, Routledge, 1994.

———. *Spurs: Nietzsche's Styles*. Translated by Barbara Harlow, U of Chicago P, 1979.
Diop, Birago. "Breath." *African Philosophy: An Anthology*, edited by Emmanuel Eze, Blackwell-Wiley, 1998, pp. 427–28.
Diop, Omar Chérif. *Violence and Trauma in Selected African Literature*. Africa World Press, 2018.
Drewal, Henry John, et al. *Yoruba: Nine Centuries of African Art and Thought*, edited by Allen Wardwell, Center for African Art in association with Harry N. Abrams, 1989.
Drewal, Margaret. *Yoruba Ritual: Performers, Play, Agency*. Indiana UP, 1992.
Driver, Dorothy, and Meg Samuelson, "History's Intimate Invasions: Yvonne Vera's *The Stone Virgins*." *English Studies in Africa*, vol. 50, no. 2, 2007, pp. 101–20.
Durrant, Sam. *Postcolonial Narrative and the Work of Mourning: J. M. Coetzee, Wilson Harris, and Toni Morrison*. State U of New York P, 2004.
———. "Surviving Time: Trauma, Tragedy, and the Postcolonial Novel." *Journal of Literature and Trauma Studies*, vol. 1, no. 1, 2012, pp. 95–117.
———. "Undoing Sovereignty: Towards a Theory of Critical Mourning." *The Future of Trauma Theory*, edited by Gert Buelens et al., Routledge, 2013, pp. 91–110.
———. and Philip Dickinson, editors. *Animism in a Planetary Frame*, special issue of *New Formations*, no. 104–05, 2022.
———. and Ryan Topper. "Cosmological Trauma and Postcolonial Modernity." *The Routledge Companion to Literature and Trauma*, edited by Colin Davis and Hanna Meretoja, Routledge, 2020, pp. 187–200.
Edelman, Lee. *No Future: Queer Theory and the Death Drive*. Duke UP, 2004.
Eisenstadt, S. N. "Multiple Modernities." *Daedalus*, vol. 129, no. 1, 2000, pp. 1–29.
Eliot, T. S. *The Complete Poems and Plays: 1909–1950*. Harcourt Brace, 1971.
Esonwanne, Uzoma. "The 'Crisis of the Soul': Psychoanalysis and African Literature." *Research in African Literatures*, vol. 38, no. 2, 2007, pp. 140–42.
Eze, Emmanuel Chukwudi, editor. *African Philosophy: An Anthology*. Blackwell, 1998.
———. "Language and Time in Postcolonial Experience." *Research in African Literatures*, vol. 39, no. 1, 2008, pp. 24–47.
Fanon, Frantz. *Black Skin, White Masks*. Translated by Charles Markmann, Grove, 1967.
———. *The Wretched of the Earth*. Translated by Constance Farrington, Penguin, 1976.
Farrell, Kirby. *Post-traumatic Culture: Injury and Interpretation in the Nineties*. Johns Hopkins UP, 1998.
Fassin, Didier, and Richard Rechtman. *Empire of Trauma: An Inquiry into the Condition of Victimhood*. Translated by Rachel Gomme, Princeton UP, 2009.
Felman, Shoshana, and Dori Laub. *Testimony: Crises of Witnessing in Literature, Psychoanalysis, and History*. Routledge, 1992.

Fletcher, John. "The Afterwardsness of Trauma and the Theory of Seduction." *Freud and the Scene of Trauma*, Fordham UP, 2013, pp. 59–87.
Forna, Aminatta. *The Memory of Love*. Bloomsbury, 2011.
Forter, Greg. "Colonial Trauma, Utopian Carnality, Modernist Form: Arundhati Roy's *The God of Small Things* and Toni Morrison's *Beloved*." *Contemporary Approaches in Literary Trauma Theory*, edited by Michelle Balaev, Palgrave Macmillan, 2014, pp. 70–105.
———. "Freud, Faulkner, Caruth: Trauma and the Politics of Literary Form." *Narrative*, vol. 15, no. 3, 2007, pp. 259–85.
Foucault, Michel. *The History of Sexuality*. Translated by Robert Hurley, vol. 1, Pantheon, 1978.
Franke, Anselm, editor. *Animism*, special issue of *e-flux*, no. 36, 2012.
Fraser, Nancy. *Scales of Justice: Reimagining Political Space in a Globalizing World*. Columbia UP, 2008.
Fraser, Robert. *West African Poetry: A Critical History*. Cambridge UP, 1986.
Freud, Sigmund. *Beyond the Pleasure Principle*. *The Penguin Freud Library Volume 11: On Metapsychology: The Theory of Psychoanalysis*. Translated by James Strachey, edited by Albert Dickson, Penguin, 1990, pp. 269–338.
———. *Moses and Monotheism*. *The Penguin Freud Library Volume 13: The Origins of Religion: Totem and Taboo, Moses and Monotheism and Other Works*. Translated by James Strachey, edited by Albert Dickson, Penguin, 1990, pp. 237–386.
———. *The Question of Lay Analysis: An Introduction to Psychoanalysis*. *Complete Psychological Works of Sigmund Freud Volume XX*. Translated by James Strachey, Norton, 1950.
Frosh, Stephen. *Hauntings: Psychoanalysis and Ghostly Transmissions*. Palgrave Macmillan, 2013.
Gagiano, Annie. "Reading *The Stone Virgins* as Vera's Study of the Katabolism of War." *Yvonne Vera*, special section of *Research in African Literatures*, vol. 38, no. 2, 2007, pp. 64–76.
Garuba, Harry. "Explorations in Animist Materialism: Notes on Reading/Writing African Literature, Culture, and Society." *Public Culture*, vol. 15, no. 2, 2003, pp. 261–86.
———. "On Animism, Modernity/Colonialism, and the African Order of Knowledge: Provisional Reflections." *Animism*, special issue of *e-flux*, no. 36, 2012.
Gates, Henry Louis, Jr. "Being, the Will, and the Semantics of Death." *Harvard Educational Review*, vol. 51, no. 1, 1981, pp. 163–73.
George, Olakunle. "Cultural Criticism in Wole Soyinka's *Death and the King's Horseman*." *Representations*, vol. 67, 1999, pp. 67–91.
———. *Relocating Agency: Modernity and African Letters*. State U of New York P, 2003.
Gibbs, James. *Wole Soyinka*. Macmillan, 1986.

Gikandi, Simon. "Preface: Modernism in the World." *Modernism/modernity*, vol. 13, no. 3, 2006, pp. 419–24.
Girard, René. *Violence and the Sacred*. Translated by Patrick Gregory, Continuum, 2005.
Glissant, Édouard. *Caribbean Discourse: Selected Essays*. Translated by J. Michael Dash, UP of Virginia, 1989.
———. *Poetics of Relation*. Translated by Betsy Wing, U of Michigan P, 1997.
Gobodo-Madikizela, Pumla. "Psychological Repair: The Intersubjective Dialogue of Remorse and Forgiveness in the Aftermath of Gross Human Rights Violations." *Journal of the American Psychoanalytic Association*, vol. 63, no. 6, 2015, pp. 1085–123.
Goodwin, Ken. *Understanding African Poetry: A Study of Ten Poets*. Heinemann, 1982.
Graham, James. "'A Country with Land But No Habitat': Women, Violent Accumulation and Negative-Value in Yvonne Vera's *The Stone Virgins*." *Journal of Postcolonial Writing*, vol. 53, no. 3, 2017, pp. 355–66.
Grant, Ben. "'Inhuman Voices': Reflections on the Place of Ancestors in the Work of Frantz Fanon." *Textual Practice*, vol. 28, no. 4, 2014, pp. 593–610.
Green, Lesley. *Rock/Water/Life: Ecology and Humanities for a Decolonial South Africa*. Duke UP, 2020.
Green, Louise. *Fragments from the History of Loss: The Nature Industry and the Postcolony*. Penn State UP, 2020.
———. "Thinking Outside the Body: New Materialism and the Challenge of the Fetish." *Cambridge Journal of Postcolonial Literary Inquiry*, vol. 5, no. 3, 2018, pp. 304–17.
Gyekye. Kwame. *An Essay on African Philosophical Thought: The Akan Conceptual Scheme*. Cambridge UP, 1987.
Habermas, Jürgen. "Religion in the Public Sphere." *European Journal of Philosophy*, vol. 14, no. 1, 2006, pp. 1–25.
Harris, Ashleigh. "'An Ingenious Tenderness': The Choreography of Violence in Yvonne Vera's *The Stone Virgins*." *Scrutiny2*, vol. 12, no. 2, 2007, pp. 32–48.
———. "Toni Morrison and Yvonne Vera: An Associative Fugue." *Scrutiny2*, vol. 9, no. 1, 2004, pp. 6–18.
Hartman, Geoffrey. "On Traumatic Knowledge and Literary Studies." *New Literary History*, vol. 26, no. 3, 1995, pp. 537–63.
Hartman, Saidiya. *Lose Your Mother: A Journey Along the Atlantic Slave Route*. Farrar, Straus and Giroux, 2007.
———. *Scenes of Subjection: Terror, Slavery, and Self-Making in Nineteenth-Century America*. Oxford UP, 1997.
Harvey, Graham. *Animism: Respecting the Living World*. Columbia UP, 2005.
———. "Introduction." *The Handbook of Contemporary Animism*, edited by Graham Harvey, Routledge, 2013, pp. 1–14.

———. editor. *The Handbook of Contemporary Animism*. Routledge, 2013.
Hayden, Lucy. "*The Man Died*, Prison Notes of Wole Soyinka: A Recorder and Visionary." *CLA Journal*, vol. 18, no. 4, 1975, pp. 542–52.
Head, Bessie. *A Question of Power*. Heinemann, 1974.
Heidegger, Martin. "Falling and Thrownness." *Being and Time*. 1927. Translated by John Macquarrie and Edward Robinson, Harper and Row, 1962, pp. 219–24.
Hena, Omaar. *Global Anglophone Poetry: Literary Form and Social Critique in Walcott, Muldoon, de Kok, and Nagra*. Palgrave Macmillan, 2015.
Hepburn, Joan. "Mediators of Ritual Closure." *Black American Literature Forum*, vol. 22, no. 3, 1988, pp. 577–614.
Herman, Judith. *Trauma and Recovery: The Aftermath of Violence—From Domestic Abuse to Political Terror*. Basic Books, 1992.
Hirsch, Marianne. *The Generation of Postmemory: Writing and Visual Culture after the Holocaust*. Columbia UP, 2012.
Horkheimer, Max, and Theodor Adorno. *Dialectic of Enlightenment: Philosophical Fragments*. Translated by Edmund Jephcott, edited by Gunzelin Chmid Noerr, Stanford UP, 2002.
Hornborg, Alf. "Animism, Fetishism, and Objectivism as Strategies for Knowing (or not Knowing) the World." *Ethnos: Journal of Anthropology*, vol. 71, no. 1, 2006, pp. 21–32.
Hountondji, Paulin. *African Philosophy: Myth and Reality*. Translated by Henri Evans, Indiana UP, 1983.
Hopkins, Gerard Manley. "God's Grandeur." *Poems and Prose*, edited by W. H. Gardner, Penguin, 1985, p. 27.
Huggan, Graham. "Is the 'Post' in 'Postsecular' the 'Post' in 'Postcolonial'?" *MFS: Modern Fiction Studies*, vol. 56, no. 4, 2010, pp. 751–68.
Hunter, Walt. *Forms of a World: Contemporary Poetry and the Making of Globalization*. Fordham UP, 2019.
Huyssen, Andreas. *Present Pasts: Urban Palimpsests and the Politics of Memory*. Stanford UP, 2003.
Ibrisim, Deniz Gundogan. "Trauma, Critical Posthumanism and New Materialism." *The Routledge Companion to Literature and Trauma*, edited by Colin Davis and Hanna Meretoja, Routledge, 2020, pp. 230–40.
Ifowodo, Ogaga. *History, Trauma, and Healing in Postcolonial Narratives: Reconstructing Identities*. Palgrave Macmillan, 2013.
Iheka, Cajetan. *African Ecomedia: Network Forms, Planetary Politics*. Duke UP, 2021.
———. *Naturalizing Africa: Ecological Violence, Agency, and Postcolonial Resistance in African Literature*. Cambridge UP, 2018.
Imma, Z'étoile. "Rewriting the SLTRC: Masculinities, the Arts of Forgetting, and Intimate Space in Delia Jarrett-Macauley's *Moses, Citizen, and Me* and Aminatta Forna's *The Memory of Love*." *Research in African Literatures*, vol. 48, no. 2, 2017, pp. 129–51.

Ingold, Tim. "Rethinking the Animate, Re-animating Thought." *Ethnos: Journal of Anthropology*, vol. 71, no. 1, 2006, pp. 9–20.
Irele, F. Abiola. "African Poetry of English Expression," *Présence Africaine*, vol. 57, 1966, p. 264.
———. *The African Imagination: Literature in Africa and the Black Diaspora*. Oxford UP, 2001.
Iweala, Uzodinman. *Beasts of No Nation*. John Murray, 2005.
Izevbaye, D. S. "Mediation in Soyinka: The Case of the King's Horseman." *Critical Perspectives on Wole Soyinka*, edited by James Gibbs, Heinemann, 1980, pp. 116–25.
Jackson, Jeanne-Marie. *The African Novel of Ideas: Philosophy and Individualism in the Age of Global Writing*. Princeton UP, 2021.
———. and Nathan Suhr-Sytsma. "Introduction: Religion, Secularity, and African Writing." *Research in African Literatures*, vol. 48, no. 2, 2017, pp. vii–xvi.
Jackson, Zakiyyah Iman. *Becoming Human: Matter and Meaning in an Antiblack World*. NYU P, 2020.
Jacobus, Mary, editor. *Trauma and Psychoanalysis*, special issue of *Diacritics*, vol. 28, no. 4, 1998.
Jarrett-Macauley, Delia. *Moses, Citizen, and Me*. Granta, 2005.
Jean-Charles, Régine Michelle. "Toward a Victim-Survivor Narrative: Rape and Form in Yvonne Vera's *Under the Tongue* and Calixthe Beyala's *Tu t'appelleras Tanga*." *Research in African Literatures*, vol. 45, no. 1, 2014, pp. 39–62.
Jeyifo, Biodun. *Wole Soyinka: Politics, Poetics and Postcolonialism*. Cambridge UP, 2004.
Jolly, Rosemary, and Alexander Fyfe, editors. *Reflections on Postcolonial Animations of the Material*, special issue of *Cambridge Journal of Postcolonial Literary Inquiry*, vol. 5, no. 3, 2018.
Kahiu, Wanuri. "Afrofuturism in Popular Culture: Wanuri Kahiu at TEDxNairobi." *YouTube*, uploaded by TEDx Talks, 14 Sept. 2012. www.youtube.com/watch?v=PvxOLVaV2YY.
———. "No More Labels: Wanuri Kahiu at TEDxEuston." *YouTube*, uploaded by TEDx Talks, 4 Feb. 2014. www.youtube.com/watch?v=4--BIlZE_78.
———. director. *Pumzi*. Focus Features, 2009.
Kaplan, E. Ann. *Trauma Culture: The Politics of Terror and Loss in Media and Literature*. Rutgers UP, 2005.
Katrak, Ketu. *Wole Soyinka and Modern Tragedy: A Study of Dramatic Theory and Practice*. Greenwood Press, 1986.
Kaufman, Eleanor. "Falling from the Sky: Trauma in Perec's 'W' and Caruth's 'Unclaimed Experience.'" *Diacritics*, vol. 28, no. 4, 1998, pp. 44–53.
Kazeem, Fayemi Ademola. "Time in Yorùbá Culture." *Al-Hikmat*, vol. 36, 2016, pp. 27–41.

Khanna, Ranjana. *Dark Continents: Psychoanalysis and Colonialism.* Duke UP, 2003.
Kilby, Jane, and Antony Rowland, editors. *The Future of Testimony: Interdisciplinary Perspectives on Witnessing.* Routledge, 2014.
Kipling, Rudyard. "The Burial." *The Collected Poems of Rudyard Kipling,* edited by R. T. Jones, Wordsworth Editions Limited, 1994, pp. 220–21.
Kopf, Martina. "Narratives of Wounded Time: Yvonne Vera's Poetics of Trauma." *Style in African Literature: Essays on Literary Stylistics and Narrative Styles,* edited by J. K. S. Makokha et al., Rodopi, 2012, pp. 91–110.
Kostelac, Sofia. "The Body Is His, Pulse and Motion": Violence and Desire in Yvonne Vera's *The Stone Virgins.*" *Research in African Literatures,* vol. 41, no. 3, 2010, pp. 75–87.
———. " 'The Voices of Drowned Men Cannot Be Heard': Writing Subalternity in Yvonne Vera's *Butterfly Burning* and *The Stone Virgins.*" *English Studies in Africa,* vol. 50, no. 2, 2007, pp. 121–32.
Kramer, Fritz. *The Red Fez: Art and Spirit Possession in Africa.* 1987. Translated by Malcolm Green, Verso, 1993.
Krishnan, Madhu. *Writing Spatiality in West Africa: Colonial Legacies in the Anglophone/Francophone Novel,* James Currey, 2018.
Kristeva, Julia. *The Sense and Non-Sense of Revolt: The Powers and Limits of Psychoanalysis, Volume 1.* Translated by Jeanine Herman, Columbia UP, 2000.
Kumavie, Delali. "The Para-Worlds of Lelsey Nneka Arimah's: What It Means When a Man Falls from the Sky." *Qui Parle: Critical Humanities and Social Sciences,* vol. 31, no. 1, 2022, pp. 37–65.
Kurtz, Roger. *Trauma and Transformation in African Literature.* Routledge, 2022.
Lacan, Jacques. *The Four Fundamental Concepts of Psychoanalysis. The Seminar of Jacques Lacan.* Translated by Alan Sheridan, edited by Jacques-Alain Miller, Norton, 1978.
———. "The Mirror Stage as Formative of the I Function, as Revealed in Psychoanalytic Experience." *Écrits. A Selection,* translated by Bruce Fink, edited by Jacques-Alain Miller, Norton, 2006, pp. 75–81.
LaCapra, Dominick. *Writing History, Writing Trauma.* Johns Hopkins UP, 2001.
Laplanche, Jean. "Notes on Afterwardsness." *Essays on Otherness,* translated by John Fletcher, edited by John Fletcher, Routledge, 1999, pp. 264–69.
———. "The Unfinished Copernican Revolution." *Essays on Otherness,* translated by Luke Thurston, edited by John Fletcher, Routledge, 1999, pp. 53–85.
Lemm, Vanessa. "Introduction: Biopolitics and Community in Roberto Esposito." *Terms of the Political: Community, Immunity Biopolitics,* by Roberto Esposito, Fordham UP, 2013, pp. 1–13.
Leys, Ruth. *Trauma: A Genealogy.* Chicago: U of Chicago P, 2000.
Lindfors, Bernth. "The Early Writings of Wole Soyinka," *Critical Perspectives on Wole Soyinka,* edited by James Gibbs, Heinemann, 1981, pp. 19–44.

Lloyd, David. "Colonial Trauma/Postcolonial Recovery?" *Interventions*, vol. 2, no. 2, 2000, pp. 212–28.

Losambe, Lokangaka. "Death, Power and Cultural Translation in Wole Soyinka's *Death and the King's Horseman*." *Journal of Commonwealth Literature*, vol. 42, no. 1, 2007, pp. 21–30.

Luckhurst, Roger. *The Trauma Question*. Routledge, 2008.

Macebuh, Stanley. "Poetics and Mythic Imagination," *Critical Perspectives on Wole Soyinka*, edited by James Gibbs, Heinemann, 1981, pp. 200–12.

Maduakor, Obi. "Soyinka's Animystic Poetics." *African Studies Review*, vol. 25, no. 1, 1982, pp. 37–48.

Mahmood, Saba. "Secularism, Hermeneutics, and Empire: The Politics of Islamic Reformation." *Public Culture*, vol. 18, no. 2, 2006, pp. 323–47.

Malabou, Catherine. "Go Wonder: Subjectivity and Affects in Neurobiological Times." *Self and Emotional Life: Philosophy, Psychoanalysis, and Neuroscience*, by Adrian Johnston and Catherine Malabou, Columbia UP, 2013, pp. 1–63.

———. *The New Wounded: From Neurosis to Brain Damage*. Translated by Steven Miller, Fordham UP, 2012.

———. *Ontology of the Accident: An Essay on Destructive Plasticity*. Translated by Carolyn Shread, Polity, 2012.

———. "Plasticity and Elasticity in Freud's 'Beyond the Pleasure Principle.'" *Diacritics*, vol. 37, no. 4, 2007, pp. 78–85.

———. *What Should We Do with Our Brain?* Translated by Sebastian Rand, Fordham UP, 2008.

Mao, Douglas, and Rebecca Walkowitz. "The New Modernist Studies," *PMLA*, vol. 123, no. 3, 2008, pp. 737–48.

Marriott, David. *Whither Fanon? Studies in the Blackness of Being*. Stanford UP, 2018.

Mbembe, Achille. "African Modes of Self-Writing," translated by Steven Rendall. *Public Culture*, vol. 14, no. 1, 2022, pp. 239–73.

———. "Necropolitics," translated by Libby Meintjes. *Public Culture*, vol. 15, no. 1, 2003, pp. 11–40.

———. *On the Postcolony*. Translated by A. M. Berrett et al., U of California P, 2001.

Mbiti, John. *Introduction to African Religion Introduction to African Religion*. Heinemann, 1975.

McGiffin, Emily. *Of Land, Bones, and Money: Toward a South African Ecopoetics*. UVA P, 2019.

McLuckie, Craig. "The Structural Coherence of Wole Soyinka's *Death and the King's Horseman*." *College Literature*, vol. 31, no. 2, 2004, pp. 143–63.

McNulty, Eugene. "Before the Law(s): Wole Soyinka's *Death and the King's Horseman* and the Passages of 'Bare Life.'" *Postcolonial Text*, vol. 6, no. 3, 2011, https://www.postcolonial.org/index.php/pct/article/view/1284. Accessed 1 Jan. 2019.

McPheron, William. "Wole Soyinka: Transforming Myth." *Prague Writers' Festival*, 29 Jan. 2008. www.pwf.cz.arhivy/texts/readings/wole-soyinka-transforming-myth_410.html. Accessed 1 Mar. 2023.
Moore, Gerald. "Soyinka's New Play." *Critical Perspectives on Wole Soyinka*, edited by James Gibbs, Heinemann, 1980, pp. 126–27.
Morrison, Toni. *Beloved*. 1987. Plume, 1988.
Mowitt, John. "Trauma Envy." *Cultural Critique*, no. 46, 2000, 272–97.
Msiska, Mpalive-Hangson. *Postcolonial Identity in Wole Soyinka*. Rodopi, 2007.
Mtambo, Nandipha. *Europa*. Andrehn-Schiptjenko.com, 2008.
Mtshali, Oswald Mbuyiseni. *Sounds of a Cowhide Drum: Imisindo Yesigubhu Sesikhumba Senkomo*. Jacana, 2012.
Muchemwa, Kizito. "Language, Voice and Presence in *Under the Tongue* and *Without a Name*." *Sign and Taboo: Perspectives on the Poetic Fiction of Yvonne Vera*, edited by Robert Muponde and Mandi Taruvinga, Weaver, 2002, pp. 3–14.
Mudimbe, V. Y. *The Invention of Africa: Gnosis, Philosophy, and the Order of Knowledge*. Indiana UP, 1988.
Muponde, Robert. "Reading Girlhood Under the Tongue." *Yvonne Vera*, special section of *Research in African Literatures*, vol. 38, no. 2, 2007, pp. 36–48.
———. and Mandi Taruvinga, editors. *Sign and Taboo: Perspectives on the Poetic Fiction of Yvonne Vera*, Weaver, 2002.
Murray, Jessica. "A Post-colonial and Feminist Reading of Selected Testimonies to Trauma in Post-liberation South Africa and Zimbabwe." *Journal of African Cultural Studies*, vol. 21, no. 1, 2009, pp. 1–21.
Mwangi, Evan Maina. *The Postcolonial Animal: African Literature and Posthuman Ethics*. U of Michigan P, 2019.
Naess, Arne. *Ecology, Community and Lifestyle: An Outline of Ecosophy*. Translated by David Rothenberg, Cambridge UP, 1989.
Nancy, Jean-Luc. "Deconstruction of Monotheism." Trans. Amanda Macdonald. *Postcolonial Studies*, vol. 6, no. 1, 2003, pp. 37–46.
Negarestani, Reza. "Globe of Revolution: An Afterthought on Geophilosophical Realism." *Identities: Journal for Politics, Gender and Culture*, vol. 8, no. 2, 2011, pp. 25–54.
Ngũgĩ wa Thiong'o. *Decolonising the Mind: The Politics of Language in African Literature*. James Currey, 1986.
Nichanian, Marc. *The Historiographic Perversion*. Translated by Gil Anidjar, Columbia UP, 2009.
Nicholls, Brendon. "Africas of the Mind: From Indigenous Medicine to Environmental Psychoanalysis." *Cultural Critique*, no. 111, 2021, pp. 52–80.
Nixon, Rob. *Slow Violence and the Environmentalism of the Poor*. Harvard UP, 2011.

Njovane, Thando. "Colonial Monuments, Postcolonial Selves: History, Trauma and Silence in Yvonne Owuor's *Dust*." *The Journal of Commonwealth Literature*, vol. 58, no. 1, 2023, pp. 169–82.

Norridge, Zoe. *Perceiving Pain in African Literature*. Palgrave, 2013.

Novak, Amy. "Who Speaks? Who Listens? The Problem of Address in Two Nigerian Trauma Novels." *Studies in the Novel*, vol. 40, no. 1, 2008, pp. 31–51.

Ntiru, Richard. "To the Living." *Poems of Black Africa*, edited by Wole Soyinka, Heinemann, 1975, pp. 48–50.

Nuttall, Sara. "Inside the City: Reassembling the Township in Yvonne Vera's Fiction." *Versions of Zimbabwe: New Approaches to Literature and Culture*, edited by Robert Muponde and Ranka Primorac, Weaver, 2005, pp. 177–91.

Nyamnjoh, Francis. *Drinking from the Cosmic Gourd: How Amos Tutuola Can Change Our Minds*. Langaa RPCIG, 2017.

Ogundele, Wole. "'Death and the King's Horseman': A Poet's Quarrel with His Culture." *Research in African Literatures*, vol. 25, no. 1, 1994, pp. 47–60.

Ojaide, Tanure. "Teaching Wole Soyinka's 'Death and the King's Horseman' to American College Students." *College Literature*, vols. 19–20, nos. 3–1, 1992–93, pp. 210–14.

———. *The Poetry of Wole Soyinka*. Malthouse Press, 1994.

O'Key, Dominic. "Aminatta Forna's Postcolonial Romance: Borders, Foxes, and Natural Resilience in *Happiness*." *Contemporary Literature*, vol. 63, no. 4, 2022, pp. 559–584.

———. *Creaturely Forms in Contemporary Literature: Narrating the War Against Animals*. Bloomsbury, 2022.

Olaniyan, Tejumola. "Wole Soyinka: 'Race Retrieval' and Cultural Self-Apprehension." *Scars of Conquest/Masks of Resistance: The Invention of Cultural Identities in African, Africa-American, and Caribbean Drama*, Oxford UP, 1995, pp. 42–66.

Olupona, Jacob. *African Religions: A Very Short Introduction*. Oxford UP, 2014.

———, editor. *Beyond Primitivism: Indigenous Religious Traditions and Modernity*. Routledge, 2004.

Oluwole, Sophie. "The Labyrinth Conception of Time as Basis of Yoruba View of Development." *Studies in Intercultural Philosophy*, vol. 8, 1997, pp. 139–50.

Onega, Susana, and Jean-Michel Ganteau, editors. *Contemporary Trauma Narratives: Liminality and the Ethics of Form*. Routledge, 2014.

Patke, Rajeev Shridhar. *Postcolonial Poetry in English*. Oxford UP, 2006.

Patterson, Orlando. *Slavery and Social Death: A Comparative Study*. Harvard UP, 1982.

p'Bitek, Okot. *Song of Lawino and Song of Ocol*. Waveland Press, 1967.

Peek, Philip M., editor. *African Divination Systems: Ways of Knowing*. Indiana UP, 1991.

Peel, J. D. Y. "Making History: The Past in the Iljesha Present." *Man*, vol. 19, no. 1, 1984, pp. 111–32.

Peters, Lenrie. "On a Wet September Morning." *Poems of Black Africa*, edited by Wole Soyinka, Heinemann, 1975, pp. 65–68.

Phalafala, Uhuru Portia. *Mine Mine Mine*. U of Nebraska P, 2023.

———. "Time Is Always NOW: Animist Materialism in Keorapetse Kgositsile's Temporal Order." *Scrutiny2*, vol. 22, no. 2, 2017, pp. 33–48.

Pietz, William. "The Problem of the Fetish I." *RES: Anthropology and Aesthetics*, vol. 9, 1985, pp. 5–17.

Posmentier, Sonya. *Cultivation and Catastrophe: The Lyric Ecology of Modern Black Literature*. Johns Hopkins UP, 2017.

Primorac, Ranka. "Crossing into the Space-Time of Memory: Borderline Identities in Novels by Yvonne Vera." *Journal of Commonwealth Literature*, vol. 36, no. 2, 2001, pp. 77–93.

———. "The Poetics of State Terror in Twenty-First Century Zimbabwe." *Interventions: International Journal of Postcolonial Studies*, vol. 9, no. 3, 2007, pp. 434–50.

Quayson, Ato. "'All of the People, Some of the Time': The Ethics of Choice in a Soyinkan Action." *Essays in Honour of Wole Soyinka at 80*, edited by Ivor Agyeman-Duah and Ogochukwu Promise, Ayebia Clarke, 2014, pp. 65–74.

———. *Strategic Transformations in Nigerian Writing*. Indiana UP, 1997.

———. *Tragedy and Postcolonial Literature*. Cambridge UP, 2021.

———. "Wole Soyinka: Disability, Maimed Rites, and the Systemic Uncanny." *Aesthetic Nervousness. Disability and the Crisis of Representation*, Columbia UP, 2007, pp. 115–46.

Rajiva, Jay. *Postcolonial Parabola: Literature, Tactility, and the Ethics of Representing Trauma*. Bloomsbury, 2017.

Ramadanovic, Petar. "Introduction: Trauma and Crisis." *Postmodern Culture*, vol. 11, no. 2, 2001.

———. "The Time of Trauma: Rereading *Unclaimed Experience* and *Testimony*." *Journal of Literature and Trauma Studies*, vol. 3, no. 2, 2014, pp. 1–23.

Ramazani, Jahan. *The Hybrid Muse: Postcolonial Poetry in English*. U of Chicago P, 2011.

Ranger, Terence. "Missionaries, Migrants, and the Manyika: The Invention of Ethnicity in Zimbabwe." *The Creation of Tribalism in Southern Africa*, edited by Leroy Vail, U of California P, 1989, pp. 118–46.

———. "Nationalist Historiography, Patriotic History and the History of the Nation: The Struggle over the Past in Zimbabwe." *Journal of Southern African Studies*, vol. 30, no. 2, 2004, pp. 215–34.

———. *Voices from the Rocks: Nature, Culture and History in the Matopos Hills of Zimbabwe*. Indiana UP, 1999.

Ratti, Manav. *The Postsecular Imagination: Postcolonialism, Religion, and Literature*. Routledge, 2013.

Reading Frantz Fanon Here and Now. "Yvonne Vera interviewed by Jane Bryce: Interview with Yvonne Vera, 1st August 2000, Bulawayo, Zimbabwe. Weaver Press." *The Frantz Fanon Blog*, 17 Nov. 2011, http://readingfanon.blogspot.com/2011/11/yvonne-vera-interviewed-by-jane-bryce.html. Accessed 1 Apr. 2022.

Rhodes, Cecil John. *The Last Will and Testament of Cecil John Rhodes: with Elucidatory Notes to Which are Added Some Chapters Describing the Political and Religious Ideas of the Testator*, edited by W. T. Stead, Review of Reviews, 1902.

Richards, David. *Masks of Difference: Cultural Representations in Literature, Anthropology and Art*. Cambridge UP, 1994.

Richards, Paul. *Fighting for the Rainforest: War, Youth, and Resources in Sierra Leone*. Currey, 1996.

Ricoeur, Paul. *Freud and Philosophy: An Essay on Interpretation*. Translated by Denis Savage, Yale UP, 1970.

Rohmer, Martin. "Wole Soyinka's 'Death and the King's Horseman,' Royal Exchange Theatre, Manchester." *New Theatre Quarterly*, vol. 10, no. 37, 1994, pp. 57–69.

Rooney, Caroline. *African Literature, Animism and Politics*. Routledge, 2000.

———. *Decolonising Gender: Literature and a Poetics of the Real*. Routledge, 2007.

Rose, Arthur. *Asbestos—The Last Modernist Object*. Edinburgh UP, 2022.

Rothberg, Michael. "Beyond Tancred and Clorinda—Trauma Studies for Implicated Subjects." *The Future of Trauma Theory*, edited by Gert Buelens et al., Routledge, 2013, pp. xi–xviii.

———. "Decolonizing Trauma Studies: A Response." *Studies in the Novel*, vol. 40, no. 2, 2008, pp. 224–33.

———. *The Implicated Subject: Beyond Victims and Perpetrators*. Stanford UP, 2019.

———. *Multidirectional Memory: Remembering the Holocaust in the Age of Decolonization*. Stanford UP, 2009.

———. "Trauma Theory, Implicated Subjects, and the Question of Israel/Palestine." *Profession*, 2 May 2014.

Sachs, Wulf. *Black Hamlet*. 1937. Johns Hopkins UP, 1996.

Said, Edward. *Culture and Imperialism*. Vintage, 1994.

———.*Freud and the Non-European*. Verso, 2014.

———. *The World, the Text, and the Critic*. Harvard UP, 1983.

Samuelson, Meg. "Re-membering the Body: Rape and Recovery in *Without a Name* and *Under the Tongue*." *Sign and Taboo: Perspectives on the Poetic Fiction of Yvonne Vera*, edited by Robert Muponde and Mandi Taruvinga, Weaver, 2002, pp. 93–100.

———. "Yvonne Vera's Bulawayo: Modernity, (Im)mobility, Music, and Memory." *Research in African Literatures*, vol. 38, no. 2, 2007, pp. 22–35.

Santner, Eric. *On Creaturely Life: Rilke, Benjamin, Sebald*. U of Chicago P, 2006.

Schmitt, Carl. *Political Theology: Four Chapters on the Concept of Sovereignty*. 1922. Translated by George Schwab, U of Chicago P, 2005.

Scott, David. *Conscripts of Modernity: The Tragedy of Colonial Enlightenment.* Duke UP, 2004.
Shakespeare, William. *Julius Caesar*, edited by Arthur Humphreys, Oxford UP, 2008.
Shepler, Susan. *Childhood Deployed: Remaking Child Soldiers in Sierra Leone.* NYU P, 2014.
———. "The Rites of the Child: Global Discourses of Youth and Reintegrating Child Soldiers in Sierra Leone." *Journal of Human Rights*, vol. 4, no. 2, 2005, pp. 197–211.
Sithole, Tendayi. *The Black Register.* Polity, 2020.
Soyinka, Wole. *Aké: The Years of Childhood.* Random House, 1981.
———. *Art, Dialogue, and Outrage: Essays on Literature and Culture*, edited by Biodun Jeyifo, Pantheon Books, 1993.
———. *The Burden of Memory, The Muse of Forgiveness.* Oxford UP, 1999.
———. *The Man Died: Prison Notes of Wole Soyinka.* Spectrum, 1972.
———. *Climate of Fear: The Quest for Dignity in a Dehumanized World.* Random House, 2004.
———. *Death and the D.O.* n.d. Leeds University Library Special Collections (BCMS20C Soyinka 2/1), Leeds.
———. *Death and the King's Horseman: Norton Critical Edition*, edited by Simon Gikandi, Norton, 2003.
———. "*Death and the King's Horseman* Playwright Wole Soyinka Answers Director Alby James' Questions." 21 June 1995. Leeds University Library Special Collections (MS1748/1), Leeds.
———. *Early Poems.* Oxford UP, 1998.
———. Figure 1. BC MS 20c Soyinka 12/1 'The Man Died: Prison Notes' (1972). File 4 of Box 4. Wole Soyinka Literary Papers. Brotherton Library Special Collections, University of Leeds.
———. Figure 2. BC MS 20c Soyinka 12/1 'The Man Died: Prison Notes' (1972). File 4 of Box 4. Wole Soyinka Literary Papers. Brotherton Library Special Collections, University of Leeds.
———. "Introduction." *Poems of Black Africa*, edited by Wole Soyinka, Heinemann, 1975.
———. *Myth, Literature and the African World.* Cambridge UP, 1992.
———. "Narcissus and Other Pall Bearers: Morbidity as Ideology." *Leeds African Studies Bulletin*, no. 77, 2015–16.
———. "Ritual as the Medium: A Modest Proposal." *African Affairs*, vol. 96, no. 382, 1997, pp. 5–23.
———. "Theatre in West Africa: A Conversation between Wole Soyinka and Martin Banham." n.d. Leeds University Library Special Collections (MS1748/1), Leeds.
Spillers, Hortense. "Mama's Baby, Papa's Maybe: An American Grammar Book." *Diacritics*, vol. 17, no. 2, 1987, pp. 64–81.
Steiner, George. *The Death of Tragedy.* 1961. Yale UP, 1996.

Stoller, Paul. *Embodying Colonial Memories: Spirit Possession, Power, and the Hauka in West Africa*. Routledge, 1995.
Suhr-Sytsma, Nathan. *Poetry, Print, and the Making of Postcolonial Literature*. Cambridge UP, 2017.
Tal, Kalí. *Worlds of Hurt: Reading the Literatures of Trauma*. Cambridge UP, 1996.
Taussig, Michael. *Mimesis and Alterity: A Particular History of the Senses*. Routledge, 1993.
———. *Shamanism, Colonialism, and the Wild Man: A Study in Terror and Healing*. U of Chicago P, 1986.
Taylor, Charles. *A Secular Age*. Harvard UP, 2007.
———. "Two Theories of Modernity." *The Hastings Center Report*, vol. 25, no. 2, 1995, pp. 24–33.
Tempels, Placide. *Bantu Philosophy*, translated by Colin King, Paris: Présence Africaine, 1969.
Terdiman, Richard. *Present Past: Modernity and the Memory Crisis*. Cornell UP, 1993.
Thompson, Jeff. "The Politics of the Shuttle: Wole Soyinka's Poetic Space." *Research in African Literatures*, vol. 27, no. 2, 1996, pp. 94–101.
Tighe, C. "In Detentio Preventione in Aeternum: Wole Soyinka's *A Shuttle in the Crypt*." *The Journal of Commonwealth Literature*, vol. 10, no. 3, 1976, pp. 9–22.
Toivanen, Anna-Leena. "Remembering the Nation's Aching Spots: Yvonne Vera's Authorial Position of a Witness and Healer." *Postcolonial Text*, vol. 5, no. 4, 2009, https://postcolonial.org/index.php/pct/article/view/1080.
Tutuola, Amos. *The Palm-Wine Drinkard and My Life in the Bush of Ghosts*. Grove, 1994.
Twitchin, Mischa, and Carl Lavery, editors. *On Animism*, special issue of *Performance Research*, vol. 24, no. 6, 2019.
Tylor, Edward B. *Primitive Culture: Researches into the Development of Mythology, Philosophy, Religion, Art, and Custom*. London: John Murray, 1871.
Vambe, Maurice. "Problems of Representing the Zimbabwean War of Liberation in Mutsasa's *The Contact*, Samupindi's *Pawns* and Vera's *The Stone Virgins*." *War in African Literature Today*, no. 26, 2008, pp. 87–102.
van Dooren, Thom, and Deborah Bird Rose. "Lively Ethography: Storying Animist Worlds." *Environmental Humanities*, vol. 8, no. 1, 2016, pp. 77–94.
Vera, Yvonne. "A Blue and Pallid people." Email sent 8 Mar. 2003. Box 8 File 2, Yvonne Vera Fonds, Clara Thomas Archives and Special Collections, York University, Toronto.
———. "Letter to John Jose, 7 Dec 2001." Box 2 File 1, Yvonne Vera Fonds, Clara Thomas Archives and Special Collections, York University, Toronto.
———. *Nehanda*. Toronto: TSAR, 1994.

———. "Nkomo's Burial Full of Emotion." *The Chronicle*, Wednesday, 7 Jul. 1999. Page 7. Box 4 File 1, Yvonne Vera Fonds, Clara Thomas Archives and Special Collections, York University, Toronto.

———. "Preface." *Opening Spaces: Contemporary African Women's Writing*, edited by Yvonne Vera, Heinemann, 1999.

———. *The Prison of Colonial Space: Narratives of Resistance*. 1995. York University, Toronto, PhD dissertation.

———. "'Shaping the Truth of the Struggle'" An Interview with Yvonne Vera." Eva Hunter. *Current Writing*, vol. 10, no. 1, 1998, pp. 75–86.

———. *The Stone Virgins: A Novel*. Farrar, Straus and Giroux, 2003.

———. "The Writer's World Resembles Some Kind of Kaleidoscope." Box 4 File 1, Yvonne Vera Fonds, Clara Thomas Archives and Special Collections, York University, Toronto.

———. "Yvonne" (VHS of POV Women segment on *Fiery Spirits*). Box 12 File 1. Yvonne Vera Fonds, Clara Thomas Archives and Special Collections, York University, Toronto.

Viditz-Ward, Vera. "Studio Photography in Freetown." *Anthology of African and Indian Ocean Photography*. Revue Noire, 1999, pp. 34–41.

Visser, Irene. "Trauma Theory and Postcolonial Literary Studies." *Journal of Postcolonial Writing*, vol. 47, no. 3, 2011, pp. 270–82.

Ward, Abigail, editor. *Postcolonial Traumas: Memory, Narrative, Resistance*. Palgrave, 2015.

Warwick Research Collective. *Combined and Uneven Development: Towards a New Theory of World-Literature*. Liverpool UP, 2015.

Watters, Ethan. *Crazy like Us: The Globalization of the American Psyche*. Free Press, 2010.

Weber, Max. *Science as a Vocation. From Max Weber: Essays in Sociology*, translated by H. H. Gerth and C. Wright Mills, edited by Gerth and Mills. Routledge, 2009, pp. 129–56.

Weheliye, Alexander Ghedi. *Habeas Viscus: Racializing Assemblages, Biopolitics, and Black Feminist Theories of the Human*. Duke UP, 2014.

Wenzel, Jennifer. *The Disposition of Nature: Environmental Crises and World Literature*. Fordham UP, 2019.

Whitehead, Anne. "Journeying Through Hell: Wole Soyinka, Trauma, and Postcolonial Nigeria." *Studies in the Novel*, vol. 40, no. 1, 2008, pp. 13–30.

Wilderson III, Frank B. *Afropessimism*. Liveright P, 2020.

Williams, Adebayo. "Ritual and the Political Unconscious: The Case of Death and the King's Horseman." *Research in African Literatures*, vol. 24, no. 1, 1993, pp. 67–79.

Wilson, Rodrick. "Complexity and Confusion in Soyinka's Shorter Poems," *The Journal of Commonwealth Literature*, vol. 8, no. 1, 1973, pp. 69–80.

Wiredu, Kwasi. *Philosophy and an African Culture.* Cambridge UP, 1980.
Wolfe, Cary. *What Is Posthumanism?* U of Minnesota P, 2009.
Wynter, Sylvia. "Columbus and the Poetics of the *Propter Nos. Annals of Scholarship*, vol. 8, no. 2, 1991, pp. 251–86.
———. with David Scott. "The Re-Enchantment of Humanism: An Interview with Sylvia Wynter." *Small Axe*, vol. 8, 2000, p. 207.
Young, Allan. *The Harmony of Illusions: Inventing Post-Traumatic Stress Disorder.* Princeton UP, 1995.

Index

Abani, Chris, 4, 29
Abraham, Nicolas, 197
Abram, David, 15, 235n14
Achebe, Chinua, 4, 40, 47; *Morning Yet on Creation Day*, 34, 47; *Things Fall Apart*, 3, 12, 13, 32, 181, 198–99, 203
Acts of the Apostles, 40
Adéèkó, Adélékè, 160, 233n6
Adorno, Theodor, 27–28, 39, 52, 227; *Dialectic of Enlightenment*, 6, 174
African studies, 33, 231n1, 233n8
African literary criticism, 5, 6
Afrofuturism, 11–12, 70
Afropessimism, 8, 145, 150–51, 176
Agamben, Giorgio, 12, 63–64, 161–62; on Holocaust, 36, 148, 161; *Homo Sacer*, 18, 146, 148–50; *The Coming Community*, 181
Aidoo, Ama Ata, 3
Alaimo, Stacy, 20, 58, 108
Alexander, Jeffrey, 45
Allen-Paisant, Jason, 17
alternative states, 78, 80–83, 189
Althusser, Louis, 160–61, 239n19
ancestral trauma, 2–3, 9, 32, 144, 227–28; of apartheid, 25; Fanon on, 24; realism-ritual spectrum of, 67; Soyinka on, 2, 24; temporality of, 7; Vera on, 197–98, 201. *See also* cosmological rupture
Anderson, Benedict, 85
Angelou, Maya, 245n19
Angira, Jared, 13
animal studies, 15, 231–32n2
animism, 14, 227–28; cosmopolitan, 141; definition of, 5; extirpation of, 227; Fanon on, 59; Garuba on, 17–18, 24, 67–68; logic of, 6; memory representation and, 63–66; "new," 14; psychoanalytic, 88–91; regeneration of, 27–29; shamanic rituals and, 72–73, 76–78, 84, 231n1; Soyinkan, 109–16; structural, 92; Tasso on, 37–41; Vera on, 187–88, 199–203. *See also* animist cosmologies, Indigenous cosmologies, and Indigenous knowledge systems
animist cosmologies, 8, 40, 47, 58–59. *See also* cosmic personhood
animist criticism, 9, 66, 227–30
animist lyric, 101–108, 141, 183
animist materialism, 17–18, 70–73
animist poetics, 1–9, 35, 63, 183; of Achebe, 40; Afrofuturism and, 12; contemporary theories of, 14–23; defined, 9, 227, 234n10; of Garuba,

animist poetics *(continued)*
71; as logic of survival, 41; *polis* and, 65; of realism-ritual spectrum, 67–73; of Soyinka, 68, 109–16, 128–29, 139; of Vera, 187–88, 200
animist realism, 17–18, 69, 76–78, 91; definition of, 18; Garuba on, 77–78, 91, 240n1
animist tragedy, 26, 143–46, 176, 183
"animystic" perception of death (Soyinka), 116–22, 201–202
anthropocentrism, 3, 6, 8, 15, 38, 43, 104–105, 181, 187, 190. *See also* posthumanism
Anzaldúa, Gloria, 20
Anzieu, Didier, 222
apartheid, 92–97; Group Areas Act of, 93; trauma of, 25, 68–69
Appiah, Anthony, 153
Apter, Andrew, 242n2
Arendt, Hannah, 193, 194
Ashcroft, Bill, 18
Augustine of Hippo, 55
Austen, Jane, 238n6

Balaev, Michelle, 238n13
Baldwin, James, 34
baobab trees, 195–99, 203
Barad, Karen, 20, 58, 108
Barnaby, Andrew, 154
Barthes, Roland, 51
Benjamin, Walter, 164; on "divine violence," 57, 65; "homogenous, empty time," 128; "natural history," 164; Schmitt and, 63–64, 240n22
Bennett, Jane, 20, 58, 108
Berlant, Lauren, 38, 238n11
Bhabha, Homi, 32–33, 242n9
Biafran War (1967–1970), 129–32, 148, 242n8, 246n30
Biopolitics 25–26, 145–46; biopolitical mediation, 143–46; biopolitical theology, 146–53, 161–62, 230; Black biopolitics, 26, 146, 148–50, 176, 180. *See also* political theology
Bird-David, Nurit, 15
Black Consciousness movement, 92
Black studies, 24, 29, 33, 64, 149. *See also* biopolitics (Black biopolitics)
Blood Diamond (film), 87–88
Brahma (deity), 137
Braidotti, Rosi, 15, 17
Brew, Kwesi, 21–22
British South Africa Company (BSAC), 209, 213, 255n38
Brown, Laura, 46, 81
Brown, Wendy, 18
Brutus, Dennis, 92
Buelens, Gert, 74
Bulawayo, NoViolet, 3
Butler, Judith, 49, 193

capitalism, 2, 9, 14, 17–18, 70, 98, 173, 193, 234n10, 236n20, 250n11
Cartesian dualism, 5, 14, 29, 183
Caruth, Cathy, 36; Butler and, 49; Freud and, 48–49; on implicated subjectivity, 90, 196; on literary criticism, 51–52; Rothberg and, 140; trauma theory of, 48–54, 139, 187, 238n12; *Literature in the Ashes of History*, 48; *Unclaimed Experience*, 37, 38, 187
Caulker, Tcho Mbaimba, 84–85
Coetzee, J. M., 33–34
Coleridge, Samuel Taylor, 132
colonial modernity, 35, 69–70, 156, 185
colonial spatiality, 202
commodity fetishism, 18, 71, 239n20
Conrad, Joseph, 7, 85
cosmic personhood, 101–108
cosmological rupture, 27–29
cosmologies, 6–8, 58–59; defined, 233n8; Indigenous, 3, 25, 40, 47,

204; Shona, 213, 252n8, 255n29; Yoruba, 26, 101, 144, 154–55, 171, 241n2, 243n12, 250n19
Couto, Mia, 12–13
Craps, Stef, 46, 74–76, 79, 81
creative-destructive principle, 26, 101, 122–28, 155, 171–81, 188, 202, 248n35, 250n19. *See also* cyclic time, regeneration, *and* regenerative death drive
cryptonomy, 197
Culler, Jonathan, 103
cultural memory: ecopoetics of, 25; erasure of, 49; Rothberg on, 186–90, 192–94, 241n7; Vera on, 184–85, 190–94. *See also* memory *and* multidimensional memory
Cvetkovich, Ann, 38
cyclic time, 101, 122–28, 242n2; consciousness of, 163–64, 166–71. *See also* creative-destructive principle

"daemonic power" (Freud), 60, 119
Dangarembga, Tsitsi, 34
Darwinianism, 55
Das, Veena, 38
Dauda, Bola, 245n21
death drive, 26, 54–63, 228; Edelman on, 8–9, 13–14; Malabou on, 138. *See also* regenerative death drive
"death-worlds" (Mbembe), 81, 83, 161
Decker, J. P., 84
Decker, Thomas, 84–87
decolonization: Fanon on, 57, 59; Grant on, 63; of trauma studies, 74–75
Deleuze, Gilles, 20
de Man, Paul, 50–51; on Kleist, 51; on literary criticism, 51
"de(re)sacralization," 163, 179

Derrida, Jacques, 22, 63–64, 153; Soyinka and, 161; on "Western worldification," 47; *The Beast and the Sovereign*, 145–47, 240n23; "Geopsychoanalysis," 35–37; *Specters of Marx*, 50, 51, 249n9; *Spurs*, 23
destructive plasticity, 116–22, 138. *See also* creative-destructive principle
Diop, Birago, 230; "Breath," 18–23, 94–95; "Sarzan," 19
Dooren, Thom van, 236n20
Driver, Dorothy, 208
drums, 65–66, 114–15, 157–58, 177, 241n8
Dunbar, Paul Laurence, 245n19
Durrant, Sam, 6, 39, 40–41, 49, 152

ecocriticism, 15, 58, 104, 196, 229. *See also* ecology, ecopoetics, environmental humanities, *and* environmental wound
ecology, 141, 196; deep, 235n16; lyric, 104; new materialist, 102, 108, 115, 132, 230; racialized, 92; transfigured, 199. *See also* ecosystem
ecopoetics, 3, 65, 104, 232n4
ecosystem, 2, 7, 13, 43, 100, 103–104, 115, 184, 196, 222, 227, 229
Edelman, Lee, 8–9, 13–14
egungun rituals, 34–35, 171–75
ekoneni, 204, 212
Elder, Arlene, 211
Eliot, T. S., 246n30
Emezi, Akwaeke, 3
environmental humanities, 6, 14, 29, 66, 196, 229, 235n14, 236n20. *See also* ecocriticism
environmental wound, 40, 185, 196. *See also* cosmological rupture, geographical violence, *and* tree-prisons

Esonwanne, Uzoma, 237n5
Esposito, Roberto, 36
Exodus, Book of, 40
Eze, Emmanuel Chukwudi, 34, 41, 71, 95

Fagunwa, D. O., 54, 236n17
Fanon, Frantz, 2–4; on animist cosmologies, 59; on "cleansing violence," 65; on colonialism, 31–32, 35, 197; on decolonization, 57, 59; on Freud, 24; Grant on, 62–63; on "new man," 249n2; on *polis*, 11, 56–57; on psychoanalysis, 3, 41–42, 43, 228; on "settler's violence," 128; Soyinka on, 137, 157–58; on Third World, 11, 59; Vera on, 185, 203, 206, 253n20; *Black Skin, White Masks*, 42, 59; *The Wretched of the Earth*, 11, 31–32, 56–57, 59, 253n20
Fassin, Didier, 45
Faulkner, William, 238n12
felix culpa, 55
Forna, Aminatta, 91–93, 95, 96, 100; *Happiness*, 88; *The Memory of Love*, 24, 68–69, 73–83
Forter, Greg, 74, 238n12
Foucault, Michel, 12, 45, 51, 161; on biopolitics, 146–47; on sovereignty, 160; Vera and, 253n17, 253n20
Franklin, Benjamin, 166
Fraser, Nancy, 193, 194
Frazer, James, 14, 165
Freud, Sigmund, 2, 8, 36, 42; on animism, 14; Caruth and, 48–49; on "daemonic power," 60; Darwinism of, 55; on death drive, 54–63, 228; Fanon on, 24; humanism of, 181; on *Nachträglichkeit*, 48–49, 139, 154; Said on, 35, 240n21; on Tasso, 54, 196, 197; on trauma, 5, 7–8, 77, 239n16; on wish fulfillment, 56; *Beyond the Pleasure Principle*, 5, 37–38, 54–60, 77, 239n17; *Civilization and Its Discontents*, 28; *The Interpretation of Dreams*, 50, 56, 88–90; *Moses and Monotheism*, 28, 43–44, 56, 62, 90; *Totem and Taboo*, 57
Frosh, Stephen, 239n14

Garuba, Harry, 5, 70–73; on animism, 17–18, 24, 67–68; on animist realism, 77–78, 91, 240n1; on re-enchantment, 17–18, 48, 70
Gates, Henry, Jr., 169
genealogical approach (trauma studies), 45
Genesis, Book of, 164, 254n25
geographical violence, 195–206, 214, 220, 253, 266n37. *See also* environmental wound *and* tree-prisons
George, Olakunle, 151, 159, 171–72, 236n17
Gerima, Haile, 181
Gilroy, Paul, 4, 237n3, 249n8
Girard, René, 159–60, 240n21
Glissant, Édouard, 42–43
Gobodo-Madikizela, Pumla, 233n7
Gowon, Yakubu, 131, 246nn29–30, 248n37
Grant, Ben, 32, 62–63
Greek tragedy, 153, 159
Green, Louise, 236n19
griots, 19
Gukurahundi massacres, 186, 191–92, 205, 212, 216, 222, 226

Hartman, Geoffrey, 49
Hartman, Saidiya, 33, 149, 150, 235n12
Harvey, Graham, 14

Hauka spirit possession ritual, 72
hauntology, 50–52
Hayden, Lucy, 244n18
Head, Bessie, 12–13
Heidegger, Martin, 6, 22
Herman, Judith, 45–46
hermeneutics, 43–44, 46–48; animist vs metaphysical, 23; *Osugbo*, 177; regenerative, 29; strategy, 9; tool, 14
historical materialism, 5, 232n5; 252n9
historicism, 38–39, 237n2
Hirsch, Marianne, 32
Holocaust, 21, 190; Agamben on, 36, 148, 161; Mbembe on, 31; Rothberg on, 186
Hopkins, Gerard Manley, 131
Horkheimer, Max, 27–28, 39, 52, 227; *Dialectic of Enlightenment*, 6, 174
Hughes, Langston, 19
humanism, 11, 59, 181; planetary, 20. See also posthumanism

identity politics, 109, 186, 194
Ifowodo, Ogaga, 154
Iheka, Cajetan, 6, 58, 104
Ijala chants, 248n35
Indigenous cosmologies, 2–3, 7, 204; animist poetics of, 69–70; reinvention of, 227–28. See also cosmologies and Indigenous knowledge systems
Indigenous knowledge systems, 232n5, 233n8. See also animism *and* animist cosmologies
ipseity, 5, 14, 25, 50, 52, 59, 113, 130, 133, 139, 167, 198, 229. See also Cartesian dualism and sovereign subjectivity
Irele, F. Abiola, 234n10
Iweala, Uzodinma, 13

Jackson, Jeanne-Marie, 235n15

Jackson, Zakiyyah Iman, 149, 162
James, Alby, 153
Jameson, Leander Starr, 209
Jarrett-Macauley, Delia, 91–93, 95, 96, 100; *Moses, Citizen, and Me.*, 24, 68–69, 73–80, 84–91
Jeyifo, Biodun, 159–60, 244nn16–17

Kahiu, Wanuri, 9–10, 12, 92
Kaufman, Eleanor, 238n12
Keynes, John Maynard, 194
Kgositsile, Keorapetse, 92
Khanna, Ranjana, 36
Kipling, Rudyard, 255n37
Kleist, Heinrich von, 51
Krishnan, Madhu, 251n2
Kristeva, Julia, 57
Kumavie, Delali, 235n12
kwela music, 203, 252n14

Lacan, Jacques, 42, 44; dream interpretation of, 50, 89–90; on "missed encounter," 61, 156
Laplanche, Jean, 62, 139
Latour, Bruno, 20
Levinas, Emmanuel, 38, 50
Lévi-Strauss, Claude, 234n9
Leys, Ruth, 37, 38, 39, 45
literary and cultural theory, 3, 8–9, 14–15, 17, 21, 24, 28, 35, 50, 51, 63, 102, 108, 140–41, 146, 180, 192, 227, 230
Lloyd, David, 40–41
Luckhurst, Roger, 45

magical realism, 11–12, 18
Makumbi, Jennifer Nansubuga, 4
Malabou, Catherine, 26, 61, 128, 131, 133, 138
Manichaeism, postcolonial, 24, 35, 41, 52, 69, 83, 91
Marriot, David, 65

Marxism, 18, 71, 122–23, 234n10, 239n20. *See also* historical materialism
mazhanje tree, 216, 219
Mbembe, Achille, 128, 162, 174; on "death-worlds," 81, 83, 161; on witchcraft, 31, 34, 62; "African Modes of Self-Writing," 31, 32; "Necropolitics," 81, 148, 161, 162
McNulty, Eugene, 170
Memmi, Albert, 206
memory: animism and, 63–66; Laplanche on, 62; multidirectional, 27, 32, 38, 186–90, 192–94, 225–26; reminiscence versus, 62. *See also* cultural memory *and* multidimensional memory
memory studies, 65, 184–86, 189–90, 192, 194, 196, 225, 229
Middle Passage, 33, 42–43, 99
mimesis, 72–73, 87, 173
Mntambo, Nandipha, 11, 12, 92
modernism: 58, 186; African, 25–26; animist poetics as, 3, 7, 228, 234n10; animist tragedy as, 177; global, 29; Soyinka's poetry as, 136, 244n15, 244n17
modernist studies, 14; "new modernist studies," 25, 234n10
monotheism, 28, 39, 52, 56, 65, 136, 149
Moore, Wayétu, 71
Morrison, Toni, 4, 36, 71
Moten, Fred, 149
Msiska, Mpalive-Hangson, 159, 242n9, 245n20, 246n27
Mtshali, Oswald Mbuyiseni, 25; "An Abandoned Bundle," 68–69, 91–96, 99–100
Mugabe, Robert, 191–92, 208–12, 215–16, 251n5

multidimensional memory, 184–85, 189, 192, 213, 215, 224–26
musuo ("harms to the soul"), 151
Mutu, Wangechi, 10, 12, 92
Mwangi, Evan Maina, 5
mythic logic, 28, 234n9
mythopoetics, 152, 190, 202

Nachträglichkeit (deferred action), 48–49, 154
Naess, Arne, 235n16
Nancy, Jean-Luc, 65
Napier, William, 207
negative ontology, 8–9, 13, 150–51
Nehanda Charwe Nyakasikana, 200, 201
new materialism, 15, 230, 236n21; comparison to animism via Diop, 19–20; of Malabou, 26, 61, 128, 131, 133, 138; comparison to Soyinka, 101–108, 115–16, 139–40
Newton, Isaac, 50
Ngũgĩ wa Thiong'o, 46, 201
Nicholls, Brendon, 8
Nietzsche, Friedrich, 179, 250n19
Nigeria, 24, 202; Biafran War of, 129–32, 148, 242n8, 246n30
Nikchanian, Marc, 237n1
Nixon, Rob, 38
Njovane, Thando, 4
Nkomo, Joshua, 211–12, 251n5
Novak, Amy, 38
novel studies, 250–51, n1
Ntiru, Richard, 21, 22
Nuttall, Sarah, 205
Nyamnjoh, Francis, 23

Ogun (deity), 135–36, 155, 243n12, 245n21, 248n35
Ojaide, Tanure, 131, 135, 156, 243n12, 246n30

Okara, Gabriel, 103, 200–201
Okigbo, Christopher, 4, 103
Okorafor, Nnedi, 4, 71
Okri, Ben, 7, 12, 71
Oyo Kingdom, 144, 145, 154, 160, 163, 248n1

Patterson, Orlando, 11, 150
Perec, Georges, 238n12
Peters, Lenri, 16–17
Phalafala, Uhuru Portia, 7; *Mine Mine Mine*, 25, 68–69, 91–92, 95–100
Pietz, William, 239n20
Poe, Edgar Allan, 44
poetry studies, 103–104, 242n3
political theology, 47, 63–65, 147–50. See also biopolitics (biopolitical theology)
polis, 1–2, 27–28, 230; animist poetics and, 65; of apartheid, 95; Fanon on, 11, 56–57; global, 35–36; monotheism and, 28; neocolonial, 136–37; Soyinka on, 153–54, 180; Vera on, 194, 213, 222
postcolonial studies, 3–4, 8, 14, 24, 25, 29, 32–33, 37, 42, 48, 64, 66, 103, 227–28
posthumanism, 3, 5–8, 9, 15–17, 28, 65, 66, 100, 108, 139, 181, 187, 196, 203, 213–14, 225, 229, 231n2. See also humanism
postsecular, 3, 6, 9, 15, 21, 28, 40, 65, 66, 100, 102, 108, 132, 139, 160, 176, 181, 187, 196, 198–99, 203, 222, 225, 229, 232n3.
post-traumatic stress disorder (PTSD), 45, 80–82
Pound, Ezra, 228
Primorac, Ranka, 189
psychoanalysis, 2, 28, 35–37, 44, 66; as critique of Eurocentrism, 46; contrapuntal reading of, 35, 39, 58, 228, 237–238n6; Fanon on, 3, 41–42, 43, 228; new materialism and, 128. See also death drive, Freud, Lacan, Malabou, repetition compulsion, *and* trauma theory
psychoanalytic animism, 88–91
Putumayo shamanism, 72

Quayson, Ato, 151, 156, 234n9, 248n1
queer theory, 9

racialized ecology, 92
Ramadanovic, Petar, 44–45, 50
Ranger, Terence, 191, 251n5, 252n10, 254n28
realism-ritual spectrum, 67–73
Rechtman, Richard, 45
re-enchantment, 17–18, 23, 48, 70
regeneration, 34, 59–60; ancestral, 63, 201; auto-destructive, 118, 120–21, 136–37; cosmological, 7; dialectical, 228; of kinship, 28–29, 104, 229; multispecies, 58; ritual, 130; of subjectivity, 184, 224, 229; of time, 108. See also regenerative death drive
regenerative death drive, 35, 54–63, 183; affirmative nature, 8–9, 13–14; ancestral trauma and, 3, 7–9; in animist tragedy, 152–53, 155, 178–81; in "animystic spells," 128–38; creative-destructive principle in, 122–28; definitions of, 2, 228; of Mtshali and Phalafala, 92–93, 100; of Vera, 201, 221, 226. See also creative-destructive principle *and* death drive
repetition compulsion, 37–39, 55–56, 60
Rhodes, Cecil, 209, 223, 255n37

Rhodesia. *See* Zimbabwe
Richards, Paul, 85–87
Ricoeur, Paul, 241n9
ritual: aesthetics *and* poetics, 9, 34, 65, 91, 100, 132–38, 146, 151, 221–23, 228; recovery, 84–88. *See also* shamanic rituals *and* self-burial
Rohmer, Martin, 169
Rooney, Caroline, 5, 21–23, 60–61, 252n6; *African Literature, Animism and Politics,* 18–19, 20, 54
Rose, Arthur, 241n9
Rothberg, Michael, 32, 74–75, 241n7; Caruth and, 140, 196; *The Implicated Subject,* 251n3; *Multidirectional Memory,* 27, 32, 38, 186–90, 192–94, 225–26
Roy, Arundhati, 181

Sachs, Wulf, 238n7
sacrifice, 134, 143–46, 154–57, 161, 176–78, 220–22, 248n1; Derrida on, 144; Girard on, 159–60; Hartman on, 149; Sithole on, 149; of time, 162–71; Wilderson on, 150; Wynter on, 149
Said, Edward, 90, 165, 195; *Culture and Imperialism,* 237nn6–7; *Freud and the Non-European,* 35, 90, 240n21
Samuelson, Meg, 208
Sankoh, Foday, 86
Santner, Eric, 36
Schiller, Friedrich, 17
Schmitt, Carl, 145, 147, 160–61; Benjamin and, 63–64, 240n22; Soyinka and, 161; Weber and, 64
Scott, David, 152
Selborne Memorandum (1907), 208
self-burial (ritualized), 221–23
sexuality, 36, 117, 135, 214, 247n32, 247–46n34

Shakespeare, William, 171, 249n9; *Julius Caesar,* 84–85, 88
shamanic rituals, 72–73, 76–78, 84, 231n1. *See also* animism
Sharpe, Christina, 149
Shepler, Susan, 80
Shona cosmology, 213, 252n8, 255n29
Sierra Leone civil war (1991–2002), 24, 68, 73–80, 240n2
silicosis, 97
Sithole, Tenddayi, 149
skin-ego, 222
slave trade, 98, 166; Glissant on, 43; Hartman on, 33; Mbembe on, 31; Spillers on, 33. *See also* Middle Passage
Smelser, Neil J., 4
social death, 11, 150
sovereign subjectivity, 23, 53, 58, 27–28, 47, 65, 230; contra creative-destructive principle, 120; contra cosmic personhood, 113; contra cyclic time and "secular social vision," 164–65; contra "metaphysics of the irreducible" and "inter-relation with Nature," 167–68; Wynter on, 163. *See also* sovereignty
sovereignty, 28, 52, 64, 145–47, 160, 161, 183; Foucault on, 160; Mbembe on, 162.; post-sovereign logic, 183–84. *See also* biopolitics
Soyinka, Wole, 15, 19, 26, 29, 101–108; on ancestral trauma, 24; animist poetics of, 68, 109–16, 128–29, 139; "animystic" perception of death, 116–22, 201–202; on creative-destructive principle, 64, 178–79; "excremental genesis" of, 95; Fanon and, 137, 157–58; on Greek tragedy, 153, 159; on "inter-relation with Nature," 167–68; on

"metaphysics of irreducible," 170; on organized religion, 242n10; on reptilian eschaton, 9, 18; on "ritual repression," 174; on secularization, 161; on "secular social vision," 164–65; U Tam'si and, 140–41; Vera and, 201–203, 252n13; on Yoruba tragedy, 47; "Animystic Spells," 106, 110–12, 128–38; *Death and the King's Horseman*, 143–82; *Idanre and Other Poems*, 137, 242n6, 243n12, 243n15, 247n32; *The Man Died*, 1–6, 148; *Myth, Literature, and the African World*, 138, 145–46, 161, 201, 234n8, 242n5
Spillers, Hortense, 149, 150
spirit possession, 19, 62, 86, 97, 157, 173, 231n1; Allen-Paisant on, 17; Hauka ritual of, 72; postcolonial, 67–68, 72–73, 77–78, 228
Steiner, George, 167
Stoller, Paul, 25, 67, 72–73, 77–78, 91, 231n1

Tal, Kali, 74
Tasso, Torquato, 37–41, 51; Freud on, 54, 196, 197
Taussig, Michael, 67, 72–73, 77–78, 91, 231n1
Taylor, Charles, 234n10
Tempels, Placide, 236n18, 237n22
Terdiman, Richard, 193
Thompson, Jeff, 244n18
Tighe, C., 243n13
Till, Emmett, 141
time. *See* cyclic time
Török, Mária, 197
transcendentalism, 141
transfigurations, posthumous, 9–14; 39
trauma, 45; cosmological, 6–7; Freud on, 5, 7–8, 77, 239n16; Gilroy on, 4, 237n3. *See also* ancestral trauma

trauma studies, 8, 43–48, 139, 236n20, 240n4
trauma theory, 24, 57; animism and, 3, 91–100; canonical, 49; Caruth on, 48–54, 139, 187, 238n12; Fanon on, 2–4, 24; hermeneutics of, 44; Malabou on, 128, 138; Njovane on, 4; postcolonial, 35–43, 228–29; psychoanalytic, 88–91; Soyinka on, 153–54; task of, 50; Yale School of, 52, 74–75
tree-prisons, 195–203, 223
Tutuola, Amos, 4, 64; *My Life in the Bush of Ghosts*, 65–66, 239n15; *The Palm-Wine Drinkard*, 53–54, 200–201, 239n15
Tylor, E. B., 15, 114

unconscious: Laplanche on, 62; cultural, 70; creating alternative states, 82; primal scene, 117
U Tam'si, Tchicaya, 140–41

Vambe, Maurice, 252n11
Vera, Yvonne, 25, 64, 184–85; Achebe and, 198–99, 203; animist poetics of, 68, 187–88; architectural criticism, 203–13; *Bulawayo Chronicle*, 211–12, 225; Fanon and, 185, 203, 206; Foucault and, 253n17, 253n20; on movement as combat, 203–13; Soyinka and, 201–203, 252n13; *Butterfly Burning*, 252n10; *Nehanda*, 187, 202–203, 225; on prophecy, 200–201; on Rhodesia's pavement law, 207; on spirit mediumship, 203; "The Prison of Colonial Space," 185, 188, 204–206, 223; *The Stone Virgins*, 25, 185–226; *Why Don't You Carve Other Animals?*, 202. *See also ekoneni*, geographical violence,

Vera, Yvonne *(continued)*
    multidimensional memory, *and* tree-prisons
vulnerability, politics of, 49

Walcott, Derek, 104
Warwick Research Collective, 234n10
Watters, Ethan, 75
wawa aba, 22
Weber, Max, 70–71, 159; on "disenchantment of the world," 17; Schmitt and, 64, 160–91
Weheliye, Alexander G., 149
Wilderson, Frank B., III, 8–9, 13, 26, 180–81; *Afropessimism*, 8, 145, 150–51, 176
Williams, Adebayo, 159
witchcraft, 31, 34, 62
Wordsworth, William, 125–26, 163–64, 246n26
Wynter, Sylvia, 20, 64, 149, 150; on biopower, 174; on creation, 163; Fanon and, 59

Yale School of trauma theory, 52, 74–75
Yeats, W. B., 234n11
Yoruba cosmology, 26, 101, 144, 154–55, 171, 241n2, 243n12, 250n19
Young, Allan, 45

Zimbabwe, 24, 27, 184, 215–16, 251n5; *Gukurahundi* massacres in, 186, 191–92, 205, 212, 216, 222, 226; "Operation Clean-Up" in, 208

www.ingramcontent.com/pod-product-compliance
Lightning Source LLC
Chambersburg PA
CBHW021959220426
43663CB00007B/889